IMS for the COBOL programmer

Part 1: Data base processing with IMS/VS and DL/I DOS/VS

IMS for the COBOL programmer

Part 1: Data base processing with IMS/VS and DL/I DOS/VS

Steve Eckols

Development Team

Technical editor:	Doug Lowe
Production editor:	Judy Taylor
Programmer:	Michele Milnes
Designer and production director:	Steve Ehlers
Artists:	Lori Davis Carl Kisling

Related Products

IMS for the COBOL Programmer, Part 2: Data Communications and Message Format Service by Steve Eckols

Structured ANS COBOL, Part 1: A Course for Novices by Mike Murach and Paul Noll

Structured ANS COBOL, Part 2: An Advanced Course by Mike Murach and Paul Noll

CICS for the COBOL Programmer, Part 1: An Introductory Course by Doug Lowe

CICS for the COBOL Programmer, Part 2: An Advanced Course by Doug Lowe

MVS JCL by Doug Lowe

DOS/VSE JCL (Second Edition) by Steve Eckols and Michele Milnes

20 19 18 17 16 15 14 13 12 11 10 9 8 7 6 5 4

Library of Congress Catalog Card Number: 85-51811

ISBN: 0-911625-29-1

Contents

Preface

If you're an application programmer in an IBM mainframe shop, sooner or later you're going to have to develop programs that use the facilities of a data base management system. Although several data base management software packages are available for System/370 family systems, IBM's DL/I (Data Language/I) is one of the most popular. In the DOS/VSE environment, DL/I is available as DL/I DOS/VS; in the MVS environment, DL/I is part of a larger product called IMS/VS.

IMS for the COBOL Programmer is a two-part series that teaches you how to use the facilities of IMS/VS in COBOL programs. This book, *Part 1,* covers data base processing using DL/I. Because DL/I for data base processing is basically the same under IMS/VS and DL/I DOS/VS, you can use this book whether yours is an OS or a DOS shop. *Part 2* teaches data communications, a feature that's unique to IMS/VS; as a result, *Part 2* isn't relevant for DOS users.

Who this book is for

If you're a COBOL programmer who works on an IBM mainframe system that uses DL/I, or you want to be, you need to know what this book teaches. Even if your current job doesn't require that you know

DL/I, you should be familiar with it anyway. Although DL/I isn't used in every shop, it's a standard by which other data base management systems are judged, for better or worse.

This book has two prerequisites. First and most important, you need a working knowledge of COBOL, enough so you can code simple report-preparation and update programs. If you aren't familiar with COBOL, I recommend *Structured ANS COBOL, Part 1* and *Part 2*, by Mike Murach and Paul Noll. These books are available from Mike Murach & Associates, Inc., and you can use the form at the end of this book to order them.

Second, you need an elementary knowledge of one of the operating systems that support DL/I, either OS or DOS, including its job control language. You can learn what you need from either Wayne Clary's *OS JCL* or from my book *DOS/VSE JCL*. You can get these books from Mike Murach & Associates too.

How to use this book

I planned this book so you can read just the parts that interest you after you've read section 1 (chapters 1 and 2) and section 2 (chapters 3 through 6). Section 1 introduces the concepts and terms you need to understand to learn DL/I. And section 2 presents the COBOL considerations for using DL/I in batch programs.

When you've finished sections 1 and 2, you can select what you're interested in from the more advanced topics in sections 3, 4, and 5. Section 3 (chapters 7 through 10) presents advanced features of DL/I data base processing that you may need to know. You can read the chapters in section 3 in any order you like.

Section 4 (chapters 11, 12, and 13) presents a brief introduction to DL/I programming in an interactive environment using IMS data communications (OS only) or CICS (OS or DOS/VSE). Chapter 11 describes interactive processing considerations common to both IMS and CICS. So you should read it first, whether you're using IMS, CICS, or both. Then, if you're using IMS for interactive programming, you can read chapter 12. If you're using CICS, read chapter 13.

Section 5 (chapters 14, 15, and 16) describes how DL/I data is actually stored. I cover this material last because you really don't have to know it to use DL/I and because it's technical and complex. However, if you do learn the internals of DL/I data organization, you'll be a better, more confident programmer.

Related reference manuals

IBM provides an extensive set of manuals for both IMS/VS and DL/I DOS/VS. Most contain information that's primarily for systems programmers. For IMS application programmers, the most useful manual is *IMS/VS Version 1 Application Programming* (SH20-9026). You'll also probably want to refer to *IMS/VS Version 1 Data Base Administration Guide* (SH20-9025) for technical descriptions of data base structures and processing considerations and to *IMS/VS Version 1 Utilities Reference Manual* (SH20-9029) for information on defining data bases. The equivalent manuals for DL/I DOS/VS users are: *DL/I DOS/VS Application Programming: CALL and RQDLI Interfaces* (SH12-5411); *Data Language/I Disk Operating System/Virtual Storage (DL/I DOS/VS) Data Base Administration* (SH24-5011); and *Data Language/I Disk Operating System/Virtual Storage (DL/I DOS/VS) Resource Definition and Utilities* (SH24-5021).

A note on the sample programs

All of the batch programs in this book were tested under both OS and DOS. For OS, I used IMS/VS Version 1 Release 3 running under MVS 3.8 on an IBM 3083 system. For DOS, I used DL/I DOS/VS Version 1 Release 6 running under VSE/AF 1.3 on an IBM 4331 system. Although the listings in this book are from the MVS system, the only change necessary to convert them to VSE is in the SELECT statements for standard files. The DL/I elements of the programs are identical, regardless of the operating system.

The interactive programs were run on only one system. The IMS DC program (chapter 12) was developed on the 3083 system using Batch Terminal Simulator II. The CICS program (chapter 13) was developed on the 4331 system under CICS/VS 1.5, but it should run the same under later releases of CICS (1.6 or 1.7).

Conclusion

I'm convinced that this book provides the most efficient and easiest way for you to learn how to process DL/I data bases in COBOL programs. But I'd certainly like to know what you think, so I encourage you to use the postage-paid comment form at the end of this book. I'd like to hear about how you use the book, how it has helped you, and what its strong and weak points are.

Steve Eckols
Fresno, California
September, 1985

Section 1

Required background

This section provides the background you need before you can begin to develop application programs that process DL/I data bases. DL/I, which stands for Data Language/I, is supported by both of IBM's main operating systems. Under DOS, DL/I is available as DL/I DOS/VS. Under OS, DL/I is part of a larger product called IMS/VS. Because DL/I data base processing is practically identical under IMS/VS and DL/I DOS/VS, the material in this section—and in most of this book—applies equally to both operating systems.

This section consists of two chapters. In chapter 1, you'll learn what DL/I data bases are and how they're organized. In chapter 2, you'll learn how DL/I data bases are defined and how they relate to your application programs.

Chapter 1

An introduction to DL/I data bases

"Data base" means different things to different people. Depending on the system you use and your shop's customs, "data base" can have a specific, technical meaning or a general meaning that varies from one application to another. And in some cases, "data base" can have a meaning as broad as an organization's entire "base of data."

In DL/I, a *data base* is a group of data elements organized to meet the requirements of one or more applications. In that sense, a DL/I data base is like a standard file. For instance, if a shop that has an employee master file, an inventory master file, and a customer master file converted them to DL/I, the result would probably be separate employee, inventory, and customer data bases. In fact, I think the easiest way for an application programmer to understand a DL/I data base is to think of it as a file with a hierarchical structure.

Hierarchical structures

Within a DL/I data base, data elements are organized in a *hierarchical structure*. In other words, some data elements are dependent on others. Although hierarchical data structures aren't unique to DL/I, DL/I supports hierarchies that are difficult to implement with standard files.

To understand how hierarchical data structures can be implemented with standard files, consider figure 1-1. It presents the record

Record layout for the VSAM VENDORS data set

```
*
 01  VENDOR-RECORD.
*
     05  VR-VENDOR-CODE                  PIC X(3).
     05  VR-VENDOR-NAME                  PIC X(30).
     05  VR-VENDOR-ADDRESS               PIC X(30).
     05  VR-VENDOR-CITY                  PIC X(17).
     05  VR-VENDOR-STATE                 PIC XX.
     05  VR-VENDOR-ZIP-CODE              PIC X(9).
     05  VR-VENDOR-TELEPHONE             PIC X(10).
     05  VR-VENDOR-CONTACT               PIC X(30).
```

Record layout for the VSAM INVMAST data set

```
*
 01  INVENTORY-RECORD.
*
     05  IR-ITEM-KEY.
         10  IR-VENDOR                   PIC X(3).
         10  IR-NUMBER                   PIC X(5).
     05  IR-DESCRIPTION                  PIC X(35).
     05  IR-UNIT-PRICE                   PIC S9(5)V99     COMP-3.
     05  IR-AVG-UNIT-COST                PIC S9(5)V99     COMP-3.
     05  IR-LOCATION-QUANTITY-DATA       OCCURS 20 TIMES.
         10  IR-LOCATION                 PIC X(3).
         10  IR-QUANTITY-ON-HAND         PIC S9(7)        COMP-3.
         10  IR-REORDER-POINT            PIC S9(7)        COMP-3.
         10  IR-QUANTITY-ON-ORDER        PIC S9(7)        COMP-3.
         10  IR-LAST-REORDER-DATE        PIC X(6).
```

Figure 1-1 Record layouts that illustrate a hierarchical structure

descriptions for two VSAM data sets that are part of an inventory application. The first record description is for the vendor master file. Here, each record contains a code that uniquely identifies a vendor (that's the key field VR-VENDOR-CODE) and the vendor's company name, address data, telephone number, and contact. The second record description in figure 1-1 is for the inventory master file. In this file, each record contains an inventory item key and the item's description, price, average cost, and stocking data for up to 20 warehouse locations.

There are two hierarchical relationships here that I want you to notice. First, every record in the inventory file is related to one and only one record in the vendor file. The three-character vendor code is not only the key to the vendor file, but it's also part of the key to the inventory file. (The complete key to the inventory file is the vendor code and a five-character item number.) As a result, it's possible to access all the inventory records for a particular vendor simply by starting at the right record and reading them in key sequence. And there's no practical limit to the number of inventory records that can be added subordinate to a single vendor record. (The actual limit is determined by the size of the item number component of the inventory file's key; here, it's far greater than the number of records that will ever be required for a single vendor.)

Although this design can work well, it's the responsibility of the system designer and the application programmers to insure that it does. Although the two files are separate, they must be treated as a single entity. An inappropriate change to either can destroy the integrity of the system.

For instance, if a program adds an inventory record that has no corresponding vendor record, the files will no longer be synchronized. And the same is true if a vendor record is deleted when active inventory records include its code as part of their keys. So although this kind of file design can be used effectively, it does have potential problems.

The second hierarchical relationship figure 1-1 illustrates is within the inventory record itself. In it, stock data for up to 20 warehouse locations can be stored. For each location, the record contains the location code, quantity on hand, reorder point, reorder quantity, quantity on order, and last reorder date.

Again, depending on application requirements, this design can work well. Although all the programs that process this data will contain table-handling logic, that's fairly straightforward. However, there's a problem if the same location code is used for two table entries in one record. Even worse, what happens if one record requires data for 21 locations? That would probably require reorganizing the file and changing all the application programs that process it. And, in most item records, only a few of the 20 location table entries would be used; that's a waste of valuable DASD space.

When you use DL/I data bases, difficulties like these don't come up. That's because DL/I was designed specifically to handle hierarchical structures and the potential problems that come with them. If you were to convert the vendor and inventory files illustrated in figure 1-1 for use under DL/I, you'd use a single hierarchical structure like the one in figure 1-2. Here, the data from two separate files is combined into one DL/I data base.

Segments

Each grouping of data in figure 1-2 (vendor, item, and stock location) is called a *segment*. A segment is the unit of data that DL/I transfers to

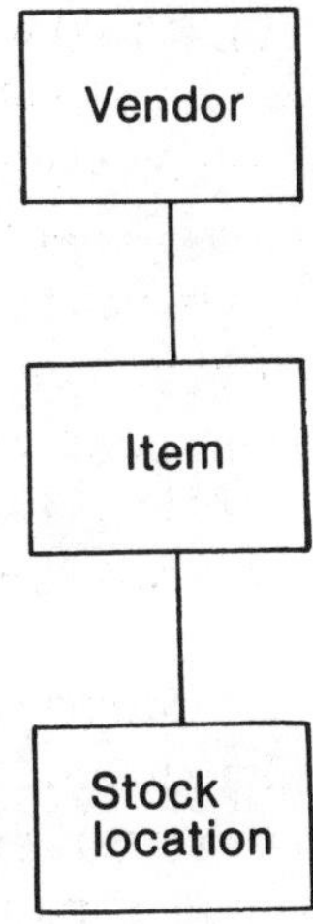

Figure 1-2 Hierarchical structure of the inventory data base

and from your program in an I/O operation. Like a record, each segment consists of one or more *fields*. As you can see in figure 1-3, you define each segment with a data description, much like you define a file record.

Now, you have to learn the difference between two similar terms: segment type and segment occurrence. A *segment type* is simply a category of data. In the inventory data base structure in figure 1-2, there are three segment types: vendor, item, and stock location. In contrast, a *segment occurrence* is one specific segment of a particular type containing user data. So although there is only one segment of the type VENDOR in the inventory data base, there may be many occurrences of it. If there are 250 vendors from whom the firm buys stock, there will be 250 occurrences of the vendor segment type in the inventory data base. Within a data base, there is only one of each segment type—it's part of the data base's definition—but there can be an unlimited number of *occurrences* of each segment type.

If you compare the segment layouts in figure 1-3 with the record layouts in figure 1-1, you'll notice that they contain the same data elements. However, the mechanisms used to implement the hierarchical structure (the combined key field and the 20-occurrence table in the inventory record) are missing in the segment descriptions. That's because DL/I manages the hierarchical relationships between segments. In the next chapter, you'll see how these relationships are specified.

```
*
 01  INVENTORY-VENDOR-SEGMENT.
*
     05  IVS-VENDOR-CODE          PIC X(3).
     05  IVS-VENDOR-NAME          PIC X(30).
     05  IVS-VENDOR-ADDRESS       PIC X(30).
     05  IVS-VENDOR-CITY          PIC X(17).
     05  IVS-VENDOR-STATE         PIC XX.
     05  IVS-VENDOR-ZIP-CODE      PIC X(9).
     05  IVS-VENDOR-TELEPHONE     PIC X(10).
     05  IVS-VENDOR-CONTACT       PIC X(30).
*
 01  INVENTORY-ITEM-SEGMENT.
*
     05  IIS-NUMBER               PIC X(5).
     05  IIS-DESCRIPTION          PIC X(35).
     05  IIS-UNIT-PRICE           PIC S9(5)V99    COMP-3.
     05  IIS-AVG-UNIT-COST        PIC S9(5)V99    COMP-3.
*
 01  INVENTORY-STOCK-LOC-SEGMENT.
*
     05  ISLS-LOCATION            PIC X(3).
     05  ISLS-QUANTITY-ON-HAND    PIC S9(7)       COMP-3.
     05  ISLS-REORDER-POINT       PIC S9(7)       COMP-3.
     05  ISLS-QUANTITY-ON-ORDER   PIC S9(7)       COMP-3.
     05  ISLS-LAST-REORDER-DATE   PIC X(6).
*
```

Figure 1-3 Segment layouts for the inventory data base

A data base need not have just a single segment type at each *level*, as in figure 1-2. Figure 1-4 is the structure of a customer data base with four levels and multiple segments at some levels. DL/I lets you implement structures that are more complex than this, with up to 15 levels and 255 different segment types. In practice, though, most data bases are relatively simple.

One additional comment about the terms "segment type" and "segment occurrence." You'll often hear the term "segment" used by itself to mean either type or occurrence. Usually, the meaning is clear from the context. For example, if someone asks, "What's the layout of the vendor segment?," it's clear that the question is about the vendor segment *type*. Or, if someone says, "The vendor segment's code field value is 411," it's obvious that the comment is about a specific segment *occurrence*.

The root segment and the data base record The segment type at the top of a hierarchy is called the *root segment*. Sometimes a hierarchical

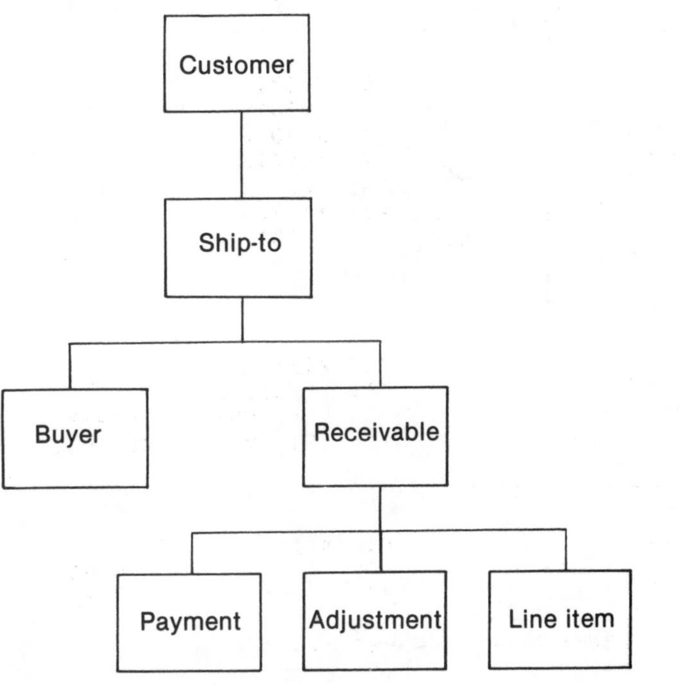

Figure 1-4 Hierarchical structure of the customer data base

data structure is called a *tree structure*. If you think of a data hierarchy diagram like the one in figure 1-2 or 1-4 as an upside-down tree, the segment at the top of the hierarchy—the one from which all the other segments eventually derive—is the root segment.

Each occurrence of the root segment plus all the segment occurrences that are subordinate to it make up one *data base record*. Every data base record has one and only one root segment, although it may have any number of subordinate segment occurrences. To illustrate, figure 1-5 shows three data base records from the inventory data base. As you can see, each record contains one occurrence of the vendor segment type (the root segment), as well as all segments subordinate to it.

Don't let the term "data base *record*" confuse you. In standard file processing, a record is the unit of data that programs operate upon. Under DL/I, that unit is the segment. A single data base record typically has many segment occurrences. For example, suppose a vendor segment occurrence in the inventory data base has 100 item segments subordinate to it, and each of them has 10 subordinate stock-location

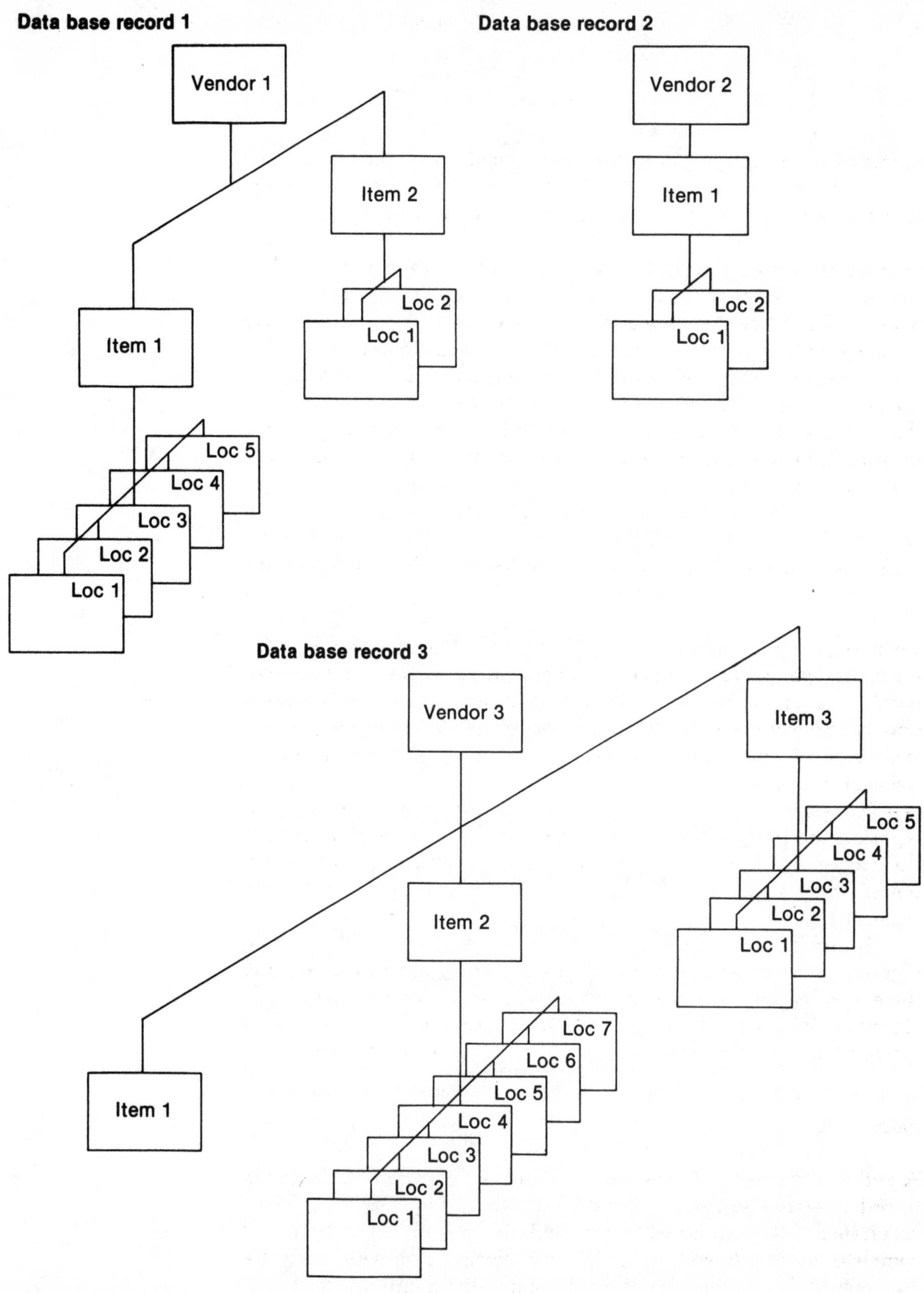

Figure 1-5 Three data base records from the inventory data base

segments. Here, 1101 segment occurrences make up a single data base record: there's one occurrence of the vendor segment type, 100 of the item segment type, and 1000 of the stock-location segment type.

Dependent, parent, and child segments All of the segments in a data base record other than the root segment are called *dependent segments* because they depend on one or more segments for their complete meaning. In the inventory data base, the item segment depends on the vendor segment, and the stock-location segment depends directly on the item segment and indirectly on the vendor segment. Each segment that has one or more dependent segments is a *parent segment* (or just *parent*). Similarly, each dependent segment in the hierarchy is a *child segment* (or just *child*).

You should also recognize that the root segment is the only segment in a data base record that is *not* a child segment. And all segments in a data base record except those at the bottom of the hierarchy are also parent segments.

Twin segments The terms "parent" and "child" apply both to segment types within a data structure and to segment occurrences within a data base. However, the term *twins*, or *twin segments*, applies only to segment occurrences. Two or more segment occurrences of the same type and with the same segment occurrence as their parent are twins of one another.

For example, in the inventory data base, two or more item segments are twins if they're dependent on the same vendor segment occurrence. But if they're dependent on different vendor segment occurrences, they aren't twin segments, even though they're the same segment type.

To understand, look again at figure 1-5. Here, the two item segment occurrences in the first data base record are twins. And the three item segment occurrences subordinate to vendor 3 are twins too. However, item 1 subordinate to vendor 1 and item 1 subordinate to vendor 3 are *not* twins because they don't have the same parent.

Paths

A *path* is the series of segments that lead from the top of a data base record (the root segment occurrence) down to any specific segment occurrence. Although a path down through the hierarchy need not be complete to the lowest possible level, what is present must be continuous. In other words, you can't skip intermediate levels.

For example, notice in figure 1-5 that item 1 subordinate to vendor 3 doesn't have any dependent stock-location segments. That's acceptable. However, it's not acceptable to have a stock-location segment that's a child of a vendor segment because that path is not continuous; there must be an item segment between them.

Logical data bases

DL/I's rigid hierarchical structure limits the data relationships that can be implemented. For example, in a *physical data base,* which is what I've described so far in this chapter, it's not possible for a segment to have two parents. But that kind of relationship is common even in relatively simple applications.

For example, figure 1-6 shows how you might combine information from the customer data base (figure 1-4) and the inventory data base (figure 1-2). Here, the line item segment is subordinate to two segment types: the receivable segment in the customer data base and the item segment in the inventory data base. With this structure, you can access inventory data through the customer data base. For instance, you can retrieve price and stocking data for an item on a particular receivable. Or, you can access customer data through the inventory data base (to access all customers who have ordered a particular item, for example).

Although DL/I doesn't support multiple-parent relationships in physical data bases, it does let you define *logical data bases* that combine two physical data bases (or create additional relationships within one physical data base). In chapter 8, I'll have more to say about the structure of logical data bases. For now, I just want to introduce some basic terminology.

In figure 1-6, the line item segment is the *logical child segment* (or just *logical child*) of the item segment. Likewise, the item segment is the *logical parent segment* (or just *logical parent*) of the line item segment. The path between two segments which would otherwise be unrelated is called a *logical relationship.*

Basic DL/I data base processing

Programs that access standard indexed files can process them sequentially or randomly, depending on the requirements of your application. The same is true for most DL/I data bases. You'll see

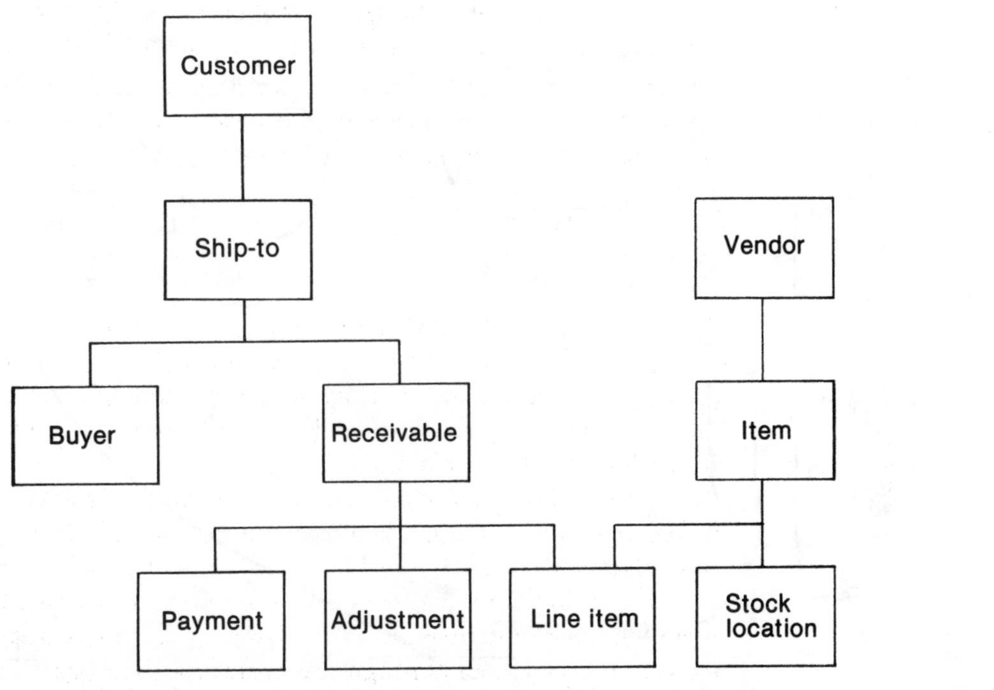

Figure 1-6 A logical relationship can connect two data bases

programs that illustrate both kinds of processing later in this book; for now, I want to describe how sequential and random processing work with DL/I data bases.

Sequential processing When you retrieve segments from a data base sequentially, DL/I follows a predictable pattern: down the hierarchy, then right. Figure 1-7 illustrates this pattern by showing how segment occurrences from three data base records in the inventory data base would be retrieved during simple sequential processing.

The first segment in a data base record that's retrieved is the root segment. Then, DL/I moves down the first leg as far as it can. When it reaches the lowest level of the first leg, it retrieves all twin segment occurrences at that level. In figure 1-7, the segments of the first leg are retrieved in this order: vendor 1, item 1, and stock locations 1, 2, 3, 4, and 5. After all the twin segments at that level have been retrieved, DL/I moves back up in the hierarchy and retrieves any twins of the previous parent. In figure 1-7, that's item 2 subordinate to vendor 1. Then, any dependents of that segment are processed.

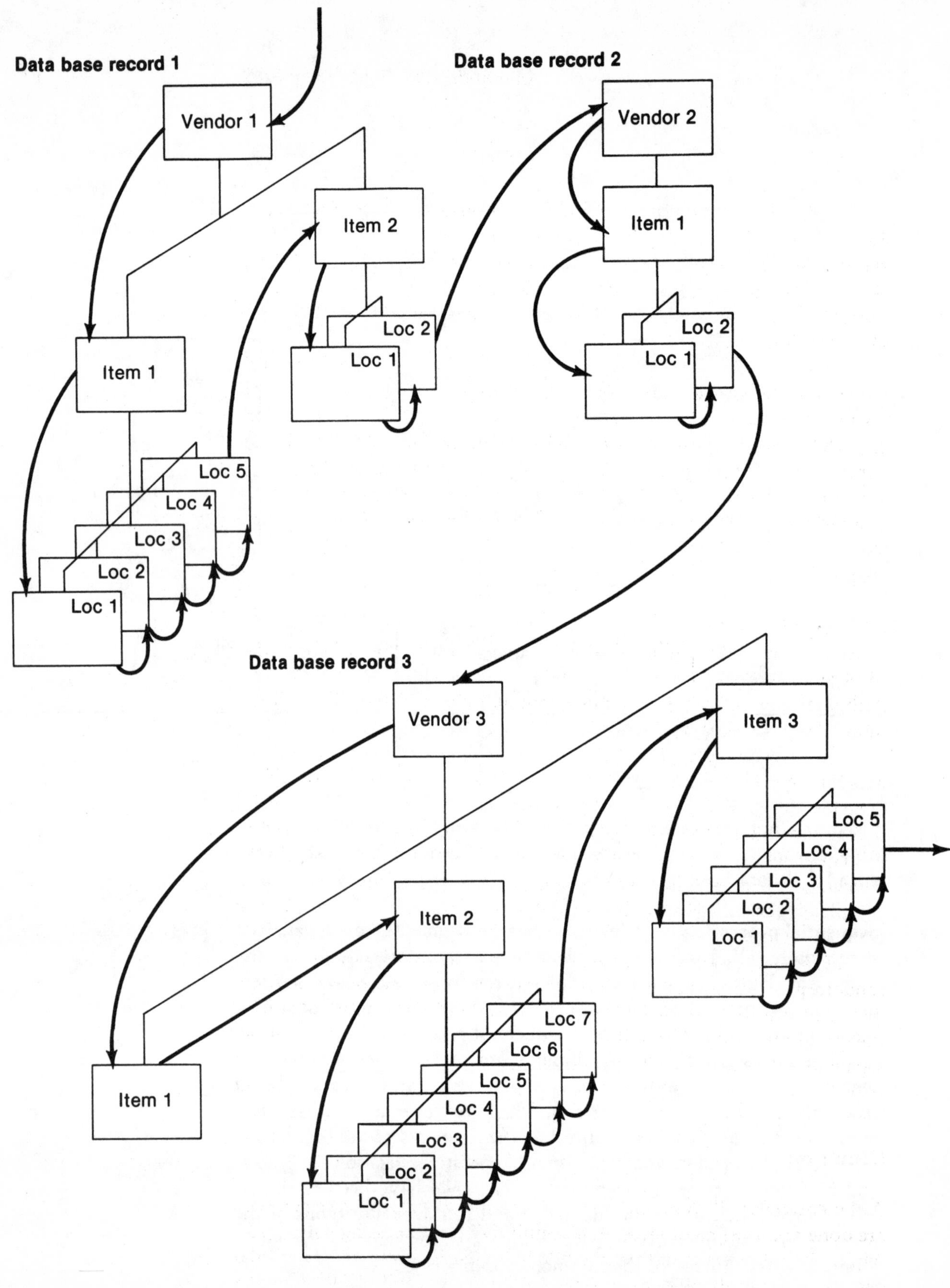

Figure 1-7 Normal path through the three records from the inventory data base

After all the segment occurrences in a single data base record have been processed, DL/I moves to the next data base record. Again, it starts at the root segment and moves down and right. If you follow the arrows through figure 1-7, the sequence should be clear. In a more complex data base, with many segment types at many levels, the sequence is the same.

At any point, your program has a *position* in the data base. That position can affect not only how segments are retrieved, but how new segments are inserted as well. In other words, when you add a new segment to a data base, that segment's location within the hierarchy can depend on your program's current position within the data base. So when you develop programs that process a DL/I data base sequentially, you need to consider how changes in position can affect your program's logic. You'll learn more about how positioning affects insertions in chapter 6.

Random processing Many applications require that a data base be processed randomly rather than sequentially. Segments that you need to access randomly normally contain a *key field* (or *sequence field*). Although you can define key fields that allow duplicate values, you're more likely to use unique keys for random retrieval.

To retrieve a specific segment occurrence randomly, an application program supplies the values for the key fields of all the segments it depends upon. For example, to retrieve the stock-location segment that's shaded in figure 1-8, you'd supply the key field values for vendor 3, item 2, and stock location 4. Together, these three values form the *concatenated key* of the segment occurrence. The concatenated key completely identifies the path from the root segment to the segment you want to retrieve.

In actual practice, many applications combine sequential and random processing. For example, a program might randomly retrieve item 2 of vendor 3 in figure 1-8. That would establish position so that the program could sequentially retrieve each of the seven location segments subordinate to item 2 of vendor 3.

Discussion

As I mentioned, all DL/I operations your application programs perform are done at the segment level. In addition, DL/I's processing pattern for sequential processing and its keying technique for random processing can affect program logic. As a result, if you're not comfortable with the

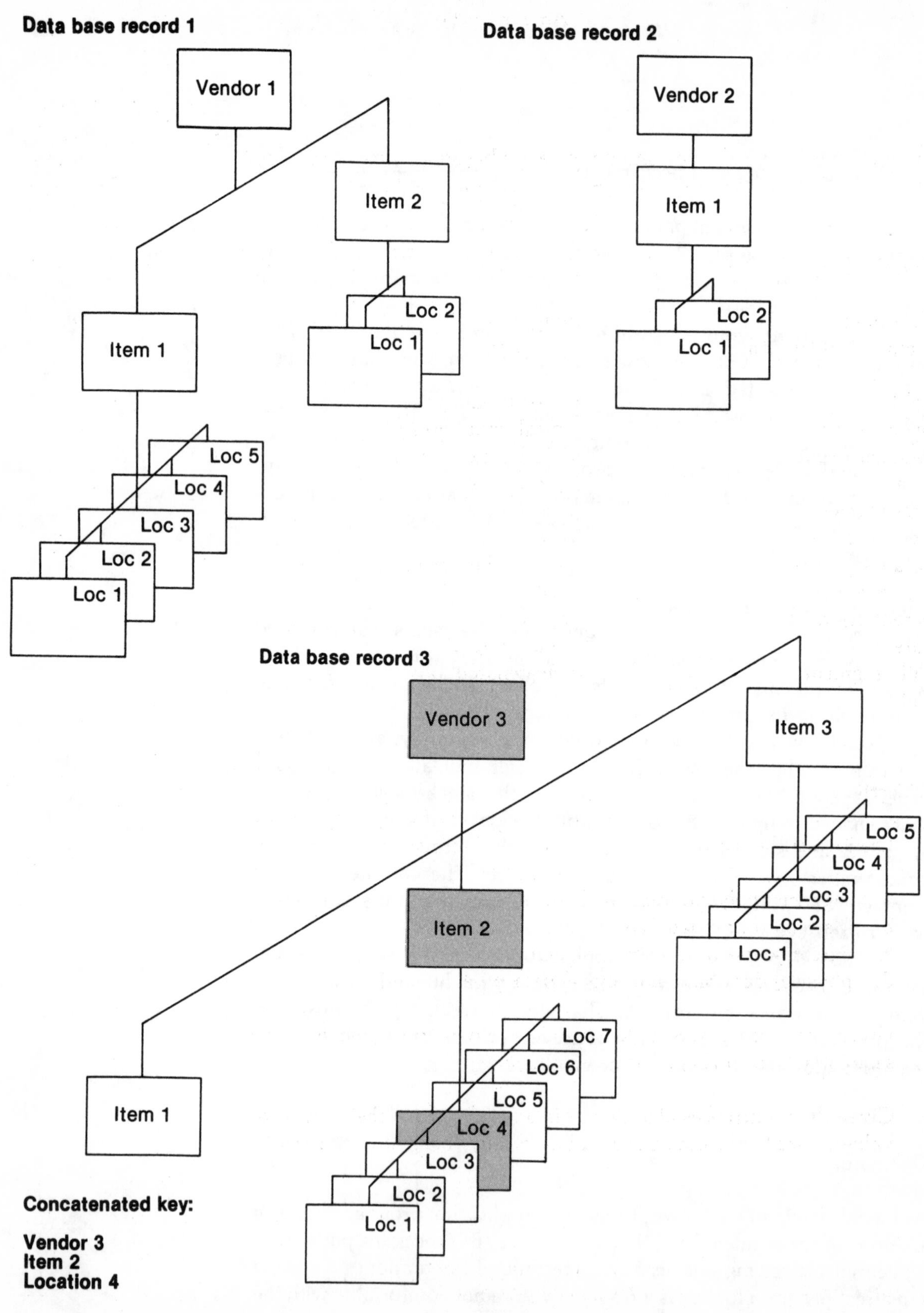

Figure 1-8 Using a concatenated key to access a specific segment occurrence

material in this chapter, you should review it before you try to develop an application program that processes a DL/I data base.

Terminology

data base
hierarchical structure
segment
field
segment type
segment occurrence
level
root segment
tree structure
data base record
dependent segment
parent segment
parent
child segment
child
twin
twin segment
path
physical data base
logical data base
logical child segment
logical child
logical parent segment
logical parent
logical relationship
position
key field
sequence field
concatenated key

Objectives

1. Distinguish between:

   a. segment type and segment occurrence
   b. file record and data base record
   c. parent segment and child segment
   d. physical data base and logical data base

2. Given the occurrences of segments in a data base, identify the sequential path through those segments.

3. Given the occurrences of segments in a data base and their key field values, specify the concatenated key of any segment occurrence.

Chapter 2

An introduction to DL/I programs and control blocks

This chapter introduces you to the environment in which DL/I programs execute. First, you'll learn how DL/I (either as IMS/VS or DL/I DOS/VS) stands between your application program and the physical structure of data in a data base. Then, you'll learn how DL/I uses control blocks to define its environment. And finally, you'll learn how to run a DL/I application program.

How DL/I relates to your application programs

The best way to understand how DL/I relates to your application programs is to compare that relationship with the way access methods relate to application programs during standard file processing. That's what figure 2-1 does. The left side of that figure shows how standard file processing works; the right side illustrates DL/I data base processing.

For standard file processing, application programs issue standard COBOL statements like READ and WRITE. These statements invoke the appropriate access method, like VSAM, to transfer data between your program and disk storage. Although the access method takes care of such details as locating your data on disk and deblocking your

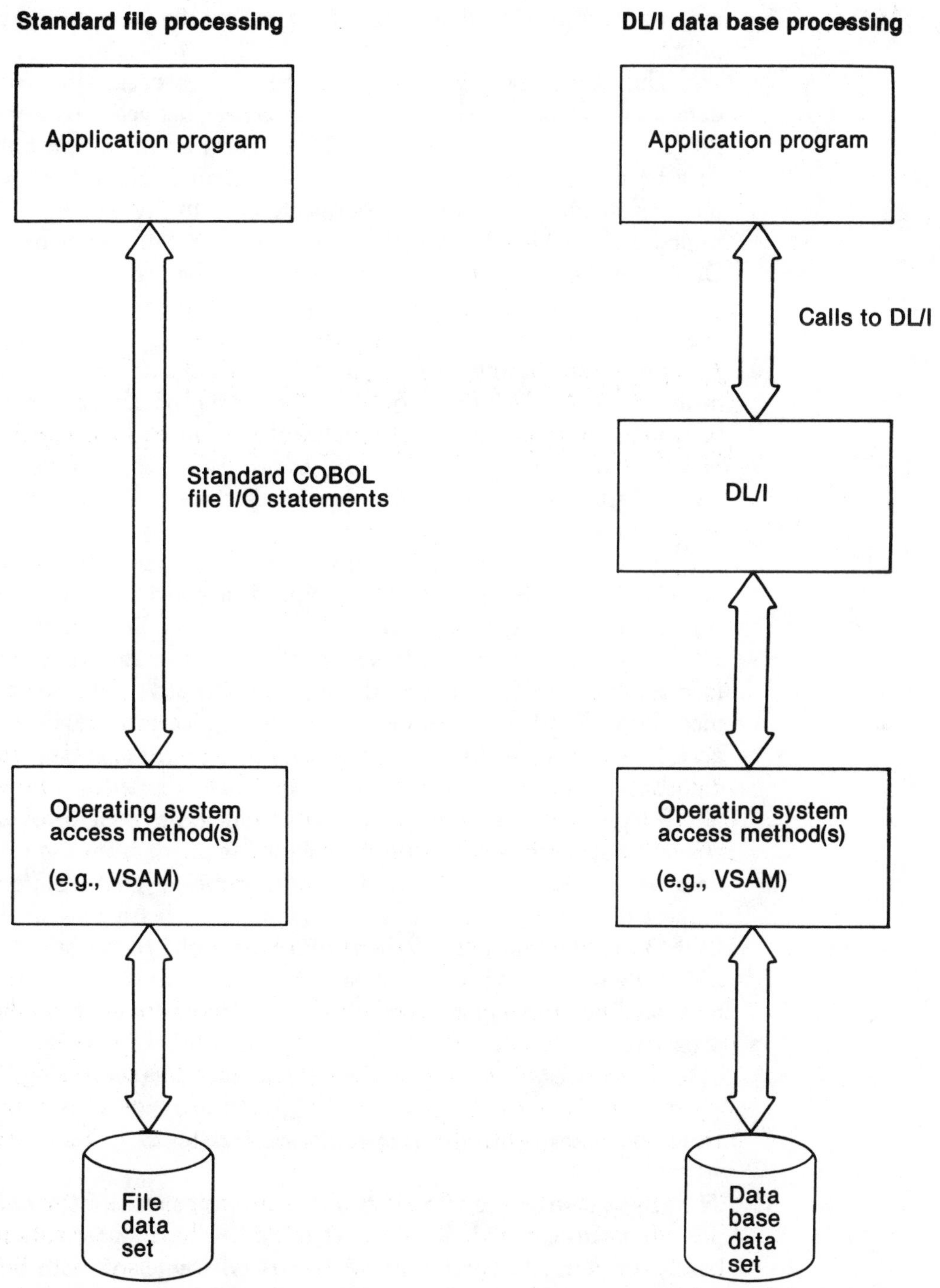

Figure 2-1 Standard file processing compared to DL/I data base processing

records if necessary, the format of the record that's processed by your program is the same as the format of the record on disk.

The right side of figure 2-1 shows the same process, only for a DL/I data base. Here, DL/I acts as an interface between an application program and the access method. To perform an operation on a DL/I data base, a program doesn't issue a standard COBOL file I/O statement. Instead, it executes a CALL statement to invoke DL/I. The parameters passed by the call tell DL/I what operation to perform. Then, DL/I, not the application program, invokes the access method.

I want you to realize that DL/I uses a standard access method—usually VSAM—to store data base data on disk. In fact, the access method doesn't know that a particular data set contains a data base instead of a standard file. However, the format of the records in a data base data set probably doesn't match the layouts of the segments that make up the data base. As a result, the way the program sees the data base differs from the way the access method sees it; that's not the case with a standard file.

For example, consider the inventory data base I described in the last chapter. To the application program, it consists of three segment types: the 131-byte vendor segment, the 48-byte item segment, and the 21-byte location segment. However, all three segment types are stored in one VSAM entry-sequenced data set with 2041-byte records. The modules of DL/I that stand between the application program and the access method take care of storing data in or retrieving data from the data base's data set.

Suppose, for example, that an application program wants to retrieve a specific occurrence of a vendor segment from the inventory data base. The program executes an appropriate CALL statement to request the segment. (In the next section, you'll learn how to code the COBOL to do that.) DL/I then invokes VSAM to retrieve the right 2041-byte record from the data base data set. From it, DL/I extracts the requested vendor segment occurrence and passes it to the application program.

How DL/I uses control blocks to define data bases

The physical structure of a DL/I data base isn't specified in application programs. Instead, DL/I uses a set of *control blocks* to define a data base's structure. In particular, DL/I uses two types of control blocks: DBDs and PSBs. A *DBD*, or *Data Base Description,* describes the complete structure of a data base. An installation must create one DBD for each DL/I data base.

Although each data base has a single physical structure that's defined by a DBD, the application programs that process it can have different *views* of it. These views, also called *application data structures,* specify the data bases (one or more) a program can access, the data elements the program can "see" in those data bases, and the processing the program can do. You specify this information in a *PSB,* or *Program Specification Block*. Although each application program can have its own PSB, it's not uncommon for application programs that have similar data base processing requirements to share a PSB.

You can see that it's more complex to create a DL/I data base than it is to create a standard file. Typically, creating DL/I blocks is the responsibility of a *data base administrator* (*DBA*). The data base administrator codes the assembler language statements necessary to define a DBD or PSB, then assembles and links them, storing the resulting load module in a partitioned data set (OS) or a core image library (DOS). This process is called control block generation; generating a DBD is usually called *DBDGEN,* and generating a PSB is called *PSBGEN.*

DBDGEN To generate a DBD, the data base administrator codes a job stream that contains a set of assembler language macro instructions that define the structure of the data base. I want to stress that you probably don't need to know how to code the statements for a DBDGEN: that's the data base administrator's job. Even so, I want to show you the DBDGEN statements for the inventory data base. After you've seen them, it should be easy for you to interpret other DBDGEN jobs for the data bases you'll use.

Look back to figures 1-2 and 1-3 to review the structure of the inventory data base and the fields that make up each of its segments. Now, consider figure 2-2, the assembler source listing for the inventory data base's DBDGEN. This listing is for IMS/VS, although the macro statements are virtually identical for DL/I DOS/VS. (However, the JCL to assemble them and link the resulting object module differs.)

The first macro, DBD, identifies the data base. The DBD macro names the data base (NAME=INDBD) and specifies the DL/I access method that will be used for it (ACCESS=HIDAM). DL/I access methods are completely internal to DL/I and are *not* the same thing as operating system access methods like VSAM and ISAM. You'll find more information on the DL/I access methods in section 5.

```
STMT   SOURCE STATEMENT

   1  PRINT          NOGEN
   2  DBD            NAME=INDBD,ACCESS=HIDAM
   3  DATASET        DD1=IN,DEVICE=3380
   4+*,                3380 DISK STORAGE
   5 *
   6  SEGM           NAME=INVENSEG,PARENT=0,POINTER=TB,BYTES=131
   7  LCHILD         NAME=(INPXPNTR,INPXDBD),POINTER=INDX
   8  FIELD          NAME=(INVENCOD,SEQ),BYTES=3,START=1,TYPE=C
   9  FIELD          NAME=INVENNAM,BYTES=30,START=4,TYPE=C
  10  FIELD          NAME=INVENADR,BYTES=30,START=34,TYPE=C
  11  FIELD          NAME=INVENCIT,BYTES=17,START=64,TYPE=C
  12  FIELD          NAME=INVENSTA,BYTES=2,START=81,TYPE=C
  13  FIELD          NAME=INVENZIP,BYTES=9,START=83,TYPE=C
  14  FIELD          NAME=INVENTEL,BYTES=10,START=92,TYPE=C
  15  FIELD          NAME=INVENCON,BYTES=30,START=102,TYPE=C
  16 *
  17  SEGM           NAME=INITMSEG,PARENT=INVENSEG,BYTES=48
  18  FIELD          NAME=(INITMNUM,SEQ),BYTES=5,START=1,TYPE=C
  19  FIELD          NAME=INITMDES,BYTES=35,START=6,TYPE=C
  20  FIELD          NAME=INITMPRC,BYTES=4,START=41,TYPE=P
  21  FIELD          NAME=INITMCST,BYTES=4,START=45,TYPE=P
  22 *
  23  SEGM           NAME=INLOCSEG,PARENT=INITMSEG,BYTES=21
  24  FIELD          NAME=(INLOCLOC,SEQ),BYTES=3,START=1,TYPE=C
  25  FIELD          NAME=INLOCONH,BYTES=4,START=4,TYPE=P
  26  FIELD          NAME=INLOCROP,BYTES=4,START=8,TYPE=P
  27  FIELD          NAME=INLOCONO,BYTES=4,START=12,TYPE=P
  28  FIELD          NAME=INLOCDAT,BYTES=6,START=16,TYPE=C
  29 *
  30  DBDGEN
  72+*,* * * * * * * * * * * * * * * * * * * * * * * * *
  73+*,*
  74+*,   RECOMMENDED VSAM DEFINE CLUSTER PARAMETERS
  75+*,*
  76+*,* * * * * * * * * * * * * * * * * * * * * * * * *
  78+*,* * * * * * * * * * * * * * * * * * * * * * * * *
  79+*,*
  80+*,*                         *NOTE2
  81+*,*  DEFINE CLUSTER (NAME(IN) NONINDEXED -
  82+*,*           RECORDSIZE (2041,2041) -
  83+*,*           CONTROLINTERVALSIZE (2048))
  84+*,*
  85+*,* *NOTE2 - SHOULD SPECIFY DSNAME FOR DD IN
  86+*,*
  87+*,* * * * * * * * * * * * * * * * * * * * * * * * *
 162+*,****** SEQUENCE FIELD ******
 211+*,****** SEQUENCE FIELD ******
 236+*,****** SEQUENCE FIELD ******
 325  FINISH
 326  END
```

Figure 2-2 Assembler source listing for the inventory data base DBDGEN

The second macro in figure 2-2, DATASET, identifies the file that will contain the data base. In this case, its symbolic name will be IN (DD1=IN), and it will reside on a 3380 disk unit (DEVICE=3380). The symbolic name is used in the JCL (the OS DD statement or the DOS DLBL statement) to identify the data set at execution time.

Notice lines 72 through 87 in figure 2-2. These lines, produced at assembly time, give recommendations for the VSAM file that will contain the inventory data base. In other words, based on the characteristics of the data base defined in this DBD, DL/I recommends that the data base data should be stored in a VSAM file with 2041-byte records and 2048-byte control intervals. The record length DL/I suggests does *not* correspond directly to the length of any of the data base's segments. That's because each file record typically contains several segment occurrences, as well as the control information necessary to maintain the hierarchical structure of the data base. In any event, you don't generally need to worry about the VSAM file recommendations that appear in DBDGEN output. Defining the VSAM data base file, like creating the DBDGEN, is the responsibility of your data base administrator.

Next in the DBDGEN source listing is the code that specifies the structure of the data base. Each of the three segment types is defined with a SEGM macro. For each, the DBA specifies a one- to eight-character name that DL/I will use to refer to the segment. The segment names for the inventory data base are INVENSEG (for the vendor segment type), INITMSEG (for the item segment type), and INLOCSEG (for the stock-location segment type). You'll use segment names in your application programs, so you need to know how to find them in the DBDGEN job.

Throughout this book, I use meaningful names for DL/I elements (or at least as meaningful as possible within eight characters). However, in a production environment, the number of DL/I elements is huge, so naming becomes a critical consideration. It's almost certain that your shop follows rigid naming conventions for DL/I elements that result in cryptic names that don't bear any apparent relationship to what they identify. For example, the vendor segment in the inventory data base might have a name like ZINS0VDR. Of course, you should learn what your shop's naming standards are and follow them.

The DBA specifies the hierarchical relationships among the segments by coding the PARENT parameter on each SEGM macro. For example, the SEGM macro for the INITMSEG segment specifies INVENSEG as its parent. The root segment is a special case; for it, the

DBA can code PARENT=0 or omit the PARENT parameter altogether. If two or more segments have the same parent, their sequence in the DBDGEN job determines their sequence in the data base hierarchy.

The last parameter on the SEGM macros in figure 2-2 is BYTES. For it, the DBA codes the length of the segment. Although it's possible to create variable-length segments, it's more common for segments to be fixed length, as they are in the inventory data base.

The POINTER parameter in the first SEGM macro and the LCHILD macro which follows are required because the data base administrator specified HIDAM in the DBD macro. It's strictly the DBA's responsibility to code these correctly, so you don't need to worry about them.

Within a segment, the data base administrator can define one or more fields. DL/I knows how long each segment is based on the BYTES parameter of the SEGM macro. The DBA doesn't have to define each field in the segment, because application programs identify fields within it in a segment layout, like the one in figure 1-3. Sometimes, though, a program needs to specify a particular field to DL/I. For example, a program might request DL/I to retrieve a vendor segment that has a particular value in its code field. To do that, the field must be defined in the DBD.

In practice, whether or not a DBD contains definitions of all fields or just those that are required depends on application requirements, shop standards, and the practices of the data base administrator. The point is this: If all of the fields within each segment are defined in the DBD, as they are in figure 2-2, the DBDGEN output is all you need to understand the complete structure of the data base. But if some of the fields are omitted from the DBD, you'll need additional documentation (such as the segment layout) to determine the contents of those portions of the segment that aren't defined in the DBD.

To define a field in the DBD, the DBA codes a FIELD macro that gives the field a unique one- to eight-character name (the NAME parameter), specifies its length and position within the segment (the BYTES and START parameters), and indicates the kind of data it contains (the TYPE parameter). Most of the fields in the inventory data base contain character data (TYPE=C). However, two fields in the item segment and three in the stock-location segment contain packed decimal data (TYPE=P). These and other data types you might encounter are shown in figure 2-3.

If you compare the segment layouts in figure 1-3 with the DBDGEN macros in figure 2-2, you'll see that they agree. For example, the item segment uses 48 bytes: 5 bytes of character data in the first 5

FIELD macro TYPE codes	Data type
C	Character
P	Packed decimal
Z	Zoned decimal
X	Hexadecimal
H	Halfword binary
F	Fullword binary

Figure 2-3 FIELD macro TYPE parameter codes

positions for the item number, 35 bytes of character data for the item description, and two 4-byte packed decimal fields for unit price and cost. The segment description shows that the packed decimal fields are defined with PIC S9(5)V99 COMP-3.

Notice that the data base administrator specified SEQ on the NAME parameter for one field in each of the three segments in the inventory data base: INVENCOD in the vendor segment, INITMNUM in the item segment, and INLOCLOC in the stock-location segment. That indicates that these are sequence fields. In other words, when occurrences of these segments are added to the data base, they're added in sequence by the values in these fields.

Again, I want to stress that you don't need to be able to code macros like those in figure 2-2, but you do need to be able to read them. It's not unusual to receive DBDGEN output as part of your program specifications rather than a hierarchy diagram like figure 1-2 and final segment layouts like the ones in figure 1-3. Then, it's up to you to code your own segment descriptions and to recognize the hierarchical relationships in the data base. However, just interpreting the DBDGEN output isn't enough to understand your program's view of a data base completely. You also need to be able to read the PSBGEN output.

PSBGEN Generating a PSB is much like generating a DBD: the data base administrator codes a job stream to assemble and link the macro instructions that specify an application program's view of one or more data bases. The resulting load module is stored in a partitioned data set (OS) or a core image library (DOS).

In this section, I'll describe the simplest sort of PSB: one for a program that accesses a single data base with *segment level sensitivity*. That means that the program's access to parts of the data base is identified at the segment level. In other words, a program might have access to the vendor segment type in the inventory data base, but not to the item or stock-location segment types. However, within the segments to which it's sensitive, the program has access to all fields.

A program can also have *field level sensitivity*. That means that within sensitive segments, only specific fields are identified as sensitive fields. Then, when the program accesses that segment, only sensitive fields are presented.

A PSBGEN is simpler than a DBDGEN. However, there will be more PSBs in a DL/I system than DBDs; that's because there's only one DBD per data base, but there can be one PSB for each program. Figure 2-4 shows the assembler source listing for the PSBGEN for the program that will load the inventory data base.

The first macro in the PSBGEN job stream is PCB. The *PCB* (*Program Communication Block*) describes one data base. A PSBGEN job contains one PCB macro for each data base the application program can access. So if a program will access three data bases, its PSB will contain three PCBs. The TYPE parameter specifies that the PCB is for a data base. Under DL/I DOS/VS, DB is the only value you can code for the TYPE parameter; under IMS/VS, the TYPE parameter indicates whether the PCB is for a data base or for data communications.

The DBDNAME parameter on the PCB macro specifies the name of the DBD for the data base to which the PCB corresponds. The KEYLEN parameter specifies the length of the longest concatenated key the program can process in the data base. For the inventory data base, that's 11 (3 bytes for the vendor-code sequence field, 5 bytes for the item-number sequence field, and 3 more bytes for the stock-location sequence field).

The last parameter on the PCB macro, PROCOPT, specifies the program's *processing options*. They indicate what processing the program is allowed to perform on the data base. In figure 2-4, LS indicates that the program can perform only load operations. Other values can authorize programs to retrieve, insert, replace, and delete segments.

For each PCB macro, subordinate SENSEG macros identify the segments in the data base to which the application program is sensitive. The names specified on the SENSEG macros must be segment names from the DBDGEN for the data base named in the DBDNAME parameter of the PCB macro. All SENSEG macros for segments other

```
STMT   SOURCE STATEMENT

   1  PRINT         NOGEN
   2  PCB           TYPE=DB,DBDNAME=INDBD,KEYLEN=11,PROCOPT=LS
   3  SENSEG        NAME=INVENSEG
   4  SENSEG        NAME=INITMSEG,PARENT=INVENSEG
   5  SENSEG        NAME=INLOCSEG,PARENT=INITMSEG
   6  PSBGEN        PSBNAME=INLOAD,LANG=COBOL
  87  END
```

Figure 2-4 Assembler source listing for the inventory data base load program's PSBGEN

than the root segment must include the PARENT parameter. Also, the DBA can code the PROCOPT parameter on the SENSEG macro to control access to the data base more selectively than is possible at the data base level. However, figure 2-4 doesn't show this.

The last PSBGEN macro in figure 2-4 is PSBGEN. It indicates there are no more statements in the PSBGEN job. Its PSBNAME parameter specifies the name to be given to the output PSB module that's stored in either an OS partitioned data set or a DOS core image library. The LANG parameter specifies the language in which the related application program(s) will be written (COBOL in figure 2-4).

How to run an application program that uses DL/I

When you run a batch program that processes a DL/I data base, you don't execute the program directly. Instead, you supply JCL to invoke the *DL/I batch initialization module,* which in turn loads your application program and the DL/I modules required to service it. Under IMS, the batch initialization module is DFSRRC00, and under DL/I DOS/VS, it's DLZRRC00. (DFS and DLZ are standard prefixes for DL/I module names under IMS and DL/I DOS/VS, respectively.)

Within its region (OS) or partition (DOS), your program and DL/I modules execute together. You may hear someone in your shop say that an application program that uses DL/I runs as a subprogram of DL/I. In a sense that's true, because the program is invoked under the control of the DL/I batch initialization module. That can confuse you, though, because the application program invokes DL/I services by issuing calls to DL/I, which makes it look like DL/I is the subprogram. Actually, the application program and DL/I execute together.

Terminology

control block
DBD
Data Base Description
view
application data structure
PSB
Program Specification Block
data base administrator
DBA
DBDGEN
PSBGEN
segment level sensitivity
field level sensitivity
PCB
Program Communication Block
processing option
DL/I batch initialization module

Objectives

1. Describe how application programs are insulated from the physical structure of data stored in DL/I data bases.

2. Given DBDGEN and PSBGEN output relevant to a specific program, code segment layouts and describe the program's view of the data base.

3. Describe how to invoke a DL/I batch program.

Section 2

Basic DL/I data base processing

This section contains four chapters that teach you a subset of DL/I for processing data bases in batch programs. You must learn the information in this section to use advanced DL/I features or to use DL/I in interactive programs. As a result, you should be willing to invest all the time and effort necessary to master this material.

Chapter 3 introduces you to DL/I programming. It teaches you how to code required DL/I elements in COBOL, then illustrates them with a program that produces a report based on data it extracts from a data base. Chapter 4 shows you how to code and use a specific DL/I element: the segment search argument, or SSA. Chapter 5 describes the programming considerations for retrieving data from a DL/I data base. Finally, chapter 6 presents DL/I calls for adding, deleting, and updating data base segments.

Chapter 3

COBOL basics for processing a DL/I data base

This chapter introduces you to the mechanisms a COBOL program and DL/I use to communicate with one another. Although you have to include a variety of elements in your programs to use DL/I, they're all fairly straightforward.

First, I'll describe two statements that are always required in a DL/I program: ENTRY and GOBACK. Then, I'll show you how to code a DL/I call and thoroughly describe three of the four elements of the call: the DL/I function, the PCB mask, and the segment I/O area. The fourth part of a call, the segment search argument, is introduced here, but described fully in the next chapter. After I've described how you code calls to request DL/I services, I'll show you how to specify a field that DL/I uses to pass status data to your program after each call. Finally, I'll illustrate all of these elements with a simple DL/I report-preparation program.

THE ENTRY AND GOBACK STATEMENTS

The first DL/I coding elements I want you to learn are the special COBOL statements you must code to start your program and end it: ENTRY and GOBACK. Although coding these statements is probably the most trivial aspect of DL/I programming, understanding what they

```
ENTRY 'DLITCBL' USING PCB-name1
                      [PCB-name2...]
```

Figure 3-1 Format of the DL/I ENTRY statement

do is important to your understanding of how DL/I and your program relate to one another.

You should recall from the last chapter that your program is invoked under the control of the DL/I batch initialization module. DL/I first loads the appropriate control blocks and modules, then loads your application program and passes control to it using a standard entry point named DLITCBL. As a result, you must declare DLITCBL as an entry point to your program by coding an ENTRY statement.

When DL/I passes control to your program, it also supplies the address of each PCB defined in your program's PSB, in much the same way as you would pass parameters to a called subprogram. Because these PCBs reside outside your program, you must define them in the Linkage Section, just as you would define passed parameters in a subprogram. The Linkage Section definition of a PCB is called a *PCB mask*; I'll describe its format and how you use it later in this chapter. For now, I just want you to realize that the way you establish addressability to the PCBs—that is, the way you relate PCB masks in your program's Linkage Section to actual PCBs in storage—is by listing the PCB masks on the ENTRY statement.

Figure 3-1 gives the format of the ENTRY statement as you code it for DL/I programs. As you can see, it specifies 'DLITCBL' as your program's entry point. And the USING clause lists the names of the PCB masks you code in the Linkage Section. Although the order in which you code the PCB masks in the Linkage Section doesn't matter, you *must* list them on the ENTRY statement in the same sequence as they appear in your program's PSBGEN.

The ENTRY statement provides the mechanism for DL/I to transfer control to your program. When your program ends, it must pass control back to DL/I so that DL/I can deallocate its resources and close your data base data sets. To do that, you code a GOBACK statement, *not* a STOP RUN statement. If you end a DL/I program with a STOP RUN statement, control returns directly to the operating system; DL/I never has a chance to perform its termination functions. So always use GOBACK rather than STOP RUN in your DL/I programs.

```
CALL 'CBLTDLI' USING DLI-function
                     PCB-mask
                     segment-io-area
                    [segment-search-argument(s)]
```

Figure 3-2 Format of the DL/I call

HOW YOUR PROGRAM REQUESTS DL/I SERVICES: THE DL/I CALL

As you learned in the last chapter, you use CALL statements to request DL/I services. The parameters you code on the CALL statement specify, among other things, the operation you want DL/I to perform.

Figure 3-2 presents the format of a DL/I call in COBOL. CBLTDLI, which stands for COBOL to DL/I, is the name of an interface module that's link edited with your program's object module. (If you were working in PL/I, you'd specify PLITDLI; for assembler language, you'd specify ASMTDLI.) Now, I'll describe each of the four parameters you can include on the CALL statement.

DL/I function

The first parameter you code on any DL/I CALL statement is the DL/I function you want to perform. For this parameter, you supply the name of a four-character working-storage field that contains the code for the function you want. Figure 3-3 presents a COBOL group item that contains the DL/I function codes you're likely to use. Notice that the figure contains a single 01-level group item with twelve 05-level items, each four bytes long. To specify a DL/I function, you'd code one of the 05-level item data names (like DLI-GN) in a DL/I call.

Because COBOL doesn't let you code literals on a CALL statement, all DL/I programmers in your shop will have to use a set of fields like this. As a result, your shop may have a COPY member similar to figure 3-3 that specifies function names. You should find out if one is available and use it. If one isn't available, figure 3-3 is a good model.

Get functions The first six 05-level items in figure 3-3 are *get functions*. You use them to retrieve segments from a DL/I data base,

```
 01  DLI-FUNCTIONS.
*
     05  DLI-GU                        PIC X(4)   VALUE 'GU  '.
     05  DLI-GHU                       PIC X(4)   VALUE 'GHU '.
     05  DLI-GN                        PIC X(4)   VALUE 'GN  '.
     05  DLI-GHN                       PIC X(4)   VALUE 'GHN '.
     05  DLI-GNP                       PIC X(4)   VALUE 'GNP '.
     05  DLI-GHNP                      PIC X(4)   VALUE 'GHNP'.
     05  DLI-ISRT                      PIC X(4)   VALUE 'ISRT'.
     05  DLI-DLET                      PIC X(4)   VALUE 'DLET'.
     05  DLI-REPL                      PIC X(4)   VALUE 'REPL'.
     05  DLI-CHKP                      PIC X(4)   VALUE 'CHKP'.
     05  DLI-XRST                      PIC X(4)   VALUE 'XRST'.
     05  DLI-PCB                       PIC X(4)   VALUE 'PCB '.
*
```

Figure 3-3 DL/I function codes

much as you use a READ statement to retrieve records from a standard file. Although I'll have much more to say about the get functions later in this chapter and in chapter 5, I want to describe them briefly now.

First, notice that you can divide the six get functions into two groups: those that contain an H in the function code and those that don't. I'll describe the three that don't contain an H (GU, GN, and GNP) first.

GU is the code for the *get unique function*. It causes DL/I to retrieve a specific segment occurrence based on field values you specify. In this respect, it's like a standard COBOL READ statement for random access.

GN is for the *get next function*. You use it to retrieve segment occurrences in sequence. It's like a standard COBOL READ statement for sequential access or a standard COBOL READ NEXT.

GNP is for the *get next within parent function*. It lets you retrieve segment occurrences in sequence, but only subordinate to an established parent segment. Because this function depends on the hierarchical structure of a DL/I data base, it doesn't have a direct parallel in standard COBOL.

The three get function codes that contain an H are get hold functions. You use them to specify an intent to update a segment after you retrieve it. GHU (the *get hold unique function*) corresponds to GU; GHN (the *get hold next function*) corresponds to GN; and GHNP (the *get hold next within parent function*) corresponds to GNP.

Update functions The next three functions in figure 3-3 (ISRT, DLET, and REPL) are *update functions*. You use them when you want to change data in a data base. ISRT (the *insert function*) is used to add a new segment occurrence to a data base. You use it to add data to an existing data base or to load a new data base. It's like the standard COBOL WRITE statement. DLET (the *delete function*) is used to remove a segment from a data base. It's like standard COBOL's DELETE statement. Finally, REPL (the *replace function*) is used to replace a segment occurrence; it's like standard COBOL's REWRITE statement.

Other functions The next two function codes in figure 3-3 (CHKP and XRST) are used in programs that take advantage of IMS's recovery and restart features. The last function code, PCB, is used in CICS programs. I'll describe these functions later in this book. In addition to the functions listed in figure 3-3, other call functions are available for use in IMS data communications programs.

PCB mask

The second parameter you must supply on your DL/I call is the name of a PCB mask defined in your program's Linkage Section. As I've already mentioned, the ENTRY statement establishes a correspondence between PCB masks in the Linkage Section and PCBs within your program's PSB. So when you code a particular PCB mask on a DL/I call, you tell DL/I which data base to use for the operation you're requesting. In that sense, it's like the file name you specify on a standard COBOL READ statement or the record name you specify on a WRITE statement. No additional COBOL elements—like SELECTs, ASSIGNs, or OPEN or CLOSE statements—are required to define a data base.

The PCB mask has other uses besides identifying which data base you want to access. For example, after each DL/I call, DL/I stores a status code in the PCB. Your program can use that code to determine whether the call succeeded or failed. You'll learn more about the information that's stored in the PCB later in this chapter.

Segment I/O area

The third parameter you code on a DL/I call is the name of a working-storage field into which DL/I will return retrieved data or from which it will get data for an update operation. This is like the field name you'd code on the INTO option of a standard COBOL READ statement or on the FROM option of a standard COBOL WRITE statement.

Segment search arguments

The first three DL/I call parameters (DL/I function, PCB mask, and I/O area) are required on DL/I data base calls. After them, you may code one or more *segment search arguments,* or *SSAs.* An SSA identifies the segment occurrence you want to access. Depending on the call you're issuing and the structure of the data base, you may have to code several SSAs on a single DL/I call. And the structure of the SSAs can vary from simple to complex. In the next chapter, you'll learn the different ways you can code and use SSAs. For now, I just want you to distinguish between the two kinds of SSAs: unqualified and qualified.

Unqualified SSAs An *unqualified SSA* simply supplies the name of the next segment *type* that you want to operate upon. For instance, if you issue a GN (get next) call with an unqualified SSA, DL/I will return the next occurrence of the segment type you specify.

Qualified SSAs A *qualified SSA* combines a segment name with additional information that specifies the segment *occurrence* to be processed. For example, a GU call with a qualified SSA might request a particular occurrence of a named segment type by providing a key value. Or, a GN call with a qualified SSA might request the next occurrence of the named segment type whose key value is greater than the value specified in the SSA. That's useful to establish a data base position for subsequent sequential retrieval.

I want you to distinguish now between the terms *qualified call* and *unqualified call.* An unqualified call is one that doesn't contain any SSAs; a qualified call is one that contains one or more SSAs. Don't confuse these terms with qualified and unqualified SSAs. A call that specifies only a single unqualified SSA is still considered to be a qualified call.

HOW DL/I COMMUNICATES WITH YOUR PROGRAM: THE PCB

As I've already mentioned, for each data base your program accesses, DL/I maintains an area of storage called the program communication block (PCB). You define masks for those areas of storage in the Linkage Section of your program. Then, after establishing the proper linkage to them at the start of your program, you can evaluate data DL/I stores there for information about the data bases your program processes.

Figure 3-4 shows the COBOL coding for the PCB mask for the inventory data base I described in chapters 1 and 2. Now, I'll describe each of the fields in this PCB mask. Keep in mind that these fields are defined in the Linkage Section, not the Working-Storage Section. Because they're not within your program's data area, your program shouldn't try to modify them.

Data base name

The first field in the PCB is the name of the data base being processed. It's an eight-byte field that contains character data. For the most part, you won't need to evaluate this field. After all, you know what data base you're using because you specified the PCB for it in your call. You should remember from chapter 2 that the DBA specifies the data base name on the DBDNAME parameter of the PCB statement during PSBGEN. Because the PSBGEN job in figure 2-4 specifies INDBD for the DBDNAME parameter, the data base name field in this PCB mask will always contain the value INDBD.

Segment level

The second field in the PCB is a two-byte character data field that specifies the current segment level in the data base. After a successful call, DL/I stores the level of the segment just processed in this field. For example, after a GU call that retrieves an occurrence of the vendor segment type from the inventory data base, the segment level field will contain 01. Similarly, it will contain 02 after DL/I retrieves an item segment occurrence, and 03 after it retrieves a stock-location segment occurrence. The segment level field will never have a value greater than 15 because that's the maximum number of levels permitted in a DL/I data base.

Status code

The third PCB field is another two-byte character field that contains data your program will evaluate after almost every DL/I call: the DL/I *status code*. When DL/I successfully completes the processing you request in a call, it indicates that to your program by moving spaces to the status code field in the PCB. On the other hand, if a call is

```
*
 01   INVENTORY-PCB-MASK.
*
      05   IPCB-DBD-NAME               PIC X(8).
      05   IPCB-SEGMENT-LEVEL          PIC XX.
      05   IPCB-STATUS-CODE            PIC XX.
      05   IPCB-PROC-OPTIONS           PIC X(4).
      05   FILLER                      PIC S9(5)        COMP.
      05   IPCB-SEGMENT-NAME           PIC X(8).
      05   IPCB-KEY-LENGTH             PIC S9(5)        COMP.
      05   IPCB-NUMB-SENS-SEGS         PIC S9(5)        COMP.
      05   IPCB-KEY                    PIC X(11).
*
```

Figure 3-4 PCB mask for the inventory data base

unsuccessful or raises some condition that isn't normal, DL/I moves some non-blank value to the status code field.

Problems that would cause an abend during standard file processing don't necessarily cause an abend under DL/I. Instead, DL/I provides the program with a non-blank status code, but continues to run. So even though processing can be completely wrong, your DL/I program can *appear* to be executing normally. As a result, you need to evaluate the status code after you issue most calls.

However, it's not as simple as just looking for non-blank status code values because some of them don't indicate error conditions. For example, when the end of a data base is reached during sequential (GN) retrieval, DL/I supplies the status code GB. You can handle this just like the AT END condition that can be raised during sequential processing with the standard COBOL READ statement. Similarly, a get unique (GU) operation can yield a GE status code if the requested segment isn't found. This is just like the INVALID KEY condition that can be raised with the standard COBOL READ statement during random processing.

Although you can expect some status codes other than blanks during normal processing, most status code values indicate data base or programming errors. In chapters 5 and 6, I'll describe the status codes you should know about for the various DL/I data base calls. In addition, appendix A presents a complete reference summary for all DL/I status codes. I encourage you to use it regularly.

Processing options

The fourth field in the PCB is a four-byte character data field that indicates what processing the program is authorized to do on the data base. As with the PCB's data base name field, the value of the processing options field is derived from the PSBGEN for the program. You probably won't need to use this field.

The next field in the PCB is reserved for DL/I's use. It's a FILLER item, defined with PIC S9(5) and COMP usage in figure 3-4.

Segment name feedback area

The next field in the PCB mask in figure 3-4 is IPCB-SEGMENT-NAME; it's the segment name feedback area. After each call, DL/I stores the eight-character name of the segment just processed in this field. The segment name is from the DBDGEN and PSBGEN. As the program example in this chapter will illustrate, you can use the value of this field to figure out where you are in the data base when you don't use qualified calls.

Key length feedback area

The next PCB field in figure 3-4 is a binary field (COMP, PIC S9(5)) that DL/I uses to report the length of the concatenated key of the lowest level segment processed during the previous call. It's used with the key feedback area, which I'll describe in a moment.

Number of sensitive segments

The next field in the PCB mask is another binary field (COMP, PIC S9(5)). Its value, like data base name and processing options, is determined by the PSBGEN. DL/I uses this field to report the number of SENSEG macros subordinate to the PCB macro for this data base. The chances are that you won't need to evaluate this field.

Key feedback area

The last field in the PCB mask, unlike all the others, varies in length from one PCB to another. It's as long as the longest possible concatenated key that can be used with the program's view of the data base. For the inventory data base, that's 11 (three bytes for the vendor code, five for the item number, and three more for the stock location). For data bases with more segment levels and larger key fields, the key feedback area will be longer.

After a data base operation, DL/I returns the concatenated key of the lowest level segment processed in this field, and it returns the key's length in the key length feedback area. You may need to evaluate the concatenated key, but because its format can vary depending on the structure of the data base and your current position in it, you have to be careful to use the correct format at any given time.

A SAMPLE REPORT-PREPARATION PROGRAM

Figure 3-5 is the layout for an inventory-availability report that's to be prepared from data stored in the inventory data base. Basically, one report line will be printed for each item segment occurrence in the data base. Each report line contains five data items.

The first data item on the report is the item's number. It's actually a combination of two data items from the data base: the three-character vendor code from the vendor segment and the five-character item number from the item segment. The next two data items on the report line (item description and unit price) are extracted directly from the item segment.

For the last two items on the report line, however, the situation isn't as simple. For locations, the report should show the number of occurrences of the stock-location segment that are subordinate to the item segment. And for on-hand, the report line should show the total number of units in stock at *all* locations. To derive these two data items, the program will have to process all the stock-location segments subordinate to a given item segment occurrence before printing the report line for that item.

The program's design

The design for a batch program that processes DL/I data bases is much like that for a program that accesses standard files. All the examples in this book use the structured programming design and coding techniques presented in *How to Design and Develop COBOL Programs* by Paul Noll and Mike Murach.

The structure of this program is in figure 3-6. Because it's much like the structure of a simple report-preparation program that extracts data

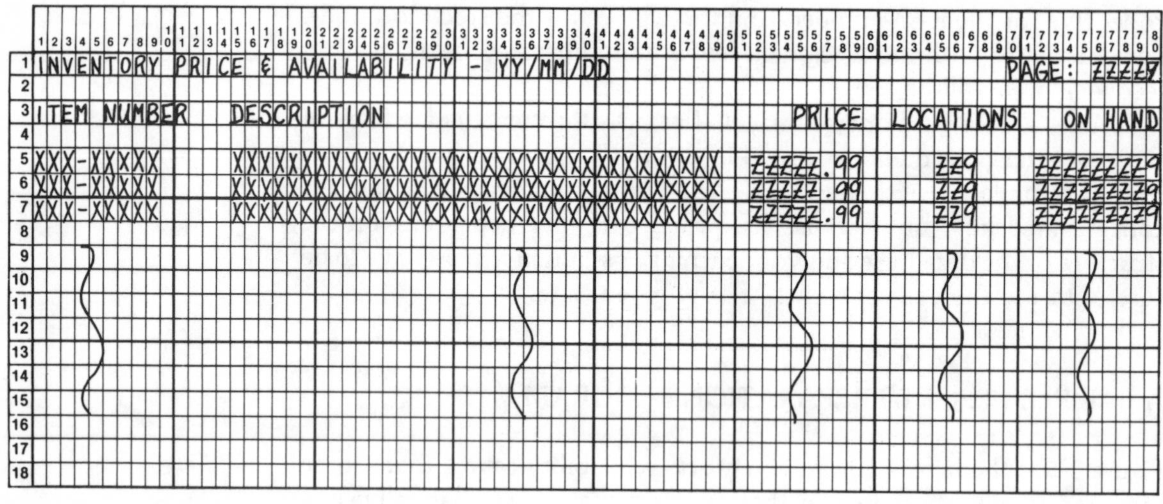

Figure 3-5 Print chart for the inventory-availability report

from standard files, it should be easy for you to understand. As a result, you can focus on the DL/I elements the program illustrates.

The top-level module is named 000-PREPARE-INVENTORY-AVAILABILITY-REPORT, and it represents the overall function of the program. Its purpose is to execute the main processing module of the program, 100-PROCESS-INVENTORY-SEGMENT, until the end of the data base is reached.

Module 100, in turn, performs two subordinate modules. The first, 110-GET-INVENTORY-SEGMENT, retrieves a segment from the data base. Module 110 will issue a DL/I call and evaluate the status code DL/I returns to determine if the call was successful or if the end of the data base was reached. (As a general rule, you should code DL/I calls in independent modules.) Then, based on the segment type retrieved (indicated in the PCB's segment name feedback area), module 100 does some preparatory processing and/or performs the second module, 120-PRINT-REPORT-LINE.

Module 120 and its subordinates don't contain any code that's especially relevant to learning DL/I. They format the report line, handle page overflow, and write the lines of the report. Because I don't want you to get bogged down in the details of report preparation itself, you don't need to worry too much about the processing modules 120 through 150 do.

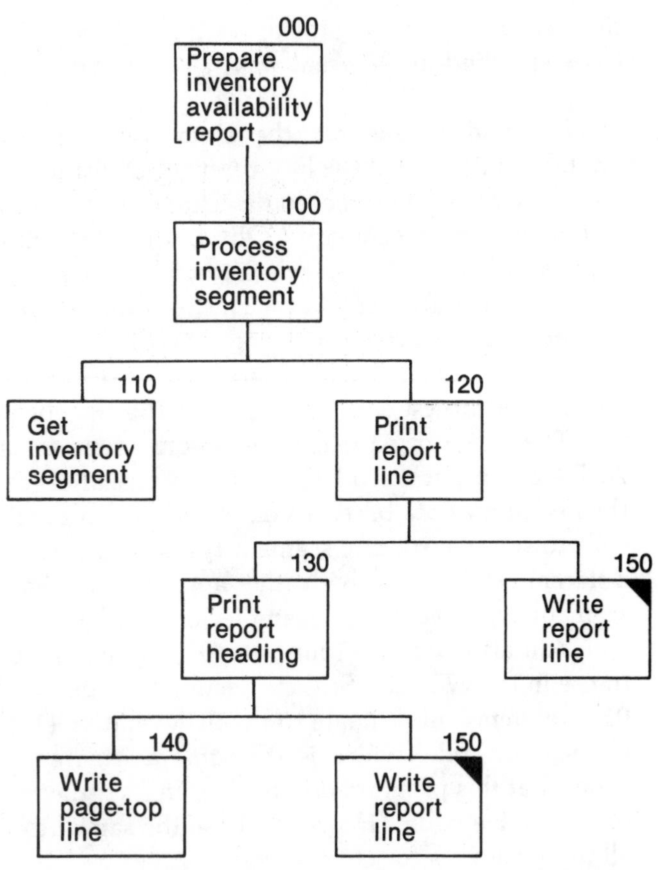

Figure 3-6 Structure chart for the inventory-availability report program

The program's code

Figure 3-7 is the complete COBOL source listing for the inventory-availability report program. The shaded sections relate directly to DL/I processing. Now, I want to describe the points you need to understand about this program.

DL/I considerations for the Environment Division Notice what's missing from this program's Environment Division: a FILE-CONTROL entry for the data base. That's because the data base has already been specified to DL/I. The application program refers to it indirectly through calls to DL/I, not through standard COBOL I/O statements, so there's no need for it to be defined here. However, notice also that files that are processed using the operating system's access methods still have to be specified in the usual way, as with the report file (PRTOUT).

DL/I considerations for the Data Division Just as there's no SELECT statement in the Environment Division for the DL/I data base, there's no FD and no record description for it in the File Section of the Data Division. In standard COBOL, the File Section record description is the area used to transfer data to and from your program. When you use DL/I, that area isn't in the File Section, but in the Working-Storage Section. In the program listing, it's the shaded 01-level item called SEGMENT-I-O-AREA. The area you use must be large enough to contain the largest data base segment that will be processed through it.

The inventory-availability report program uses SEGMENT-I-O-AREA as a generalized I/O field to receive all three segment types from the inventory data base. If you're coding a program that uses qualified calls to retrieve specific segment types, it makes more sense to specify different I/O areas with the appropriate characteristics for each segment type. You'll see examples of that later in this book.

You also code the four-byte DL/I function code fields you'll need to use in the Working-Storage Section. In figure 3-7, they're the twelve 05-level items subordinate to the 01-level item DLI-FUNCTIONS. This segment of code, which is the same as figure 3-3, includes function codes that this program doesn't use. In fact, the program only uses one of the twelve codes. However, I use the same block of twelve codes in all my programs for consistency.

Although they're not shaded in figure 3-7, the Working-Storage Section also includes three segment descriptions: INVENTORY-VENDOR-SEGMENT, INVENTORY-ITEM-SEGMENT, and INVENTORY-STOCK-LOC-SEGMENT. If you look back to figure 1-3, you'll see that these items and the segment descriptions there are the same.

You can think of the segment descriptions in the same way as you would a working-storage description of a standard file's record. For example, you might code a READ statement to retrieve a record, then follow it with a MOVE statement to transfer the entire record from the File Section record description to another area defined in the Working-Storage Section. Or, you could code a READ with the INTO option to do both in one step. Similarly, in the inventory-availability report program, a DL/I call retrieves a segment and stores it in SEGMENT-I-O-AREA. Then, based on the segment name in the PCB mask, the program moves the data from SEGMENT-I-O-AREA to the appropriate segment description.

```
 IDENTIFICATION DIVISION.
*
 PROGRAM-ID.  INV2100.
*
 ENVIRONMENT DIVISION.
*
 INPUT-OUTPUT SECTION.
*
 FILE-CONTROL.
*
     SELECT PRTOUT ASSIGN TO UT-S-PRTOUT.
*
 DATA DIVISION.
*
 FILE SECTION.
*
 FD  PRTOUT
     LABEL RECORDS ARE OMITTED
     RECORD CONTAINS 132 CHARACTERS.
*
 01  PRTOUT-RECORD                     PIC X(132).
*
 WORKING-STORAGE SECTION.
*
 01  SWITCHES.
*
     05  END-OF-DATA-BASE-SW           PIC X         VALUE 'N'.
         88  END-OF-DATA-BASE                        VALUE 'Y'.
     05  FIRST-ITEM-SW                 PIC X         VALUE 'Y'.
         88  FIRST-ITEM                              VALUE 'Y'.
*
 01  COUNT-FIELDS                                    COMP-3.
*
     05  QUANTITY-SEGMENT-COUNT        PIC S9(3)     VALUE ZERO.
     05  QUANTITY-ON-HAND-TOTAL        PIC S9(9)     VALUE ZERO.
*
 01  PRINT-FIELDS                                    COMP-3.
*
     05  PAGE-COUNT                    PIC S9(5)     VALUE ZERO.
     05  LINE-COUNT                    PIC S9(3)     VALUE +999.
     05  LINES-ON-PAGE                 PIC S9(3)     VALUE +50.
     05  SPACE-CONTROL                 PIC S9(3)     VALUE +1.
*
 01  HEADING-LINE-1.
*
     05  FILLER             PIC X(20)     VALUE 'INVENTORY PRICE & AV'.
     05  FILLER             PIC X(13)     VALUE 'AILABILITY - '.
     05  HL1-DATE           PIC 99/99/99.
     05  FILLER             PIC X(28)     VALUE SPACE.
     05  FILLER             PIC X(6)      VALUE 'PAGE: '.
     05  HL1-PAGE           PIC Z(4)9.
     05  FILLER             PIC X(52)     VALUE SPACE.
*
```

Figure 3-7 Source listing for the inventory-availability report program (part 1 of 5)

```
 01   HEADING-LINE-2.
*
      05   FILLER              PIC X(20)   VALUE 'ITEM NUMBER    DESCRI'.
      05   FILLER              PIC X(20)   VALUE 'PTION                '.
      05   FILLER              PIC X(20)   VALUE '               PRICE '.
      05   FILLER              PIC X(20)   VALUE ' LOCATIONS    ON HAND'.
      05   FILLER              PIC X(52)   VALUE SPACE.
*
 01   REPORT-LINE.
*
      05   RL-VENDOR-CODE                  PIC X(3).
      05   FILLER                          PIC X         VALUE '-'.
      05   RL-NUMBER                       PIC X(5).
      05   FILLER                          PIC X(5)      VALUE SPACE.
      05   RL-DESCRIPTION                  PIC X(35).
      05   FILLER                          PIC XX        VALUE SPACE.
      05   RL-UNIT-PRICE                   PIC Z(5).99.
      05   FILLER                          PIC X(5)      VALUE SPACE.
      05   RL-LOCATION-COUNT               PIC ZZ9.
      05   FILLER                          PIC X(4)      VALUE SPACE.
      05   RL-QUANTITY-TOTAL               PIC Z(8)9.
      05   FILLER                          PIC X(52)     VALUE SPACE.
*
 01   DLI-FUNCTIONS.
*
      05   DLI-GU                          PIC X(4)      VALUE 'GU  '.
      05   DLI-GHU                         PIC X(4)      VALUE 'GHU '.
      05   DLI-GN                          PIC X(4)      VALUE 'GN  '.
      05   DLI-GHN                         PIC X(4)      VALUE 'GHN '.
      05   DLI-GNP                         PIC X(4)      VALUE 'GNP '.
      05   DLI-GHNP                        PIC X(4)      VALUE 'GHNP'.
      05   DLI-ISRT                        PIC X(4)      VALUE 'ISRT'.
      05   DLI-DLET                        PIC X(4)      VALUE 'DLET'.
      05   DLI-REPL                        PIC X(4)      VALUE 'REPL'.
      05   DLI-CHKP                        PIC X(4)      VALUE 'CHKP'.
      05   DLI-XRST                        PIC X(4)      VALUE 'XRST'.
      05   DLI-PCB                         PIC X(4)      VALUE 'PCB '.
*
 01   SEGMENT-I-O-AREA                     PIC X(131).
*
 01   INVENTORY-VENDOR-SEGMENT.
*
      05   IVS-VENDOR-CODE                 PIC X(3).
      05   IVS-VENDOR-NAME                 PIC X(30).
      05   IVS-VENDOR-ADDRESS              PIC X(30).
      05   IVS-VENDOR-CITY                 PIC X(17).
      05   IVS-VENDOR-STATE                PIC XX.
      05   IVS-VENDOR-ZIP-CODE             PIC X(9).
      05   IVS-VENDOR-TELEPHONE            PIC X(10).
      05   IVS-VENDOR-CONTACT              PIC X(30).
*
```

Figure 3-7 Source listing for the inventory-availability report program (part 2 of 5)

```
 01   INVENTORY-ITEM-SEGMENT.
*
      05   IIS-NUMBER                    PIC X(5).
      05   IIS-DESCRIPTION               PIC X(35).
      05   IIS-UNIT-PRICE                PIC S9(5)V99      COMP-3.
      05   IIS-AVG-UNIT-COST             PIC S9(5)V99      COMP-3.
*
 01   INVENTORY-STOCK-LOC-SEGMENT.
*
      05   ISLS-LOCATION                 PIC X(3).
      05   ISLS-QUANTITY-ON-HAND         PIC S9(7)         COMP-3.
      05   ISLS-REORDER-POINT            PIC S9(7)         COMP-3.
      05   ISLS-QUANTITY-ON-ORDER        PIC S9(7)         COMP-3.
      05   ISLS-LAST-REORDER-DATE        PIC X(6).
*
 LINKAGE SECTION.
*
 01   INVENTORY-PCB-MASK.
*
      05   IPCB-DBD-NAME                 PIC X(8).
      05   IPCB-SEGMENT-LEVEL            PIC XX.
      05   IPCB-STATUS-CODE              PIC XX.
      05   IPCB-PROC-OPTIONS             PIC X(4).
      05   FILLER                        PIC S9(5)         COMP.
      05   IPCB-SEGMENT-NAME             PIC X(8).
      05   IPCB-KEY-LENGTH               PIC S9(5)         COMP.
      05   IPCB-NUMB-SENS-SEGS           PIC S9(5)         COMP.
      05   IPCB-KEY                      PIC X(11).
*
 PROCEDURE DIVISION.
*
      ENTRY 'DLITCBL' USING INVENTORY-PCB-MASK.
*
 000-PREPARE-INV-AVAIL-REPORT.
*
      ACCEPT HL1-DATE FROM DATE.
      OPEN OUTPUT PRTOUT.
      PERFORM 100-PROCESS-INV-SEGMENT
           UNTIL END-OF-DATA-BASE.
      CLOSE PRTOUT.
      GOBACK.
*
 100-PROCESS-INV-SEGMENT.
*
      PERFORM 110-GET-INVENTORY-SEGMENT.
      IF END-OF-DATA-BASE
           PERFORM 120-PRINT-REPORT-LINE
      ELSE
           IF IPCB-SEGMENT-NAME = 'INLOCSEG'
                MOVE SEGMENT-I-O-AREA TO INVENTORY-STOCK-LOC-SEGMENT
                ADD 1                    TO QUANTITY-SEGMENT-COUNT
                ADD ISLS-QUANTITY-ON-HAND TO QUANTITY-ON-HAND-TOTAL
```

Figure 3-7 Source listing for the inventory-availability report program (part 3 of 5)

```
           ELSE
               IF IPCB-SEGMENT-NAME = 'INVENSEG'
                   MOVE SEGMENT-I-O-AREA TO INVENTORY-VENDOR-SEGMENT
               ELSE
                   IF IPCB-SEGMENT-NAME = 'INITMSEG'
                       IF FIRST-ITEM
                           MOVE 'N'              TO FIRST-ITEM-SW
                           MOVE SEGMENT-I-O-AREA
                               TO INVENTORY-ITEM-SEGMENT
                           MOVE IVS-VENDOR-CODE TO RL-VENDOR-CODE
                           MOVE IIS-NUMBER      TO RL-NUMBER
                           MOVE IIS-DESCRIPTION TO RL-DESCRIPTION
                           MOVE IIS-UNIT-PRICE  TO RL-UNIT-PRICE
                       ELSE
                           PERFORM 120-PRINT-REPORT-LINE
                           MOVE SEGMENT-I-O-AREA
                               TO INVENTORY-ITEM-SEGMENT
                           MOVE IVS-VENDOR-CODE TO RL-VENDOR-CODE
                           MOVE IIS-NUMBER      TO RL-NUMBER
                           MOVE IIS-DESCRIPTION TO RL-DESCRIPTION
                           MOVE IIS-UNIT-PRICE  TO RL-UNIT-PRICE.
      *
       110-GET-INVENTORY-SEGMENT.
      *
           CALL 'CBLTDLI' USING DLI-GN
                                INVENTORY-PCB-MASK
                                SEGMENT-I-O-AREA.
           IF IPCB-STATUS-CODE = 'GB'
               MOVE 'Y' TO END-OF-DATA-BASE-SW
           ELSE
               IF      IPCB-STATUS-CODE NOT = 'GA'
                   AND IPCB-STATUS-CODE NOT = SPACE
                   MOVE 'Y' TO END-OF-DATA-BASE-SW
                   DISPLAY 'INV2100 I 1 DATA BASE ERROR - STATUS CODE '
                           IPCB-STATUS-CODE.
      *
       120-PRINT-REPORT-LINE.
      *
           IF LINE-COUNT > LINES-ON-PAGE
               PERFORM 130-PRINT-REPORT-HEADING
               MOVE 1 TO LINE-COUNT.
           MOVE QUANTITY-SEGMENT-COUNT TO RL-LOCATION-COUNT.
           MOVE QUANTITY-ON-HAND-TOTAL TO RL-QUANTITY-TOTAL.
           MOVE REPORT-LINE TO PRTOUT-RECORD.
           PERFORM 150-WRITE-REPORT-LINE.
           ADD 1      TO LINE-COUNT.
           MOVE 1     TO SPACE-CONTROL.
           MOVE ZERO TO QUANTITY-SEGMENT-COUNT
                        QUANTITY-ON-HAND-TOTAL.
      *
```

Figure 3-7 Source listing for the inventory-availability report program (part 4 of 5)

```
 130-PRINT-REPORT-HEADING.
*
     ADD 1 TO PAGE-COUNT.
     MOVE PAGE-COUNT TO HL1-PAGE.
     MOVE HEADING-LINE-1 TO PRTOUT-RECORD.
     PERFORM 140-WRITE-PAGE-TOP-LINE.
     MOVE 2 TO SPACE-CONTROL.
     MOVE HEADING-LINE-2 TO PRTOUT-RECORD.
     PERFORM 150-WRITE-REPORT-LINE.
*
 140-WRITE-PAGE-TOP-LINE.
*
     WRITE PRTOUT-RECORD
         AFTER ADVANCING PAGE.
*
 150-WRITE-REPORT-LINE.
*
     WRITE PRTOUT-RECORD
         AFTER SPACE-CONTROL LINES.
*
```

Figure 3-7 Source listing for the inventory-availability report program (part 5 of 5)

In the Linkage Section of the program, I coded the PCB mask for the inventory data base. It's the same as the sample PCB mask in figure 3-4. Because this program accesses just one data base, it needs only one PCB mask. For a program that accesses more than one data base, you would have to include one PCB mask for each.

DL/I considerations for the Procedure Division Now, I want to describe the DL/I elements in the Procedure Division. Actually, the statements in the Procedure Division that are immediately relevant to DL/I are few: ENTRY, GOBACK, and the DL/I CALL. They're shaded in figure 3-7.

As you should recall, the first statement in the Procedure Division of a program that processes a DL/I data base must be an ENTRY statement. In the USING clause, you have to supply the names of the PCB masks you coded in the Linkage Section. The program in figure 3-7 uses only one PCB mask. However, if a program accesses more than one data base, you must code PCB masks for each and list them in the USING clause in the order they're coded in the PSBGEN job for your program.

The next shaded item in figure 3-7 is the GOBACK statement that ends the application program and transfers control back to DL/I, which then deallocates its resources and closes the data bases it was using. Remember, always end a DL/I COBOL program with GOBACK, not with STOP RUN.

The third and last shaded item in the Procedure Division of the program is the CALL statement itself:

```
CALL 'CBLTDLI' USING DLI-GN
                     INVENTORY-PCB-MASK
                     SEGMENT-I-O-AREA.
```

First, notice that this is an unqualified call: it *doesn't* include any segment search arguments. As a result, each time DL/I is invoked with this call, processing proceeds from the current position in the data base; all occurrences of all segment types are retrieved.

Next, notice the three parameters the call does specify. The first is the four-byte field (subordinate to the 01-level item DLI-FUNCTIONS) that specifies the function code for the get next operation (GN). The second is the name of the PCB mask for the inventory data base. This is how the call specifies the data base on which the function should be performed. The last, SEGMENT-I-O-AREA, names the working-storage field DL/I will use as the I/O area for the operation to be performed.

Understanding the logic of the program Now that you're familiar with the DL/I elements in the inventory-availability report program, I want to describe how the program works. After you've read this section, you should have a better understanding of the DL/I call, the sequence through a DL/I data base, and how to use fields in the PCB.

As I've already mentioned, the primary function of module 000 is to execute the main processing module (100) repeatedly to process each segment in the data base. In addition, module 000 takes care of work that needs to be done before the main module is executed for the first time and work that needs to be done after the main module has been executed for the last time.

First, module 000 gets the system date using an ACCEPT statement. The date is stored in HL1-DATE, a field in the report heading. Next, the report file (PRTOUT) is opened for output. Then, module 000 executes a PERFORM UNTIL statement to invoke module 100 to process the entire data base one segment at a time. The

PERFORM UNTIL specifies a condition name (END-OF-DATA-BASE) that's associated with a switch that the program turns on when DL/I indicates (via the PCB status code) that the last segment in the data base has been processed. You'll see how that works when I describe module 110. After module 100 has been executed for the last time, module 000 closes the report file PRTOUT and ends the program with a GOBACK statement. After that, DL/I releases the resources it had acquired for the program and closes the data base.

Module 100 contains most of the decision-making code in the program. Much of it is determined by the structure of the data base, so I want to be sure you understand it. The first thing module 100 does is perform module 110 to retrieve a data base segment. So before I explain the logic of module 100, I'll describe module 110.

The first statement in module 110 is the DL/I call I've already described. You should be familiar with it. Because it uses the get next function, it will retrieve segments from the inventory data base one after another, from beginning to end, in the normal DL/I sequence.

The rest of the code in module 110 evaluates the PCB status code. You should recall that DL/I sets the PCB status code to spaces when it processes a call and doesn't detect any unusual conditions. However, if it does detect something out of the ordinary, it moves a non-blank value to the PCB status code. Your program is responsible for evaluating those status code values and deciding what to do based on them.

The inventory-availability report program needs to check for two non-blank status values which don't represent real errors: GB and GA. GB you already know about: it indicates that the end of the data base has been reached. When the program detects a GB status code, it sets the END-OF-DATA-BASE-SW field to Y. Both modules 100 and 000 use the value of this switch to control their processing.

For sequential retrieval of segments from the inventory data base, still another status code will be raised: GA. This means that a hierarchical boundary has been crossed. To understand, consider figure 3-8. This is a version of the figure from chapter 1 that illustrated the normal DL/I sequence through three data base records in the inventory data base. In addition, for each step through the segment occurrences, figure 3-8 shows the PCB status code value that will be returned by DL/I. (This example assumes that there are only these three records in the data base.) Notice that the DL/I get next call issued after the last segment has already been retrieved causes the GB status code. But also notice that each time the current position goes up one or more levels, the status code returned is GA.

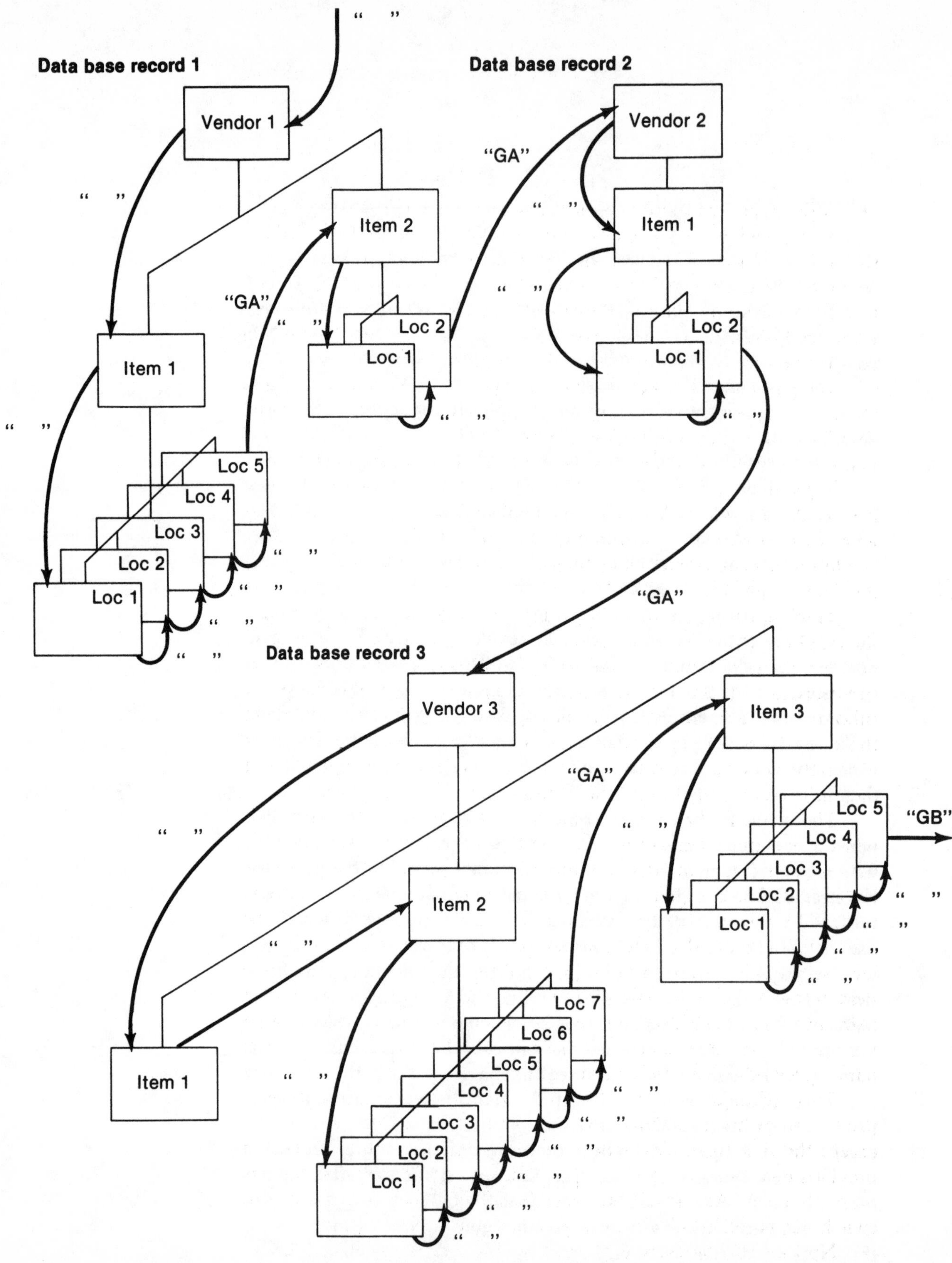

Figure 3-8 Status codes returned during sequential retrieval of segments from the inventory data base

Any other non-blank status codes encountered by the program represent genuine errors and should be handled accordingly. Many shops have a standard error routine that application programs call whenever an unexpected error is detected. In this program, I assume that such a routine isn't available. As a result, when an unexpected status code is detected, the program ends in a controlled way and advises the user of the problem by displaying an error message.

The particular status codes that are expected during processing and those that represent errors vary from application to application. As I describe the DL/I data base calls in more detail in later chapters, I'll tell you what status codes can occur and when they're likely to be errors.

Regardless of the status code value module 110 detects, control goes back to module 100 after it's complete, and execution continues with the next statement. All that remains in module 100 is a complex condition that determines when to print a report line and how to handle the data supplied by the DL/I call.

Think again about how this program will have to work to prepare the required report. To print a report line for an item, it has to process not just the item segment itself, but also all stock-location segments subordinate to it. But for the program to know it has processed all the subordinate stock location segments, it must read beyond the last of those segments for the current item, either to another item segment within the same data base record, to another vendor segment in the next data base record, or beyond the last segment in the data base.

The result is that a report line is printed at two different times: when a new item segment is retrieved (then the data for the *previous* item segment is formatted and printed) or when the end of the data base is detected. The program can tell when a new item segment has been retrieved by evaluating the contents of the segment name field in the PCB. DL/I updates this field after each call with the name of the lowest level segment it processed during the call. So when the segment name field in the PCB has the value INITMSEG, the program knows an item segment was just retrieved and that it's time to write a report line. (To use the PCB segment name field like this, you have to know the DL/I name specified for the field in the DBDGEN.)

This technique is tricky, however, because the program needs to print a report line each time it encounters an item segment occurrence, *except* the first time. That's because the program is reporting on the previous item segment, and the first item segment in the data base has no predecessor. As a result, module 100 contains the code (based on a switch named FIRST-ITEM-SW) to handle this special case.

Notice that the section of module 100 that's executed if IPCB-SEGMENT-NAME is equal to INITMSEG (and it's not the first time) causes the appropriate fields for the item segment just retrieved to be moved to the report line *after* the report line for the previous item is written. That way, the new data won't overlay the previous data before it's written to the report.

Module 100 also contains the code to process occurrences of the other two segment types. If the segment name field in the PCB indicates the segment just retrieved was a vendor segment, the contents of the I/O area used by the call (SEGMENT-I-O-AREA) are moved to the segment description for the vendor segment. Other than the vendor number field, the data in the vendor segment is ignored.

Similarly, if the segment just retrieved was a stock location segment, the contents of SEGMENT-I-O-AREA are moved to the segment description for the stock-location segment. Then, the counter for the number of locations stocking the item (QUANTITY-SEGMENT-COUNT) is increased by one and the number of units on hand from the stock-location segment (ISLS-QUANTITY-ON-HAND) is added to the total number of units on hand for the item (QUANTITY-ON-HAND-TOTAL). These totals are reset to zero in module 120, when the report line is printed.

The code in the remaining modules (120 through 150) is simple standard COBOL for report preparation. Because it doesn't illustrate any special DL/I considerations, I won't describe it here.

DISCUSSION

The program example in this chapter has introduced you to the basics of DL/I programming. The chapters that follow expand the information in this chapter so you can do sophisticated data base processing and use advanced data base features. All of the information that follows depends on your mastery of the material in this chapter. As a result, if you're not comfortable with it, I encourage you to review the chapter. The time you spend will be worthwhile.

Although the inventory-availability report program is just a simple example of DL/I processing, it can serve as a model for much more complex programs. However, I don't want to mislead you. Although the simple get next processing the inventory-availability report program uses works in this instance, it won't work for *all* DL/I data bases. Whether it does or not depends on the DL/I organization of a particular data base. For example, in a data base with a particular DL/I organization (HDAM), data base records aren't stored sequentially, but rather in another sequence determined by a randomizing module. If this program were to process an HDAM inventory data base, the items wouldn't appear in sequence as they should.

At this point, I'm not going to describe the technical differences between the different options that are available for DL/I data base organization. That's an advanced topic I'll cover in section 5. For now, you can assume that you won't be asked to develop programs that require functions that don't work for the data base access method being used.

Terminology

PCB mask
get functions
get unique function
get next function
get next within parent function
get hold unique function
get hold next function
get hold next within parent function
update functions
insert function
delete function
replace function
segment search argument
SSA
unqualified SSA
qualified SSA
qualified call
unqualified call
status code

Objectives

1. Describe the format of the DL/I call and explain the function of each of the call's parameters.

2. Distinguish between:

   a. an unqualified SSA and a qualified SSA
   b. an unqualified call and a qualified call

3. Describe the purpose of a PCB mask.

4. Given the specifications for a data base, code a PCB mask for it.

5. Explain why a non-blank status code value doesn't necessarily indicate an error condition, and give two examples where that's the case.

Chapter 4

How to use segment search arguments

The last chapter described three of the four elements that can be part of a DL/I call: the DL/I function, the PCB mask, and the segment I/O area. In addition, it introduced the fourth element, the segment search argument (SSA), but it didn't show you how to code it or how to use it. That's what you'll learn in this chapter.

The inventory-availability report program in the last chapter used an unqualified GN call—that is, one without SSAs—to retrieve segments from the inventory data base in the standard DL/I sequence. Although there are cases where such simple sequential processing is useful, more often you'll need to use a more sophisticated retrieval scheme. And when you do, you have to use qualified calls, ones that *do* include SSAs.

You should recall from the last chapter that an SSA identifies the segment occurrence you want to access and can itself be either qualified or unqualified. An unqualified SSA simply names the type of segment you want to use. A qualified SSA, on the other hand, specifies not only the segment type, but also a specific occurrence of it. A qualified SSA includes a field value DL/I uses to search for the segment you request. In that sense, an SSA is like a key field for a standard indexed file. However, you're not restricted to using just a segment's sequence field in an SSA; you can use any field to which your program is sensitive.

Because of the hierarchical structure DL/I uses, you often have to specify several levels of SSAs to access a segment at a low level in a data

Unqualified SSA format

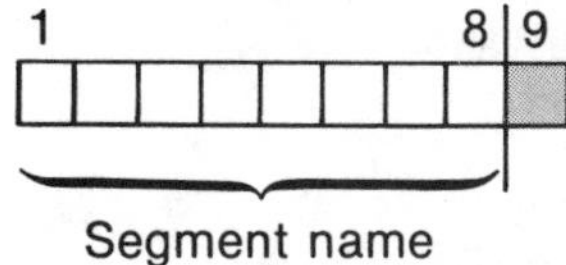

COBOL code for an unqualified SSA

```
 01  UNQUALIFIED-SSA.
*
     05  UNQUAL-SSA-SEGMENT-NAME      PIC X(8).
     05  FILLER                       PIC X         VALUE SPACE.
*
```

Figure 4-1 An unqualified SSA

base. That's no problem, though, because you can code as many SSAs on a single call as you need. And you can combine qualified and unqualified SSAs on a single call. In the chapters that follow, I'll explain the implications of coding multiple SSAs on various types of DL/I calls.

How to use unqualified SSAs

Simply put, an SSA is an area of storage that contains data which identifies the segment to which a DL/I call applies. The contents of that storage area depend on whether the SSA is qualified or unqualified. Figure 4-1 shows the format of the simpler type of SSA—the unqualified SSA—and an example of how you can code this storage area in COBOL. You code all SSAs—unqualified and qualified—in your program's Working-Storage Section.

As you can see, a basic unqualified SSA is nine bytes long. The first eight bytes contain the name of the segment you want to process; the ninth byte contains a blank. The segment name must be one the DBA assigned during DBDGEN. If the name is less than eight characters long, you must pad it on the right with blanks. The ninth position of a basic unqualified SSA always contains a blank. Because DL/I uses the value in position 9 to decide what kind of SSA you're providing, you'll encounter errors if you omit it.

The unqualified SSA in figure 4-1 is generalized; to access a particular segment type, you must modify the segment name during program execution by moving an appropriate eight-character segment name to the field UNQUAL-SSA-SEGMENT-NAME. For example, if I code

```
MOVE 'INVENSEG' TO UNQUAL-SSA-SEGMENT-NAME
```

and then issue a get call that specifies UNQUALIFIED-SSA, DL/I will return a vendor segment from the inventory data base. However, if I code

```
MOVE 'INITMSEG' TO UNQUAL-SSA-SEGMENT-NAME
```

and issue the same call, DL/I will return an item segment.

Alternatively, you can code the segment name as a literal when you define an unqualified SSA. For example, you could code

```
 01  UNQUAL-VENDOR-SSA     PIC X(9) VALUE 'INVENSEG '.
*
 01  UNQUAL-ITEM-SSA       PIC X(9) VALUE 'INITMSEG '.
*
 01  UNQUAL-STOCK-LOC-SSA  PIC X(9) VALUE 'INLOCSEG '.
```

Then, to retrieve a vendor segment, you'd specify UNQUAL-VENDOR-SSA on the get call; to retrieve an item segment, you'd specify UNQUAL-ITEM-SSA; and to retrieve a stock-location segment, you'd specify UNQUAL-STOCK-LOC-SSA.

To understand how to use an unqualified SSA in a program, consider figures 4-2 and 4-3. This is a simple report-preparation program that accesses only vendor segment occurrences in the inventory data base. For each vendor segment, the program prints a line containing the vendor's code and name. The contents of the item and stock-location segment occurrences are irrelevant for this program.

The structure of the vendor-listing program in figure 4-2 is just what you'd expect for a simple report-preparation program. In practice, a program like this would probably produce a more complex report. But all I want you to notice here is how to use an unqualified SSA to request a specific segment type.

Figure 4-3 is the complete source listing for this program. The program is much like the example in the last chapter, so it should be easy for you to understand. In it, I've shaded the code I particularly want you to notice.

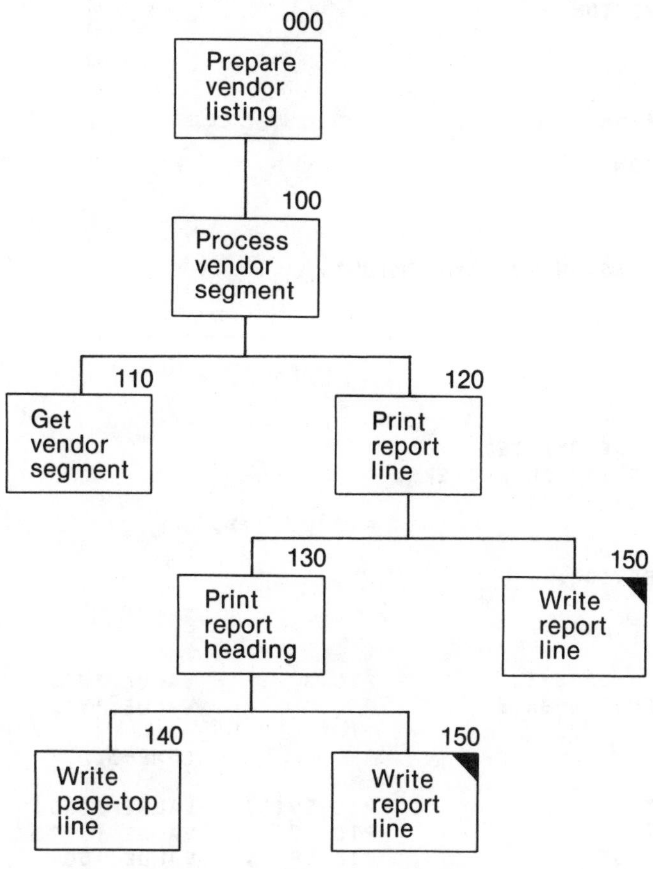

Figure 4-2 Structure chart for the vendor listing program

First, look at the CALL statement. You'll notice that in addition to the three parameters I described in the last chapter, it includes an SSA. In this case, it's the SSA from figure 4-1: UNQUALIFIED-SSA. (The name you choose for an SSA is irrelevant; even so, I encourage you to use names that are as meaningful as possible.)

Before this call can be executed successfully, the value of the segment-name variable in UNQUALIFIED-SSA has to be set properly. That's what the statement

```
MOVE 'INVENSEG' TO UNQUAL-SSA-SEGMENT-NAME
```

in module 000 does. Because this program uses only one segment type, I could just as well have coded the unqualified SSA with INVENSEG as a literal.

```
 IDENTIFICATION DIVISION.
*
 PROGRAM-ID.  INV2300.
*
 ENVIRONMENT DIVISION.
*
 INPUT-OUTPUT SECTION.
*
 FILE-CONTROL.
*
     SELECT PRTOUT ASSIGN TO UT-S-PRTOUT.
*
 DATA DIVISION.
*
 FILE SECTION.
*
 FD  PRTOUT
     LABEL RECORDS ARE OMITTED
     RECORD CONTAINS 132 CHARACTERS.
*
 01  PRTOUT-RECORD                     PIC X(132).
*
 WORKING-STORAGE SECTION.
*
 01  SWITCHES.
*
     05  END-OF-DATA-BASE-SW           PIC X          VALUE 'N'.
         88  END-OF-DATA-BASE                         VALUE 'Y'.
*
 01  PRINT-FIELDS                                     COMP-3.
*
     05  PAGE-COUNT                    PIC S9(5)      VALUE ZERO.
     05  LINE-COUNT                    PIC S9(3)      VALUE +999.
     05  LINES-ON-PAGE                 PIC S9(3)      VALUE +50.
     05  SPACE-CONTROL                 PIC S9(3)      VALUE +1.
*
 01  HEADING-LINE-1.
*
     05  FILLER             PIC X(20)    VALUE 'VENDOR LISTING
     05  FILLER             PIC X(13)    VALUE SPACE.
     05  HL1-DATE           PIC 99/99/99.
     05  FILLER             PIC X(28)    VALUE SPACE.
     05  FILLER             PIC X(6)     VALUE 'PAGE: '.
     05  HL1-PAGE           PIC Z(4)9.
     05  FILLER             PIC X(52)    VALUE SPACE.
*
 01  REPORT-LINE.
*
     05  RL-VENDOR-CODE                PIC X(3).
     05  FILLER                        PIC X(3)       VALUE SPACE.
     05  RL-VENDOR-NAME                PIC X(30).
     05  FILLER                        PIC X(96)      VALUE SPACE.
```

Figure 4-3 Source listing for the vendor listing program (part 1 of 4)

```
*
 01  DLI-FUNCTIONS.
*
     05  DLI-GU                            PIC X(4)      VALUE 'GU  '.
     05  DLI-GHU                           PIC X(4)      VALUE 'GHU '.
     05  DLI-GN                            PIC X(4)      VALUE 'GN  '.
     05  DLI-GHN                           PIC X(4)      VALUE 'GHN '.
     05  DLI-GNP                           PIC X(4)      VALUE 'GNP '.
     05  DLI-GHNP                          PIC X(4)      VALUE 'GHNP'.
     05  DLI-ISRT                          PIC X(4)      VALUE 'ISRT'.
     05  DLI-DLET                          PIC X(4)      VALUE 'DLET'.
     05  DLI-REPL                          PIC X(4)      VALUE 'REPL'.
     05  DLI-CHKP                          PIC X(4)      VALUE 'CHKP'.
     05  DLI-XRST                          PIC X(4)      VALUE 'XRST'.
     05  DLI-PCB                           PIC X(4)      VALUE 'PCB '.
*
 01  UNQUALIFIED-SSA.
*
     05  UNQUAL-SSA-SEGMENT-NAME           PIC X(8).
     05  FILLER                            PIC X         VALUE SPACE.
*
 01  INVENTORY-VENDOR-SEGMENT.
*
     05  IVS-VENDOR-CODE                   PIC X(3).
     05  IVS-VENDOR-NAME                   PIC X(30).
     05  IVS-VENDOR-ADDRESS                PIC X(30).
     05  IVS-VENDOR-CITY                   PIC X(17).
     05  IVS-VENDOR-STATE                  PIC XX.
     05  IVS-VENDOR-ZIP-CODE               PIC X(9).
     05  IVS-VENDOR-TELEPHONE              PIC X(10).
     05  IVS-VENDOR-CONTACT                PIC X(30).
*
 LINKAGE SECTION.
*
 01  INVENTORY-PCB-MASK.
*
     05  IPCB-DBD-NAME                     PIC X(8).
     05  IPCB-SEGMENT-LEVEL                PIC XX.
     05  IPCB-STATUS-CODE                  PIC XX.
     05  IPCB-PROC-OPTIONS                 PIC X(4).
     05  FILLER                            PIC S9(5)     COMP.
     05  IPCB-SEGMENT-NAME                 PIC X(8).
     05  IPCB-KEY-LENGTH                   PIC S9(5)     COMP.
     05  IPCB-NUMB-SENS-SEGS               PIC S9(5)     COMP.
     05  IPCB-KEY                          PIC X(11).
*
 PROCEDURE DIVISION.
*
     ENTRY 'DLITCBL' USING INVENTORY-PCB-MASK.
*
```

Figure 4-3 Source listing for the vendor listing program (part 2 of 4)

```
 000-PREPARE-VENDOR-LISTING.
*
     ACCEPT HL1-DATE FROM DATE.
     MOVE 'INVENSEG' TO UNQUAL-SSA-SEGMENT-NAME.
     OPEN OUTPUT PRTOUT.
     PERFORM 100-PROCESS-VENDOR-SEGMENT
         UNTIL END-OF-DATA-BASE.
     CLOSE PRTOUT.
     GOBACK.
*
 100-PROCESS-VENDOR-SEGMENT.
*
     PERFORM 110-GET-VENDOR-SEGMENT.
     IF NOT END-OF-DATA-BASE
         PERFORM 120-PRINT-REPORT-LINE.
*
 110-GET-VENDOR-SEGMENT.
*
     CALL 'CBLTDLI' USING DLI-GN
                          INVENTORY-PCB-MASK
                          INVENTORY-VENDOR-SEGMENT
                          UNQUALIFIED-SSA.
     IF IPCB-STATUS-CODE = 'GB'
         MOVE 'Y' TO END-OF-DATA-BASE-SW
     ELSE
         IF IPCB-STATUS-CODE NOT = SPACE
             MOVE 'Y' TO END-OF-DATA-BASE-SW
             DISPLAY 'INV2300 I 1 DATA BASE ERROR - STATUS CODE '
                     IPCB-STATUS-CODE.
*
 120-PRINT-REPORT-LINE.
*
     IF LINE-COUNT > LINES-ON-PAGE
         PERFORM 130-PRINT-REPORT-HEADING
         MOVE 1 TO LINE-COUNT.
     MOVE IVS-VENDOR-CODE TO RL-VENDOR-CODE.
     MOVE IVS-VENDOR-NAME TO RL-VENDOR-NAME.
     MOVE REPORT-LINE     TO PRTOUT-RECORD.
     PERFORM 150-WRITE-REPORT-LINE.
     ADD 1                TO LINE-COUNT.
     MOVE 1               TO SPACE-CONTROL.
*
 130-PRINT-REPORT-HEADING.
*
     ADD 1               TO PAGE-COUNT.
     MOVE PAGE-COUNT     TO HL1-PAGE.
     MOVE HEADING-LINE-1 TO PRTOUT-RECORD.
     PERFORM 140-WRITE-PAGE-TOP-LINE.
     MOVE 2              TO SPACE-CONTROL.
*
```

Figure 4-3 Source listing for the vendor listing program (part 3 of 4)

```
 140-WRITE-PAGE-TOP-LINE.
*
     WRITE PRTOUT-RECORD
         AFTER ADVANCING PAGE.
*
 150-WRITE-REPORT-LINE.
*
     WRITE PRTOUT-RECORD
         AFTER SPACE-CONTROL LINES.
*
```

Figure 4-3 Source listing for the vendor listing program (part 4 of 4)

This program also illustrates a different way to specify the segment I/O area. The program in the last chapter used a common I/O area for all three segment types. After it determined what type of segment had been retrieved, the program moved the contents of the I/O area to the appropriate segment description. However, because the vendor-listing program retrieves only vendor segments, it's practical to use the segment description directly as the call's I/O area. So the CALL statement in figure 4-3 specifies INVENTORY-VENDOR-SEGMENT as its I/O area. As a general rule, when you use SSAs to control the segment type that's going to be returned, you can use the segment description as the call's I/O area.

How to use qualified SSAs

Although unqualified SSAs give you more control over data base operations than unqualified calls do, you often need to specify that a call is for a specific occurrence of a particular segment type. To do that, you have to use a qualified SSA. Simply put, a qualified SSA lets you specify a particular segment occurrence based on a condition that a field within the segment must meet. For example, you could specify a particular occurrence of the vendor segment type by specifying that the vendor code field must have a specific value.

Figure 4-4 shows the general format of a qualified SSA and gives a COBOL example. Like an unqualified SSA, you code qualified SSAs in the Working-Storage Section of your program, then refer to them by name in your DL/I calls. However, the format of a qualified SSA is more complex than that of an unqualified SSA. Both begin with the

Qualified SSA format

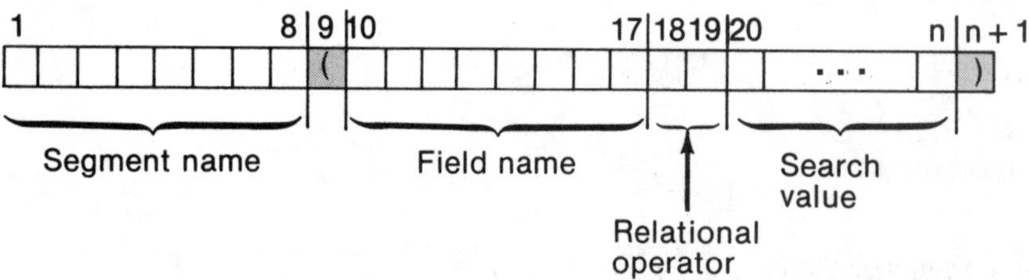

COBOL code for a qualified SSA

```
 01   VENDOR-SSA.
*
      05   FILLER                       PIC X(9)   VALUE 'INVENSEG('.
      05   FILLER                       PIC X(10)  VALUE 'INVENCOD ='.
      05   VENDOR-SSA-CODE              PIC X(3).
      05   FILLER                       PIC X      VALUE ')'.
*
```

Figure 4-4 A qualified SSA

eight-character segment name. The ninth position of a qualified SSA is a left parenthesis: (.

Immediately following the left parenthesis in positions 10 through 17 is an eight-character field name. As with the segment name, the field name must be specified in the data base's DBDGEN. And if the field name is fewer than eight characters, you must pad it on the right with spaces. After the field name, in positions 18 and 19, you code a two-character *relational operator* to indicate the kind of checking DL/I should do on the field in the segment. (More on the values you can use for the relational operator in a moment.)

After the relational operator, you code a variable field into which you move the search value you want to use for the call. The length of the search value field can vary depending on the size of the field in the segment; it's the only part of a basic qualified SSA that doesn't have a fixed length. Finally, the last character in the qualified SSA is a right parenthesis:).

The two-character value you use for the relational operator depends on the sort of comparison you want to make between the

	Letters	Symbols	
Equal to	EQ	=□	□=
Not equal to	NE	¬=	=¬
Greater than	GT	>□	□>
Greater than or equal to	GE	>=	=>
Less than	LT	<□	□<
Less than or equal to	LE	<=	=<

Figure 4-5 Qualified SSA relational operators

search value you specify and the value of the field you name. As figure 4-5 shows, you can use either letters or symbols to indicate six possible relationships. To retrieve a particular segment occurrence with a GU call, you'll want to specify that the search field has a value that's equal to the one you specify. In that case, you'd code EQ or = (either preceded or followed by a space) as the relational operator. In other cases, most likely to establish a position for subsequent sequential processing, you can use any of the other values in figure 4-5.

In the chapters that follow, you'll see program examples that use qualified SSAs. For now, I just want to describe how to use one. In VENDOR-SSA, illustrated in figure 4-4, I defined one variable field: VENDOR-SSA-CODE. It's the same length as the code field (INVENCOD) in the vendor segment (INVENSEG). Notice that I coded both the field and segment names in the proper positions in the SSA. I specified the equal sign as the relational operator, so when I issue a call that specifies VENDOR-SSA, the vendor segment that's processed will be the one with the vendor code value I've moved to VENDOR-SSA-CODE. For example, suppose these statements are executed when the value of the field TR-VENDOR-CODE is 411:

```
MOVE TR-VENDOR-CODE TO VENDOR-SSA-CODE.
CALL 'CBLTDLI' USING DLI-GU
                     INVENTORY-PCB-MASK
                     INVENTORY-VENDOR-SEGMENT
                     VENDOR-SSA.
```

Command code	Meaning
C	Concatenated key
D	Path call
F	First occurrence
L	Last occurrence
N	Path call ignore
P	Set parentage
Q	Enqueue segment
U	Maintain position at this level
V	Maintain position at this and all superior levels
—	Null command code

Figure 4-6 SSA command codes

The result is that the specific vendor segment occurrence whose code field has the value 411 is returned, if one is present in the data base.

At this point, you know all you have to know about SSAs for most data base processing. However, DL/I provides additional SSA features that can be particularly useful in some situations: command codes and multiple qualification.

How to use SSAs with command codes

You can use SSA *command codes* to extend the functions of DL/I calls. In some cases, command codes can simplify your programs because they let you perform a function in a single DL/I call that otherwise would require two or more. And that also means a performance improvement, because issuing DL/I calls is expensive in terms of the system resources it requires.

Figure 4-6 lists the command code values you can use. As you can see, each command code is a single-character value that indicates a specific function. In this chapter, I'll show you how to use the "-"

Unqualified SSA format with a single command code

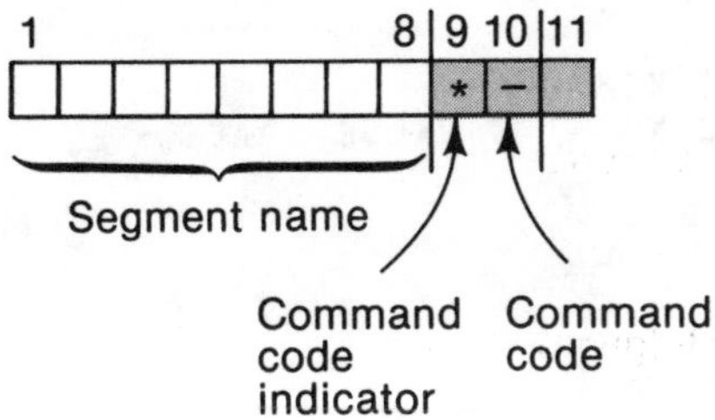

Qualified SSA format with a single command code

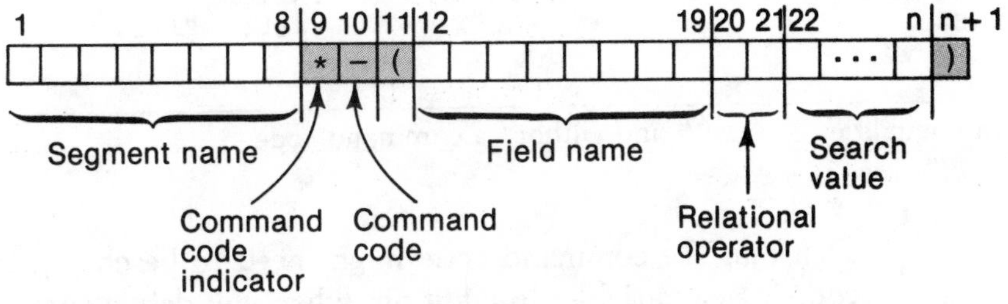

Figure 4-7 Formats of unqualified and qualified SSAs with a single command code

command code. Then, in the chapters that follow, I'll describe the others along with the calls in which you use them. First, however, you need to know how to include command codes in your SSAs.

To use command codes, code an asterisk in position 9 of the SSA. Then, code your command codes starting in position 10. When DL/I finds an asterisk in position 9, it knows command codes follow. From position 10 on, DL/I considers all characters to be command codes until it encounters a space (for an unqualified SSA) or a left parenthesis (for a qualified SSA). However, it's unusual to use more than one command code in a single SSA. As a result, most SSAs you use with command codes will have one of the formats shown in figure 4-7.

Like other SSA components, you can code a command code either as a literal value or as a variable. If you use an SSA for the same call function with the same command code all the time, you might as well include the command code as a literal. However, if your application is

Basic unqualified SSA

```
 01  UNQUALIFIED-SSA.
*
     05  UNQUAL-SSA-SEGMENT-NAME     PIC X(8).
     05  FILLER                      PIC X        VALUE SPACE.
*
```

Unqualified SSA with a single, variable command code

```
 01  UNQUALIFIED-SSA.
*
     05  UNQUAL-SSA-SEGMENT-NAME     PIC X(8).
     05  FILLER                      PIC X        VALUE "*".
     05  UNQUAL-SSA-COMMAND-CODE     PIC X        VALUE "-".
     05  FILLER                      PIC X        VALUE SPACE.
*
```

Figure 4-8 An unqualified SSA with and without a command code

such that the command code might need to be changed, you should code it as a variable. In addition, when you define command codes as variables, you have the option not only of changing them, but also of turning them off altogether using a special command code value: the *null command code.*

The null command code (-) When the value of a command code field is a hyphen (-), it's considered to be a null command code. In other words, although the command code position is present, DL/I ignores it. This can be particularly useful if you'd like to be able to use the same SSA with and without command codes.

For example, consider the two unqualified SSA descriptions in figure 4-8. The one in the top of the figure is like the one you're already familiar with: an eight-character segment name followed by one space. The SSA in the bottom of the figure includes a variable command code field that's initialized to a hyphen, the null command code.

In terms of function, the two SSAs in figure 4-8 are the same. Because the command code in the second SSA is a hyphen, DL/I ignores it. However, if the program needs to use the SSA with a command code, it can move the appropriate one-letter value to UNQUAL-SSA-COMMAND-CODE before issuing the call. Then, to make the SSA again function as though it doesn't have a command

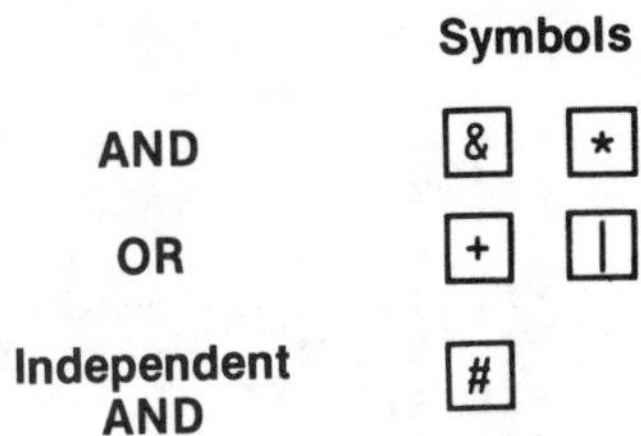

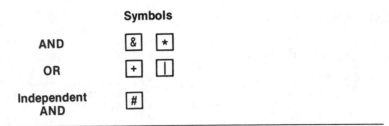

Figure 4-9 Boolean operators for use in SSAs with multiple qualification

code, the program will move a hyphen back to UNQUAL-SSA-COMMAND-CODE.

How to use SSAs with multiple qualification

Another advanced feature of SSAs that you might want to use for some applications is *multiple qualification*. There are two cases in which you'd use SSAs with multiple qualification. The first is when you want to process a segment based on the contents of two or more fields within it. The second is when you want to process a segment based on a range of possible values for a single field.

To use multiple qualification, you connect two or more qualification statements (a field name, a relational operator, and a comparison value) within the parentheses of the SSA. To connect them, you use the *Boolean operators* AND and OR. As figure 4-9 shows, you can use either of two symbols for both of these operators. (The third Boolean operator in figure 4-9, the independent AND, is used for special operations with secondary indexes, which I'll describe in chapter 7.)

To illustrate, suppose you want to retrieve vendor segments whose vendor codes fall within a certain range. Figure 4-10 shows how you could construct an SSA with multiple qualification to do that. Here, two qualification statements are connected by an AND operator (&). The first qualification statement specifies that the vendor code field must be greater than or equal to a particular value; that's the low end of the range. The second qualification statement specifies that the vendor code field must be less than or equal to a particular value; that's the high end of the range. To retrieve the vendor segments that fall within this range, you would first move values for the low and high ends of the range to VENDOR-SSA-LOW-CODE and VENDOR-SSA-HIGH-CODE. Then, you would execute GN calls that include VENDOR-SSA.

```
 01  VENDOR-SSA.
*
     05  FILLER                    PIC X(9)     VALUE 'INVENSEG('.
     05  FILLER                    PIC X(10)    VALUE 'INVENCOD>='.
     05  VENDOR-SSA-LOW-CODE       PIC X(3).
     05  FILLER                    PIC X        VALUE '&'.
     05  FILLER                    PIC X(10)    VALUE 'INVENCOD<='.
     05  VENDOR-SSA-HIGH-CODE      PIC X(3).
     05  FILLER                    PIC X        VALUE ')'.
```

Figure 4-10 An SSA that provides multiple qualification

You can code SSAs of considerable complexity when you use multiple qualification. Keep in mind, though, that you'll seldom use SSAs with multiple qualification. And when you do, it will almost always be with just two qualification statements. When that's the case, the relationship the Boolean operator implies will be obvious.

When you use more than two qualification statements, you need to understand that DL/I evaluates them from left to right. In addition, you need to understand the concept of a *qualification set*. An OR operator or the end of an SSA marks the end of a set, and an AND operator connects individual qualifications *within* a set. For an SSA's qualification to be satisfied, at least one set must be satisfied. And for one set to be satisfied, all of the qualifications within it (which are connected by ANDs) must be satisfied.

Discussion

Although you should now know how to code both unqualified and qualified SSAs with or without command codes and multiple qualification, I don't expect you to understand how SSAs are used for the various types of DL/I calls. That's what you'll learn in the next two chapters: chapter 5 shows you how to use the get calls, and chapter 6 shows you how to use the update calls (insert, delete, and replace). In those chapters, I'll describe in detail how you can use SSAs to influence the way those calls operate.

Terminology

relational operator
command code
null command code
multiple qualification
Boolean operator
qualification set

Objectives

1. Given data base specifications, code a fully qualified SSA with single or multiple qualification for any segment in the data base.

2. Describe how to specify a command code on an SSA.

3. Describe the function of the null command code.

Chapter 5

How to retrieve data from a data base

Now that you're familiar with the basics of using DL/I through COBOL, you're ready to learn more details about data base retrieval calls. This chapter has five main sections. The first shows you how to retrieve data from a data base randomly using GU calls qualified with SSAs. The second shows you how to retrieve segments sequentially using GN and GNP calls. The third presents another report-preparation program example that illustrates how to use these calls. The fourth section shows you how to use SSA command codes in retrieval calls. Finally, the fifth section shows you how to use multiple positioning.

Random processing: The GU call

Random processing using DL/I is similar to random processing with standard files: you know what data you want to retrieve, and you want to get to it directly. In standard COBOL, you supply a key value, then execute a READ statement with the INVALID KEY option. When you use DL/I, you issue a GU (get unique) call, usually with a set of qualified SSAs. A GU call is independent of the position established by previous calls, unlike the GN calls used in the report-preparation programs you've already seen.

In terms of application, random processing is easiest to understand in an interactive environment. For example, suppose a terminal operator wants to know how many units of a given inventory item are stocked at a particular location. He invokes an inquiry program and supplies the vendor code, item number, and location. The inquiry program uses these values to build three qualified SSAs, then issues a DL/I call like this:

```
CALL 'CBLTDLI' USING DLI-GU
                     INVENTORY-PCB-MASK
                     INVENTORY-STOCK-LOC-SEGMENT
                     VENDOR-SSA
                     ITEM-SSA
                     STOCK-LOCATION-SSA.
```

If the call is successful, the program formats the data it retrieved and displays the result for the user.

In batch programs, random processing is typically used when a relatively small number of updates are posted to a large data base. And sometimes you'll use random processing to establish position in a data base for subsequent sequential retrieval. You'll see program examples that illustrate both applications in this book.

Most of the time when you use a GU call, you'll supply a complete set of qualified SSAs down to and including the level of the segment you want to retrieve, as I just described. A complete set of SSAs to retrieve a segment includes one for each segment level in the hierarchical path to the segment type you want to retrieve. That's a *fully qualified call.*

Since the path to a location segment in the inventory data base has three segments, a fully qualified call for a location segment occurrence has three qualified SSAs, as in the example above. Similarly, the path to the item segment type has two segments, so a fully qualified GU call to retrieve an item has two qualified SSAs. And the path to the vendor type has just one segment, so a GU call for a vendor segment occurrence requires just one SSA. In each case, the lowest level SSA you specify is the one for the segment type you want to retrieve.

Usually, GU processing is based on sequence (key) fields with unique values. However, for some applications, it's necessary to access a segment whose sequence field allows non-unique values. Or, you can issue a GU call for a segment based on a field that's not the segment's key field. When you do that, DL/I returns the first segment occurrence with the specified search value. The data base designer should tell you if a field you'll use in a GU call can have non-unique values. Then, you can use a GU call to retrieve the first segment with that value and GN calls to retrieve the rest.

Special considerations for GU calls without a full set of qualified SSAs Although most of the GU calls you use will be fully qualified, there are times when you may want to use different techniques. When you do, you need to be aware of some special DL/I processing considerations.

First, when you use an unqualified SSA in a GU call, DL/I accesses the first segment occurrence in the data base that meets the criteria you specify. Of course, if you include qualified SSAs in the call, DL/I tries to adhere to their specifications. For example, to locate the item in the inventory data base with number 52301, you could issue a GU call with an unqualified SSA for the vendor segment and a qualified SSA for the item segment. DL/I then searches through the data base until it finds the first item occurrence with number 52301, regardless of the value of the sequence field of the parent vendor segment.

You can also use this technique to establish position at the first occurrence of a dependent segment within a path. For instance, to establish position at the first location segment subordinate to the item segment with number 52301, you could issue a GU call with a qualified SSA for the item segment and with an unqualified SSA for the location segment.

If you issue a GU call without any SSAs, DL/I returns the first occurrence of the root segment in the data base. This can be useful to reset position at the beginning of a data base for sequential processing applications.

If you omit some SSAs for intermediate levels in a hierarchical path, the action DL/I takes depends on your current position and on the SSAs that are missing. DL/I either uses the established position or defaults to an unqualified SSA for the segment. Because this can become tricky, I recommend you always code a qualified or unqualified SSA for each level in the path from the root segment to the segment you want to retrieve. For more information about the effects of omitting SSAs on a GU call, consult either the IMS or DL/I DOS/VS application programming manual.

Status codes you can expect during random processing When you issue GU calls in typical programs, you only need to consider two status code values. Spaces means the call was successful and the requested segment was returned in your program's I/O area. And a GE status code indicates that DL/I couldn't find a segment that met the criteria you specified in the call. This is equivalent to the INVALID KEY condition that can be raised during standard file processing.

If you issue a GU call that results in a GE status code, the action you take depends on the application. In an interactive program, it probably means the operator entered an inaccurate key value and should try again. In batch processing, it can mean that an invalid transaction was detected. In both cases, processing can proceed normally with the next entry or transaction, as long as notification of the error is provided so it can be corrected.

Sequential processing: The GN and GNP calls

You can use either the GN or GNP call to retrieve segments sequentially. In this section, I'll show you how to use both, and I'll describe the status codes you can expect during sequential processing.

Basic sequential processing: The GN call The report-preparation programs you've seen in the last two chapters used simple sequential processing, with the GN call, to retrieve data from the inventory data base. In this section, I'll give you more information on how to use GN calls.

To understand sequential retrieval, you have to understand data base position. After a successful call, your data base position is immediately before the *next* segment occurrence in the normal hierarchical sequence. Before your program issues any calls, position is before the root segment of the first data base record.

The GN call moves forward through the data base from the position established by the previous call. In the program in chapter 3, the GN call was unqualified. As a result, it returned each segment occurrence in the data base, regardless of type, in hierarchical sequence. The program in the last chapter used a single unqualified SSA in a GN call to access only vendor segment occurrences. Even so, that qualified GN call still moved forward through the data base from the current position.

When you issue a GN call, you can include SSAs. Then, DL/I retrieves only segments that meet the requirements of all the SSAs you specify. If you include an unqualified SSA or omit an SSA altogether for a segment type, DL/I allows any occurrence of that segment type to satisfy the call. But when you specify a qualified SSA, DL/I selects only those segment occurrences that meet the criteria you specify. For example, suppose you want to retrieve all location segment occurrences that have a sequence field value of NYC. To do that, you could set up a qualified SSA that specifies NYC as the location code and then issue this call:

```
CALL 'CBLTDLI' USING DLI-GN
                     INVENTORY-PCB-MASK
                     SEGMENT-I-O-AREA
                     STOCK-LOCATION-SSA.
```

The next occurrence of the location segment whose sequence field has the value NYC will be returned to the I/O area, regardless of the sequence field values of the vendor and item segment occurrences that are above it in the hierarchy.

Often, you want to retrieve a series of segments in hierarchical sequence, but you only want the segments that are dependent on a particular segment occurrence. For example, you might want to retrieve all the item segment occurrences for a particular vendor segment. To do that, you issue a GU call to establish position at the proper vendor segment, then issue GN calls to retrieve item segments. However, your program's logic then has to determine when an item segment is returned that isn't subordinate to the vendor segment you're interested in. Because this kind of processing is common, DL/I includes a special call to make it easier: GNP.

Sequential processing within parentage: The GNP call The GNP call works just like the GN call, except it retrieves only segments that are subordinate to the currently established parent. To use GNP calls, you have to understand *parentage*. To establish parentage, your program must issue either a GU or a GN call, and the call must be successful. The segment returned by that call becomes the established parent. Then, subsequent GNP calls return only segment occurrences that are dependent on that parent. When there are no more segments within the established parentage, DL/I returns GE as the status code.

Don't assume that parentage is automatically established because of the hierarchical structure of the data base. For example, the fact that the location segment type in the inventory data base is the child of the item segment type does *not* imply that parentage is in effect between a given occurrence of the item segment and subordinate occurrences of the location segment type. To establish parentage, you *must* issue a GU or GN call to retrieve the parent segment.

To understand parentage and the GNP call, consider figure 5-1. Both parts of this figure represent a simple inventory data base record that contains two item segment occurrences, each with three location segment occurrences. In both parts of the figure, GNP calls will be issued repeatedly to return location segment occurrences.

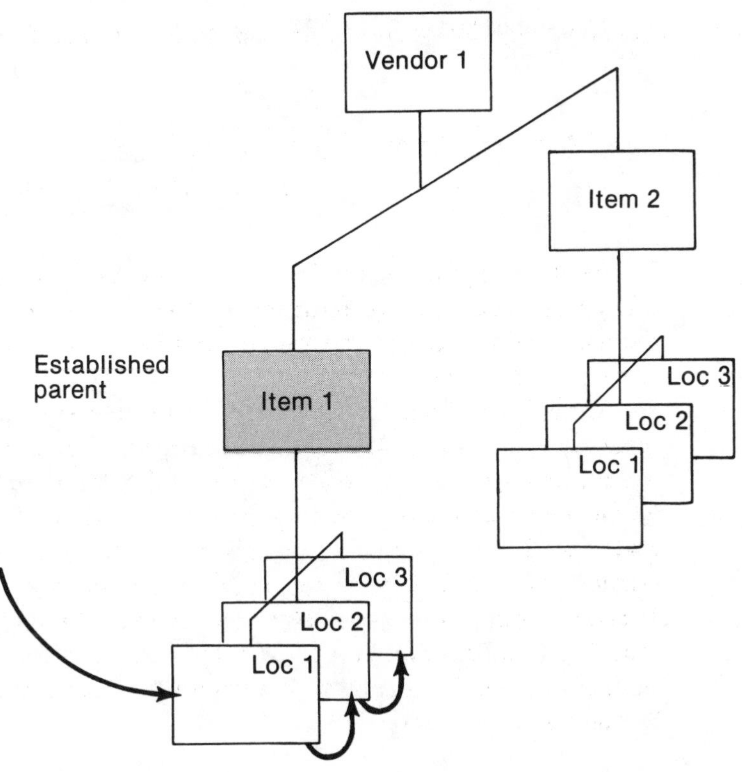

Figure 5-1 Sequential retrieval with GNP calls (part 1 of 2)

In part 1, a GU call establishes position and parentage at item 1. Then, GNP calls are issued for the location segments. The arrows show the sequence of segments that are retrieved: locations 1, 2, and 3, all subordinate to item 1. The fourth GNP call results in a GE status code because there are no more location segment occurrences subordinate to the established parent.

Part 2 of the figure shows what happens if parentage is established by a GU call at the vendor segment level. In this case, GNP calls that specify an unqualified SSA for the location segment retrieve all six location occurrences in the first data base record. If you issued unqualified GNP calls with vendor 1 as the established parent, item segments would be retrieved as well, in this sequence: item 1, locations 1, 2, and 3 of item 1, item 2, and locations 1, 2, and 3 of item 2.

The GNP call can make programming easier for some applications. When you use it, just be careful to establish parentage where you want

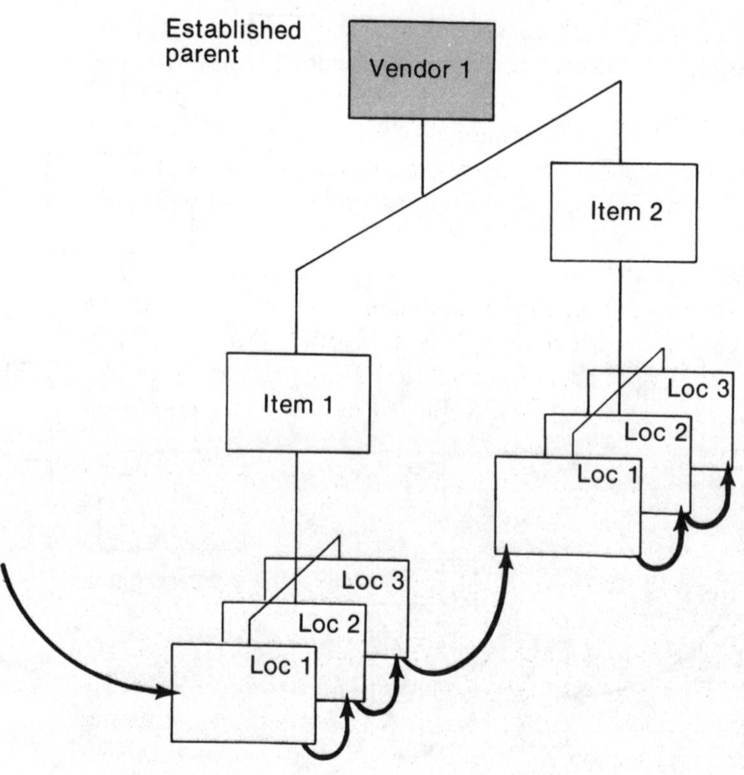

Figure 5-1 Sequential retrieval with GNP calls (part 2 of 2)

it. If you make a mistake establishing parentage before issuing a GNP call, the results you get can be dramatically wrong.

When you code a qualified GNP call, don't include SSAs for segments at a level higher than or equal to that of the currently established parent segment. If you do, you'll get a GP status code.

Status codes you can expect during sequential processing As with the GU call, blanks in the PCB status code field after a GN or GNP call indicate that the call was successful. And as with a GU call, a GE status code indicates that a segment occurrence that meets the requirements of the SSAs you specified couldn't be found. That doesn't necessarily mean that such segments don't exist; it means there are none *after* the current data base position. Remember, GN and GNP calls look forward in the data base.

Other status codes can occur during sequential processing, too. You've already seen examples of two in the program example in chapter 3: GB and GA.

The GB status code, which can occur with a GN but not a GNP call, indicates that you've tried to retrieve a segment but are at the end of the data base. It's like the AT END condition that's raised during sequential processing with the standard COBOL READ statement. If you're processing a data base from beginning to end, GB is a status code value you should expect. (When you reach the end of a data base with the GNP call, DL/I returns the GE status code.)

The GA status code, to which you also were introduced in chapter 3, is raised when an unqualified GN or GNP call moves up a level in the data base hierarchy to retrieve a segment. Notice that I said an *unqualified* call: GA never occurs for qualified calls. Depending on the requirements of your application, a GA may or may not be a condition your program needs to handle.

The GK status code is similar to GA. It's raised by an unqualified GN or GNP call when a segment type other than the one just retrieved is accessed, but at the *same* hierarchical level. Again, depending on the requirements of your application, a GK may or may not represent a condition you need to handle.

If you issue a GNP call without first establishing parentage, you get a GP status code. You might also get a GP if there's an error in the SSAs you use in a GNP call. A GP almost always represents a programming error: either your program didn't issue a GU or GN call to establish parentage or the call wasn't successful, but the program attempted the GNP anyway. An unusual but possible case in which you might get a GP is if an established parent segment is deleted before the GNP calls that depend on it have all been issued.

A more complex report-preparation program

Now that you've seen how to use the get calls, I want to illustrate them in a more complex report-preparation program. Figure 5-2 is the print chart for a program that produces a reorder report from the inventory data base. To determine if an item should be listed, the program reads through the location segments subordinate to the item to see if any has a stock level (quantity on hand plus quantity on order) that's at or below its reorder point. Then, if stock needs to be reordered for any location, the data for *all* locations stocking the item should be printed. That way, purchasing personnel have the option of transferring stock from one location to another instead of reordering.

The program works through the data base sequentially, accessing item segments with GN calls. After it accesses an item, a series of GNP

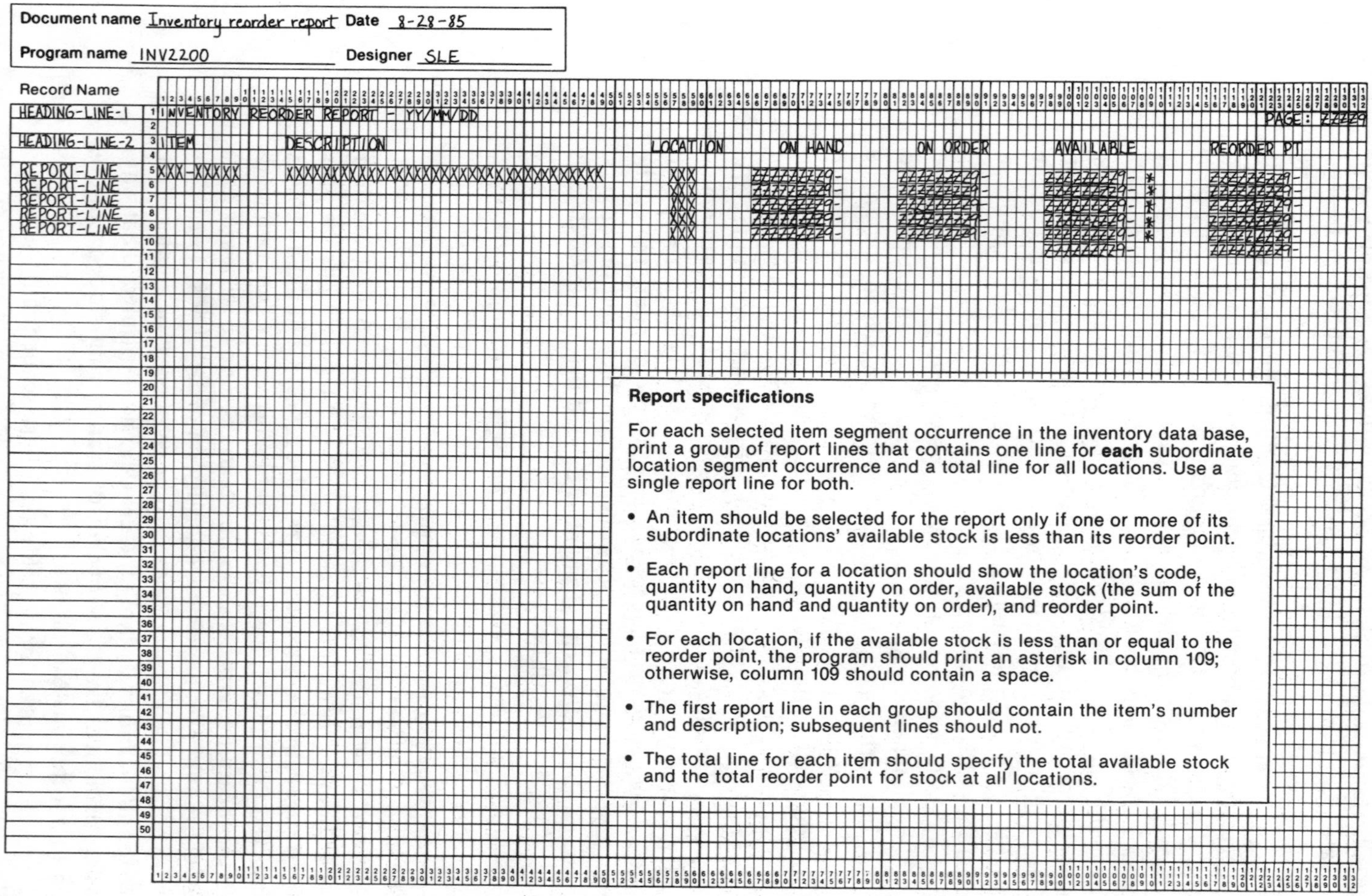

Document name Inventory reorder report Date 8-28-85

Program name INV2200 Designer SLE

Record Name	Line	Print layout
HEADING-LINE-1	1	INVENTORY REORDER REPORT - YY/MM/DD PAGE: ZZZZ9
	2	
HEADING-LINE-2	3	ITEM DESCRIPTION LOCATION ON HAND ON ORDER AVAILABLE REORDER PT
	4	
REPORT-LINE	5	XXX-XXXXX XXXXXXXXXXXXXXXXXXXXXXXXXXXXXXXXXXXX XXX ZZZZZZZ9- ZZZZZZZ9- ZZZZZZZ9- * ZZZZZZZ9-
REPORT-LINE	6	XXX ZZZZZZZ9- ZZZZZZZ9- ZZZZZZZ9- * ZZZZZZZ9-
REPORT-LINE	7	XXX ZZZZZZZ9- ZZZZZZZ9- ZZZZZZZ9- * ZZZZZZZ9-
REPORT-LINE	8	XXX ZZZZZZZ9- ZZZZZZZ9- ZZZZZZZ9- * ZZZZZZZ9-
REPORT-LINE	9	XXX ZZZZZZZ9- ZZZZZZZ9- ZZZZZZZ9- * ZZZZZZZ9-
	10	ZZZZZZZ9- ZZZZZZZ9-

Report specifications

For each selected item segment occurrence in the inventory data base, print a group of report lines that contains one line for **each** subordinate location segment occurrence and a total line for all locations. Use a single report line for both.

- An item should be selected for the report only if one or more of its subordinate locations' available stock is less than its reorder point.
- Each report line for a location should show the location's code, quantity on hand, quantity on order, available stock (the sum of the quantity on hand and quantity on order), and reorder point.
- For each location, if the available stock is less than or equal to the reorder point, the program should print an asterisk in column 109; otherwise, column 109 should contain a space.
- The first report line in each group should contain the item's number and description; subsequent lines should not.
- The total line for each item should specify the total available stock and the total reorder point for stock at all locations.

Figure 5-2 Print chart and report specifications for the inventory reorder report program

calls retrieve the subordinate location segments. As each location segment is retrieved, it's evaluated to determine if it meets the condition required for reporting. If it doesn't, processing continues with the next location segment (via a GNP call) or, if there are no more subordinate location segments, with the next item (via a GN).

On the other hand, if a given location segment does meet the reporting requirement, position must be reestablished at the parent item segment so any preceding location segments can be accessed for reporting. To do that, the program issues a GU call with fully qualified SSAs for the vendor and item segments. Then, all of its subordinate location segments can again be retrieved by a series of GNP calls. This time, though, a report line is printed for each location segment, according to the print chart in figure 5-2. And data from each location segment is accumulated to print a total line for the item.

Figures 5-3 and 5-4 present the structure chart and source code for the program. As you can see, it's more complex than the two report-preparation programs you've already studied. The sections of the program that I shaded are the ones I particularly want you to notice.

First, notice that I coded an unqualified SSA with a variable I'll set to indicate whether I want to retrieve an item (INITMSEG) segment occurrence with a GN call or a location (INLOCSEG) segment occurrence with a GNP call. And I coded qualified SSAs for the vendor and item segment types; I use them in the GU call that reestablishes position when it's necessary to back up in the data base.

Also, notice that there's no segment description for the vendor segment type in this program. That's because no calls retrieve the vendor segment. All that's required is that the value of the vendor segment sequence field be available when it's necessary to issue a GU call for an item segment, and the program can always get that from the concatenated key field of the PCB mask. To make it easy to extract the current vendor code from the PCB, I defined the IPCB-KEY field with three subordinate fields, one of which, IPCB-VENDOR-CODE, will contain the current vendor code.

Now, I want to describe the three calls I coded in the Procedure Division. The first, in module 110, is the GN call to retrieve the next item segment in hierarchical sequence from the data base:

```
CALL 'CBLTDLI' USING DLI-GN
                     INVENTORY-PCB-MASK
                     INVENTORY-ITEM-SEGMENT
                     UNQUALIFIED-SSA.
```

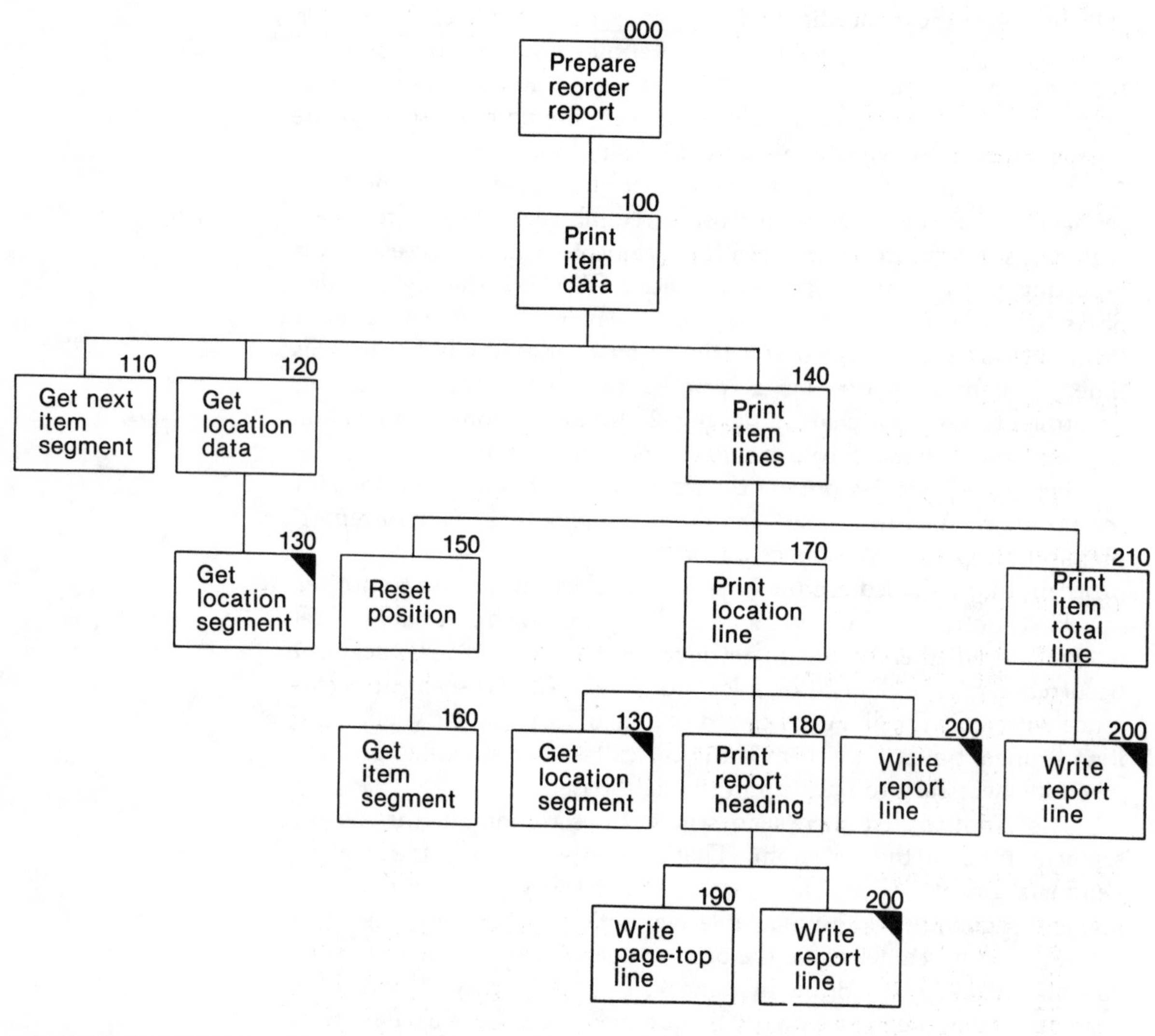

Figure 5-3 Structure chart for the inventory reorder report program

The first shaded MOVE statement in module 100 formats the unqualified SSA with the proper segment name. And because this call will return only an item segment occurrence, I specified the item segment description (INVENTORY-ITEM-SEGMENT) as the call's I/O area.

Notice the status code checking I use in module 110. First, I evaluate the PCB status code field for GB; that would indicate that the end of the data base has been reached and the program should end.

```
IDENTIFICATION DIVISION.
*
PROGRAM-ID.  INV2200.
*
ENVIRONMENT DIVISION.
*
INPUT-OUTPUT SECTION.
*
FILE-CONTROL.
*
    SELECT PRTOUT ASSIGN TO UT-S-PRTOUT.
*
DATA DIVISION.
*
FILE SECTION.
*
FD  PRTOUT
    LABEL RECORDS ARE OMITTED
    RECORD CONTAINS 132 CHARACTERS.
*
01  PRTOUT-RECORD                   PIC X(132).
*
WORKING-STORAGE SECTION.
*
01  SWITCHES.
*
    05  PRINT-ITEM-SW               PIC X        VALUE 'N'.
        88  PRINT-ITEM                           VALUE 'Y'.
    05  FIRST-LOCATION-SW           PIC X        VALUE 'N'.
        88  FIRST-LOCATION                       VALUE 'Y'.
    05  ALL-LOCATIONS-PROCESSED-SW  PIC X        VALUE 'N'.
        88  ALL-LOCATIONS-PROCESSED              VALUE 'Y'.
    05  END-OF-DATA-BASE-SW         PIC X        VALUE 'N'.
        88  END-OF-DATA-BASE                     VALUE 'Y'.
*
01  COUNT-FIELDS                                 COMP-3.
*
    05  LOCATION-COUNT              PIC S9(3)    VALUE ZERO.
    05  ON-HAND-TOTAL               PIC S9(9)    VALUE ZERO.
    05  AVAILABLE-STOCK             PIC S9(9)    VALUE ZERO.
    05  TOTAL-AVAILABLE-STOCK       PIC S9(9)    VALUE ZERO.
    05  TOTAL-REORDER-POINT         PIC S9(9)    VALUE ZERO.
*
01  PRINT-FIELDS                                 COMP-3.
*
    05  PAGE-COUNT                  PIC S9(5)    VALUE +1.
    05  LINE-COUNT                  PIC S9(3)    VALUE +999.
    05  LINES-ON-PAGE               PIC S9(3)    VALUE +50.
    05  SPACE-CONTROL               PIC S9(3)    VALUE ZERO.
*
```

Figure 5-4 Source listing for the inventory reorder report program (part 1 of 7)

```
 01  HEADING-LINE-1.
*
     05  FILLER            PIC X(20)   VALUE 'INVENTORY REORDER RE'.
     05  FILLER            PIC X(7)    VALUE 'PORT - '.
     05  HL1-SYSTEM-DATE PIC 99/99/99.
     05  FILLER            PIC X(86)   VALUE SPACE.
     05  FILLER            PIC X(6)    VALUE 'PAGE: '.
     05  HL1-PAGE          PIC Z(4)9.
*
 01  HEADING-LINE-2.
*
     05  FILLER            PIC X(20)   VALUE 'ITEM          DESCRI'.
     05  FILLER            PIC X(20)   VALUE 'PTION               '.
     05  FILLER            PIC X(20)   VALUE '              LOCATI'.
     05  FILLER            PIC X(20)   VALUE 'ON       ON HAND    '.
     05  FILLER            PIC X(20)   VALUE '   ON ORDER       AV'.
     05  FILLER            PIC X(20)   VALUE 'AILABLE        REORD'.
     05  FILLER            PIC X(12)   VALUE 'ER PT       '.
*
 01  REPORT-LINE.
*
     05  RL-VENDOR-CODE                PIC X(3).
     05  RL-HYPHEN                     PIC X.
     05  RL-NUMBER                     PIC X(5).
     05  FILLER                        PIC X(5)    VALUE SPACE.
     05  RL-DESCRIPTION                PIC X(35).
     05  FILLER                        PIC X(7)    VALUE SPACE.
     05  RL-LOCATION                   PIC X(3).
     05  FILLER                        PIC X(6)    VALUE SPACE.
     05  RL-ON-HAND                    PIC Z(8)9-.
     05  FILLER                        PIC X(6)    VALUE SPACE.
     05  RL-ON-ORDER                   PIC Z(8)9-.
     05  FILLER                        PIC X(6)    VALUE SPACE.
     05  RL-AVAILABLE                  PIC Z(8)9-.
     05  FILLER                        PIC X       VALUE SPACE.
     05  RL-STAR                       PIC X.
     05  FILLER                        PIC X(6)    VALUE SPACE.
     05  RL-REORDER-POINT              PIC Z(8)9-.
     05  FILLER                        PIC X(7)    VALUE SPACE.
*
 01  DLI-FUNCTIONS.
*
     05  DLI-GU                        PIC X(4)    VALUE 'GU  '.
     05  DLI-GHU                       PIC X(4)    VALUE 'GHU '.
     05  DLI-GN                        PIC X(4)    VALUE 'GN  '.
     05  DLI-GHN                       PIC X(4)    VALUE 'GHN '.
     05  DLI-GNP                       PIC X(4)    VALUE 'GNP '.
     05  DLI-GHNP                      PIC X(4)    VALUE 'GHNP'.
     05  DLI-ISRT                      PIC X(4)    VALUE 'ISRT'.
     05  DLI-DLET                      PIC X(4)    VALUE 'DLET'.
     05  DLI-REPL                      PIC X(4)    VALUE 'REPL'.
     05  DLI-CHKP                      PIC X(4)    VALUE 'CHKP'.
     05  DLI-XRST                      PIC X(4)    VALUE 'XRST'.
     05  DLI-PCB                       PIC X(4)    VALUE 'PCB '.
```

Figure 5-4 Source listing for the inventory reorder report program (part 2 of 7)

```
*
 01  UNQUALIFIED-SSA.
*
     05  UNQUAL-SSA-SEGMENT-NAME PIC X(8).
     05  FILLER                  PIC X       VALUE SPACE.
*
 01  VENDOR-SSA.
*
     05  FILLER                  PIC X(9)    VALUE 'INVENSEG('.
     05  FILLER                  PIC X(10)   VALUE 'INVENCOD ='.
     05  VENDOR-SSA-CODE         PIC X(3).
     05  FILLER                  PIC X       VALUE ')'.
*
 01  ITEM-SSA.
*
     05  FILLER                  PIC X(9)    VALUE 'INITMSEG('.
     05  FILLER                  PIC X(10)   VALUE 'INITMNUM ='.
     05  ITEM-SSA-NUMBER         PIC X(5).
     05  FILLER                  PIC X       VALUE ')'.
*
 01  INVENTORY-ITEM-SEGMENT.
*
     05  IIS-NUMBER              PIC X(5).
     05  IIS-DESCRIPTION         PIC X(35).
     05  IIS-UNIT-PRICE          PIC S9(5)V99     COMP-3.
     05  IIS-AVG-UNIT-COST       PIC S9(5)V99     COMP-3.
*
 01  INVENTORY-STOCK-LOC-SEGMENT.
*
     05  ISLS-LOCATION           PIC X(3).
     05  ISLS-QUANTITY-ON-HAND   PIC S9(7)        COMP-3.
     05  ISLS-REORDER-POINT      PIC S9(7)        COMP-3.
     05  ISLS-QUANTITY-ON-ORDER  PIC S9(7)        COMP-3.
     05  ISLS-LAST-REORDER-DATE  PIC X(6).
*
 LINKAGE SECTION.
*
 01  INVENTORY-PCB-MASK.
*
     05  IPCB-DBD-NAME           PIC X(8).
     05  IPCB-SEGMENT-LEVEL      PIC XX.
     05  IPCB-STATUS-CODE        PIC XX.
     05  IPCB-PROC-OPTIONS       PIC X(4).
     05  FILLER                  PIC S9(5)        COMP.
     05  IPCB-SEGMENT-NAME       PIC X(8).
     05  IPCB-KEY-LENGTH         PIC S9(5)        COMP.
     05  IPCB-NUMB-SENS-SEGS     PIC S9(5)        COMP.
     05  IPCB-KEY.
         10  IPCB-VENDOR-CODE    PIC X(3).
         10  IPCB-ITEM-NUMBER    PIC X(5).
         10  IPCB-LOCATION       PIC X(3).
*
```

Figure 5-4 Source listing for the inventory reorder report program (part 3 of 7)

```
 PROCEDURE DIVISION.
*
     ENTRY 'DLITCBL' USING INVENTORY-PCB-MASK.
*
 000-PREPARE-REORDER-REPORT.
*
     OPEN OUTPUT PRTOUT.
     ACCEPT HL1-SYSTEM-DATE FROM DATE.
     PERFORM 100-PRINT-ITEM-DATA
         UNTIL END-OF-DATA-BASE.
     CLOSE PRTOUT.
     GOBACK.
*
 100-PRINT-ITEM-DATA.
*
     MOVE 'INITMSEG' TO UNQUAL-SSA-SEGMENT-NAME.
     PERFORM 110-GET-NEXT-ITEM-SEGMENT.
     IF NOT END-OF-DATA-BASE
         MOVE 'N'          TO ALL-LOCATIONS-PROCESSED-SW
                              PRINT-ITEM-SW
         MOVE 'INLOCSEG' TO UNQUAL-SSA-SEGMENT-NAME
         PERFORM 120-GET-LOCATION-DATA
             UNTIL ALL-LOCATIONS-PROCESSED
         IF PRINT-ITEM
             PERFORM 140-PRINT-ITEM-LINES.
*
 110-GET-NEXT-ITEM-SEGMENT.
*
     CALL 'CBLTDLI' USING DLI-GN
                          INVENTORY-PCB-MASK
                          INVENTORY-ITEM-SEGMENT
                          UNQUALIFIED-SSA.
     IF IPCB-STATUS-CODE = 'GB'
         MOVE 'Y' TO END-OF-DATA-BASE-SW
     ELSE
         IF IPCB-STATUS-CODE NOT = SPACE
             MOVE 'Y' TO END-OF-DATA-BASE-SW
             DISPLAY 'INV2200 I 1 DATA BASE ERROR - STATUS CODE '
                     IPCB-STATUS-CODE.
*
 120-GET-LOCATION-DATA.
*
     PERFORM 130-GET-LOCATION-SEGMENT.
     IF NOT ALL-LOCATIONS-PROCESSED
         ADD ISLS-QUANTITY-ON-HAND ISLS-QUANTITY-ON-ORDER
             GIVING AVAILABLE-STOCK
         IF AVAILABLE-STOCK NOT > ISLS-REORDER-POINT
             MOVE 'Y' TO ALL-LOCATIONS-PROCESSED-SW
                         PRINT-ITEM-SW.
*
```

Figure 5-4 Source listing for the inventory reorder report program (part 4 of 7)

```
 130-GET-LOCATION-SEGMENT.
*
     CALL 'CBLTDLI' USING DLI-GNP
                          INVENTORY-PCB-MASK
                          INVENTORY-STOCK-LOC-SEGMENT
                          UNQUALIFIED-SSA.
     IF IPCB-STATUS-CODE = 'GE'
         MOVE 'Y' TO ALL-LOCATIONS-PROCESSED-SW
     ELSE
         IF IPCB-STATUS-CODE NOT = SPACE
             MOVE 'Y' TO ALL-LOCATIONS-PROCESSED-SW
                         END-OF-DATA-BASE-SW
             DISPLAY 'INV2200 I 2 DATA BASE ERROR - STATUS CODE '
                     IPCB-STATUS-CODE.
*
 140-PRINT-ITEM-LINES.
*
     MOVE 'Y' TO FIRST-LOCATION-SW.
     MOVE 'N' TO ALL-LOCATIONS-PROCESSED-SW.
     PERFORM 150-RESET-POSITION.
     MOVE ZERO                TO TOTAL-AVAILABLE-STOCK
                                 TOTAL-REORDER-POINT.
     MOVE IPCB-VENDOR-CODE TO RL-VENDOR-CODE.
     MOVE '-'                 TO RL-HYPHEN.
     MOVE IIS-NUMBER          TO RL-NUMBER.
     MOVE IIS-DESCRIPTION     TO RL-DESCRIPTION.
     PERFORM 170-PRINT-LOCATION-LINE
         UNTIL ALL-LOCATIONS-PROCESSED.
     PERFORM 210-PRINT-ITEM-TOTAL-LINE.
*
 150-RESET-POSITION.
*
     MOVE IPCB-VENDOR-CODE TO VENDOR-SSA-CODE.
     MOVE IPCB-ITEM-NUMBER TO ITEM-SSA-NUMBER.
     PERFORM 160-GET-ITEM-SEGMENT.
*
 160-GET-ITEM-SEGMENT.
*
     CALL 'CBLTDLI' USING DLI-GU
                          INVENTORY-PCB-MASK
                          INVENTORY-ITEM-SEGMENT
                          VENDOR-SSA
                          ITEM-SSA.
     IF IPCB-STATUS-CODE NOT = SPACE
         MOVE 'Y' TO END-OF-DATA-BASE-SW
         DISPLAY 'INV2200 I 3 DATA BASE ERROR - STATUS CODE '
                 IPCB-STATUS-CODE.
*
```

Figure 5-4 Source listing for the inventory reorder report program (part 5 of 7)

```
 170-PRINT-LOCATION-LINE.
*
     PERFORM 130-GET-LOCATION-SEGMENT.
     IF NOT ALL-LOCATIONS-PROCESSED
         COMPUTE AVAILABLE-STOCK = ISLS-QUANTITY-ON-HAND +
                                   ISLS-QUANTITY-ON-ORDER
         ADD AVAILABLE-STOCK          TO TOTAL-AVAILABLE-STOCK
         ADD ISLS-QUANTITY-ON-HAND    TO ON-HAND-TOTAL
         ADD ISLS-REORDER-POINT       TO TOTAL-REORDER-POINT
         MOVE AVAILABLE-STOCK         TO RL-AVAILABLE
         MOVE ISLS-LOCATION           TO RL-LOCATION
         MOVE ISLS-QUANTITY-ON-HAND   TO RL-ON-HAND
         MOVE ISLS-QUANTITY-ON-ORDER  TO RL-ON-ORDER
         MOVE ISLS-REORDER-POINT      TO RL-REORDER-POINT
         IF AVAILABLE-STOCK > ISLS-REORDER-POINT
             MOVE SPACE TO RL-STAR
         ELSE
             MOVE '*'   TO RL-STAR.
     IF NOT ALL-LOCATIONS-PROCESSED
         IF LINE-COUNT > LINES-ON-PAGE
             PERFORM 180-PRINT-REPORT-HEADING
             MOVE REPORT-LINE TO PRTOUT-RECORD
             PERFORM 200-WRITE-REPORT-LINE
         ELSE
             MOVE REPORT-LINE TO PRTOUT-RECORD
             PERFORM 200-WRITE-REPORT-LINE.
     IF FIRST-LOCATION
         MOVE 'N'   TO FIRST-LOCATION-SW
         MOVE SPACE TO RL-VENDOR-CODE
                       RL-HYPHEN
                       RL-NUMBER
                       RL-DESCRIPTION.
*
 180-PRINT-REPORT-HEADING.
*
     MOVE 1               TO LINE-COUNT.
     MOVE PAGE-COUNT      TO HL1-PAGE.
     ADD 1                TO PAGE-COUNT.
     MOVE HEADING-LINE-1 TO PRTOUT-RECORD.
     PERFORM 190-WRITE-PAGE-TOP-LINE.
     MOVE 2               TO SPACE-CONTROL.
     MOVE HEADING-LINE-2 TO PRTOUT-RECORD.
     PERFORM 200-WRITE-REPORT-LINE.
     MOVE 2               TO SPACE-CONTROL.
*
 190-WRITE-PAGE-TOP-LINE.
*
     WRITE PRTOUT-RECORD
         AFTER ADVANCING PAGE.
*
```

Figure 5-4 Source listing for the inventory reorder report program (part 6 of 7)

```
 200-WRITE-REPORT-LINE.
*
     WRITE PRTOUT-RECORD
         AFTER ADVANCING SPACE-CONTROL LINES.
     ADD SPACE-CONTROL TO LINE-COUNT.
     MOVE 1 TO SPACE-CONTROL.
*
 210-PRINT-ITEM-TOTAL-LINE.
*
     MOVE SPACE TO REPORT-LINE.
     MOVE TOTAL-AVAILABLE-STOCK TO RL-AVAILABLE.
     MOVE TOTAL-REORDER-POINT   TO RL-REORDER-POINT.
     MOVE REPORT-LINE           TO PRTOUT-RECORD.
     PERFORM 200-WRITE-REPORT-LINE.
     MOVE 2                     TO SPACE-CONTROL.
*
```

Figure 5-4 Source listing for the inventory reorder report program (part 7 of 7)

Then, if an unexpected status code (one other than spaces or GB) is detected, the program sets END-OF-DATA-BASE-SW to "Y" and displays an error message. As a result, the program ends without doing additional data base processing, and it provides information about the failure that can be used for debugging.

Remember, many installations use error-handling routines for situations like these. Such a routine typically provides more complete information about the problem for use in debugging and abends the program so that a storage dump is produced and subsequent steps in the job are bypassed. If your shop uses a standard error routine, find out how to invoke it and be sure to provide the necessary code for it in your programs.

The second call, the GNP call in module 130, retrieves location segments subordinate to the previously established parent item segment. Parentage is established either by the GN call in module 110 (for the initial scan of the dependent location segments) or by the GU call in module 160 (to retrieve location segments for printing).

The GNP call in module 130 is much like the GN in module 110. It also uses a single, unqualified SSA. However, UNQUALIFIED-SSA specifies the location segment type (INLOCSEG) when the GNP call is issued, so I used the field INVENTORY-STOCK-LOC-SEGMENT as the call's I/O area. (The location segment name was moved to UNQUAL-SSA-SEGMENT-NAME by the second MOVE statement in module 100.)

The last call in the program, the GU call in module 160, resets the current data base position back to the parent item segment. This fully qualified call specifies two qualified SSAs (VENDOR-SSA and ITEM-SSA), which were properly formatted by the shaded MOVE statements in module 150. Because the sequence field values used in this call were derived directly from the data base itself, there's no normal way a GE (segment not found) status code can be generated by this call. As a result, if module 160 detects a non-blank status code, it causes the program to end after displaying an appropriate error message.

Although this program works, the programming technique I used in it isn't necessarily the best one for the application. A better approach would be to use an SSA command code.

Using command codes with retrieval calls

When you code retrieval calls, you can use most of the SSA command codes I introduced in the last chapter. In this section, I'll show you examples of the F, D, C, and P command codes, and I'll describe the L, U, V, and Q command codes.

The F and L command codes The F and L command codes are related in function. When you issue a call with an SSA that includes the F command code, the call processes the *first* occurrence of the segment named by that SSA, subject to the call's other qualifications. Similarly, when you issue a call with an SSA that includes the L command code, the call processes the *last* occurrence of the segment named by that SSA. In this section, I'll show you how to use the F command code; that should make it easy for you to understand how to use the L command code.

You can use the F command code when you're doing sequential processing and you need to back up in the data base. In other words, you can use the F command code for sequential retrieval using GN and GNP calls. When you use GU calls, the F command code is meaningless because GU normally retrieves the first segment occurrence that meets the criteria you specify anyway.

Figure 5-5 shows you how I could have used the F command code in the inventory reorder report program. The figure compares code from the original version of the program (part 1) with another section of code that achieves the same result with one less call by using the F command code (part 2). The shaded sections in part 2 replace those in

Code to back up in the inventory data base without using the F command code

```
 .
*
 01  UNQUALIFIED-SSA.
*
     05  UNQUAL-SSA-SEGMENT-NAME      PIC X(8).
     05  FILLER                       PIC X   VALUE SPACE.
*
 .
 .
 .
*
 140-PRINT-ITEM-LINES.
*
 .
 .
 .
     PERFORM 150-RESET-POSITION.
 .
 .
 .
     PERFORM 170-PRINT-LOCATION-LINE
         UNTIL ALL-LOCATIONS-PROCESSED.
 .
 .
 .
*
 150-RESET-POSITION.
*
     MOVE IPCB-VENDOR-CODE TO VENDOR-SSA-CODE.
     MOVE IPCB-ITEM-NUMBER TO ITEM-SSA-NUMBER.
     PERFORM 160-GET-ITEM-SEGMENT.
*
 160-GET-ITEM-SEGMENT.
*
     CALL "CBLTDLI" USING DLI-GU
                          INVENTORY-PCB-MASK
                          INVENTORY-ITEM-SEGMENT
                          VENDOR-SSA
                          ITEM-SSA.
     IF IPCB-STATUS-CODE NOT = SPACE
         MOVE "Y" TO END-OF-DATA-BASE-SW
         DISPLAY "INV2200 I 3 DATA BASE ERROR - STATUS CODE "
                 IPCB-STATUS-CODE.
*
 170-PRINT-LOCATION-LINE.
*
     PERFORM 130-GET-LOCATION-SEGMENT.
 .
 .
 .
```

Figure 5-5 The F command code (part 1 of 2)

Code to back up in the inventory data base using the F command code

```
 .
 .
 .
*
 01  UNQUALIFIED-SSA.
*
     05  UNQUAL-SSA-SEGMENT-NAME       PIC X(8).
     05  FILLER                        PIC X   VALUE "*".
     05  UNQUAL-SSA-COMMAND-CODE       PIC X   VALUE "-".
     05  FILLER                        PIC X   VALUE SPACE.
*
 .
 .
 .
*
 140-PRINT-ITEM-LINES.
*
 .
 .
 .
     MOVE "F" TO UNQUAL-SSA-COMMAND-CODE.
     PERFORM 170-PRINT-LOCATION-LINE
         UNTIL ALL-LOCATIONS-PROCESSED.
 .
 .
 .
*
 170-PRINT-LOCATION-LINE.
*
     PERFORM 130-GET-LOCATION-SEGMENT.
     MOVE "-" TO UNQUAL-SSA-COMMAND-CODE.
 .
 .
 .
```

Figure 5-5 The F command code (part 2 of 2)

part 1. In both cases, you can assume that the field UNQUAL-SSA-SEGMENT-NAME has the value INLOCSEG.

In part 2 of figure 5-5, you can see that I defined UNQUALIFIED-SSA with a single command code and that I initialized the command code field with a hyphen: the null command code. As a result, this program can modify the SSA to turn the command code function on and off by moving either a hyphen or an F to UNQUAL-SSA-COMMAND-CODE.

In the segment of Procedure Division code in part 2 of figure 5-5, the program moves F to the command code field just before it repeatedly performs module 170 to print location lines. This causes the first GNP call (issued by module 130) to return to the first occurrence of the location segment type under the current parent item segment. Then, after the position is reset by the first GNP call, module 170 turns the command code function off by moving a hyphen to the command code field. As a result, as module 170 is executed again and again, the call in module 130 proceeds forward through *all* the location segment occurrences subordinate to the parent item segment.

Compare the more awkward way the original version of the program handled this same function (part 1 of figure 5-5). Instead of simply providing a command code field and manipulating its value properly, the program had to issue a GU call to back up to the parent item segment to insure that the position in the data base was right for the following GNP calls. Not only does this complicate the program, but it also reduces the program's efficiency because it has to issue one additional DL/I call for each item to be listed.

The L command code works like the F command code, only it processes the *last* occurrence of the specified segment type. However, unlike the F command code, you can use the L command code with a GU call. You might want to do this when you want the last occurrence of a segment with a specific key value, and the segment's key field can have non-unique values. The L command code overrides DL/I's normal function of returning the *first* segment occurrence that fully satisfies the call's SSAs.

The D command code Normally, DL/I operates on the lowest level segment you specify in an SSA. So if you issue a GU call like this:

```
CALL 'CBLTDLI' USING DLI-GU
                     INVENTORY-PCB-MASK
                     INVENTORY-STOCK-LOC-SEGMENT
                     VENDOR-SSA
                     ITEM-SSA
                     STOCK-LOCATION-SSA.
```

DL/I returns just the appropriate occurrence of the location segment.

In many cases, you want data not just from the lowest level in the call, but from other levels as well. In the inventory data base, you might want to retrieve not only the location segment occurrence, but also its parent item and vendor segments.

To do that, you could issue three separate GU calls: one to retrieve the vendor segment, one to retrieve the item segment, and one to retrieve the location segment. However, DL/I provides a facility that makes it easier for you to retrieve an entire path of segments. A call with an SSA that includes the D command code is a *path call*. It operates on a path of two or more segments rather than just one segment. As a general rule, the fewer DL/I calls your program issues, the more efficient it is. Therefore, path calls can improve the overall performance of programs that process paths of segments.

For a program to be able to issue path calls, its PCB must specifically enable them. If P is one of the values specified in the PCB macro's PROCOPT parameter in the program's PSBGEN, path calls are supported. If you try to do a path call when it's not explicitly enabled by the PSBGEN job, you'll get an AM status code.

Figure 5-6 compares the code to retrieve three segments from the inventory data base with separate calls (part 1) and with a single path call (part 2). It illustrates two points you need to keep in mind as you use path calls. First, the I/O area you specify on a path call has to be large enough to contain *all* the segments that will be processed by the call. In this example, the I/O area has to be at least 200 bytes long (131 for the vendor segment, 48 for the item segment, and 21 for the location segment). Second, you need to specify the D command code on the SSA for each segment in the path that's to be operated upon by the call, except the last; DL/I always returns the lowest level segment you specify. (I included the D command code on the SSA for the location segment just for consistency; it's not necessary there.)

If you omit the D command code on one or more of the SSAs involved in a path get call, DL/I doesn't return those segments in the I/O area. For example, figure 5-7 shows the code to do a path call to retrieve a vendor and location segment from the inventory data base, but without returning an item segment as well. Note that the item segment's SSA doesn't have the D command code, and room isn't provided for it in the I/O area. However, the item SSA is nevertheless specified in the call so the program can retrieve the correct location segment. Again, the lowest level segment you specify in the call is always returned whether you specify the D command code on its SSA or not.

The C command code If you're developing a program that retrieves just lower-level segment occurrences from a data base, you don't have to code separate SSAs for each level in the hierarchical path. Instead, you can use a single SSA with the C command code. Then, rather than coding a field name, relational operator, and search value, you specify the concatenated key for the segment you're interested in. Figure 5-8 shows the code to retrieve a specific location segment occurrence from

Code to retrieve a path of three segments from the inventory data base with three separate calls

```
*
 01  VENDOR-SSA.
*
     05  FILLER                    PIC X(9)     VALUE "INVENSEG(".
     05  FILLER                    PIC X(10)    VALUE "INVENCOD =".
     05  VENDOR-SSA-CODE           PIC X(3).
     05  FILLER                    PIC X        VALUE ")".
*
 01  ITEM-SSA.
*
     05  FILLER                    PIC X(9)     VALUE "INITMSEG(".
     05  FILLER                    PIC X(10)    VALUE "INITMNUM =".
     05  ITEM-SSA-NUMBER           PIC X(5).
     05  FILLER                    PIC X        VALUE ")".
*
 01  LOCATION-SSA.
*
     05  FILLER                    PIC X(9)     VALUE "INLOCSEG(".
     05  FILLER                    PIC X(10)    VALUE "INLOCLOC =".
     05  LOCATION-SSA-CODE         PIC X(3).
     05  FILLER                    PIC X        VALUE ")".
*
 01  INVENTORY-VENDOR-SEGMENT            PIC X(131).
*
 01  INVENTORY-ITEM-SEGMENT              PIC X(48).
*
 01  INVENTORY-STOCK-LOC-SEGMENT         PIC X(21).
*
.
.
.
*
     CALL "CBLTDLI" USING DLI-GU
                          INVENTORY-PCB-MASK
                          INVENTORY-VENDOR-SEGMENT
                          VENDOR-SSA.
     CALL "CBLTDLI" USING DLI-GU
                          INVENTORY-PCB-MASK
                          INVENTORY-ITEM-SEGMENT
                          VENDOR-SSA
                          ITEM-SSA.
     CALL "CBLTDLI" USING DLI-GU
                          INVENTORY-PCB-MASK
                          INVENTORY-STOCK-LOC-SEGMENT
                          VENDOR-SSA
                          ITEM-SSA
                          LOCATION-SSA.
```

Figure 5-6 The D command code (part 1 of 2)

Code to retrieve a path of three segments from the inventory data base with a single call

```
*
 01   VENDOR-SSA.
*
      05  FILLER                    PIC X(11)    VALUE "INVENSEG*D(".
      05  FILLER                    PIC X(10)    VALUE "INVENCOD =".
      05  VENDOR-SSA-CODE           PIC X(3).
      05  FILLER                    PIC X        VALUE ")".
*
 01   ITEM-SSA.
*
      05  FILLER                    PIC X(11)    VALUE "INITMSEG*D(".
      05  FILLER                    PIC X(10)    VALUE "INITMNUM =".
      05  ITEM-SSA-NUMBER           PIC X(5).
      05  FILLER                    PIC X        VALUE ")".
*
 01   LOCATION-SSA.
*
      05  FILLER                    PIC X(11)    VALUE "INLOCSEG*D(".
      05  FILLER                    PIC X(10)    VALUE "INLOCLOC =".
      05  LOCATION-SSA-CODE         PIC X(3).
      05  FILLER                    PIC X        VALUE ")".
*
 01   PATH-CALL-I-O-AREA.
*
      05  INVENTORY-VENDOR-SEGMENT         PIC X(131).
      05  INVENTORY-ITEM-SEGMENT           PIC X(48).
      05  INVENTORY-STOCK-LOC-SEGMENT      PIC X(21).
*
  .
  .
  .
*
      CALL "CBLTDLI" USING DLI-GU
                           INVENTORY-PCB-MASK
                           PATH-CALL-I-O-AREA
                           VENDOR-SSA
                           ITEM-SSA
                           LOCATION-SSA.
```

Figure 5-6 The D command code (part 2 of 2)

the inventory data base using one SSA with a concatenated key and the C command code.

When you use the C command code, the SSA has a different format from that you've already seen. You don't specify a field name in the SSA because you're supplying data from two or more fields, all from different segments, in the concatenated key. And you don't

```
*
 01  VENDOR-SSA.
*
     05  FILLER                   PIC X(11)   VALUE "INVENSEG*D(".
     05  FILLER                   PIC X(10)   VALUE "INVENCOD =".
     05  VENDOR-SSA-CODE          PIC X(3).
     05  FILLER                   PIC X       VALUE ")".
*
 01  ITEM-SSA.
*
     05  FILLER                   PIC X(9)    VALUE "INITMSEG(".
     05  FILLER                   PIC X(10)   VALUE "INITMNUM =".
     05  ITEM-SSA-NUMBER          PIC X(5).
     05  FILLER                   PIC X       VALUE ")".
*
 01  LOCATION-SSA.
*
     05  FILLER                   PIC X(11)   VALUE "INLOCSEG*D(".
     05  FILLER                   PIC X(10)   VALUE "INLOCLOC =".
     05  LOCATION-SSA-CODE        PIC X(3).
     05  FILLER                   PIC X       VALUE ")".
*
 01  PATH-CALL-I-O-AREA.
*
     05  INVENTORY-VENDOR-SEGMENT         PIC X(131).
     05  INVENTORY-STOCK-LOC-SEGMENT      PIC X(21).
*
 .
 .
 .
*
     CALL "CBLTDLI" USING DLI-GU
                          INVENTORY-PCB-MASK
                          PATH-CALL-I-O-AREA
                          VENDOR-SSA
                          ITEM-SSA
                          LOCATION-SSA.
```

Figure 5-7 Excluding a segment from a path call

specify a relational operator, either. Figure 5-8 should make this clear. Before the call in the figure is executed, the program moves the proper field values to the three shaded variables in LOCATION-SSA.

The P command code When you issue a GU or a GN call, DL/I normally establishes parentage at the lowest level segment that's retrieved. However, if you want to override that and cause parentage to be established at a higher-level segment in the hierarchical path, you can use the P command code in its SSA. For example, a GN call without the P command code for an item segment from the inventory data base

```
*
 01  LOCATION-SSA.
*
     05  FILLER                    PIC X(11)    VALUE 'INLOCSEG*C('.
     05  LOCATION-SSA-VENDOR       PIC X(3).
     05  LOCATION-SSA-ITEM         PIC X(5).
     05  LOCATION-SSA-LOCATION     PIC X(3).
     05  FILLER                    PIC X        VALUE ')'.
*
 .
 .
 .
     CALL 'CBLTDLI' USING DLI-GU
                          INVENTORY-PCB-MASK
                          INVENTORY-STOCK-LOC-SEGMENT
                          LOCATION-SSA.
```

Figure 5-8 The C command code

would establish parentage at the item segment. You could issue the call to retrieve the same item segment, but establish parentage at the vendor segment level by using the P command code on the vendor segment's SSA.

You can also use the P command code in a GNP call. Don't let this confuse you, though. Before you can issue a GNP successfully, parentage must have *already* been established. The parentage you specify with the P command code in an SSA used in a GNP call doesn't go into effect until *after* the segment is retrieved.

Also, you should specify the P command code at just one hierarchical level. If you issue a call with two or more SSAs that contain the P command code, DL/I ignores all except the one at the lowest level in the hierarchical path.

Figure 5-9 gives an example of how you might use the P command code. (As you look at this figure, keep in mind that it illustrates just the DL/I elements required to meet this program's specifications—not other application considerations.) Suppose an inquiry program allows an operator to key in a vendor code and item number, then displays all the location data for that item. Part 1 of figure 5-9 shows a segment of code to retrieve the appropriate location segment occurrences using SSAs without command codes. A GU call establishes parentage at the right item segment occurrence, then GNP calls are executed repeatedly to return all the location segments subordinate to that item; that's like the processing the reorder report program does.

Code to establish parentage without the P command code

```
*
 01  VENDOR-SSA.
*
     05  FILLER                    PIC X(9)     VALUE "INVENSEG(".
     05  FILLER                    PIC X(10)    VALUE "INVENCOD =".
     05  VENDOR-SSA-CODE           PIC X(3).
     05  FILLER                    PIC X        VALUE ")".
*
 01  ITEM-SSA.
*
     05  FILLER                    PIC X(9)     VALUE "INITMSEG(".
     05  FILLER                    PIC X(10)    VALUE "INITMNUM =".
     05  ITEM-SSA-NUMBER           PIC X(5).
     05  FILLER                    PIC X        VALUE ")".
*
 01  UNQUALIFIED-SSA.
*
     05  FILLER                    PIC X(9)     VALUE "INLOCSEG ".
*
 01  INVENTORY-VENDOR-SEGMENT           PIC X(131).
*
 01  INVENTORY-ITEM-SEGMENT             PIC X(48).
*
 01  INVENTORY-STOCK-LOC-SEGMENT        PIC X(21).
*
 .
 .
 .
*
     CALL "CBLTDLI" USING DLI-GU
                          INVENTORY-PCB-MASK
                          INVENTORY-ITEM-SEGMENT
                          VENDOR-SSA
                          ITEM-SSA.
     IF IPCB-STATUS-CODE = SPACE
         MOVE "Y" TO MORE-LOCATION-SEGS-SW
         PERFORM 150-GET-NEXT-LOCATION-SEGMENT
             UNTIL NOT MORE-LOCATION-SEGS.
*
 150-GET-NEXT-LOCATION-SEGMENT.
*
     CALL "CBLTDLI" USING DLI-GNP
                          INVENTORY-PCB-MASK
                          INVENTORY-STOCK-LOC-SEGMENT
                          VENDOR-SSA
                          ITEM-SSA
                          UNQUALIFIED-SSA.
     IF IPCB-STATUS-CODE NOT = SPACE
        MOVE "N" TO MORE-LOCATION-SEGS-SW.
```

Figure 5-9 The P command code (part 1 of 2)

Code to establish parentage with the P command code

```
*
 01   VENDOR-SSA.
*
      05   FILLER                      PIC X(9)     VALUE "INVENSEG(".
      05   FILLER                      PIC X(10)    VALUE "INVENCOD =".
      05   VENDOR-SSA-CODE             PIC X(3).
      05   FILLER                      PIC X        VALUE ")".
*
 01   ITEM-SSA.
*
      05   FILLER                      PIC X(11)    VALUE "INITMSEG*P(".
      05   FILLER                      PIC X(10)    VALUE "INITMNUM =".
      05   ITEM-SSA-NUMBER             PIC X(5).
      05   FILLER                      PIC X        VALUE ")".
*
 01   UNQUALIFIED-SSA.
*
      05   FILLER                      PIC X(9)     VALUE "INLOCSEG ".
*
 01   INVENTORY-VENDOR-SEGMENT               PIC X(131).
*
 01   INVENTORY-ITEM-SEGMENT                 PIC X(48).
*
 01   INVENTORY-STOCK-LOC-SEGMENT            PIC X(21).
*
 .
 .
*
      CALL "CBLTDLI" USING DLI-GU
                           INVENTORY-PCB-MASK
                           INVENTORY-STOCK-LOC-SEGMENT
                           VENDOR-SSA
                           ITEM-SSA
                           UNQUALIFIED-SSA.
      IF IPCB-STATUS-CODE = SPACE
          .
          (Insert code to process first segment occurrence here)
          .
          MOVE "Y" TO MORE-LOCATION-SEGS-SW
          PERFORM 150-GET-NEXT-LOCATION-SEGMENT
              UNTIL NOT MORE-LOCATION-SEGS.
*
 150-GET-NEXT-LOCATION-SEGMENT.
*
      CALL "CBLTDLI" USING DLI-GNP
                           INVENTORY-PCB-MASK
                           INVENTORY-STOCK-LOC-SEGMENT
                           VENDOR-SSA
                           ITEM-SSA
                           UNQUALIFIED-SSA.
      IF IPCB-STATUS-CODE NOT = SPACE
          MOVE "N" TO MORE-LOCATION-SEGS-SW.
```

Figure 5-9 The P command code (part 2 of 2)

Part 2 of figure 5-9 is a segment of code that achieves the same result as that in part 1 using an SSA with the P command code to establish parentage. Here, a GU call retrieves not an item segment, but the first occurrence of a location segment subordinate to a specified item. Qualified SSAs for vendor and item establish position properly, and an unqualified SSA for location causes the first occurrence to be returned by the GU call.

Because I coded the P command code in ITEM-SSA, parentage is established at the item segment. As a result, subsequent GNP calls can retrieve the other location segments subordinate to that item segment occurrence. Although the two sections of code in figure 5-9 produce the same result, the code in the second part is more efficient because it uses one less DL/I call for each inquiry.

Other command codes you can use with get calls There are three other command codes you can use in SSAs for get calls: U, V, and Q. Frankly, they're for special purposes, and I don't think you'll have much reason to use them. As a result, I'll just describe them briefly here. Then, if you have a use for them, you can refer to the DL/I manuals for more information.

The U and V command codes provide similar functions. When you use an unqualified SSA that specifies the U command code in a GN call, DL/I restricts the search for the segment you request to dependents of the segment with the U command code. With the U command code on an unqualified SSA, you can achieve the same result you'd get if you issued a call that contained a qualified SSA for the current position. When you use the V command code at any hierarchical level, its effect is the same as if you had coded the U command code at that level and all levels above it in the hierarchy. You use the U and V command codes only with unqualified SSAs; if you use either with a qualified SSA, DL/I ignores the command code.

The last of the command codes you can use with get calls is the Q command code. You use it to *enqueue*, or reserve for your exclusive use, a segment or path of segments. You only need to use the Q command code in an interactive environment where there's a chance that another program might make a change to a segment between the time you first access it and the time you're finished with it. For more information about the Q command code, refer to your appropriate application programming manual.

Multiple processing

The data base examples you've seen so far have used *single positioning*. In other words, as each DL/I call is processed, the program's current position in the data base is adjusted. Although that's the normal way to process a DL/I data base, it's not well suited for some data base structures and applications. At times, you may want to do *multiple processing*.

Multiple processing is a general term that means a program can have more than one position in a single physical data base at the same time. In this section, I'll show you the two ways DL/I lets you implement multiple processing: through multiple PCBs and through multiple positioning.

Multiple PCBs When a program needs to access more than one data base, it has a PCB for each. All you have to do is define a unique PCB mask in your program's Linkage Section and name it in the ENTRY statement at the beginning of the Procedure Division. Then, you specify what data base you want to process by naming its PCB in your call.

It's also possible for the data base administrator to define *multiple PCBs* for a *single* data base. Then, the program has two (or more) views of the data base. As with PCBs for different data bases, each has its own mask in the Linkage Section and is specified in the ENTRY statement. It's up to the program's logic to decide when to use a particular PCB to access the data base.

Of the two options for multiple processing, the multiple PCB technique is the most flexible. However, it's also the most inefficient because of the overhead imposed by the extra PCBs. So, unless your application requires the flexibility of multiple PCBs, I suggest you use the second technique: multiple positioning.

Multiple positioning *Multiple positioning* lets a program maintain more than one position within a data base using a single PCB. To do that, DL/I maintains a distinct position for each hierarchical path the program processes. Most of the time, you'll use multiple positioning to access segments of two or more types sequentially at the same time (in other words, to do parallel processing).

To understand, consider figure 5-10. This figure illustrates two data base records from a simple, three-segment-type data base. The root segment (A) has two subordinate segment types (B and C). The first data base record has three occurrences each of segment types B and C, and the second data base record has two occurrences of each.

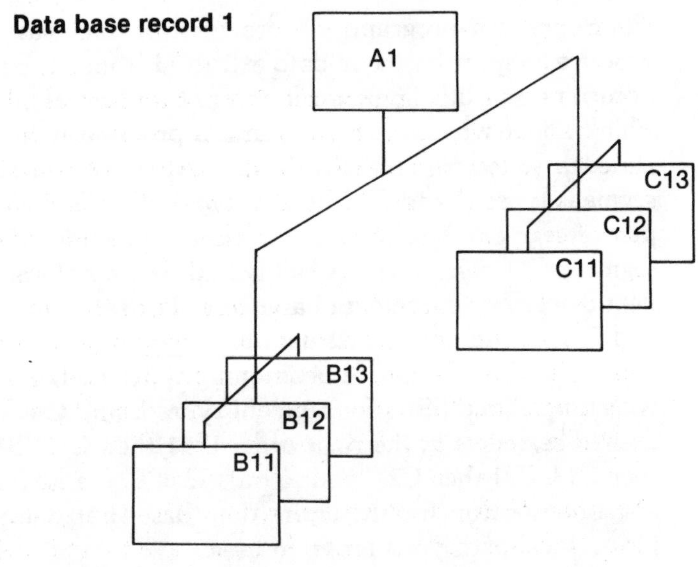

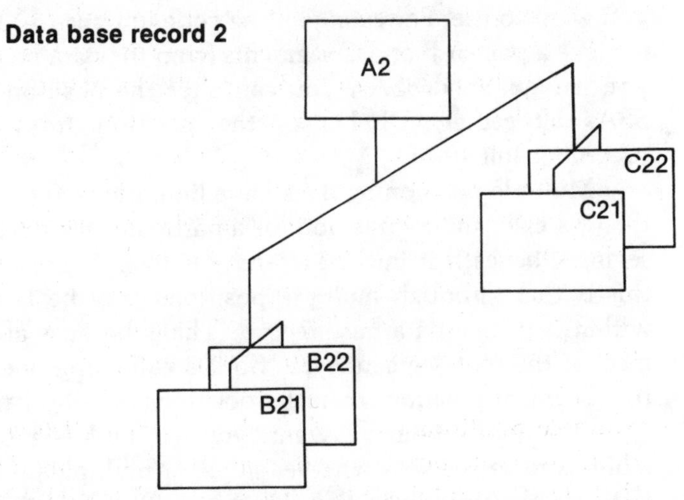

Figure 5-10 Two data base records to illustrate multiple positioning

Although it's not obvious from the figure, there's a one-to-one correspondence between segment type B and segment type C occurrences. In other words, segment B11 is related to segment C11, B12 is related to C12, and so on.

Suppose a program will process this data base sequentially and produce a report based on data extracted from paired B and C segment occurrences. With single positioning, that isn't as simple as it sounds. Think about what would happen if a program with single positioning issued a series of GN calls, alternatively with unqualified SSAs for segment types B and C. The first two GN calls would return the first pair of segments (B11 and C11). After the second call, position is after segment C11. The next GN call would return not segment B12, but the next B segment in the data base: B21. The result is that two pairs of B and C segments in the first data base record would be skipped.

However, if multiple positioning were used, alternating GN calls with unqualified SSAs for segment types B and C would return all the desired segments in the right order (B11 then C11, B12 then C12, B13 then C13, B21 then C21, and so on). That's because DL/I maintains not just one position for the entire data base, but one position for *each* hierarchical path your program uses.

When you use multiple positioning, DL/I maintains its separate positions based on segment type. As a result, you include an unqualified SSA in the call that names the segment type whose position you want to use. For example, the code in figure 5-11 might be used to retrieve a pair of B and C segments from the data base in figure 5-10. If you use qualified SSAs, you can alter the position, and if you omit SSAs altogether, DL/I uses the position from the immediately preceding call.

Multiple positioning does have limitations. The most important is that if a call changes position for a particular segment, position for any segment beneath it in the hierarchy is lost. A practical implication of this is that although multiple positions may be in effect, they're all within the same data base record. That's because all paths eventually meet at the root segment type. So if a call along one path changes the root segment position, then the positions on all other paths are lost.

One more point I want you to understand: the data base administrator specifies whether single or multiple positioning will be in effect in the program's PSB. As a result, multiple positioning isn't a characteristic of a data base, as it might seem. Instead, it's how DL/I allows a program to view a data base. The same data base can be processed with either single or multiple positioning by different programs; which technique a program uses is determined by the program's PSB. In terms of DL/I resource usage, there's practically no performance differences between the two types of positioning. However, multiple positioning can allow some applications to be met

```
MOVE 'SEGB     ' TO UNQUAL-SSA-SEGMENT-NAME.
CALL 'CBLTDLI' USING DLI-GN
                     SAMPLE-DB-PCB
                     SEGMENT-B-I-O-AREA
                     UNQUALIFIED-SSA.
MOVE 'SEGC     ' TO UNQUAL-SSA-SEGMENT-NAME.
CALL 'CBLTDLI' USING DLI-GN
                     SAMPLE-DB-PCB
                     SEGMENT-C-I-O-AREA
                     UNQUALIFIED-SSA.
```

Figure 5-11 Sample DL/I calls for parallel processing

with simpler, more efficient programs than would be possible with single positioning.

Discussion

The information in this chapter, particularly the basic information on the three kinds of get calls, is fundamental for developing DL/I programs. So if you're not comfortable with it, review it. The material on using SSA command codes and multiple processing isn't critical. But although you don't *have* to know how to use command codes and multiple processing to develop DL/I programs, you should. They can make your job easier and your programs more efficient.

In the next chapter, I'll show you how to use calls to make changes to a DL/I data base: ISRT, REPL and DLET. In addition, you'll learn how to use special variations of the get calls that let you hold segments for update: GHU, GHN, and GHNP.

Terminology

fully qualified call
parentage
path call
enqueue
single positioning
multiple processing
multiple PCBs
multiple positioning

Objective

Given complete specifications, code a retrieval program that accesses a physical data base using any of the DL/I functions this chapter presents.

Chapter 6

How to add data to and update data in a data base

Now that you know how to retrieve data from a data base, you're ready to learn how to use the calls that add segments (ISRT, insert), change segments (REPL, replace), and delete segments (DLET, delete). This chapter describes how to issue these calls. In addition, it shows you what you need to know about the get hold calls, which you must issue before you use REPL or DLET.

The ISRT call

You issue a DL/I ISRT call to add a segment occurrence to a data base, either during update processing of an existing data base or during load processing of a new data base. In this section, I'll describe how you use the ISRT call for both kinds of processing.

When you use a standard COBOL WRITE statement to add a record to a file, your program must first build the record in an I/O area by moving appropriate values to the fields of the record. The same is true when you use an ISRT call: before you issue the call, you should first build the segment occurrence by moving data to the fields of the segment description.

After formatting the segment, you issue the ISRT call with at least one SSA: an unqualified SSA for the segment type you want to add. For example, this call would cause DL/I to add a location segment to the inventory data base:

```
CALL 'CBLTDLI' USING DLI-ISRT
                     INVENTORY-PCB-MASK
                     INVENTORY-STOCK-LOC-SEGMENT
                     UNQUALIFIED-SSA.
```

Here, UNQUALIFIED-SSA specifies the segment name INLOCSEG. Because the SSA is unqualified, DL/I tries to satisfy the call based on the current position in the data base. As a result, you need to be careful about position when you issue an ISRT call that specifies only a single unqualified SSA.

A safer technique is to specify a qualified SSA for each hierarchical level above the one where you want to insert the segment. For example, assume your program issues this call to add a stock-location segment to the inventory data base:

```
CALL 'CBLTDLI' USING DLI-ISRT
                     INVENTORY-PCB-MASK
                     INVENTORY-STOCK-LOC-SEGMENT
                     VENDOR-SSA
                     ITEM-SSA
                     UNQUALIFIED-SSA.
```

If the SSAs for vendor and item were initialized with the proper key values, DL/I inserts the new segment occurrence in the correct position in the data base.

When you issue a fully qualified ISRT call like this, DL/I returns a status code of GE if any segment occurrence you specify in an SSA isn't present in the data base. As a result, you can issue an ISRT call with qualified SSAs instead of first issuing GU calls to find out if higher-level segments in the path are present. By issuing one call instead of two (or more), you can save system resources.

Where inserted segments are stored If the new segment has a unique sequence field, as most segment types do, it's added in its proper sequential position. However, some lower-level segment types in some data bases have non-unique sequence fields or don't have sequence fields at all. When that's the case, where a segment occurrence is added depends on the *rules* the data base administrator specifies for the data base.

For a segment without a sequence field, the insert rule determines how the new segment is positioned relative to existing twin segments. If the rule is "first," the new segment is added before any existing twins. If the rule is "last," the new segment is added after all existing twins. And if the rule is "here," it's added at the current position relative to existing twins, which may be first, last, or anywhere in the middle. For segments with non-unique sequence fields, the rules are similar, but they determine where the new segment is positioned relative to existing twin segments that have the same key value.

In most cases, the positioning specified by insert rules is transparent to you, so you don't need to worry about it. In special cases where you need to override the rule in effect for a segment, you can use the F or L command code to do so.

Using command codes with ISRT calls When you issue ISRT calls, you can use any of the command codes I described in the last chapter except the Q and P command codes. As with the get calls, I suspect you're most likely to use F, L, or D.

You use F or L to override the rules specified for segment insertion by the data base administrator. Because unique sequence fields always identify a segment's position in the data base, the F and L command codes have meaning only for segments that have a non-unique sequence field or no sequence field at all. If there's a need for you to use either of these command codes when adding a segment to a data base, your program's specifications should indicate it.

Incidentally, there are limits as to how you can use command codes to override the insert rules specified by the data base administrator. In particular, you can override a rule of "here" by coding F or L. And you can override "first" by coding L. But you can't override "last." Nor can you change "first" to "here" by specifying a command code.

In the last chapter, you saw how to specify the D command code to issue a path call. The D command code has a similar function for ISRT calls: It lets you insert more than one segment along a path with a single call. When adding a hierarchical path of segments to a data base, it's more efficient to issue one ISRT call with multiple SSAs, each with the D command code, than it is to issue a separate ISRT call for each segment. As with using path calls to retrieve segments, your program's PSB's PROCOPT must specify P for a path call to work.

Special considerations for load processing As I've already mentioned, you use the ISRT call to add segments to an existing data base and to load a new data base. To load a data base, two special requirements must be met. First, all segment occurrences must be inserted in hierarchical order. Second, the PSB for the load program must specify the proper PROCOPT value: either L or LS. DL/I uses the processing option value to determine whether an ISRT call is a load operation for a new data base or an addition operation for an existing data base.

In a data base load program, the only allowable calls are ISRTs. Unlike ISRT processing for an existing data base, I recommend you use only a single unqualified SSA on all ISRT calls for load processing. Although you can supply multiple SSAs for ISRT calls during a load, DL/I uses them only to double-check your accuracy. If a segment to be inserted doesn't satisfy the path you specify, DL/I returns a non-blank status code. Since you have to be sure that segments are loaded in sequence anyway, coding qualified SSAs just adds to programming complexity and makes programming errors more likely.

Status codes you can expect during insert processing When you're using ISRT to add segments to an existing data base, you can expect two non-blank status codes. The first, GE, I've already mentioned. You'll get a GE code when you use multiple SSAs and DL/I can't satisfy the call with the specified path. In other words, at least one of the segment occurrences you request isn't present.

The second status code you might get as a result of an ISRT call is II. DL/I returns an II status code when you try to add a segment occurrence that's already present in the data base.

For load processing, you might get status codes LB, LC, LD, or LE. In most cases, they indicate that you aren't inserting segments in exact hierarchical sequence. That means there's an error in your program or the files from which you're loading the data base contain incorrect data.

The get hold calls

There are three get hold functions you can specify in a DL/I call: GHU (get hold unique), GHN (get hold next), and GHNP (get hold next within parent). As you can see, these calls parallel the three retrieval calls you're already familiar with. I suspect the get hold call you'll use most often will be GHU.

Before you can replace or delete a segment, you must declare your intent to do so by retrieving the segment with one of these three calls. Then, you must issue the replace or delete call before you do any other DL/I processing in your program. If you issue any intervening calls, the effect of the get hold call is lost.

There's a practical implication to this: If you retrieve a segment with one of the get hold calls, then decide you don't want to delete or replace it, you can proceed with other processing, and the hold will no longer be in effect. You don't have to take any explicit action to cancel the effect of a get hold call.

The get hold call may be a path call; in that case, you're declaring your intent either to replace or delete an entire path of segments. As I describe the replace and delete calls, I'll show you how you can selectively operate on particular segments in a path.

The REPL call

After you've retrieved a segment with one of the get hold calls, you can make changes to the data in that segment, then issue a REPL call to replace the original segment with the new data. There are two restrictions on the changes you can make: (1) you can't change the length of the segment (this is irrelevant for most data bases, which have fixed length segments anyway) and (2) you can't change the value of the sequence field if the segment has one (this is also true for a standard file-processing replace operation using the COBOL REWRITE statement).

Never code a qualified SSA on a REPL call; if you do, the call will fail. Also, when you update a segment that was retrieved with a GHU call that wasn't a path call, the REPL call doesn't need any SSAs at all.

To see how the GHU and REPL calls work together, look at figure 6-1. It shows some code for updating stock-location segments in the inventory data base based on inventory receipts. Once the key fields in the vendor, item, and location SSAs have been set, the GHU call retrieves the appropriate stock-location segment. Then, the changes are made, and the unqualified REPL call replaces the updated segment in the data base.

Replace processing and path calls If the get hold call that immediately precedes a replace is a path call, then the replace operates on the entire path. So you can retrieve an entire hierarchical path of segment occurrences with one get hold call, make changes to one, some, or all of them, and then replace them in the data base with one REPL call. When you issue the replace, you don't have to indicate that it's a path call: DL/I knows that because the preceding get hold was a path call.

If the get hold is a path call and you don't want all of the segment occurrences you retrieved to be replaced, you can specify one or more unqualified SSAs with the N command code. Those SSAs name the

```
CALL 'CBLTDLI' USING DLI-GHU
                     INVENTORY-PCB-MASK
                     INVENTORY-STOCK-LOC-SEGMENT
                     VENDOR-SSA
                     ITEM-SSA
                     LOCATION-SSA.
ADD TRANS-RECEIPT-QTY          TO    ISLS-QUANTITY-ON-HAND.
SUBTRACT TRANS-RECEIPT-QTY FROM ISLS-QUANTITY-ON-ORDER.
CALL 'CBLTDLI' USING DLI-REPL
                     INVENTORY-PCB-MASK
                     INVENTORY-STOCK-LOC-SEGMENT.
```

Figure 6-1 Sample code to update a location segment in the inventory data base

segments you do *not* want to replace. Remember, when you're doing replace processing along a path, you specify the segment types you *don't* want to be replaced, not those you *do*.

Status codes you can expect during replace processing All of the non-blank status codes that result from a REPL call represent serious errors. If you try to use a qualified SSA on a REPL call, you'll get an AJ status code. Or, if your program issues a replace call without an immediately preceding get hold call, DL/I returns a DJ status code. And if your program makes a change to the segment's key field before issuing the REPL call, DL/I returns a DA status code.

The DLET call

The DLET call works much like REPL. You must first issue a get hold call to indicate that you intend to make a change to the segment you're retrieving. Then, you issue a DLET call to delete the segment occurrence from the data base. For example, to delete a stock location that's no longer active, you'd code a series of statements like the ones in figure 6-2. Notice that the DLET call doesn't include any SSAs. Again, as with the REPL call, you only need to include an SSA when you use a path call, and you never include a qualified SSA.

There's one particularly important point you must keep in mind whenever you use the DLET call: When you delete a segment, you automatically delete all segment occurrences subordinate to it. Although this can be a big time-saver if you really do want to delete so many segments in one call, it can cause real problems if you issue a DLET call mistakenly. So be careful.

```
CALL 'CBLTDLI' USING DLI-GHU
                     INVENTORY-PCB-MASK
                     INVENTORY-STOCK-LOC-SEGMENT
                     VENDOR-SSA
                     ITEM-SSA
                     LOCATION-SSA.
CALL 'CBLTDLI' USING DLI-DLET
                     INVENTORY-PCB-MASK
                     INVENTORY-STOCK-LOC-SEGMENT.
```

Figure 6-2 Sample code to delete a location segment from the inventory data base

Delete processing and path calls As with REPL, if the get hold call that immediately precedes a delete is a path call, then the delete operates on the entire path. With delete processing on a path, you have two choices. First, you can delete the entire path by simply issuing the delete call. Alternatively, you can limit the scope of the delete by supplying one unqualified SSA without a command code. The segment that the unqualified SSA names will be deleted, along with all of its dependents. However, segments above it along the path you retrieved will remain in the data base. This is the only case when you code an SSA on a DLET call.

Status codes you can expect during delete processing The status codes you might get after a DLET call are the same as those you can get after a REPL call. If you try to use a qualified SSA on a DLET call, you'll get an AJ status code. If your program issues a delete call without an immediately preceding get hold call, DL/I returns a DJ status code. And if your program makes a change to the segment's key field before issuing the DLET call, DL/I returns a DA status code.

An update program

Frankly, if you're familiar with how to update a file in standard COBOL, the ISRT, REPL, and DLET calls should present few difficulties for you. Even so, to help you understand how to use them, I want to describe a simple update program. Figures 6-3, 6-4, and 6-5 present the specifications, structure chart, and COBOL source code for the program.

Transaction records are read from a standard sequential file that contains 80-byte records. In this program, the transactions affect only the location segment occurrences in the inventory data base. There are

Inventory stock transaction record layout

```
 01   INVENTORY-STOCK-TRANSACTION.
*
      05  IST-TRANSACTION-TYPE          PIC X.
          88  IST-ADJUSTMENT                              VALUE "A".
          88  IST-DELETION                                VALUE "D".
          88  IST-NEW-LOCATION                            VALUE "N".
      05  IST-CONCATENATED-KEY.
          10  IST-VENDOR                PIC X(3).
          10  IST-ITEM                  PIC X(5).
          10  IST-LOCATION              PIC X(3).
      05  IST-QUANTITY-ON-HAND          PIC 9(7).
      05  IST-REORDER-POINT             PIC 9(7).
      05  IST-QUANTITY-ON-ORDER         PIC 9(7).
      05  IST-LAST-REORDER-DATE         PIC X(6).
      05  FILLER                        PIC X(41).
*
```

Transaction	Function	Quantity on hand	Reorder point	Quantity on order	Last reorder date
A	REPL	Replace with quantity on hand from transaction	Replace with reorder point from transaction	Replace with quantity on order from transaction	Replace with last reorder date from transaction
D	DLET	Irrelevant	Irrelevant	Irrelevant	Irrelevant
N	ISRT	Zero	Use transaction reorder point	Zero	Spaces

Figure 6-3 Specifications for the post inventory transactions program

three kinds of transactions: new location segment additions, old location segment deletions, and current location segment adjustments. The transaction type is indicated by a one-character value in the first position of the transaction record, as you can see in the record layout in figure 6-3. Following the type code in the transaction record is the full 11-byte concatenated key that identifies the location segment to which the transaction applies.

The bottom section of figure 6-3 shows exactly what processing the program should do for each transaction type. For an adjustment, the program uses the four data field values in the transaction record to replace the values in the corresponding fields of the location segment in the data base. For a deletion, the program simply deletes the proper location segment occurrence. And for an addition, the program inserts a new location segment occurrence, setting its reorder point field to the value specified in the transaction, but moving zero or spaces to the other fields in the segment.

Now, consider figure 6-4, the structure chart for the program. The main processing module (100) reads a transaction record (module 110). Then, depending on the transaction type, it performs module 120 (to add a new location segment), module 140 (to delete a location segment), or module 170 (to make a change to an existing segment). If a processing error is detected, module 100 performs module 190 to display an error message.

Figure 6-5 shows the complete source listing for the program. The sections that relate directly to DL/I are shaded. First, consider the module to add a new location segment occurrence to the data base (module 120). As you can see, this module simply formats the new location segment according to the processing requirements in figure 6-3, then invokes module 130 to insert the new segment in the inventory data base.

Module 130 issues an ISRT call that's qualified for vendor and item. (The code that properly formats VENDOR-SSA and ITEM-SSA is in module 100.) The call uses an unqualified SSA for the location segment.

The error checking that follows the ISRT call in module 130 is straightforward: If the status code is blanks, the call was successful; if the status code is not blanks, the call was not. If this program attempts to insert a location segment that already exists in the data base, DL/I will return a status code of II. That's the only non-blank status code that's likely to be returned as a result of this call. (It's more efficient to issue the ISRT call and handle the II status code when it occurs than to issue a GU call you expect to fail most of the time to see if a segment already exists.)

Notice that if module 130 detects a non-blank status code, it moves an error message to the field EM-TEXT. Module 100 then invokes module 190 to format and display an error message. Module 190 uses the message supplied by module 130 plus the complete key in the transaction record and the PCB status code to create the message. As a

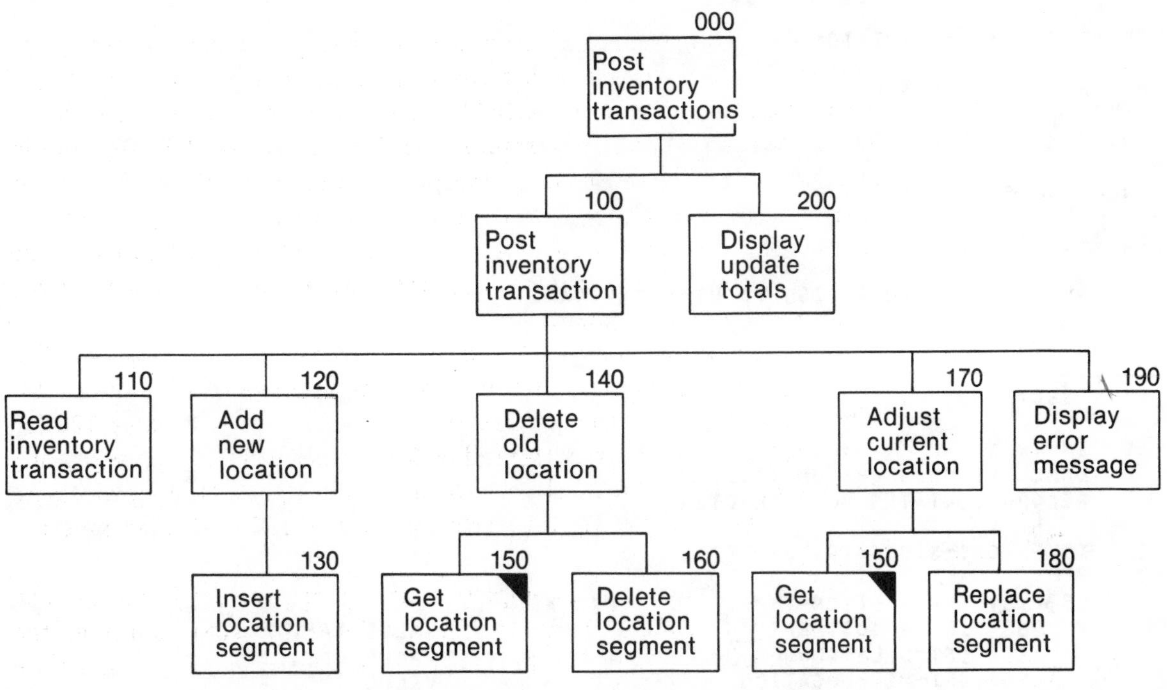

Figure 6-4 Structure chart for the post inventory transactions program

result, the message can be used to determine just what went wrong with the call.

The other two main functions the program can perform—deleting or replacing a segment—require two DL/I calls: first a get hold call, then either a DLET or REPL call. As a result, both module 140 (for DLET) and module 170 (for REPL) begin by invoking module 150 to issue a GHU call for the specific location segment the program needs. As you can see in module 150, the GHU call is fully qualified: it specifies qualified SSAs for each of the three segment levels in the inventory data base. Again, the code that moves the key values to these SSAs is in module 100.

If the GHU call in module 150 yields a status code of blanks, processing proceeds normally. If the transaction is a deletion, module 140 invokes module 160, which in turn issues a DLET call. Notice that the DLET call doesn't specify any SSAs. If the transaction is an adjustment, module 170 first formats the new version of the location segment, then invokes module 180, which issues the REPL call. The REPL call doesn't specify any SSAs either.

```
 IDENTIFICATION DIVISION.
*
 PROGRAM-ID.  INV3100.
*
 ENVIRONMENT DIVISION.
*
 INPUT-OUTPUT SECTION.
*
 FILE-CONTROL.
*
     SELECT INVTRAN ASSIGN TO UT-S-INVTRAN.
*
 DATA DIVISION.
*
 FILE SECTION.
*
 FD  INVTRAN
     LABEL RECORDS ARE OMITTED
     RECORD CONTAINS 80 CHARACTERS.
*
 01  INVENTORY-STOCK-TRANSACTION.
*
     05  IST-TRANSACTION-TYPE          PIC X.
         88  IST-ADJUSTMENT                          VALUE 'A'.
         88  IST-DELETION                            VALUE 'D'.
         88  IST-NEW-LOCATION                        VALUE 'N'.
     05  IST-CONCATENATED-KEY.
         10  IST-VENDOR                PIC X(3).
         10  IST-ITEM                  PIC X(5).
         10  IST-LOCATION              PIC X(3).
     05  IST-QUANTITY-ON-HAND          PIC 9(7).
     05  IST-REORDER-POINT             PIC 9(7).
     05  IST-QUANTITY-ON-ORDER         PIC 9(7).
     05  IST-LAST-REORDER-DATE         PIC X(6).
     05  FILLER                        PIC X(41).
*
 WORKING-STORAGE SECTION.
*
 01  SWITCHES.
*
     05  INVTRAN-EOF-SW                PIC X         VALUE 'N'.
         88  INVTRAN-EOF                             VALUE 'Y'.
     05  LOCATION-SEGMENT-FOUND-SW     PIC X         VALUE 'N'.
         88  LOCATION-SEGMENT-FOUND                  VALUE 'Y'.
*
 01  COUNT-FIELDS                                    COMP-3.
*
     05  SUCCESSFUL-REPL-COUNT         PIC S9(9)     VALUE ZERO.
     05  SUCCESSFUL-ISRT-COUNT         PIC S9(9)     VALUE ZERO.
     05  SUCCESSFUL-DLET-COUNT         PIC S9(9)     VALUE ZERO.
     05  FAILED-REPL-COUNT             PIC S9(9)     VALUE ZERO.
     05  FAILED-ISRT-COUNT             PIC S9(9)     VALUE ZERO.
     05  FAILED-DLET-COUNT             PIC S9(9)     VALUE ZERO.
*
```

Figure 6-5 Source listing for the post inventory transactions program (part 1 of 6)

```
 01   TOTAL-MESSAGE.
*
      05   TM-COUNT                      PIC Z(8)9.
      05   TM-TEXT                       PIC X(60).
*
 01   ERROR-MESSAGE.
*
      05   FILLER               PIC X(10)     VALUE 'INV3100 I '.
      05   FILLER               PIC X(8)      VALUE 'SEGMENT '.
      05   EM-KEY               PIC X(11).
      05   FILLER               PIC X(14)     VALUE ' (STATUS CODE '.
      05   EM-STATUS-CODE       PIC XX.
      05   FILLER               PIC XX        VALUE ') '.
      05   EM-TEXT              PIC X(60).
*
 01   DLI-FUNCTIONS.
*
      05   DLI-GU               PIC X(4)      VALUE 'GU  '.
      05   DLI-GHU              PIC X(4)      VALUE 'GHU '.
      05   DLI-GN               PIC X(4)      VALUE 'GN  '.
      05   DLI-GHN              PIC X(4)      VALUE 'GHN '.
      05   DLI-GNP              PIC X(4)      VALUE 'GNP '.
      05   DLI-GHNP             PIC X(4)      VALUE 'GHNP'.
      05   DLI-ISRT             PIC X(4)      VALUE 'ISRT'.
      05   DLI-DLET             PIC X(4)      VALUE 'DLET'.
      05   DLI-REPL             PIC X(4)      VALUE 'REPL'.
      05   DLI-CHKP             PIC X(4)      VALUE 'CHKP'.
      05   DLI-XRST             PIC X(4)      VALUE 'XRST'.
      05   DLI-PCB              PIC X(4)      VALUE 'PCB '.
*
 01   UNQUALIFIED-SSA           PIC X(9)      VALUE 'INLOCSEG '.
*
 01   VENDOR-SSA.
*
      05   FILLER               PIC X(9)      VALUE 'INVENSEG('.
      05   FILLER               PIC X(10)     VALUE 'INVENCOD ='.
      05   VENDOR-SSA-CODE      PIC X(3).
      05   FILLER               PIC X         VALUE ')'.
*
 01   ITEM-SSA.
*
      05   FILLER               PIC X(9)      VALUE 'INITMSEG('.
      05   FILLER               PIC X(10)     VALUE 'INITMNUM ='.
      05   ITEM-SSA-NUMBER      PIC X(5).
      05   FILLER               PIC X         VALUE ')'.
*
 01   LOCATION-SSA.
*
      05   FILLER               PIC X(9)      VALUE 'INLOCSEG('.
      05   FILLER               PIC X(10)     VALUE 'INLOCLOC ='.
      05   LOCATION-SSA-CODE    PIC X(3).
      05   FILLER               PIC X         VALUE ')'.
*
```

Figure 6-5 Source listing for the post inventory transactions program (part 2 of 6)

```
 01   INVENTORY-STOCK-LOC-SEGMENT.
*
     05  ISLS-LOCATION                  PIC X(3).
     05  ISLS-QUANTITY-ON-HAND          PIC S9(7)    COMP-3.
     05  ISLS-REORDER-POINT             PIC S9(7)    COMP-3.
     05  ISLS-QUANTITY-ON-ORDER         PIC S9(7)    COMP-3.
     05  ISLS-LAST-REORDER-DATE         PIC X(6).
*
 LINKAGE SECTION.
*
 01   INVENTORY-PCB-MASK.
*
     05  IPCB-DBD-NAME                  PIC X(8).
     05  IPCB-SEGMENT-LEVEL             PIC XX.
     05  IPCB-STATUS-CODE               PIC XX.
     05  IPCB-PROC-OPTIONS              PIC X(4).
     05  FILLER                         PIC S9(5)    COMP.
     05  IPCB-SEGMENT-NAME              PIC X(8).
     05  IPCB-KEY-LENGTH                PIC S9(5)    COMP.
     05  IPCB-NUMB-SENS-SEGS            PIC S9(5)    COMP.
     05  IPCB-KEY                       PIC X(11).
*
 PROCEDURE DIVISION.
*
     ENTRY 'DLITCBL' USING INVENTORY-PCB-MASK.
*
 000-POST-INVENTORY-TRANS.
*
     OPEN INPUT INVTRAN.
     PERFORM 100-POST-INVENTORY-TRANSACTION
         UNTIL INVTRAN-EOF.
     PERFORM 200-DISPLAY-UPDATE-TOTALS.
     CLOSE INVTRAN.
     GOBACK.
*
 100-POST-INVENTORY-TRANSACTION.
*
     PERFORM 110-READ-INVENTORY-TRANSACTION.
     IF NOT INVTRAN-EOF
         MOVE SPACE        TO EM-TEXT
         MOVE 'Y'          TO LOCATION-SEGMENT-FOUND-SW
         MOVE IST-LOCATION TO LOCATION-SSA-CODE
         MOVE IST-ITEM     TO ITEM-SSA-NUMBER
         MOVE IST-VENDOR   TO VENDOR-SSA-CODE
         IF IST-NEW-LOCATION
             PERFORM 120-ADD-NEW-LOCATION
         ELSE IF IST-DELETION
             PERFORM 140-DELETE-OLD-LOCATION
         ELSE IF IST-ADJUSTMENT
             PERFORM 170-ADJUST-CURRENT-LOCATION.
     IF NOT INVTRAN-EOF
         IF EM-TEXT NOT = SPACE
             PERFORM 190-DISPLAY-ERROR-MESSAGE.
```

Figure 6-5 Source listing for the post inventory transactions program (part 3 of 6)

```
 110-READ-INVENTORY-TRANSACTION.
*
     READ INVTRAN
         AT END
             MOVE 'Y' TO INVTRAN-EOF-SW.
*
 120-ADD-NEW-LOCATION.
*
     MOVE IST-LOCATION       TO ISLS-LOCATION.
     MOVE ZERO               TO ISLS-QUANTITY-ON-HAND
                                ISLS-QUANTITY-ON-ORDER.
     MOVE IST-REORDER-POINT TO ISLS-REORDER-POINT.
     MOVE SPACE              TO ISLS-LAST-REORDER-DATE.
     PERFORM 130-INSERT-LOCATION-SEGMENT.
*
 130-INSERT-LOCATION-SEGMENT.
*
     CALL 'CBLTDLI' USING DLI-ISRT
                          INVENTORY-PCB-MASK
                          INVENTORY-STOCK-LOC-SEGMENT
                          VENDOR-SSA
                          ITEM-SSA
                          UNQUALIFIED-SSA.
     IF IPCB-STATUS-CODE = SPACE
         ADD 1 TO SUCCESSFUL-ISRT-COUNT
     ELSE
         ADD 1 TO FAILED-ISRT-COUNT
         IF IPCB-STATUS-CODE = 'II'
             MOVE 'LOCATION SEGMENT ALREADY EXISTS' TO EM-TEXT
         ELSE
             MOVE 'INSERT CALL FAILED' TO EM-TEXT.
*
 140-DELETE-OLD-LOCATION.
*
     PERFORM 150-GET-LOCATION-SEGMENT.
     IF LOCATION-SEGMENT-FOUND
         PERFORM 160-DELETE-LOCATION-SEGMENT
     ELSE
         ADD 1 TO FAILED-DLET-COUNT
         MOVE 'MATCHING LOCATION SEGMENT FOR DELETE NOT FOUND'
             TO EM-TEXT.
*
 150-GET-LOCATION-SEGMENT.
*
     CALL 'CBLTDLI' USING DLI-GHU
                          INVENTORY-PCB-MASK
                          INVENTORY-STOCK-LOC-SEGMENT
                          VENDOR-SSA
                          ITEM-SSA
                          LOCATION-SSA.
     IF IPCB-STATUS-CODE NOT = SPACE
         MOVE 'N' TO LOCATION-SEGMENT-FOUND-SW.
*
```

Figure 6-5 Source listing for the post inventory transactions program (part 4 of 6)

```
 160-DELETE-LOCATION-SEGMENT.
*
     CALL 'CBLTDLI' USING DLI-DLET
                          INVENTORY-PCB-MASK
                          INVENTORY-STOCK-LOC-SEGMENT.
     IF IPCB-STATUS-CODE = SPACE
         ADD 1 TO SUCCESSFUL-DLET-COUNT
     ELSE
         ADD 1 TO FAILED-DLET-COUNT
         MOVE 'DELETE CALL FAILED' TO EM-TEXT.
*
 170-ADJUST-CURRENT-LOCATION.
*
     PERFORM 150-GET-LOCATION-SEGMENT.
     IF LOCATION-SEGMENT-FOUND
         MOVE IST-QUANTITY-ON-HAND  TO ISLS-QUANTITY-ON-HAND
         MOVE IST-REORDER-POINT     TO ISLS-REORDER-POINT
         MOVE IST-QUANTITY-ON-ORDER TO ISLS-QUANTITY-ON-ORDER
         MOVE IST-LAST-REORDER-DATE TO ISLS-LAST-REORDER-DATE
         PERFORM 180-REPLACE-LOCATION-SEGMENT
     ELSE
         ADD 1 TO FAILED-REPL-COUNT
         MOVE 'MATCHING LOCATION SEGMENT FOR REPLACE NOT FOUND'
             TO EM-TEXT.
*
 180-REPLACE-LOCATION-SEGMENT.
*
     CALL 'CBLTDLI' USING DLI-REPL
                          INVENTORY-PCB-MASK
                          INVENTORY-STOCK-LOC-SEGMENT.
     IF IPCB-STATUS-CODE = SPACE
         ADD 1 TO SUCCESSFUL-REPL-COUNT
     ELSE
         ADD 1 TO FAILED-REPL-COUNT
         MOVE 'REPLACE CALL FAILED' TO EM-TEXT.
*
 190-DISPLAY-ERROR-MESSAGE.
*
     MOVE IPCB-STATUS-CODE      TO EM-STATUS-CODE.
     MOVE IST-CONCATENATED-KEY TO EM-KEY.
     DISPLAY ERROR-MESSAGE.
*
 200-DISPLAY-UPDATE-TOTALS.
*
     MOVE SUCCESSFUL-REPL-COUNT                    TO TM-COUNT.
     MOVE ' REPLACE CALLS PROCESSED NORMALLY' TO TM-TEXT.
     DISPLAY TOTAL-MESSAGE.
     MOVE SUCCESSFUL-ISRT-COUNT                    TO TM-COUNT.
     MOVE ' INSERT CALLS PROCESSED NORMALLY'  TO TM-TEXT.
     DISPLAY TOTAL-MESSAGE.
     MOVE SUCCESSFUL-DLET-COUNT                    TO TM-COUNT.
     MOVE ' DELETE CALLS PROCESSED NORMALLY'  TO TM-TEXT.
     DISPLAY TOTAL-MESSAGE.
```

Figure 6-5 Source listing for the post inventory transactions program (part 5 of 6)

```
           MOVE FAILED-REPL-COUNT                    TO TM-COUNT.
           MOVE ' REPLACE CALLS FAILED'              TO TM-TEXT.
           DISPLAY TOTAL-MESSAGE.
           MOVE FAILED-ISRT-COUNT                    TO TM-COUNT.
           MOVE ' INSERT CALLS FAILED'               TO TM-TEXT.
           DISPLAY TOTAL-MESSAGE.
           MOVE FAILED-DLET-COUNT                    TO TM-COUNT.
           MOVE ' DELETE CALLS FAILED'               TO TM-TEXT.
           DISPLAY TOTAL-MESSAGE.
      *
```

Figure 6-5 Source listing for the post inventory transactions program (part 6 of 6)

Discussion

I think you'll agree that basic update processing using the ISRT, get hold, DLET, and REPL calls is fairly straightforward. And even the more sophisticated path calls aren't particularly difficult. For anyone familiar with standard COBOL file processing, the ISRT, DLET, and REPL calls should be easy to use.

Objective

Given complete specifications, code a load or update program that accesses a physical data base using any of the DL/I functions this chapter presents.

Section 3

Advanced DL/I data base processing

This section contains four chapters that expand the basic DL/I information you learned in section 2. Chapter 7 introduces secondary indexing, a technique that lets you access segments directly and efficiently even if you don't know their complete concatenated keys. Chapter 8 describes DL/I logical data bases and shows you what you need to know to process them in application programs. Chapter 9 presents DL/I recovery and restart facilities. The last chapter in this section, chapter 10, presents three other advanced DL/I features you might need to know about: variable length segments, segment edit/compression routines, and field-level sensitivity.

Each of these chapters is independent. As a result, you can read them in any order you like. However, both chapters 7 and 8 use the same data base structure as an example. So if you want to read chapter 8 before chapter 7, take a quick look at the description of the customer data base in chapter 7 first (figures 7-1 and 7-2).

Chapter 7

How to use secondary indexing

Often, you need to be able to access data in a data base in an order other than its primary hierarchical sequence. Or, you may need to access a segment in a data base record directly, without supplying its complete concatenated key. With *secondary indexing,* both are possible. In this chapter, I'll show you how DL/I implements secondary indexing and illustrate the programming considerations you need to keep in mind when you process a data base via a secondary index. Then, I'll show you an update program that uses a secondary index, and I'll describe some advanced secondary indexing features you may need to know about.

A customer data base

To describe secondary indexes, I'm not going to use the familiar inventory data base. Instead, I'll use a new data base: one for customer and receivables data, which I'll call the customer data base. Figure 7-1 shows the hierarchical structure of this data base, and figure 7-2 shows the COBOL segment layouts for each of its segment types. As you can tell from both figures 7-1 and 7-2, the customer data base has seven segment types. And, from the hierarchy chart in figure 7-1, you can see that two levels (3 and 4) have more than one segment type. So this is a

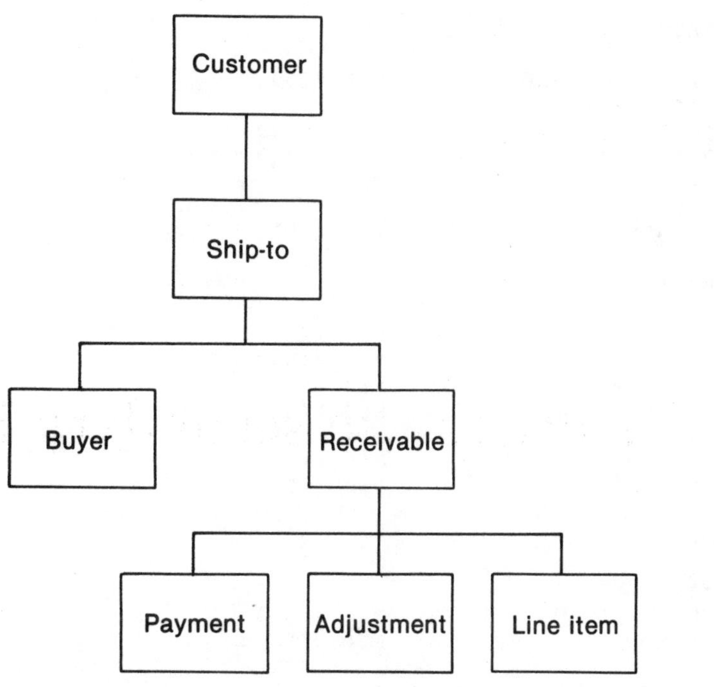

Figure 7-1 The customer data base

more complex structure than the inventory data base you're already familiar with.

The customer data base contains information on all the companies to which the firm sells products. For each of those companies, there's one data base record. The root segment has a six-character sequence field: CS-CUSTOMER-NUMBER. In addition, the customer segment contains information that's used to prepare bills for the customer: name and mailing address.

Subordinate to each occurrence of the customer segment may be one or more occurrences of the ship-to segment. Because some customers may have several ship-to locations, there needs to be a record of each. Each ship-to location is identified by a two-character sequence code (STS-SHIP-TO-SEQUENCE) and contains name and address information used to prepare packing lists for shipments.

The ship-to segment type has two subordinate segment types: buyer and receivable. The buyer segment is primarily for marketing purposes; it contains the names, titles, and telephone numbers of the persons in the customer firm who authorize purchases.

```
 01   CUSTOMER-SEGMENT.
*
      05   CS-CUSTOMER-NUMBER             PIC X(6).
      05   CS-CUSTOMER-NAME               PIC X(31).
      05   CS-ADDRESS-LINE-1              PIC X(31).
      05   CS-ADDRESS-LINE-2              PIC X(31).
      05   CS-CITY                        PIC X(18).
      05   CS-STATE                       PIC XX.
      05   CS-ZIP-CODE                    PIC X(9).
*
 01   SHIP-TO-SEGMENT.
*
      05   STS-SHIP-TO-SEQUENCE           PIC XX.
      05   STS-SHIP-TO-NAME               PIC X(31).
      05   STS-ADDRESS-LINE-1             PIC X(31).
      05   STS-ADDRESS-LINE-2             PIC X(31).
      05   STS-CITY                       PIC X(18).
      05   STS-STATE                      PIC XX.
      05   STS-ZIP-CODE                   PIC X(9).
*
 01   BUYER-SEGMENT.
*
      05   BS-BUYER-NAME                  PIC X(31).
      05   BS-TITLE                       PIC X(31).
      05   BS-TELEPHONE                   PIC X(10).
*
 01   RECEIVABLE-SEGMENT.
*
      05   RS-INVOICE-NUMBER              PIC X(6).
      05   RS-INVOICE-DATE                PIC X(6).
      05   RS-PO-NUMBER                   PIC X(25).
      05   RS-PRODUCT-TOTAL               PIC S9(5)V99      COMP-3.
      05   RS-CASH-DISCOUNT               PIC S9(5)V99      COMP-3.
      05   RS-SALES-TAX                   PIC S9(5)V99      COMP-3.
      05   RS-FREIGHT                     PIC S9(5)V99      COMP-3.
      05   RS-BALANCE-DUE                 PIC S9(5)V99      COMP-3.
*
 01   PAYMENT-SEGMENT.
*
      05   PS-CHECK-NUMBER                PIC X(16).
      05   PS-BANK-NUMBER                 PIC X(25).
      05   PS-PAYMENT-DATE                PIC X(6).
      05   PS-PAYMENT-AMOUNT              PIC S9(5)V99      COMP-3.
*
 01   ADJUSTMENT-SEGMENT.
*
      05   AS-REFERENCE-NUMBER            PIC X(6).
      05   AS-ADJUSTMENT-DATE             PIC X(6).
      05   AS-ADJUSTMENT-TYPE             PIC X.
      05   AS-ADJUSTMENT-AMOUNT           PIC S9(5)V99      COMP-3.
*
```

Figure 7-2 Segment layouts for the customer data base (part 1 of 2)

```
 01  LINE-ITEM-SEGMENT.
*
     05  LIS-ITEM-KEY.
         10  LIS-ITEM-KEY-VENDOR       PIC X(3).
         10  LIS-ITEM-KEY-NUMBER       PIC X(5).
     05  LIS-UNIT-PRICE                PIC S9(5)V99        COMP-3.
     05  LIS-QUANTITY                  PIC S9(7)           COMP-3.
*
```

Figure 7-2 Segment layouts for the customer data base (part 2 of 2)

The receivable segment corresponds to an invoice or a billing. When an invoice is issued, an occurrence of the receivable segment is inserted in the data base. It contains an invoice number (the segment's sequence field), invoice date, purchase order number, and several financial fields. The invoice total (that is, the amount billed) is the sum of RS-PRODUCT-TOTAL, RS-SALES-TAX, and RS-FREIGHT, minus RS-CASH-DISCOUNT. (The billing amount isn't stored as a separate field in the segment because it can be calculated easily.) The last field in the receivable segment, RS-BALANCE-DUE, represents the total amount of money currently due on the receivable.

The difference between the total amount billed and the current balance due must be accounted for either by payments received or adjustments made to the receivable. So subordinate to the receivable segment type are two additional segment types that correspond to these two types of transactions. The payment segment type contains the amount and date of the payment, plus its check and bank numbers. The adjustment segment type also contains an amount field, plus an identifying reference number, adjustment date, and a single-character adjustment type code.

Occurrences of the line item segment type contain data for each of the items sold under a given invoice. This segment type contains three data elements: item key, unit price, and quantity. The extended price (quantity multiplied by unit price) for all the line item segment occurrences for a single receivable equals the value in the RS-PRODUCT-TOTAL field in the receivable segment. If a program needs additional information about an item sold on an invoice, it can use the item number field of the line item segment to retrieve the corresponding item segment from the inventory data base.

Although this data base structure adequately defines the information related to a particular customer, it has some weaknesses. In particular, it's not possible to access a particular customer unless you know that customer's number. Unfortunately, that's not always the case; sometimes you need to find a customer segment based on the customer's name. In addition, many applications that use this data base will require direct access to receivable segments based on invoice number. But the structure in figure 7-1 isn't designed for that kind of access; it requires that you go through the customer path to retrieve a receivable segment.

The solution to both of these problems is a secondary index. Simply put, a secondary index could let you access customer root segments based on the customer name field rather than the customer number field. And, a secondary index could allow you to access receivable segments directly based on invoice number, without going through the customer path at all.

Secondary indexes

Figure 7-3 illustrates a possible use of secondary indexing with the customer data base. Here, the customer data base is indexed in sequence by invoice number—the sequence field not of the root segment, but of the receivable segment. As a result, this secondary index lets you access receivable segments in invoice number sequence.

DL/I maintains the alternate sequence by storing pointers to segments of the *indexed data base* in a separate *secondary index data base*. The fact that a secondary index is actually a separate data base is largely transparent to you; you don't have to provide a PCB mask for the secondary index data base because it's not explicitly defined in your program's PSB.

A secondary index data base has just one segment type, called the *index pointer segment*. The index pointer segment contains two main elements: a prefix element and a data element. The data element contains the key value from the segment in the indexed data base over which the index is built, called the *index source segment*. In figure 7-3, the index source segment is the receivable segment in the customer data base; the secondary index key derived from that segment is an invoice number. I'll have more to say about secondary index keys in just a moment.

The prefix part of the index pointer segment contains a pointer to the *index target segment*. That's the segment that's accessible via the secondary index. In figure 7-3, the index source and target segments are the same. As a result, this secondary index lets you access a receivable segment directly based on its invoice number. Later in this chapter,

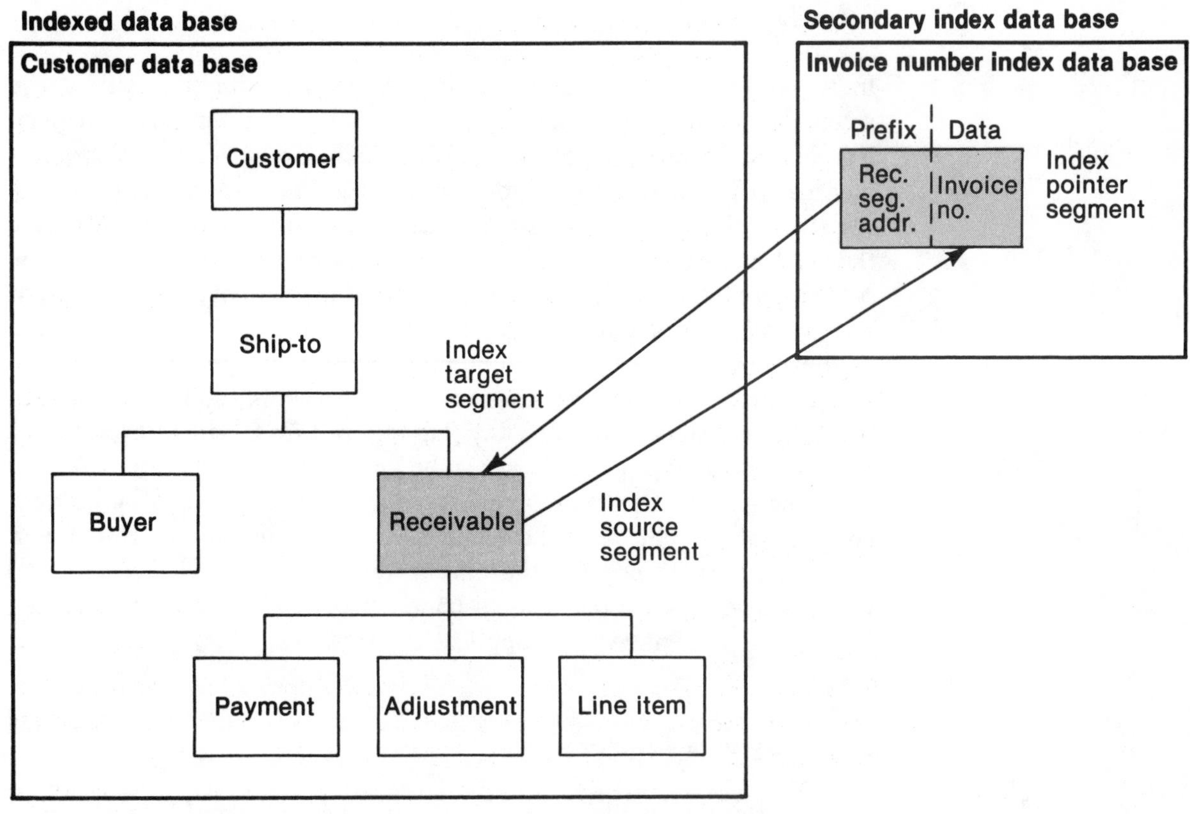

Figure 7-3 Secondary indexing example in which the index source segment and the index target segment are the same

you'll see that the index source and target segments don't have to be the same.

After a secondary index has been set up, DL/I maintains it automatically as changes are made to the indexed data base—though the index is transparent to application programs that don't use it. So even if a program that isn't sensitive to a secondary index updates a data base record in a way that would affect the index, DL/I automatically updates the index. As you can imagine, that can degrade performance if the index is built over a frequently modified segment.

If multiple access paths are required into the same data base, the DBA can define as many different secondary indexes as are necessary. Each is stored in a separate index data base. In practice, the number of secondary indexes for a given data base is kept low because each imposes additional processing overhead on DL/I.

Secondary keys

In the receivable secondary index, the invoice number field of the receivable segment is the secondary key. In this case, the secondary key happens to be the segment's sequence field. But that's not a requirement: any field within the segment can be used as a secondary key. As a result, the data base administrator can define a secondary index over the customer segment type using the customer name field as the secondary key, even though that field isn't the segment's sequence field.

Usually, a single field within the index source segment is designated as the secondary key for a secondary index. However, the data base administrator can combine more than one field in the source segment to form the complete secondary key. Up to five fields, which do *not* have to be adjacent to one another, can be combined in this way.

One last point: Secondary key values do *not* have to be unique. For example, if you used the name field of the customer segment as a secondary key, it's possible that duplicates could exist. DL/I has several ways of dealing with duplicate secondary key values, but fortunately, they're transparent to most application programs.

Secondary data structures

It's important to realize that using a secondary index like the one in figure 7-3 changes the apparent hierarchical structure of the data base. That's because when you access a data base from a secondary index, the index target segment is presented to your program as if it were a root segment, even if it isn't actually the root segment of the data base. As a result, the hierarchical sequence of the segments in the path from the index target segment to the root segment is inverted: those segments appear to be subordinate to the index target segment, even though they're actually superior to it. The resulting rearrangement of the data base structure is called a *secondary data structure*. Secondary data structures don't change the way the data base segments are stored on disk; they just alter the way DL/I presents those segments to application programs.

To illustrate, figure 7-4 shows the secondary data structure for the customer data base when accessed by the secondary index in figure 7-3. Here, the receivable segment—the index target segment—is at the top of the hierarchy, as if it were the root segment. Subordinate to it are the payment, adjustment, and line item segments, as you would expect. But the ship-to segment, which is the parent segment of the receivable

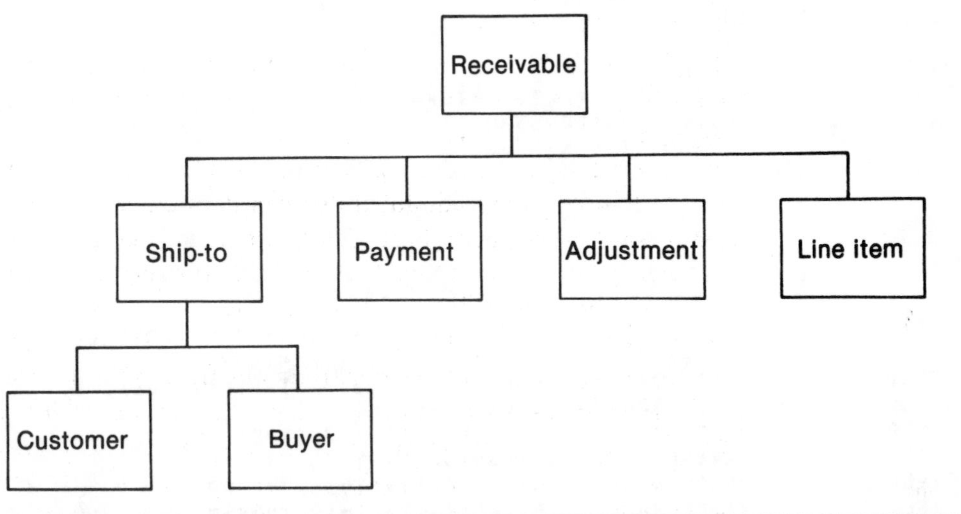

Figure 7-4 Secondary data structure for the secondary index shown in figure 7-3

segment in the actual data base, is subordinate to the receivable segment when the secondary index is used. And the customer segment appears subordinate to the ship-to segment. The buyer segment type, which was originally subordinate to the ship-to segment type, remains subordinate to it in figure 7-4.

When you code an application program that processes a data base via a secondary index, you must consider how the secondary data structure affects your program's logic. For example, suppose an application program processing the customer data base using the secondary index in figure 7-3 retrieves a receivable segment by issuing a GU call that specifies an invoice number in a qualified SSA. To retrieve the customer segment that corresponds to that receivable, the program simply issues a GN call with an unqualified SSA for the customer segment type.

DBDGEN requirements for secondary indexes

Because a secondary index relationship involves two data bases, two DBDGENs are required: one for the indexed data base, the other for the secondary index data base. Figures 7-5 and 7-6 show both DBDGEN outputs for the secondary index in figure 7-3. In figure 7-5, the DBDGEN for the customer data base, I've omitted all the SEGM macros

```
STMT   SOURCE STATEMENT

  PRINT            NOGEN
  DBD              NAME=CRDBD,ACCESS=HIDAM
  DATASET          DD1=CR,DEVICE=3380
 *,                  3380 DISK STORAGE
   .
   .
   .
 *
  SEGM             NAME=CRRECSEG,PARENT=CRSHPSEG,POINTER=T,BYTES=57
  LCHILD           NAME=(CRSXPNTR,CRSXDBD),POINTER=INDX
  FIELD            NAME=(CRRECINO,SEQ,U),BYTES=6,START=1,TYPE=C
  XDFLD            NAME=CRRECXNO,SRCH=CRRECINO
  FIELD            NAME=CRRECDAT,BYTES=6,START=7,TYPE=C
  FIELD            NAME=CRRECPO,BYTES=25,START=13,TYPE=C
  FIELD            NAME=CRRECPRT,BYTES=4,START=38,TYPE=P
  FIELD            NAME=CRRECDIS,BYTES=4,START=42,TYPE=P
  FIELD            NAME=CRRECTAX,BYTES=4,START=46,TYPE=P
  FIELD            NAME=CRRECFRT,BYTES=4,START=50,TYPE=P
  FIELD            NAME=CRRECDUE,BYTES=4,START=54,TYPE=P
 *
   .
   .
   .
```

Figure 7-5 Partial DBDGEN output for the customer data base showing the code to implement the secondary index

except the one for the receivable segment type; the others are the same with or without secondary indexing. As a result, you can focus on the code used to implement the secondary index relationship. Because all of the secondary index DBDGEN is relevant, figure 7-6 shows all of its output.

In the DBDGEN for an indexed data base, an LCHILD macro relates an index target segment to its associated secondary index data base. In figure 7-5, the shaded LCHILD macro relates the receivable segment (CRRECSEG) to the index pointer segment (CRSXPNTR) in the secondary index data base (CRSXDBD). If you look at figure 7-6, the DBDGEN for the secondary index data base, you'll see that the name specified in the DBD macro is CRSXDBD and that the only segment in the secondary index data base is CRSXPNTR. (Incidentally, ACCESS=INDEX in the DBD macro in figure 7-6 tells DL/I that an index data base is being defined.)

```
STMT   SOURCE STATEMENT

   1  PRINT          NOGEN
   2  DBD            NAME=CRSXDBD,ACCESS=INDEX
   3  DATASET        DD1=CRSX,DEVICE=3380
  4+*,                 3380 DISK STORAGE
   5 *
   6  SEGM           NAME=CRSXPNTR,PARENT=0,BYTES=6
   7  LCHILD         NAME=(CRRECSEG,CRDBD),INDEX=CRRECXNO
   8  FIELD          NAME=(CRPXINUM,SEQ,U),BYTES=6,START=1,TYPE=C
   9  DBDGEN
 52+*,* * * * * * * * * * * * * * * * * * * * * * * * * *
 53+*,*
 54+*,    RECOMMENDED VSAM DEFINE CLUSTER PARAMETERS
 55+*,*
 56+*,* * * * * * * * * * * * * * * * * * * * * * * * * *
 58+*,* * * * * * * * * * * * * * * * * * * * * * * * * *
 59+*,*
 60+*,*                        *NOTE1
 61+*,*   DEFINE CLUSTER (NAME(CRSX) -
 62+*,*          INDEXED KEYS (6,5) -
 63+*,*          RECORDSIZE (12,12)) -
 64+*,*          DATA (CONTROLINTERVALSIZE (1024))
 65+*,*
 66+*,* *NOTE1 - SHOULD SPECIFY DSNAME FOR DD CRSX
 67+*,*
 68+*,* * * * * * * * * * * * * * * * * * * * * * * * * *
107+*,****** SEQUENCE FIELD ******
172   FINISH
173   END
```

Figure 7-6 DBDGEN output for the secondary index data base

An LCHILD macro is required in the DBDGEN for the secondary index data base, too. It relates the index pointer segment to the index target segment. So the LCHILD macro in figure 7-6 specifies the name of the receivable segment (CRRECSEG) and the name of the indexed data base (CRDBD).

In addition, the INDEX parameter of the LCHILD macro in figure 7-6 specifies the name of the secondary key field: CRRECXNO. In figure 7-5, I've shaded the XDFLD macro that defines this field. The XDFLD macro supplies a field name (CRRECXNO) that's used to access the data base via the secondary key. This key field does *not* become a part of the segment. Instead, its value is derived from up to five fields defined within the segment with FIELD macros. In figure 7-5, the SRCH parameter specifies just one field: CRRECINO. It's defined by the FIELD macro that's just before the XDFLD macro.

Fortunately, coding DBDGEN jobs for secondary indexes is the responsibility of the data base administrator. So you don't need to learn how to code DBDGEN jobs yourself. I include them here only because they help you see how DL/I is able to make the connections among the related segment types and so you can appreciate what the data base administrator has to do to set up a secondary index.

PSBGEN requirements for secondary indexing

Just because a secondary index exists for a data base doesn't mean DL/I will automatically use it when one of your programs issues calls for that data base. You need to be sure that the PSBGEN for the program specifies the proper processing sequence for the data base on the PROCSEQ parameter of the PCB macro. If it doesn't, processing is done using the normal hierarchical sequence for the data base. For the PROCSEQ parameter, the DBA codes the DBD name for the secondary index data base that will be used.

Figure 7-7 shows the PSBGEN job for a program that posts payments to invoices in the customer data base (I'll show you the complete program in a moment). Notice that the SENSEG macros in figure 7-7 reflect the secondary data structure imposed by the secondary index. As a result, the first SENSEG macro specifies the receivable segment (CRRECSEG) rather than the customer segment. And the ship-to and customer segments specify parentage that reflects their inverted hierarchical sequence. The two shaded SENSEG macros in figure 7-7 are for the segment types the program will access: receivable (CRRECSEG) and payment (CRPAYSEG).

Notice the PROCSEQ parameter in the PCB macro in figure 7-7. When it's present, processing is done based on the secondary index sequence. In this case, it's the sequence provided by CRSXDBD. If a program needs to access the same indexed data base using different processing sequences, the program's PSBGEN will contain more than one PCB macro, each specifying a different value for the PROCSEQ parameter.

An update program that uses a secondary index

Now, let me show you the post payment transactions program; figures 7-8 and 7-9 present its structure chart and source code. The program reads a file of payment transactions in card format. Each transaction

```
STMT   SOURCE STATEMENT

   1   PRINT         NOGEN
   2   PCB           TYPE=DB,DBDNAME=CRDBD,KEYLEN=22,PROCOPT=A,
                     PROCSEQ=CRSXDBD
   3   SENSEG        NAME=CRRECSEG
   4   SENSEG        NAME=CRSHPSEG,PARENT=CRRECSEG
   5   SENSEG        NAME=CRCSTSEG,PARENT=CRSHPSEG
   6   SENSEG        NAME=CRBUYSEG,PARENT=CRSHPSEG
   7   SENSEG        NAME=CRPAYSEG,PARENT=CRRECSEG
   8   SENSEG        NAME=CRADJSEG,PARENT=CRRECSEG
   9   SENSEG        NAME=CRLINSEG,PARENT=CRRECSEG
  10   PSBGEN        PSBNAME=CRSIA,LANG=COBOL
 113   END
```

Figure 7-7 PSBGEN output for the post payments program

contains payment data as well as the number of the invoice to which the payment should be applied. (Although the input is on cards, it could as well be stored in another way, such as in a VSAM file.) Besides updating the receivable segment and adding a payment segment occurrence for each transaction, the program produces a printed report that lists the invoice number, check number, bank number, ending balance, payment amount, date, and comment.

The basic operation of this program should be simple enough to follow. Module 100 is the main processing module: it invokes modules to read a payment transaction, get the corresponding receivable segment, replace it, insert a payment segment, and print a report line. After module 100 has processed all of the transactions, module 200 is invoked to print the report's total lines.

I've shaded the parts of the source program (figure 7-9) I particularly want you to notice. First, look at the qualified SSA that the program uses when it issues a GHU call for a receivable segment (INVOICE-NO-SSA). The SSA specifies the segment name CRRECSEG, as you'd expect. But instead of specifying a field name from a FIELD macro in the DBDGEN job, it uses the field name from the XDFLD macro (CRRECXNO). That way, the secondary index will be used when calls are issued with this SSA.

Before the module that issues the GHU call is performed, the statement

```
MOVE PT-INVOICE-NUMBER TO INVOICE-NO-SSA-VALUE
```

sets up the SSA so it can be used to return the proper segment

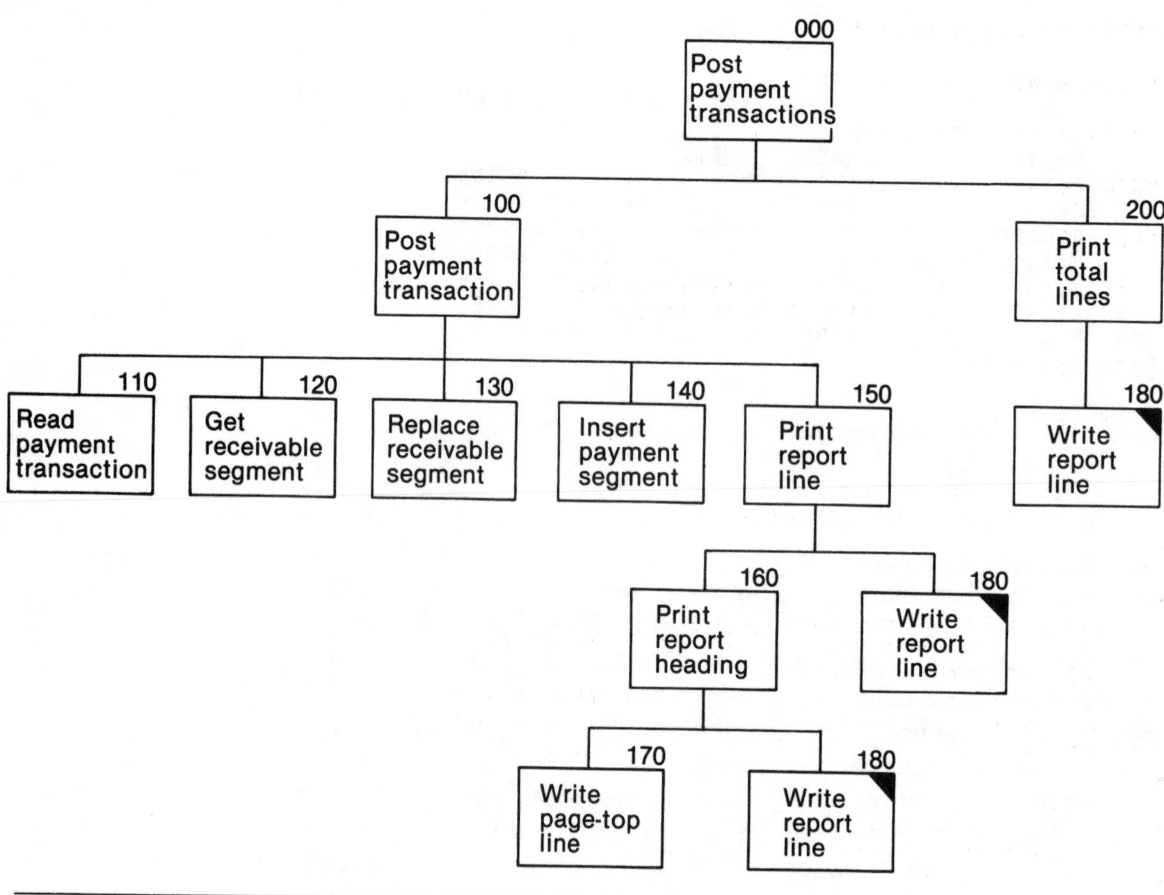

Figure 7-8 Structure chart for the post payments program

occurrence. Then, the CALL statement in module 120 retrieves the segment and holds it for update. The payment amount from the transaction record is subtracted from the balance due in the receivable segment, then module 130 is invoked to replace the segment. As you can see, there's nothing unusual about the replace call.

After the receivable segment has been replaced, a new occurrence of the payment segment containing the detail data from the current transaction is inserted by the call in module 140. Position in the data base is correct because the parent receivable segment was just processed.

```
IDENTIFICATION DIVISION.
*
PROGRAM-ID.  CR4100.
*
ENVIRONMENT DIVISION.
*
INPUT-OUTPUT SECTION.
*
FILE-CONTROL.
*
    SELECT PAYTRAN ASSIGN UT-S-PAYTRAN.
    SELECT PRTOUT  ASSIGN UT-S-PRTOUT.
*
DATA DIVISION.
*
FILE SECTION.
*
FD  PAYTRAN
    LABEL RECORDS ARE OMITTED
    RECORD CONTAINS 80 CHARACTERS.
*
01  PAYMENT-TRANSACTION-RECORD.
*
    05  PT-INVOICE-NUMBER          PIC X(6).
    05  PT-CHECK-NUMBER            PIC X(16).
    05  PT-BANK-NUMBER             PIC X(25).
    05  PT-PAYMENT-DATE            PIC X(6).
    05  PT-PAYMENT-AMOUNT          PIC 9(5)V99.
    05  FILLER                     PIC X(20).
*
FD  PRTOUT
    LABEL RECORDS ARE OMITTED
    RECORD CONTAINS 132 CHARACTERS.
*
01  PRTOUT-RECORD                  PIC X(132).
*
WORKING-STORAGE SECTION.
*
01  SWITCHES.
*
    05  PAYTRAN-EOF-SW             PIC X        VALUE 'N'.
        88  PAYTRAN-EOF                         VALUE 'Y'.
    05  RECEIVABLE-FOUND-SW        PIC X        VALUE 'Y'.
        88  RECEIVABLE-FOUND                    VALUE 'Y'.
*
01  COUNT-FIELDS                   COMP-3.
*
    05  CASH-RECEIVED              PIC S9(7)V99 VALUE ZERO.
    05  VALID-TRANSACTION-COUNT    PIC S9(5)    VALUE ZERO.
    05  INVALID-TRANSACTION-COUNT  PIC S9(5)    VALUE ZERO.
*
```

Figure 7-9 Source listing for the post payments program (part 1 of 6)

```
 01  PRINT-FIELDS                                       COMP-3.
*
     05  PAGE-COUNT                     PIC S9(5)      VALUE +1.
     05  LINE-COUNT                     PIC S9(3)      VALUE +999.
     05  LINES-ON-PAGE                  PIC S9(3)      VALUE +50.
     05  SPACE-CONTROL                  PIC S9(3)      VALUE ZERO.
*
 01  HEADING-LINE-1.
*
     05  FILLER           PIC X(20)   VALUE 'CASH RECEIPTS REGIST'.
     05  FILLER           PIC X(7)    VALUE 'ER  -  '.
     05  HL1-SYSTEM-DATE  PIC 99/99/99.
     05  FILLER           PIC X(86)   VALUE SPACE.
     05  FILLER           PIC X(6)    VALUE 'PAGE: '.
     05  HL1-PAGE         PIC Z(4)9.
*
 01  HEADING-LINE-2.
*
     05  FILLER           PIC X(20)   VALUE 'INVOICE     CHECK NUM'.
     05  FILLER           PIC X(20)   VALUE 'BER        BANK NUMBER'.
     05  FILLER           PIC X(20)   VALUE '                 NEW'.
     05  FILLER           PIC X(20)   VALUE ' BAL          PAYMENT '.
     05  FILLER           PIC X(20)   VALUE '         DATE       CO'.
     05  FILLER           PIC X(20)   VALUE 'MMENT               '.
     05  FILLER           PIC X(12)   VALUE '            '.
*
 01  REPORT-LINE.
*
     05  RL-INVOICE-NUMBER              PIC X(6).
     05  FILLER                         PIC X(5)      VALUE SPACE.
     05  RL-CHECK-NUMBER                PIC X(16).
     05  FILLER                         PIC XX        VALUE SPACE.
     05  RL-BANK-NUMBER                 PIC X(25).
     05  FILLER                         PIC XX        VALUE SPACE.
     05  RL-NEW-BALANCE                 PIC Z(5).99-.
     05  FILLER                         PIC X(6)      VALUE SPACE.
     05  RL-PAYMENT-AMOUNT              PIC Z(5).99-.
     05  FILLER                         PIC X(6)      VALUE SPACE.
     05  RL-PAYMENT-DATE                PIC 99/99/99.
     05  FILLER                         PIC X(5)      VALUE SPACE.
     05  RL-COMMENT                     PIC X(33)     VALUE SPACE.
*
 01  TOTAL-LINE-1.
*
     05  FILLER           PIC X(20)   VALUE 'VALID PAYMENTS:      '.
     05  TL1-COUNT        PIC Z(4)9.
     05  FILLER           PIC X(20)   VALUE '     CASH RECEIVED:  '.
     05  TL1-CASH         PIC Z(7).99.
     05  FILLER           PIC X(77)   VALUE SPACE.
*
```

Figure 7-9 Source listing for the post payments program (part 2 of 6)

```
 01  TOTAL-LINE-2.
*
     05  FILLER             PIC X(20)    VALUE 'INVALID PAYMENTS:
     05  TL2-COUNT          PIC Z(4)9.
     05  FILLER             PIC X(107)   VALUE SPACE.
*
 01  DLI-FUNCTIONS.
*
     05  DLI-GU                          PIC X(4)    VALUE 'GU  '.
     05  DLI-GHU                         PIC X(4)    VALUE 'GHU '.
     05  DLI-GN                          PIC X(4)    VALUE 'GN  '.
     05  DLI-GHN                         PIC X(4)    VALUE 'GHN '.
     05  DLI-GNP                         PIC X(4)    VALUE 'GNP '.
     05  DLI-GHNP                        PIC X(4)    VALUE 'GHNP'.
     05  DLI-ISRT                        PIC X(4)    VALUE 'ISRT'.
     05  DLI-DLET                        PIC X(4)    VALUE 'DLET'.
     05  DLI-REPL                        PIC X(4)    VALUE 'REPL'.
     05  DLI-CHKP                        PIC X(4)    VALUE 'CHKP'.
     05  DLI-XRST                        PIC X(4)    VALUE 'XRST'.
*
 01  RECEIVABLE-SEGMENT.
*
     05  RS-INVOICE-NUMBER               PIC X(6).
     05  RS-INVOICE-DATE                 PIC X(6).
     05  RS-PO-NUMBER                    PIC X(25).
     05  RS-PRODUCT-TOTAL                PIC S9(5)V99     COMP-3.
     05  RS-CASH-DISCOUNT                PIC S9(5)V99     COMP-3.
     05  RS-SALES-TAX                    PIC S9(5)V99     COMP-3.
     05  RS-FREIGHT                      PIC S9(5)V99     COMP-3.
     05  RS-BALANCE-DUE                  PIC S9(5)V99     COMP-3.
*
 01  PAYMENT-SEGMENT.
*
     05  PS-CHECK-NUMBER                 PIC X(16).
     05  PS-BANK-NUMBER                  PIC X(25).
     05  PS-PAYMENT-DATE                 PIC X(6).
     05  PS-PAYMENT-AMOUNT               PIC S9(5)V99     COMP-3.
*
 01  UNQUALIFIED-SSA.
*
     05  UNQUAL-SSA-SEGMENT-NAME         PIC X(8)   VALUE 'CRPAYSEG'.
     05  FILLER                          PIC X      VALUE SPACE.
*
 01  INVOICE-NO-SSA.
*
     05  FILLER                          PIC X(9)   VALUE 'CRRECSEG('.
     05  FILLER                          PIC X(10)  VALUE 'CRRECXNO ='.
     05  INVOICE-NO-SSA-VALUE            PIC X(6).
     05  FILLER                          PIC X      VALUE ')'.
*
```

Figure 7-9 Source listing for the post payments program (part 3 of 6)

```
 LINKAGE SECTION.
*
 01  CR-PCB-MASK.
*
     05  CR-PCB-DBD-NAME                   PIC X(8).
     05  CR-PCB-SEGMENT-LEVEL              PIC XX.
     05  CR-PCB-STATUS-CODE                PIC XX.
     05  CR-PCB-PROC-OPTIONS               PIC X(4).
     05  FILLER                            PIC S9(5)    COMP.
     05  CR-PCB-SEGMENT-NAME               PIC X(8).
     05  CR-PCB-KEY-LENGTH                 PIC S9(5)    COMP.
     05  CR-PCB-NUMB-SENS-SEGS             PIC S9(5)    COMP.
     05  CR-PCB-KEY                        PIC X(22).
*
 PROCEDURE DIVISION.
*
     ENTRY 'DLITCBL' USING CR-PCB-MASK.
*
 000-POST-PAYMENT-TRANSACTIONS.
*
     OPEN INPUT  PAYTRAN
          OUTPUT PRTOUT.
     ACCEPT HL1-SYSTEM-DATE FROM DATE.
     PERFORM 100-POST-PAYMENT-TRANSACTION
         UNTIL PAYTRAN-EOF.
     PERFORM 200-PRINT-TOTAL-LINES.
     CLOSE PAYTRAN
           PRTOUT.
     GOBACK.
*
 100-POST-PAYMENT-TRANSACTION.
*
     PERFORM 110-READ-PAYMENT-TRANSACTION.
     IF NOT PAYTRAN-EOF
         MOVE 'Y'               TO RECEIVABLE-FOUND-SW
         MOVE PT-INVOICE-NUMBER TO INVOICE-NO-SSA-VALUE
         PERFORM 120-GET-RECEIVABLE-SEGMENT
         IF RECEIVABLE-FOUND
             SUBTRACT PT-PAYMENT-AMOUNT FROM RS-BALANCE-DUE
             PERFORM 130-REPLACE-RECEIVABLE-SEGMENT
             MOVE PT-CHECK-NUMBER   TO PS-CHECK-NUMBER
             MOVE PT-BANK-NUMBER    TO PS-BANK-NUMBER
             MOVE PT-PAYMENT-DATE   TO PS-PAYMENT-DATE
             MOVE PT-PAYMENT-AMOUNT TO PS-PAYMENT-AMOUNT
             PERFORM 140-INSERT-PAYMENT-SEGMENT
             ADD 1                  TO VALID-TRANSACTION-COUNT
             ADD PT-PAYMENT-AMOUNT  TO CASH-RECEIVED
             PERFORM 150-PRINT-REPORT-LINE
         ELSE
             ADD 1                  TO INVALID-TRANSACTION-COUNT
             PERFORM 150-PRINT-REPORT-LINE.
```

Figure 7-9 Source listing for the post payments program (part 4 of 6)

```
*
 110-READ-PAYMENT-TRANSACTION.
*
     READ PAYTRAN
         AT END
             MOVE 'Y' TO PAYTRAN-EOF-SW.
*
 120-GET-RECEIVABLE-SEGMENT.
*
     CALL 'CBLTDLI' USING DLI-GHU
                          CR-PCB-MASK
                          RECEIVABLE-SEGMENT
                          INVOICE-NO-SSA.
     IF CR-PCB-STATUS-CODE NOT = SPACE
         MOVE 'N'                          TO RECEIVABLE-FOUND-SW
         MOVE ZERO                         TO RS-BALANCE-DUE
         MOVE 'INVALID INVOICE NUMBER'     TO RL-COMMENT.
*
 130-REPLACE-RECEIVABLE-SEGMENT.
*
     CALL 'CBLTDLI' USING DLI-REPL
                          CR-PCB-MASK
                          RECEIVABLE-SEGMENT.
     IF CR-PCB-STATUS-CODE NOT = SPACE
         MOVE 'Y' TO PAYTRAN-EOF-SW
         DISPLAY 'CR4100 I 1 INVALID STATUS ON REPLACE CALL -- '
                 CR-PCB-STATUS-CODE.
*
 140-INSERT-PAYMENT-SEGMENT.
*
     CALL 'CBLTDLI' USING DLI-ISRT
                          CR-PCB-MASK
                          PAYMENT-SEGMENT
                          UNQUALIFIED-SSA.
     IF CR-PCB-STATUS-CODE NOT = SPACE
         MOVE 'Y' TO PAYTRAN-EOF-SW
         DISPLAY 'CR4100 I 2 INVALID STATUS ON INSERT CALL -- '
                 CR-PCB-STATUS-CODE.
*
 150-PRINT-REPORT-LINE.
*
     IF LINE-COUNT > LINES-ON-PAGE
         PERFORM 160-PRINT-REPORT-HEADING.
     MOVE PT-INVOICE-NUMBER TO RL-INVOICE-NUMBER
     MOVE PT-CHECK-NUMBER   TO RL-CHECK-NUMBER
     MOVE PT-BANK-NUMBER    TO RL-BANK-NUMBER
     MOVE RS-BALANCE-DUE    TO RL-NEW-BALANCE
     MOVE PT-PAYMENT-AMOUNT TO RL-PAYMENT-AMOUNT
     MOVE PT-PAYMENT-DATE   TO RL-PAYMENT-DATE
     MOVE REPORT-LINE       TO PRTOUT-RECORD.
     PERFORM 180-WRITE-REPORT-LINE.
     MOVE SPACE             TO RL-COMMENT.
```

Figure 7-9 Source listing for the post payments program (part 5 of 6)

```
*
 160-PRINT-REPORT-HEADING.
*
     MOVE 1                 TO LINE-COUNT.
     MOVE PAGE-COUNT        TO HL1-PAGE.
     ADD 1                  TO PAGE-COUNT.
     MOVE HEADING-LINE-1 TO PRTOUT-RECORD.
     PERFORM 170-WRITE-PAGE-TOP-LINE.
     MOVE 2                 TO SPACE-CONTROL.
     MOVE HEADING-LINE-2 TO PRTOUT-RECORD.
     PERFORM 180-WRITE-REPORT-LINE.
     MOVE 2                 TO SPACE-CONTROL.
*
 170-WRITE-PAGE-TOP-LINE.
*
     WRITE PRTOUT-RECORD
         AFTER ADVANCING PAGE.
*
 180-WRITE-REPORT-LINE.
*
     WRITE PRTOUT-RECORD
         AFTER ADVANCING SPACE-CONTROL LINES.
     ADD SPACE-CONTROL TO LINE-COUNT.
     MOVE 1              TO SPACE-CONTROL.
*
 200-PRINT-TOTAL-LINES.
*
     MOVE 2                           TO SPACE-CONTROL.
     MOVE VALID-TRANSACTION-COUNT     TO TL1-COUNT.
     MOVE CASH-RECEIVED               TO TL1-CASH.
     MOVE TOTAL-LINE-1                TO PRTOUT-RECORD.
     PERFORM 180-WRITE-REPORT-LINE.
     MOVE INVALID-TRANSACTION-COUNT TO TL2-COUNT.
     MOVE TOTAL-LINE-2                TO PRTOUT-RECORD.
     PERFORM 180-WRITE-REPORT-LINE.
```

Figure 7-9 Source listing for the post payments program (part 6 of 6)

The other parts of the program are routine. Most of the code is related to preparing and printing an audit trail register that has one line for each payment transaction. The error handling the program does is straightforward too. If the GHU call yields a non-blank status code, the program assumes the transaction record contains an invalid invoice number. The program's logic handles that much like it would an invalid key condition when processing updates against a standard indexed file. On the other hand, a non-blank status code from either the ISRT or REPL call probably indicates an error condition that the program can't handle. As a result, the program takes steps to end and to advise the user of the problem with an appropriate error message.

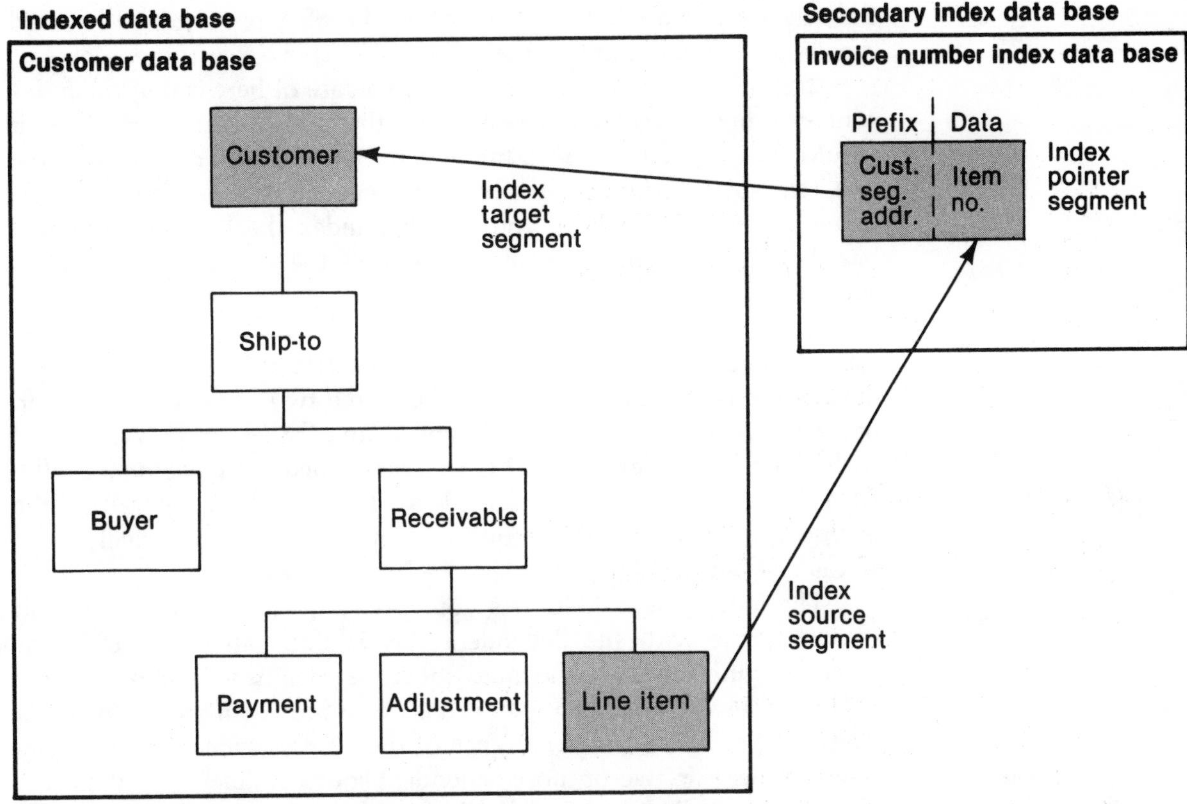

Figure 7-10 Secondary indexing example in which the index source segment and the index target segment are different

Indexing a segment based on a dependent segment

Although the secondary index example in this chapter uses the same segment for both the index source segment and the index target segment, that's not a requirement. Some applications require that a particular segment be indexed by a value that's derived from a dependent segment. In that case, the index source and target segments are different.

To illustrate, figure 7-10 shows another secondary index that might be created for the customer data base. Here, the customer segment type is indexed based on item number values that exist within line item segments. The result is that you can retrieve customers based on items they have purchased. In other words, the SSA for a get call would specify an item number, but the call would retrieve a customer segment.

The only restriction you need to be aware of here is that the index source segment must be a dependent of the index target segment. So it wouldn't be possible to index the buyer segment based on values in the line item segment, because the line item segment isn't dependent on the buyer segment. Similarly, you couldn't index the line item segment based on the customer segment, because the customer segment is superior to the line item segment.

Independent AND operators When I described how to use multiple qualifications in SSAs in chapter 4, I covered two of the three Boolean operators available to you: AND (* or &) and OR (+ or |). When used with secondary indexes, AND (* or &) is called the *dependent AND*. Also in chapter 4, I mentioned a third Boolean operator, the *independent AND* (#), and told you that it's used exclusively with secondary indexes. Now, I'll describe how it works.

The independent AND lets you specify qualifications that would be impossible with the dependent AND. You can use it only for secondary indexes where the index source segment is a dependent of the index target segment. Then, you can code an SSA with the independent AND to specify that an occurrence of the target segment be processed based on fields in two or more dependent source segments. In contrast, a dependent AND requires that all of the fields you specify in the SSA be in the same segment occurrence.

To illustrate, suppose you're developing a program that prints a list of all customers who have purchased both of two particular items. Assuming the item number secondary key field is named CRLINXNO, you could code an SSA like the one in figure 7-11. Then, after moving the correct item numbers to SSA-ITEM-KEY-1 and SSA-ITEM-KEY-2, you could issue a series of GN calls to retrieve the customers who have purchased both items.

Sparse sequencing

When the data base administrator implements a secondary index data base with *sparse sequencing* (also called *sparse indexing*), it's possible to omit some index source segments from the index. Sparse sequencing can improve performance when some occurrences of the index source segment must be indexed, but others need not be.

```
01  ITEM-SELECTION-SSA.
*
    05  FILLER            PIC X(9)    VALUE 'CRCUSSEG('.
    05  FILLER            PIC X(10)   VALUE 'CRLINXNO ='.
    05  SSA-ITEM-KEY-1    PIC X(8).
    05  FILLER            PIC X       VALUE '#'.
    05  FILLER            PIC X(10)   VALUE 'CRLINXNO ='.
    05  SSA-ITEM-KEY-2    PIC X(8).
    05  FILLER            PIC X       VALUE ')'.
```

Figure 7-11 An SSA that uses the independent AND operator

DL/I uses a *suppression value*, a *suppression routine*, or both to determine whether a segment should be indexed (either when inserting a new segment or processing an existing one). If the value of the sequence field(s) in the index source segment matches a suppression value specified by the DBA, no index relationship is established (for an insert) or expected (for any other call). The DBA can also specify a suppression routine that DL/I invokes to determine the index status for the segment. The suppression routine is a user-written program that evaluates the segment and determines whether or not it should be indexed.

To illustrate the use of sparse sequencing, consider again the example in figures 7-10 and 7-11. Suppose that nearly all of the firm's customers order item 00001. In that case, it wouldn't be very helpful to extract that information via the secondary index. So the data base administrator could use a suppression value to specify that line item segments with 00001 in the item number field should be omitted from the secondary index. That makes the secondary index smaller, and, as a result, more efficient.

When sparse sequencing is used, its functions are handled by DL/I. You don't need to make special provisions for it in your application programs.

Duplicate data fields

For some applications, it might be desirable to store user data from the index source segment in the index pointer segment. When the DBA specifies that some fields are *duplicate data fields*, this is possible. Up to five duplicate data fields can be stored in the index data base, and DL/I maintains them automatically. Duplicate data fields are useful only when the index data base is processed as a separate data base, and that's unusual.

In the receivable secondary index example (figure 7-3), the DBA might decide to store the current invoice balance due in the invoice pointer segment as a duplicate data field. Then, an application program that simply lists the current balances due for all receivables could process just the index data base to produce its report. Although this is more efficient for the report preparation program than accessing the receivable segment through the index, extra DL/I overhead and DASD storage are required to maintain the duplicate data. It's the DBA's responsibility to decide which factor outweighs the other.

Discussion

Secondary indexing is a powerful tool that lets the data base administrator get around some of the limitations of the strict hierarchical structure DL/I imposes. However, it does have a cost. Additional DASD space is required for the secondary index data base and, more important, significant DL/I overhead is involved to keep secondary index relationships up-to-date. As a result, the data base administrator has to think carefully about using secondary indexing. Often, it's more efficient not to use a secondary index, but to extract data base data into a standard file, then sort it for processing. However, for non-batch applications where response time is critical or for applications like the one in this chapter where access to a segment occurrence without first going through the root segment is required, secondary indexing is a sensible choice.

Terminology

secondary indexing
indexed data base
secondary index data base
index pointer segment
index source segment
index target segment
secondary data structure
dependent AND
independent AND
sparse sequencing
sparse indexing
suppression value
suppression routine
duplicate data field

Objective

Given complete specifications, code a program that uses secondary indexing to access segments.

Chapter 8

How to process a DL/I logical data base

So far in this book, I've shown you how to process data bases with simple hierarchical structures. Although such data bases can have many different segment types at up to 15 levels, the basic rule that each segment type can have only one parent limits the complexity of a physical data base.

However, many DL/I applications require a more complex structure: one that lets a segment have two parent segment types. As a result, DL/I lets the data base administrator implement *logical relationships* in which a segment can have both a physical parent and a logical parent. Then, new data structures called *logical data bases* can be built around those logical relationships. This chapter presents the concepts and terms you need to understand and the programming considerations you need to be aware of when you develop programs that process logical data bases or physical data bases with logical relationships.

Logical relationships

A logical relationship is a path between segments that otherwise would be unrelated. A logical relationship is always between two segments. Although those segments are usually in separate physical data bases,

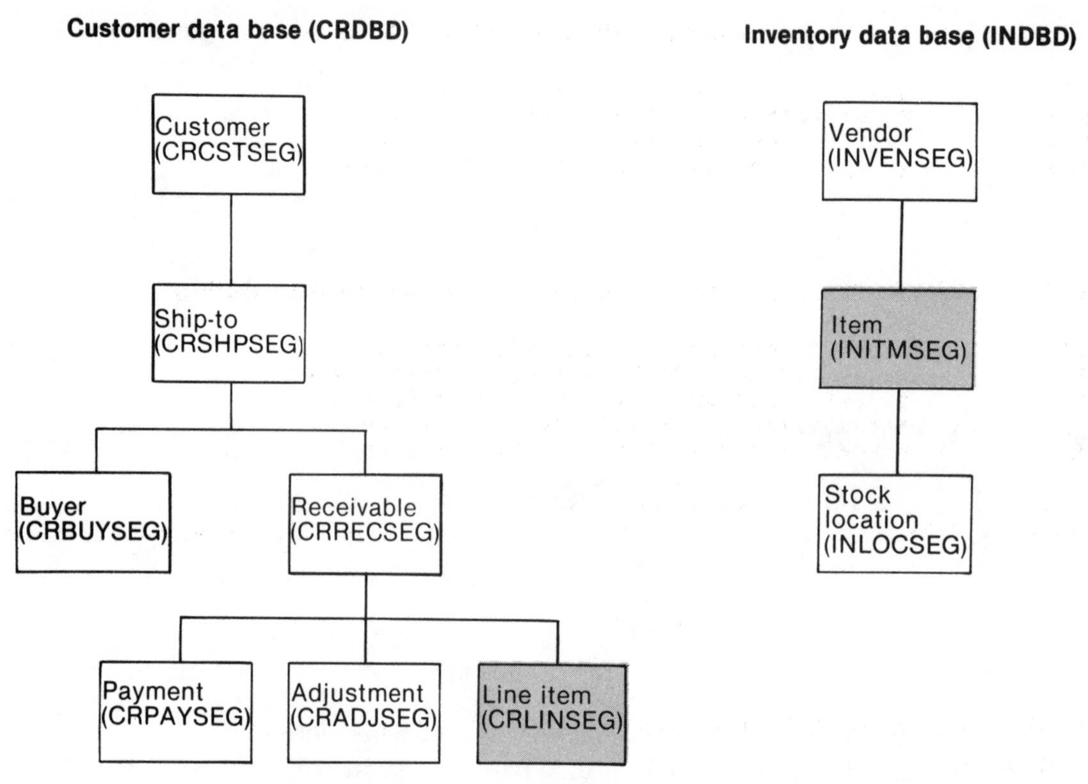

Figure 8-1 The customer and inventory data bases without a logical relationship

that doesn't have to be the case; a logical relationship can also connect two segments within the same physical data base.

To describe logical relationships, I'm going to use the inventory data base you've seen throughout this book and the customer data base I introduced in the last chapter. Figure 8-1 shows the hierarchical structures of both. The logical relationship I'm going to use as an example in this chapter will be between the two shaded segments: CRLINSEG in the customer data base and INITMSEG in the inventory data base.

To understand the way the logical relationship is specified, you first need to understand the DBDGEN code for the two segments without a logical relationship; it's in figure 8-2. As you can see, there's nothing unusual about these sections of code. Notice, however, that the customer data base line item segment (CRLINSEG) is defined with an eight-character item number in its first eight bytes. This field contains the concatenated key of a related item segment in the inventory data

DBDGEN code for the line item segment (CRLINSEG) in the customer data base (CRDBD)

```
SEGM          NAME=CRLINSEG,PARENT=CRRECSEG,BYTES=16
FIELD         NAME=CRLININO,BYTES=8,START=1,TYPE=C
FIELD         NAME=CRLINPRC,BYTES=4,START=9,TYPE=P
FIELD         NAME=CRLINQTY,BYTES=4,START=13,TYPE=P
```

DBDGEN code for the item segment (INITMSEG) in the inventory data base (INDBD)

```
SEGM          NAME=INITMSEG,PARENT=INVENSEG,BYTES=48
FIELD         NAME=(INITMNUM,SEQ),BYTES=5,START=1,TYPE=C
FIELD         NAME=INITMDES,BYTES=35,START=6,TYPE=C
FIELD         NAME=INITMPRC,BYTES=4,START=41,TYPE=P
FIELD         NAME=INITMCST,BYTES=4,START=45,TYPE=P
```

Figure 8-2 Partial DBDGEN code for the customer and inventory data bases without a logical relationship

base (the key consists of the three-byte vendor code and the five-byte item number).

Because the line item segment contains this data, a program that accesses it has all the information it needs to retrieve the associated item segment from the inventory data base. Then, the program can combine data from the two segment occurrences to produce whatever output is required. The point here is that there is a relationship between data items in two data bases, but the relationship is part of the application and is maintained by it.

Because situations like this are common in hierarchical structures, DL/I provides an advanced feature to make them easier to handle: logical relationships. Figure 8-3 illustrates the connection between the line item and inventory item segments when a logical relationship is in effect between them.

The basis of a logical relationship is a segment called the *logical child segment* (in figure 8-3, the logical child is the line item segment). The logical child is a physical data base segment, but DL/I looks at it as if it had two parents: its *physical parent segment* and its *logical parent segment*. In figure 8-3, the physical parent segment of CRLINSEG is the receivable segment in the customer data base (CRRECSEG), and the logical parent is the item segment in the inventory data base (INITMSEG).

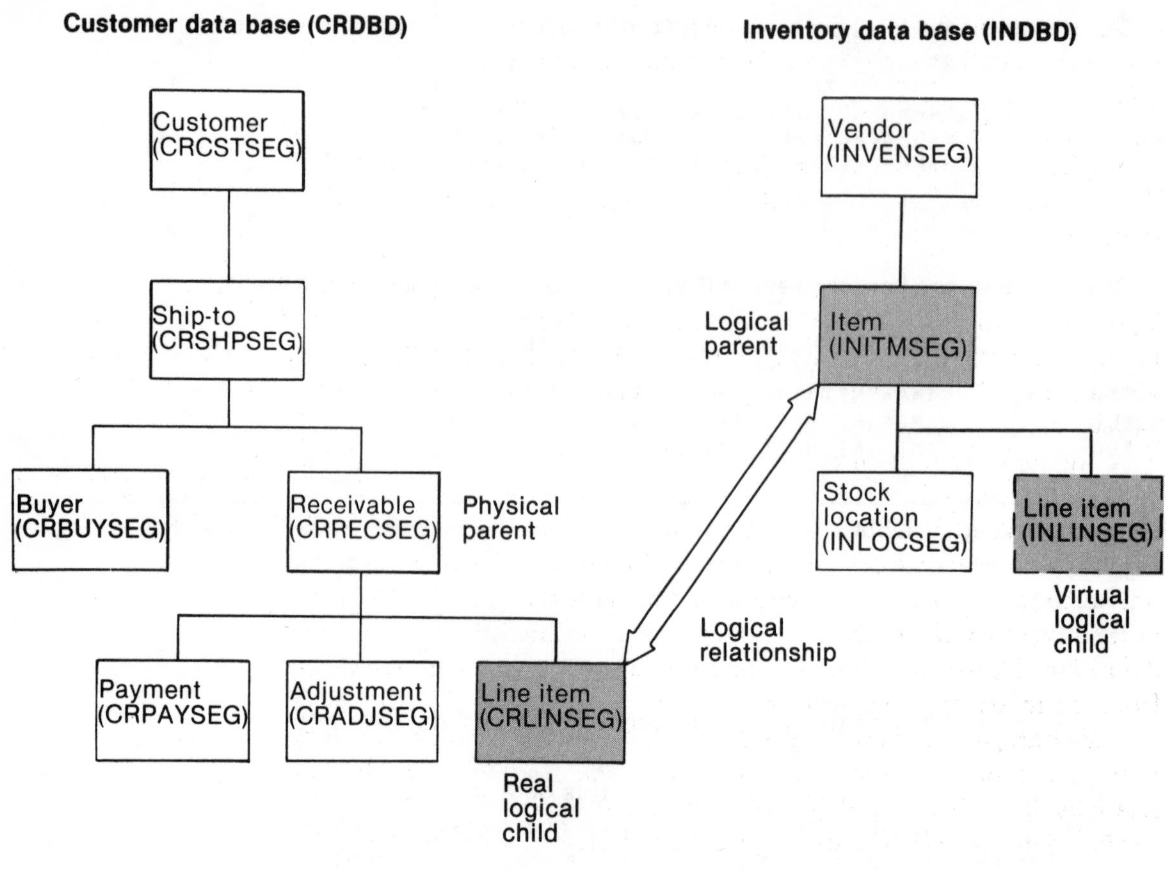

Figure 8-3 The customer and inventory data bases with a logical relationship

Think for a moment about the structure in figure 8-3. A particular receivable segment in the customer data base might have several subordinate line item segments, each for a different product. Each of those line item segments, in turn, has a different logical parent in the inventory data base. Even so, one logical child segment occurrence has only one logical parent occurrence.

Because the same inventory item is sold to different customers, there may be many line item segments in the customer data base that have the same occurrence of the inventory item segment as their logical parent. They're called *logical twins*. Logical twins are occurrences of a logical child segment type that are all subordinate to a single occurrence of the logical parent segment type.

Notice also in figure 8-3 that a new segment type was added to the inventory data base hierarchy: line item (INLINSEG). This segment, called the *virtual logical child segment*, doesn't exist physically in the inventory data base, although DL/I makes it appear to. Actually, the data that seems to be in INLINSEG is stored in the real logical child segment CRLINSEG. Although it's common for a virtual logical child to be implemented as part of a logical relationship, it doesn't have to be. Whether one exists depends on the kind of logical relationship the DBA specifies.

Types of logical relationships There are three kinds of logical relationships the DBA can specify: (1) unidirectional, (2) bidirectional virtual, and (3) bidirectional physical. This section briefly describes each.

The *unidirectional logical relationship* is the simplest of the three. When a logical relationship is defined as unidirectional, the logical connection goes from logical child (via its physical structure) to the logical parent, not the other way around. In the example in figure 8-3, a unidirectional logical relationship would provide access to product data in the inventory data base from the line item segment in the customer data base. However, it would not allow access to line item segments from the inventory item segment.

In contrast, a *bidirectional logical relationship* does allow access in both directions. There are two kinds of bidirectional logical relationships: virtual and physical. In a *bidirectional virtual logical relationship*, which is what figure 8-3 illustrates, the logical child segment can be accessed from both its physical data base and from the data base in which its logical parent is defined. That's why the line item segment in figure 8-3 appears in both the customer and inventory hierarchies. However, the segment actually exists only in its physical data base. In this kind of a logical relationship, the logical child in its physical structure and the corresponding virtual logical child are said to be *paired*. So in figure 8-3, CRLINSEG and INLINSEG are paired.

If the data base administrator implemented the same structure with a *bidirectional physical logical relationship*, it would appear in the same way to application programs as if it were implemented with a bidirectional virtual logical relationship. However, the logical child segment would be physically stored subordinate to both its physical and logical parents. Although this introduces redundancy into the data bases, it may be desirable for some applications.

Fortunately, deciding what kind of logical relationship to use for a particular situation is the responsibility of the DBA. In most cases, the bidirectional virtual logical relationship, illustrated in figure 8-3, offers the best combination of flexibility and performance.

DBDGEN code for the real logical child segment (the line item segment CRLINSEG) in the customer data base (CRDBD)

```
SEGM        NAME=CRLINSEG,                                         *
            PARENT=((CRRECSEG,DBLE),(INITMSEG,V,INDBD)),           *
            POINTER=(TWIN,LTWIN),RULES=(LLV,LAST),BYTES=16
FIELD       NAME=CRLININO,BYTES=8,START=1,TYPE=C
FIELD       NAME=CRLINPRC,BYTES=4,START=9,TYPE=P
FIELD       NAME=CRLINQTY,BYTES=4,START=13,TYPE=P
```

DBDGEN code for the logical parent segment (the item segment INITMSEG) and the virtual logical child segment (the line item segment INLINSEG) in the inventory data base (INDBD)

```
SEGM        NAME=INITMSEG,PARENT=INVENSEG,BYTES=48
LCHILD      NAME=(CRLINSEG,CRDBD),POINTER=DBLE,PAIR=INLINSEG,      *
            RULES=LAST
FIELD       NAME=(INITMNUM,SEQ),BYTES=5,START=1,TYPE=C
FIELD       NAME=INITMDES,BYTES=35,START=6,TYPE=C
FIELD       NAME=INITMPRC,BYTES=4,START=41,TYPE=P
FIELD       NAME=INITMCST,BYTES=4,START=45,TYPE=P
*
SEGM        NAME=INLINSEG,PARENT=INITMSEG,POINTER=PAIRED,          *
            SOURCE=(CRLINSEG,D,CRDBD)
```

Figure 8-4 Partial DBDGEN code for the customer and inventory data bases with a logical relationship

DBDGENs for physical data bases with logical relationships To implement a logical relationship, the DBA has to specify it in the DBDGENs for the involved physical data bases. Figure 8-4 shows the parts of the DBDGEN jobs for the customer and inventory data bases that specify the logical relationship in figure 8-3. You don't need to worry about the details of the code; I just want you to see how the DBA specifies the relationship. You can compare the code in figure 8-4 with that in figure 8-2, which is for the same segments without the logical relationship.

The top section of figure 8-4 presents the DBDGEN code for CRLINSEG, the logical child segment. As you can see, two parent segments are specified for it. The first is its physical parent (CRRECSEG); the second is its logical parent (INITMSEG). Because INITMSEG is in another data base, its DBD (INDBD) is also named.

In the second part of the figure is the code for the logical parent (INITMSEG). The LCHILD macro specifies that INITMSEG is a logical parent and identifies the logical child: CRLINSEG in CRDBD. The

PAIR parameter indicates that the virtual logical child segment is INLINSEG. For a unidirectional relationship, the DBA would have omitted the PAIR parameter.

The DBDGEN for the data base that contains the logical parent in a bidirectional virtual logical relationship also must contain a SEGM macro for the virtual logical child segment. That's what the second SEGM macro in the last part of figure 8-4 is. It specifies that the data that will appear to be in the virtual logical child will actually be stored in the line item segment in the customer data base (SOURCE=(CRLINSEG,D,CRDBD)).

Programming considerations for physical data bases with logical relationships To process segments that are involved in a logical relationship, you issue calls just as you would if the segments weren't involved in the logical relationship. Your program specifications will indicate the structure of the data base you'll be using. In some cases, you may not even know you're processing a segment that's involved in a logical relationship.

However, logical relationships add a new dimension to data base programming. In the example in this chapter, the customer and inventory physical data bases are integrated when they're combined with a logical relationship. As a result, changes to one of the data bases can affect the other. For example, deleting an item segment from the inventory data base would affect the integrity of the relationship because the chances are that it's the logical parent of many line item segment occurrences in the customer data base.

The DBA has to anticipate the results of possible data base processing on the segments involved in a logical relationship. She can control that processing by specifying appropriate processing options for involved data bases and segments. At an even finer level, she can specify rules that determine what operations are allowed for segments involved in the logical relationship.

The program specifications you receive should indicate what processing is allowed. If your program issues a call that violates a processing rule, you'll get a non-blank status code. As a result, although the potential problems of updating data bases involved in logical relationships are extensive, as an application programmer, you don't have to worry about all their ramifications.

What you do need to know is that the I/O area you use for a logical child segment always begins with the complete concatenated key of the *destination parent*. (It's called the *destination parent concatenated key*, or just *DPCK*). The destination parent is the parent other than the one from which the logical child was accessed. So when a segment that's a logical child is accessed through its *physical access path*, the destination parent is the logical parent, but when it's accessed through its *logical access path*, the destination parent is the physical parent.

For example, suppose access to the line item segment is through its logical path (in other words, from the item segment in the inventory data base). Then, the destination parent is the receivable segment in the customer data base and the segment layout has to begin with its concatenated key. Figure 8-5 shows how you'd code this. You might use a segment layout like this if you had to develop a program to list individual sales by product. In that case, the program would retrieve each item segment sequentially, then issue a series of GNP calls to retrieve the virtual logical child segments for each item.

On the other hand, suppose you need to access line item segments from their physical access path, perhaps to build an image of a customer's invoice. Figure 8-6 shows how you might code the I/O area for the line item segment in this situation. In this case, I coded the I/O area so that it begins with the logical parent's (that is, the inventory item's) concatenated key.

Although you must always code the DPCK at the start of your segment I/O area for a logical child, the data that's actually stored in the data base doesn't necessarily include the DPCK. Whether it does or not depends on how the DBA defined the segment.

Logical data bases

Although you can use logical relationships when you process physical data bases, it's limiting. For example, you know that you can access line item data within the inventory data base, perhaps to produce a report of sales by item. But what if you need customer data in addition to line item data? Or, what if you have an application that needs to access complete product data—including vendor and location information—for a line item? In both cases, you're still faced with the problem of processing two physical data bases.

To make solutions to application problems like these easier, DL/I lets the DBA define a logical data base, which is a single structure that's based on logical relationships specified in physical data bases. Although a logical data base appears to an application program to exist as a separate entity, it really doesn't. Instead, it's an alternative view of one or more physical data bases.

```
*
 01  LINE-ITEM-LOG-CHILD-SEGMENT.
*
     05  LILCS-DEST-PARENT-CONCAT-KEY.
         10  LILCS-DPCK-CUSTOMER-NUMBER       PIC X(6).
         10  LILCS-DPCK-SHIP-TO-SEQUENCE      PIC XX.
         10  LILCS-DPCK-INVOICE-NUMBER        PIC X(6).
     05  LILCS-LINE-ITEM-SEGMENT.
         10  LILCS-LIS-ITEM-KEY.
             15  LILCS-LIS-ITEM-KEY-VENDOR    PIC X(3).
             15  LILCS-LIS-ITEM-KEY-NUMBER    PIC X(5).
         10  LILCS-LIS-UNIT-PRICE             PIC S9(5)V99 COMP-3.
         10  LILCS-LIS-QUANTITY               PIC S9(7)    COMP-3.
```

Figure 8-5 Layout of the line item segment when accessed from its logical path

```
*
 01  LINE-ITEM-SEGMENT.
*
     05  LIS-DEST-PARENT-CONCAT-KEY.
         10  LIS-ITEM-KEY-VENDOR          PIC X(3).
         10  LIS-ITEM-KEY-NUMBER          PIC X(5).
     05  LIS-UNIT-PRICE                   PIC S9(5)V99 COMP-3.
     05  LIS-QUANTITY                     PIC S9(7)    COMP-3.
```

Figure 8-6 Layout of the line item segment when accessed from its physical path

To define a logical data base, the DBA has to do a DBDGEN not only for each physical data base that will be involved in the logical structure, with all the segments involved in logical relationships so indicated, but also for the logical data base itself. Then, PSBs for programs that will use the logical data base have to be created. Just as with PSBs that specify physical data bases, a PSB that specifies a logical data base can selectively present parts of it.

Concatenated segments and inverted hierarchies To use logical data bases, you need to be aware of two peculiarities of them. First, a logical data base usually contains a *concatenated segment*. A concatenated segment is a single segment type in the logical data base, but DL/I builds it by combining a logical child segment (as defined in a physical data base DBD) with one of its destination parents. And second, in a logical data base, segment types from more than one physical data base

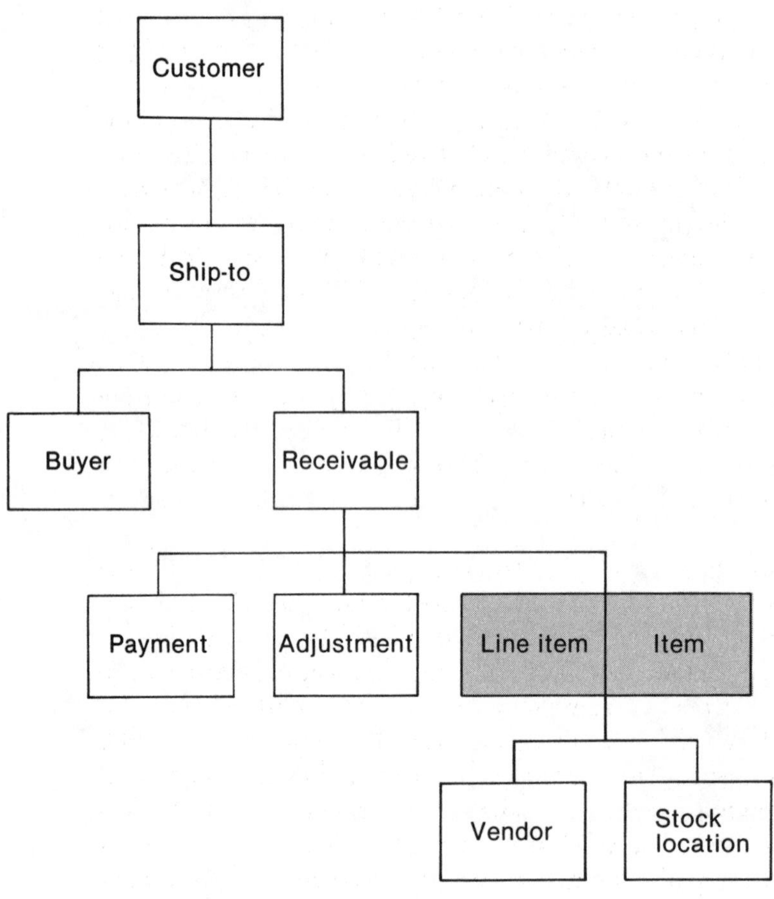

Figure 8-7 A possible logical data base using the customer and inventory physical data bases

can be combined into a single hierarchical structure, even if they aren't directly involved in a logical relationship.

Figure 8-7 illustrates the hierarchical structure for a logical data base formed around the inventory item and customer line item logical relationship. This logical data base is entered from the customer segment. As a result, the customer hierarchy is part of the logical data base and it has the same structure as in its physical data base.

The concatenated segment in figure 8-7 is a combination of the customer line item and inventory item segments. Because access to the logical child in this structure is from its physical parent, the destination parent is the logical parent. As a result, the logical parent is what's concatenated with the logical child to create the concatenated segment in this case.

Notice also that segment types from the inventory data base that don't participate directly in the logical relationship are still part of this logical data base. However, because access to the segments in the inventory physical data base is through the item segment instead of the root segment (vendor), the structure is changed. The inventory location segment, which is subordinate to the item segment in the physical data base, is still subordinate to it in the logical data base. But the vendor segment, which is superior to the item segment in the physical data base, is subordinate to it in the logical data base. This may seem strange to you. However, just realize that the segment through which the physical hierarchy is entered seems to become the root segment, and the segment types that are on the path to it in the physical data base are subordinate to it in the logical data base. (If you've read chapter 7, you'll recognize that the way a data base hierarchy is changed in a logical data base is similar to the way it's changed when a secondary index is used.)

In a logical data base, the concatenated segment makes the connection between segments that are defined in different physical data bases. As a result, you can generate two different logical data base structures from a single logical relationship, by concatenating both possible destination parent segments with the logical child.

Figure 8-8 shows the logical data base that would result if the DBA specified that the logical child should be concatenated with its physical parent (the receivable segment in the customer data base). In this structure, access to the logical child is through its logical parent. As a result, the structure of the segments from the inventory physical data base is unchanged in the logical data base.

However, the structure of segments from the customer data base is changed. The payment and adjustment segments are still subordinate to the receivable segment (in its concatenation with line item) in figure 8-8, but the other segments from the customer data base are inverted. Ship-to, the physical parent of receivable, is subordinate to it in the logical structure. And customer, the physical parent of ship-to, is subordinate to it in the logical data base. The buyer segment is subordinate to ship-to in both the physical and logical data bases. Its position isn't changed because it's not on the direct path to the receivable segment in the physical data base.

DBDGENs for logical data bases Figure 8-9 shows the DBDGEN output for the logical data base in figure 8-7. In the DBDGEN for a logical data base (ACCESS=LOGICAL and DATASET LOGICAL), all of the segment types the DBA names must have already been defined in

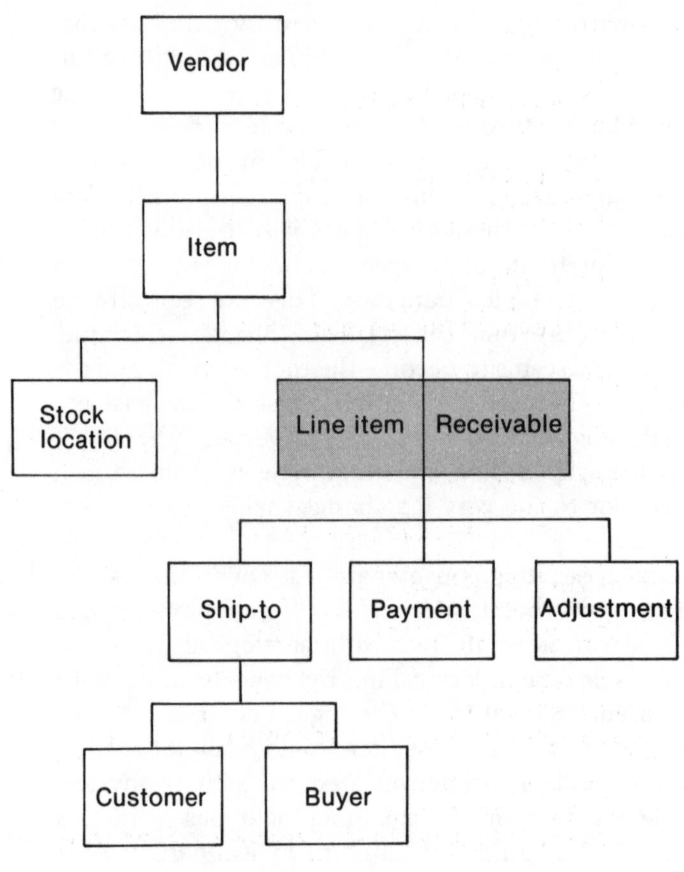

Figure 8-8 Another possible logical data base using the customer and inventory physical data bases

a physical data base DBDGEN. As a result, the DBA doesn't have to describe their sizes or the fields they contain in a logical data base DBDGEN. Instead, the SEGM macro in a logical data base DBDGEN specifies the SOURCE parameter to identify the related physical data base segment and the data base that it's a part of.

In figure 8-9, the segment at the top of the logical data structure is CRCSTSEG. Its source parameter specifies that it's actually stored in the physical data base CRDBD as the segment CRCSTSEG. Although the segment names in this logical data base and the associated physical data bases are the same, they don't have to be.

I want you to notice a couple of other points here. First, look at the SOURCE parameter in the SEGM macro for CRLINSEG (it's shaded). This is how the DBA specifies a concatenated segment. In this case, the

```
STMT   SOURCE STATEMENT

   1  PRINT         NOGEN
   2  DBD           NAME=LICRDBD,ACCESS=LOGICAL
   3  DATASET       LOGICAL
   4 *
   5  SEGM          NAME=CRCSTSEG,                                      X
                    PARENT=0,                                           X
                    SOURCE=((CRCSTSEG,D,CRDBD))
   6 *
   7  SEGM          NAME=CRSHPSEG,                                      X
                    PARENT=CRCSTSEG,                                    X
                    SOURCE=((CRSHPSEG,D,CRDBD))
   8 *
   9  SEGM          NAME=CRBUYSEG,                                      X
                    PARENT=CRSHPSEG,                                    X
                    SOURCE=((CRBUYSEG,D,CRDBD))
  10 *
  11  SEGM          NAME=CRRECSEG,                                      X
                    PARENT=CRSHPSEG,                                    X
                    SOURCE=((CRRECSEG,D,CRDBD))
  12 *
  13  SEGM          NAME=CRPAYSEG,                                      X
                    PARENT=CRRECSEG,                                    X
                    SOURCE=((CRPAYSEG,D,CRDBD))
  14 *
  15  SEGM          NAME=CRADJSEG,                                      X
                    PARENT=CRRECSEG,                                    X
                    SOURCE=((CRADJSEG,D,CRDBD))
  16 *
  17  SEGM          NAME=CRLINSEG,                                      X
                    PARENT=CRRECSEG,                                    X
                    SOURCE=((CRLINSEG,D,CRDBD),(INITMSEG,D,INDBD))
  18 *
  19  SEGM          NAME=INVENSEG,                                      X
                    PARENT=CRLINSEG,                                    X
                    SOURCE=((INVENSEG,D,INDBD))
  20 *
  21  SEGM          NAME=INLOCSEG,                                      X
                    PARENT=CRLINSEG,                                    X
                    SOURCE=((INLOCSEG,D,INDBD))
  22  DBDGEN
 301  FINISH
 302  END
```

Figure 8-9 DBDGEN output for the customer-inventory logical data base

segment CRLINSEG will be the concatenation of the physical segment CRLINSEG from CRDBD (defined there as a logical child) and the physical segment INITMSEG from INDBD (defined there as a logical parent).

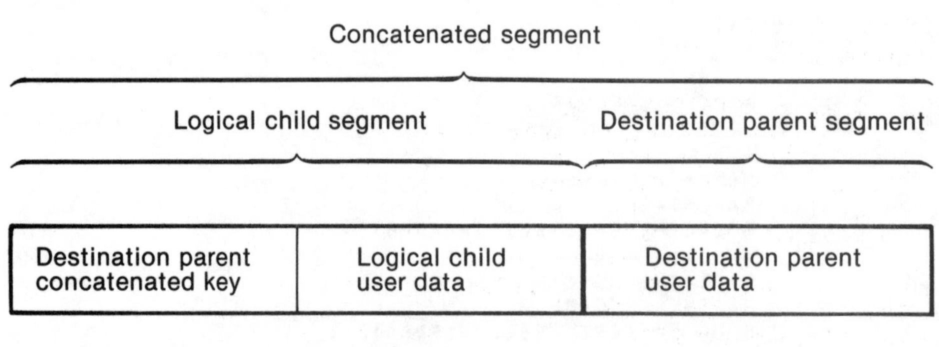

Note: Destination parent concatenated key and the sequence field in the logical child user data may overlap.

Figure 8-10 Format of a concatenated segment

Also, notice that subordinate to this concatenated segment are two segment types from the inventory data base: INVENSEG and INLOCSEG. Both specify PARENT=CRLINSEG. This name refers to CRLINSEG defined as a segment in the logical data base, not to CRLINSEG in the customer physical data base.

Programming considerations for logical data bases There's no mystery to coding programs that process logical data bases. You issue DL/I calls against the PCB mask for the data base, and you evaluate the PCB status code to determine whether or not the calls were successful.

When you process a concatenated segment, you need to keep in mind that DL/I presents it to your program as a single segment, although it actually contains data from two segments. You process the concatenated segment with a single call, and the I/O area you specify must be properly defined to contain the concatenated segment. For example, a single get call for the concatenated segment in figure 8-7 would return data from both the line item segment and from its logical parent, the inventory item segment.

Figure 8-10 shows the generalized format of a concatenated segment. As long as you remember two points, you shouldn't have any problems understanding the format of a concatenated segment. First, a concatenated segment consists of a logical child segment immediately followed by its destination parent. And second, the logical child component always begins with the full concatenated key of the destination parent. With this background, the I/O area description in figure 8-11, which is for the concatenated segment in figure 8-8, should

```
*
 01  CONCATENATED-SEGMENT.
*
     05  CS-DEST-PARENT-CONCAT-KEY.
         10  CS-DPCK-CUSTOMER-NUMBER     PIC X(6).
         10  CS-DPCK-SHIP-TO-SEQUENCE    PIC XX.
         10  CS-DPCK-INVOICE-NUMBER      PIC X(6).
     05  CS-LINE-ITEM-SEGMENT.
         10  CS-LIS-ITEM-KEY.
             15  CS-LIS-ITEM-KEY-VENDOR  PIC X(3).
             15  CS-LIS-ITEM-KEY-NUMBER  PIC X(5).
         10  CS-LIS-UNIT-PRICE           PIC S9(5)V99 COMP-3.
         10  CS-LIS-QUANTITY             PIC S9(7)    COMP-3.
     05  CS-RECEIVABLE-SEGMENT.
         10  CS-RS-INVOICE-NUMBER        PIC X(6).
         10  CS-RS-INVOICE-DATE          PIC X(6).
         10  CS-RS-PO-NUMBER             PIC X(25).
         10  CS-RS-PRODUCT-TOTAL         PIC S9(5)V99 COMP-3.
         10  CS-RS-CASH-DISCOUNT         PIC S9(5)V99 COMP-3.
         10  CS-RS-SALES-TAX             PIC S9(5)V99 COMP-3.
         10  CS-RS-FREIGHT               PIC S9(5)V99 COMP-3.
         10  CS-RS-BALANCE-DUE           PIC S9(5)V99 COMP-3.
*
```

Figure 8-11 Format of the concatenated segment that combines the line item and inventory item segments

be easy to understand. It contains the destination parent segment's concatenated key, the line item segment, and the destination parent (receivable) segment.

When you work with concatenated segments during update processing, it may be possible to add or change data in both the logical child and the destination parent with a single call. However, that depends on the rules the DBA specified for the data base. For an insert, be sure to provide the proper DPCK in the right position. And for a replace or a delete, don't change the DPCK or sequence field data in either part of the concatenated segment.

Discussion

If you're confused after reading this chapter, take heart. Logical data base processing is complicated, and some of its concepts are obscure. As I've pointed out throughout this chapter, however, most of the technical details involved with logical data bases are out of your hands; they're the responsibility of the data base administrator. If you're interested in learning more about logical relationships and logical data bases, you can refer to the data base administration manual for either IMS/VS or DL/I DOS/VS.

Terminology

logical relationship
logical data base
logical child segment
physical parent segment
logical parent segment
logical twin
virtual logical child segment
unidirectional logical relationship
bidirectional logical relationship
bidirectional virtual logical relationship
paired
bidirectional physical logical relationship
destination parent
destination parent concatenated key
DPCK
physical access path
logical access path
concatenated segment

Objectives

1. Identify the segment types involved in a logical relationship.

2. Given specifications for a program that will process a segment from a physical data base that's involved in a logical relationship, code the Data Division code to define the segment and the Procedure Division code to access and/or update it.

3. Given specifications for a program that will process a logical data base, code the Data Division code to define the concatenated segment and the Procedure Division code to access and/or update it.

Chapter 9

How to use DL/I recovery and restart features

A major part of the data base administrator's job is making sure that problems with the system have as little impact on the integrity of the data base and the efficiency of operations as possible. As a result, the DBA has to devote a lot of attention to planning for data base recovery and program restart in the event of a failure. Those failures can be of many kinds, including application program abends, system software errors, hardware errors, and power failures.

The simple approach to recovery that's been the rule in batch applications is to periodically make backup copies of important data sets. Then, from the time the backup copy is made, all transactions posted against the data sets are retained. If a failure occurs that damages a data set, the problem is corrected. Then, the accumulated transactions are reposted to the backup copy to bring it up-to-date.

Even in a simple file-based application, this approach can be inappropriate because it can take a long time to repost all the accumulated transactions. That means other applications have to wait until the file is restored, and a work backlog grows. When an application uses data bases, recovery in this fashion can take even longer than with standard files, particularly if a data base is involved in logical and secondary index relationships that have to be restored along with it.

As a result, DL/I's designers provided a sophisticated set of recovery and restart facilities. DL/I DOS/VS and IMS/VS share some features that are primarily for use in the batch environment; that's what this chapter covers. In *Part 2* of this series, I'll describe the additional IMS/VS recovery and restart facilities that make a comprehensive package for the data communications environment. In this chapter, you'll learn about a variety of DL/I recovery and restart facilities: abnormal termination routines, logging, forward and backward recovery, and checkpointing and restart facilities.

Abnormal termination routines

When a DL/I application program abends, it doesn't crash the way a non-DL/I program does because the program isn't executed directly by the operating system, but rather under the control of DL/I. So when an application program fails, DL/I intervenes to contain the damage that's done to the data bases. It does this by invoking an *abnormal termination routine*.

The abnormal termination routine makes sure the data base data sets are properly closed. If the data bases are stored in VSAM data sets (as they most likely are), this means that their catalog entries are properly updated, too. In addition to the data base data sets, the DL/I log the program was using is also closed (more about logging in a moment). The abnormal termination routine cancels the job and, if you requested it, produces a storage dump you can use to find out what caused the abend.

Keep in mind that although DL/I terminates your abending program in an orderly way, its function is to prevent additional data base damage, not to correct damage that's already been done. Just because the abnormal termination routine is executed does not insure that the data in the data bases in use is accurate. It's usually necessary to back out changes made by the abending program, correct the error, then rerun the program. And to do that, a DL/I log is required.

Logging

When logging is used, DL/I records all the changes a program makes to its data bases in a special file called a *log* that can reside on either tape or DASD. (It is possible to run a DL/I program without logging, but that's unusual in a production environment.) When a program changes a segment, DL/I logs both a *before image* and an *after image* of it. These segment images can be used to restore a data base to its proper condition in the event of a program or system failure.

DL/I uses a technique called *write-ahead logging* to record data base changes. With write-ahead logging, a data base change is written to the log data set before it's written to the actual data base data set. Because the log is always ahead of the data base, the recovery utilities can determine the status of any data base change.

As an application programmer, basic logging operations are transparent to you. When you issue a DL/I call that changes a data base segment, DL/I takes care of logging. In fact, logging often extends beyond your program's view of the data base. For example, a change you make to a segment can cause changes in the segment's parent, twins, and dependents that all have to be logged. And changes to segments involved in logical relationships or secondary indexes can cause even more log activity. You can imagine, then, that in a complex data base structure, even the simplest call to change a segment can cause extensive logging. So when the DBA plans a data base, she considers not only the data base structure itself, but also the effects that structure will have on logging performance.

Recovery

When a batch DL/I program abends, two approaches are available for recovering the damaged data bases: forward recovery and backward recovery.

Forward recovery *Forward recovery* of a data base works much like the traditional technique for recovering batch files: change data for a period of time is accumulated, then applied to a copy of the data base as it existed before the changes began. However, instead of working from original transactions to restore the data base, DL/I uses change data stored in DL/I logs for forward recovery.

Forward recovery is normally used only when a data base is physically damaged in some way. For example, if a device error makes the current version of a data base inaccessible, forward recovery is the technique the operations staff will use to restore it. To help you understand the steps in forward recovery, figure 9-1 shows the entire process.

For forward recovery to be an option, two requirements have to be met: (1) an old copy of the data base has to be available and (2) all the changes posted to the data base since the copy was made must be available. To meet the first requirement, the operations staff can periodically run the *Data Set Image Copy Utility* (for DL/I DOS/VS) or

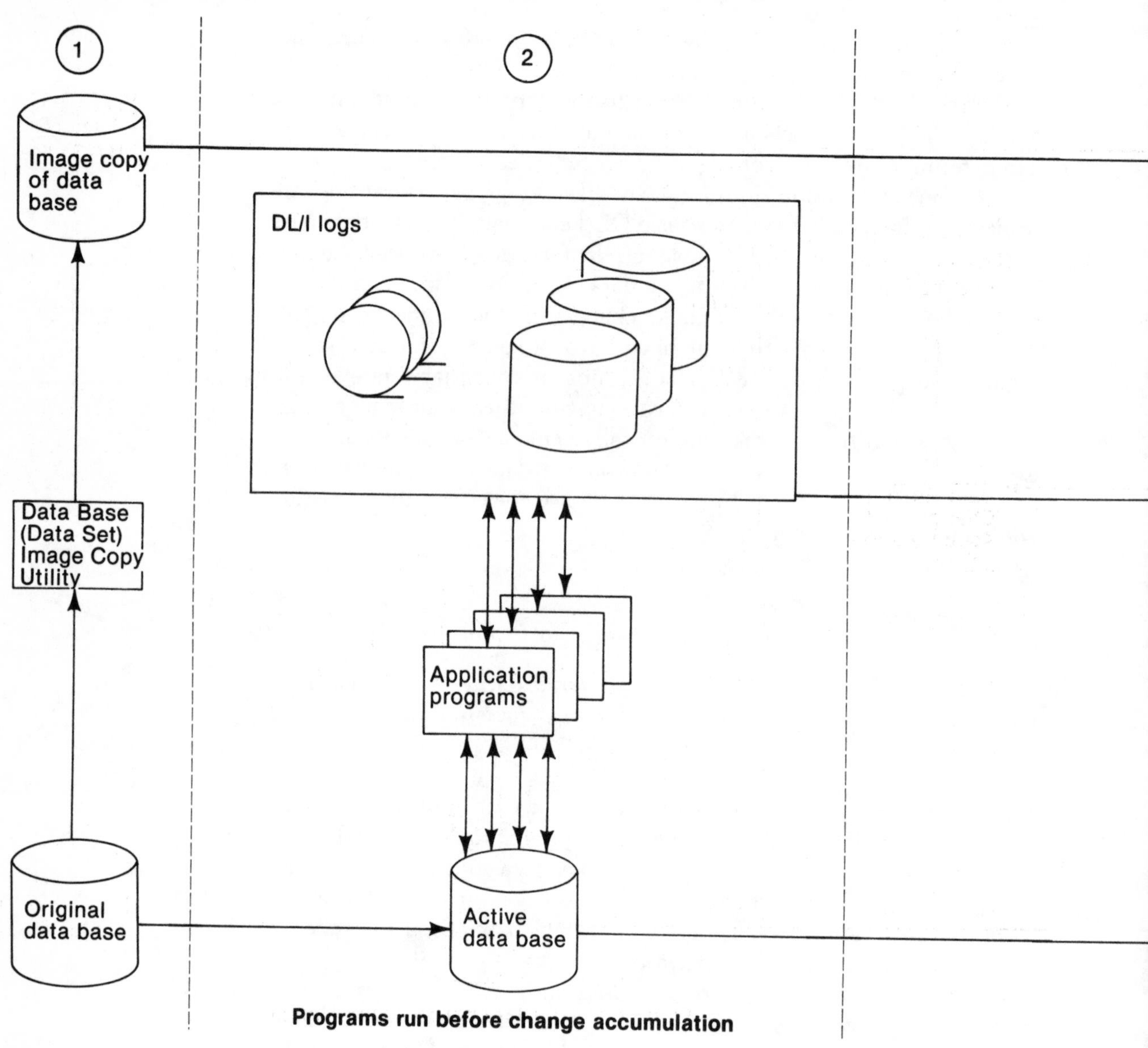

Figure 9-1 The forward recovery process

the *Data Base Image Copy Utility* (for IMS/VS). That's what section 1 of figure 9-1 illustrates.

After the image copy of the data base has been made, many application programs can be run that change the data base. That's what section 2 of figure 9-1 shows. As the figure indicates, each program

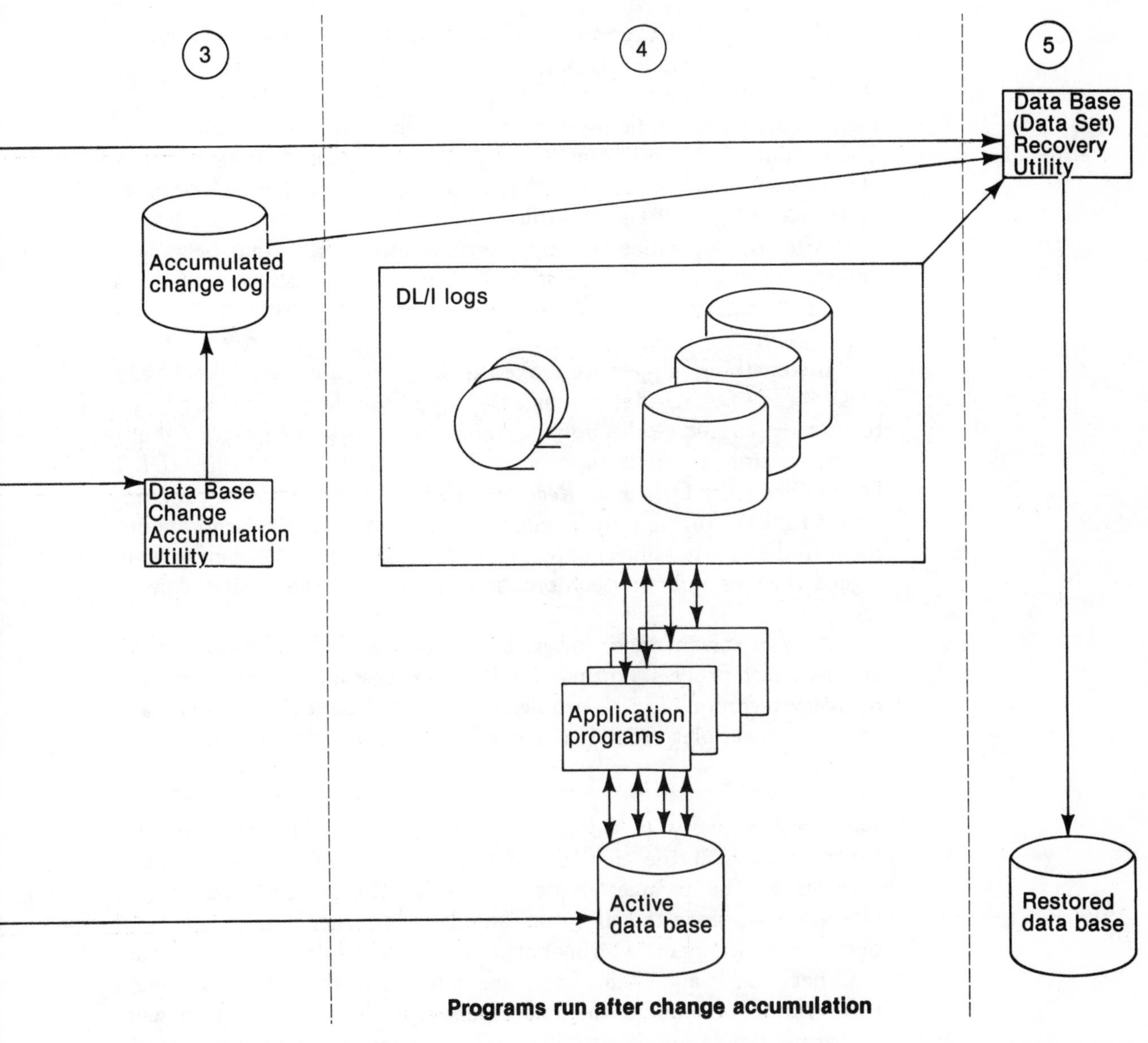

writes its own log. That meets the second requirement of forward recovery: that all changes made since the previous image copy was taken are saved.

Because every execution of a batch DL/I application program produces its own log file, it's efficient to periodically combine them in case they have to be used to recover the data base. Both DL/I DOS/VS and IMS/VS include a program called the *Data Base Change Accumulation Utility* that consolidates multiple logs and organizes the logged data so it can be used most efficiently in a recovery operation. The output of this program is called an *accumulated change log* (or *change accumulation log*), which may be stored on either disk or tape. Section 3 of figure 9-1 shows this process.

After the Data Base Change Accumulation Utility has been run, application programs that change the data base are still executed, as section 4 of figure 9-1 shows. Each of these programs also writes its own log.

If something happens to make the data base unusable (like a head crash on the DASD that contains the data base data set), it has to be forward recovered. As section 5 of figure 9-1 shows, the program that's used to restore the data base is the *Data Set Recovery Utility* (DL/I DOS/VS) or the *Data Base Recovery Utility* (IMS/VS). This program works forward through the changes made to the data base and applies them to the original image copy of the data base. The program accepts logged changes from any combination of DL/I or accumulated change logs.

As you can imagine, forward recovery can be a time-consuming and awkward process. Fortunately, it's not necessary to use the forward recovery technique for all problems with DL/I data bases. Backward recovery, a simpler process, is more appropriate for most situations.

Backward recovery *Backward recovery*, also called *backout*, uses the data base at the time of an application program's failure and reverses all the changes made to it since the program began (or, alternatively, since the program issued its last checkpoint, which I'll describe in a moment). During backout, log records for the program are read backwards and their effects are reversed in the data base. When the backout is complete, the data bases are in the same state they were in before the failure (assuming another application program hasn't altered the data base in the meantime).

Backout is appropriate when an application program ends in a controlled fashion. For example, if a program encounters an invalid situation it can't handle, such as an unexpected status code, it can end in such a way as to cause an abend. For example, it can invoke an installation-standard termination routine that records and reports the problem, then abends. This is called a *pseudoabend*. Then, backward recovery can be performed to restore the data bases to their previous

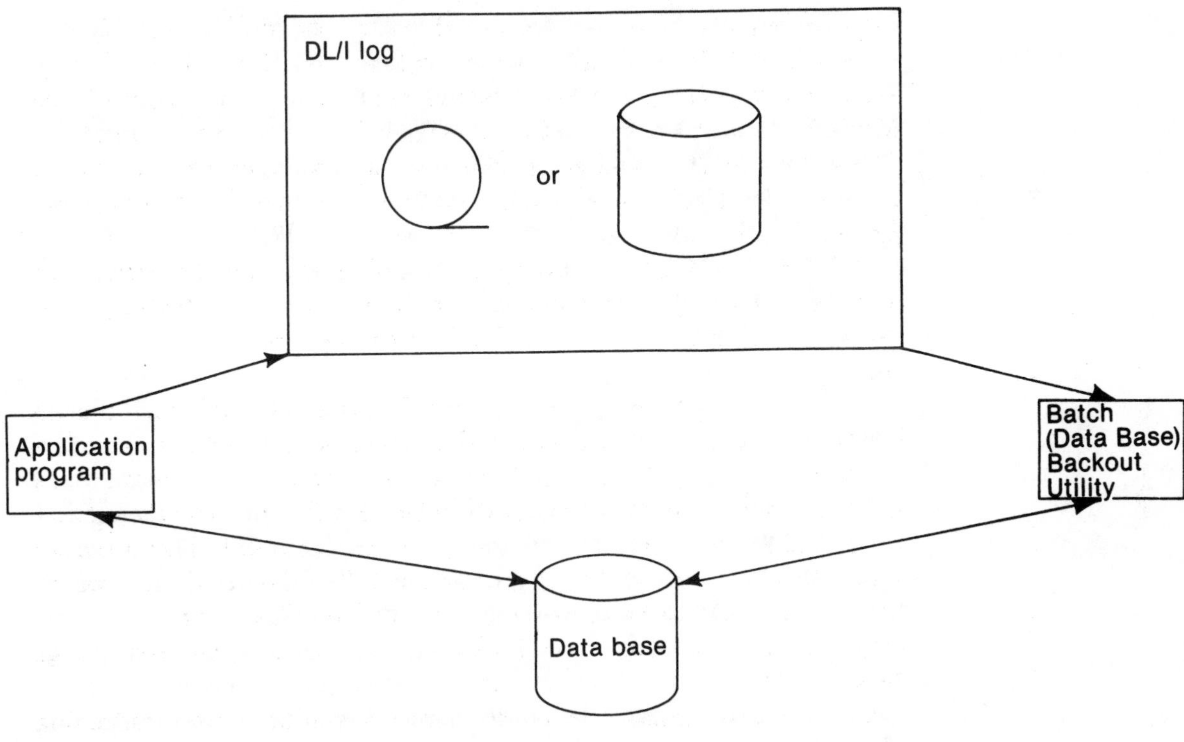

Figure 9-2 The backward recovery process

condition. After the application program or input data is corrected, the job can be run again.

Figure 9-2 shows the backward recovery process. Under DL/I DOS/VS, backward recovery is performed by a DL/I program called the *Data Base Backout Utility*. Under IMS/VS, the *Batch Backout Utility* has the same function. In both cases, the backout utility program is executed from its own job.

For backward recovery to be useful when using these utilities, jobs need to be readily available for the operations staff to use, and appropriate recovery procedures must be in place. However, as you can tell by comparing figures 9-2 and 9-1, backward recovery is a simpler, easier, and more efficient process than forward recovery.

Under IMS, a data base in use by a batch program that abends can be backward-recovered through *dynamic backout*. If the JCL that invokes the program specifies dynamic backout and the program fails, IMS automatically backs out all data base changes made since the program began (or since it issued its last checkpoint).

In addition, an application program under IMS can invoke dynamic backout by issuing a *rollback call* (ROLB). There's seldom cause to use ROLB in a typical batch program. And although the ROLB call can be used in a user-written termination routine, that's something that you probably won't be called upon to code.

As I've described backward recovery of batch programs, I've mentioned that recovery proceeds back to either the start of the program or to the last checkpoint. Now, I'll describe what checkpoints are and how you can use them in your programs to limit the scope of a required backout.

Checkpointing

In the DL/I documentation, you'll see a variety of similar terms used in similar ways: *checkpoint, synchronization point, sync point, commit point,* and *point of integrity*. All mean basically the same thing: a point in the execution of your program where the data base changes the program has made are considered complete and accurate. Data base changes made *before* the most recent checkpoint are not reversed by backward recovery. And data base changes logged *after* the most recent checkpoint are not applied to an image copy of the data base during forward recovery. So, whether backward or forward recovery is used, the data base is restored to its condition at the most recent checkpoint when the recovery process completes.

The default for batch programs is that the checkpoint is the beginning of the program. However, if you're developing programs that will process many update transactions, it's useful to be able to tell DL/I at intervals that what's been done so far is OK. Then, if the program later abends, there's no need to backout the data base changes that have been made up to that point. You can establish a checkpoint by issuing a *checkpoint call* (CHKP). The checkpoint call causes a *checkpoint record* to be written on the DL/I log. It's the presence of a checkpoint record in a log that tells the DL/I recovery utilities to stop their recovery processing.

Under either DL/I DOS/VS or IMS/VS, you can use a simple form of checkpointing called *basic checkpointing*. Basic checkpointing lets you issue checkpoint calls that the DL/I recovery utilities use during recovery processing. Under IMS/VS, you can use a more advanced form of checkpointing called *symbolic checkpointing* in combination with the *extended restart* facility. Together, symbolic checkpointing and extended restart let you code your programs so they can resume processing at the point following a checkpoint. Because basic checkpointing is simpler to understand, I'll describe it first.

Basic checkpointing To use basic checkpointing, you code your program so that it periodically issues checkpoint calls. Although it's simplest to issue a checkpoint call once for each transaction your program processes, that's uncommon. Most programs issue checkpoints at intervals like every 100 or 1,000 transactions. And some applications issue checkpoints based on elapsed time, perhaps every 10 or 15 minutes. So be sure to find out what your shop's standards are for checkpointing.

For basic checkpointing, you code the checkpoint call like this:

```
CALL 'CBLTDLI' USING DLI-CHKP
                     I-O-PCB-MASK
                     CHECKPOINT-ID.
```

Here, I specified three parameters: the call function, the PCB name, and an eight-character working storage field that contains a checkpoint-id.

Under DL/I DOS/VS, you specify a data base PCB on the checkpoint call. It doesn't matter which data base PCB you specify; the checkpoint call always applies to all of the data bases your program processes. However, for the CHKP call under IMS, you supply the name of a special PCB called the *I/O PCB*. The I/O PCB, normally used for data communications programs, has a format that's different from a data base PCB. Fortunately, you need to use just the status code field of the I/O PCB. So you can code a ten-byte FILLER item, followed by the two-byte status code field, like this:

```
 01  I-O-PCB-MASK.
*
     05  FILLER                  PIC X(10).
     05  I-O-PCB-STATUS-CODE     PIC XX.
```

Also, you must list the I/O PCB as the first PCB on the ENTRY statement in the Procedure Division.

The eight-byte *checkpoint-id* field takes the place of a segment I/O area for a checkpoint call. In it, your program places a value that identifies the checkpoint record. Then, during recovery, the operations staff can use the checkpoint-id to restart your program, assuming your program is coded to work that way.

The problem with using basic checkpointing isn't keeping track of where a program fails and restoring the data base back to that point. Instead, it's picking up execution of the failed program at the intermediate point. Your program has to provide a facility to accept the checkpoint-id, then decide what to do with it. Typically, that involves reading through any transaction files to skip transactions that were posted before the last checkpoint. And it may mean resetting working storage fields (such as total fields) to the values they had when the checkpoint was taken.

Generally, the more functions the program performs, the more complex the considerations are for restart. If you develop an update program that prepares reports and updates non-DL/I data sets, recovery will be more complex than if the program simply changes a data base according to input transactions. As a result, it's practical to limit the function of a data base update program that uses checkpointing to data base operations. Then, restart is simpler. However, these are system design considerations, so if you're given specifications for an update program that will use checkpointing, be sure to find out from your DBA or system designer how to handle restart functions.

Symbolic checkpointing Symbolic checkpointing, available only under IMS, is similar to basic checkpointing in that you use a CHKP call to write checkpoint records to a DL/I log. But symbolic checkpointing, along with extended restart, provide an advantage: they let you store program data along with the checkpoint records and retrieve that data when it's necessary to restart the program after a failure.

When you use symbolic checkpointing, the checkpoint call begins with the same three parameters as the basic checkpoint call: the function code (CHKP), the PCB mask, and the eight-byte checkpoint-id field. Then, you can code up to seven pairs of field names to specify the working storage areas you want to have saved along with the checkpoint record. In each pair, the first item is the name of a fullword binary field (PIC S9(5) COMP) that contains the length of the data area to be saved; the second is the name of the data area itself.

A program that uses extended restart should always issue an XRST call before it issues any other DL/I calls. On the XRST call, you list the same working storage fields you list on the CHKP call. Normally, the XRST call does nothing; it leaves the specified working storage fields as they are. But when the program is being restarted (DL/I knows this from the JCL used to start the program), DL/I retrieves the values stored in the checkpoint record and restores the specified fields.

Figure 9-3 illustrates how the symbolic checkpoint and extended restart calls might be used in a data base update program. Here, two

```
      .
      .
      .
 01   COUNT-FIELDS                         COMP-3.

      05  CASH-RECEIVED                    PIC S9(7)V99      VALUE ZERO.
      05  VALID-TRANSACTION-COUNT          PIC S9(5)         VALUE ZERO.
      05  INVALID-TRANSACTION-COUNT        PIC S9(5)         VALUE ZERO.
*
 01   PRINT-FIELDS                         COMP-3.
*
      05  PAGE-NUMBER                      PIC S9(5)         VALUE +1.
      05  SPACE-CONTROL                    PIC S9(3)         VALUE +1.
      05  LINE-COUNT                       PIC S9(3)         VALUE +99.
      05  LINES-ON-PAGE                    PIC S9(3)         VALUE +50.
*
 01   CHECKPOINT-ID                        PIX S9(8)         VALUE ZERO.
*
 01   RESTART-WORK-AREA                    PIC X(12)         VALUE SPACE.
*
 01   LENGTH-FIELDS                        COMP.
*
      05  LENGTH-COUNT-FIELDS              PIC S9(5)         VALUE +11.
      05  LENGTH-PRINT-FIELDS              PIC S9(5)         VALUE +9.
      05  LENGTH-LONGEST-SEGMENT           PIC S9(5)         VALUE +128.
      .
      .
      .
*
 LINKAGE SECTION.
*
 01   I-O-PCB.
*
      05  FILLER                           PIC X(10).
      05  I-O-PCB-STATUS-CODE              PIC XX.
      .
      .
      .
```

Figure 9-3 COBOL code for symbolic checkpointing and extended restart (part 1 of 2)

data areas (COUNT-FIELDS and PRINT-FIELDS) are to be saved by the checkpoint calls and restored during restart processing.

Notice that I defined two length fields (LENGTH-COUNT-FIELDS and LENGTH-PRINT-FIELDS) that correspond to the two data areas I want to save, and I initialized them with the sizes of those areas. The third length field, LENGTH-LONGEST-SEGMENT, is a PIC S9(5) binary field that contains the length of the longest I/O area the program uses (in other words, the length of the longest segment or path of segments the program processes). DL/I uses this value to acquire a buffer area.

```
*
 PROCEDURE DIVISION.
*
     ENTRY 'DLITCBL' USING I-O-PCB ...
*
 000-POST-CASH-RECEIPTS.
*
     CALL 'CBLTDLI' USING DLI-XRST
                          I-O-PCB
                          LENGTH-LONGEST-SEGMENT
                          RESTART-WORK-AREA
                          LENGTH-COUNT-FIELDS
                          COUNT-FIELDS
                          LENGTH-PRINT-FIELDS
                          PRINT-FIELDS.
     IF I-O-PCB-STATUS-CODE NOT = SPACE
         DISPLAY 'CR1000 I 1 RESTART FAILED -- STATUS CODE '
                I-O-PCB-STATUS-CODE
     ELSE
        IF RESTART-WORK-AREA NOT = SPACE
           PERFORM 100-REPOSITION-DATA-BASE.
     .
     .
     .
*
 230-ISSUE-CHECKPOINT-CALL.
*
     ADD 1 TO CHECKPOINT-ID.
     CALL 'CBLTDLI' USING DLI-CHKP
                          I-O-PCB
                          LENGTH-LONGEST-SEGMENT
                          CHECKPOINT-ID
                          LENGTH-COUNT-FIELDS
                          COUNT-FIELDS
                          LENGTH-PRINT-FIELDS
                          PRINT-FIELDS.
     IF I-O-PCB-STATUS-CODE NOT = SPACE
        DISPLAY 'CR1000 I 2 CHECKPOINT FAILED -- STATUS CODE '
               I-O-PCB-STATUS-CODE
     .
     .
     .
```

Figure 9-3 COBOL code for symbolic checkpointing and extended restart (part 2 of 2)

As the program executes, it periodically increments the CHECKPOINT-ID field and issues the checkpoint call. This call causes the specified areas to be saved on the log along with the checkpoint record.

If the program fails, the problem that caused the failure is corrected and the affected data bases are restored using forward or backward recovery. Then, the program is restarted. The operator supplies the last checkpoint-i[illegible] PARM for the EXEC that invokes the program.

Then, the XRST call, which is the first call in the program, knows the program should restart rather than begin a normal execution.

There is one difference between the XRST call in figure 9-3 and the CHKP call. Instead of specifying the CHECKPOINT-ID field, the XRST call specifies a 12-byte work area. This field, RESTART-WORK-AREA in figure 9-3, must be initialized with spaces. If your program is being restarted, DL/I places the checkpoint-id value in this field; otherwise, DL/I leaves the field blank. After these items, the XRST call specifies the length and data fields for any saved data in the same sequence as they appeared in the CHKP call. If the program is being restarted, DL/I retrieves the values for those fields from the checkpoint record. If not, DL/I doesn't change the values of those fields.

After the XRST call in figure 9-3, the program checks for two conditions. First, it checks to see if the restart call was successful: if the status code field in the I/O PCB is not spaces, the restart call failed, so an appropriate message is displayed. If the call didn't fail, the program then tests to see if this is a normal execution or a restart execution by checking the restart work area. If that field isn't spaces, the program is being restarted, so module 100 is invoked to reestablish position in the data base. (Although that's not a requirement for all restartable programs, it's often desirable.)

Discussion

I can't stress enough that before you decide to use the CHKP call, you should find out what your shop's standards for recovery are. Your DBA should tell you when it's appropriate to use the checkpoint call and should also provide you with the conventions used in your shop for writing restartable programs (and, ideally, a model program, too).

Terminology

abnormal termination routine
log
before image
after image
write-ahead logging
forward recovery
Data Set Image Copy Utility
Data Base Image Copy Utility
Data Base Change Accumulation Utility

accumulated change log
change accumulation log
Data Set Recovery Utility
Data Base Recovery Utility
backward recovery
backout
pseudoabend
Data Base Backout Utility
Batch Backout Utility
dynamic backout
rollback call
checkpoint
synchronization point
sync point
commit point
point of integrity
checkpoint call
checkpoint record
basic checkpointing
symbolic checkpointing
extended restart
I/O PCB
checkpoint-id

Objectives

1. Compare and contrast how DL/I implements forward and backward recovery.

2. Compare and contrast basic checkpointing and symbolic checkpointing/extended restart.

3. Given program specifications and installation standards, code a restartable update program.

Chapter 10

How to use other advanced DL/I features

This chapter presents some DL/I "odds and ends" that you might need to know for some applications but that are of relatively minor importance: variable length segments, segment edit/compression routines, and field level sensitivity. Frankly, these subjects are of more immediate interest to the data base administrator than the application programmer, but it won't hurt you to know about them.

Variable length segments

So far, all of the data base examples you've seen in this book have used fixed length segments. However, for some applications, the data base administrator may need to specify *variable length segments.* As common sense indicates, a variable length segment is used when the data that's stored in a segment type varies in size.

For example, suppose a segment type contains descriptive or explanatory text. In most cases, the text is brief, but in some cases, it's long. If the segment is defined with a fixed length long enough to accommodate the longest possible text string, space is wasted in most segment occurrences, which contain shorter text strings.

To create a variable length segment, the data base administrator specifies two length values on the BYTES parameter of the SEGM macro in the data base's DBDGEN job. The first value is the segment's maximum size, and the second is its minimum size. If the segment contains a sequence field, the minimum size must include all the data up to and including it. And the sequence field must appear in the same position in each segment occurrence.

Both of the length values the DBA specifies must be two bytes longer than the actual minimum and maximum amounts of user data that will be stored in the segment type. The two additional bytes are for a *length field* that DL/I uses to record the size of the segment occurrence. The length field always occupies the first two bytes of a variable length segment.

When you develop an application program that will process a variable length segment, you have to include the length field in the I/O area for the segment. You code it as a binary halfword (PIC S9(4) COMP). The I/O area should be large enough to contain the longest possible occurrence of the variable length segment, including the length field. Before you issue a call to insert, replace, or delete the segment, you move its actual length to the length field in the I/O area.

The additional considerations you have to keep in mind as you develop programs that process variable length segments depend on the data base design. Within a variable length segment, you have to know where fields begin and end, and you have to know what fields are present if some are optional. The simplest situation is where a variable length segment contains a single variable length field, and that field is at the end of the segment. But that isn't typical. When fixed length and variable length fields are mixed in a variable length segment, you might use control fields with codes and lengths to identify fields. Or, you might rely on a standard within the application that certain fields are in certain locations. In any event, accessing the individual fields within a variable length segment is a COBOL consideration, not a DL/I consideration.

Because of the way variable length segments are stored, they're most appropriate when segment occurrence lengths vary but, once created, are stable. If occurrences of a segment type will tend to grow in length, variable length segments aren't a good choice for performance reasons. When a variable length segment outgrows its original space, it's split into two parts. If the two parts aren't stored in the same physical record, two I/O operations may be required to retrieve the segment, and overall performance will drop.

Segment edit/compression routines

Although data compression is transparent to you as an application programmer, it's a DL/I feature that's worth knowing about. When the data base administrator defines a segment in the DBD, she can specify a *segment edit/compression routine* for it. Then, whenever that segment is accessed, control is passed to the routine. These routines are assembler language programs written at your installation; they're not supplied by IBM.

The most common use for a segment edit/compression routine is to compress data before it's stored on DASD and to expand it before it's processed by an application program. For example, an edit/compression routine might store consecutive occurrences of the same character as a single occurrence along with a count byte. Then, on retrieval, the routine can use the count byte to expand the segment to its original form.

Because this is the basic function of an edit/compression routine, all segments processed by such a routine must be stored as variable length segments. However, application programs may view them as fixed length segments, depending on how the routine is written. In fact, one good use of edit/compression routines is to make variable length segments look like fixed length segments. That way, the problem of locating individual fields within the segment are handled by the edit/compression routine rather than by the application programs.

In addition to data compression and expansion, edit/compression routines can also be used to encode and decode data stored on DASD. When *encryption* is used, a code scheme is applied to the data before it's written to disk. Then, a program can't make sense of the data unless it's decoded by the same routine (this process is called *decryption*).

Edit/compression routines can also perform application functions on segments, like combining or resequencing fields. Or, the routine might calculate a value based on other data in the segment and present it to the program as if it were stored in the segment.

Figure 10-1 shows how an edit/compression routine works. The top part of the figure illustrates the way DL/I handles data when an edit/compression routine isn't active. Data is transferred between your program's I/O area and disk through the DL/I *buffer pool*. The buffer pool is an area of virtual storage used to store a block of segments.

The bottom part of the figure shows how segment retrieval and update work when an edit/compression routine is active. When your program issues a get call, control is passed to the edit/compression

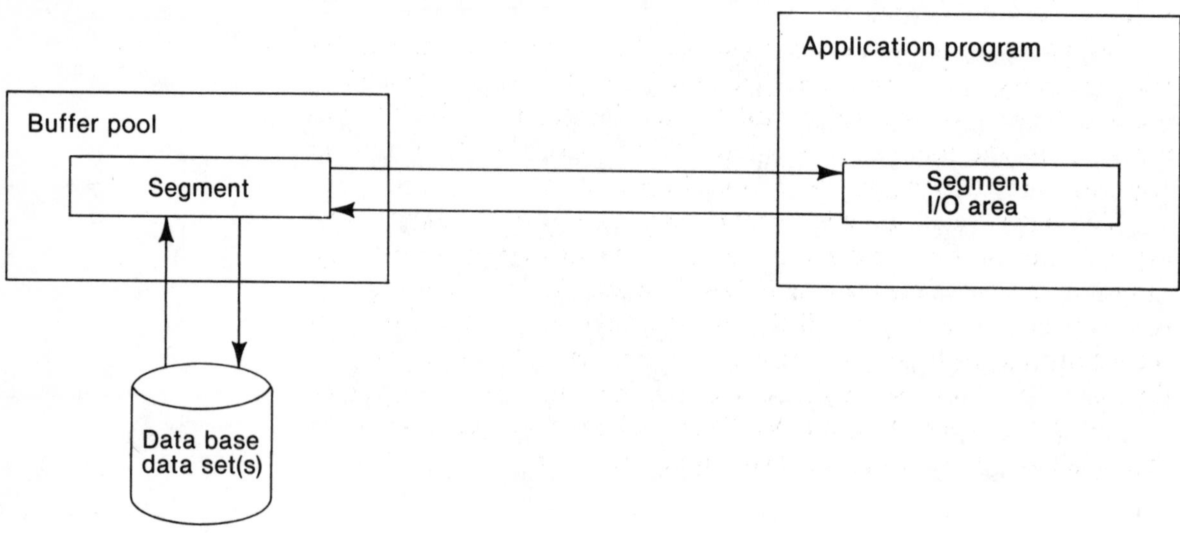

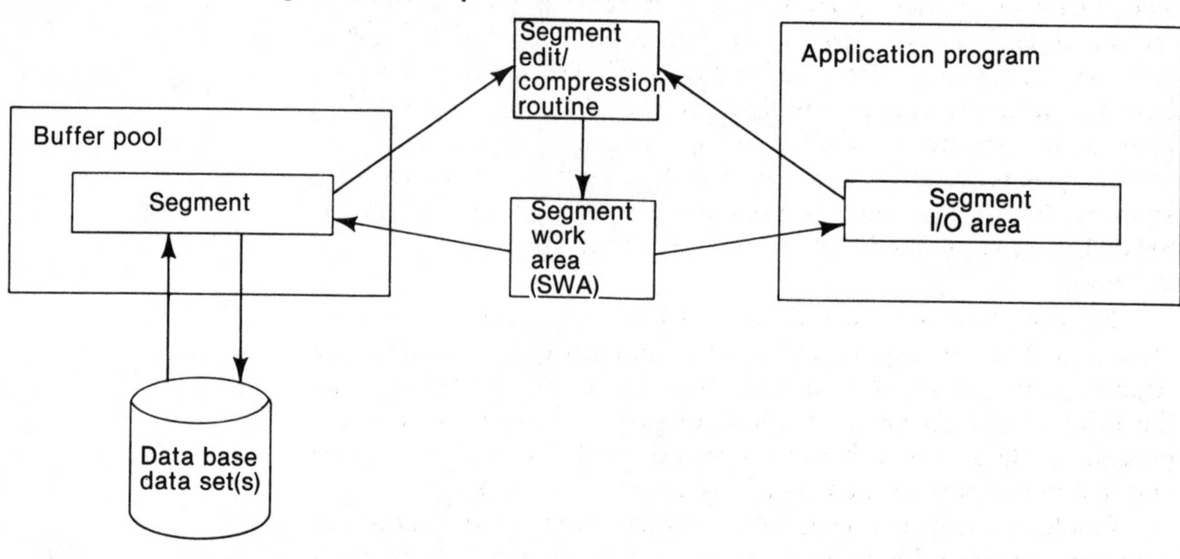

Figure 10-1 Data base I/O with and without a segment edit/compression routine

routine. It retrieves the segment from the buffer pool, manipulates it, then stores the segment as the application program will view it in the *segment work area* (*SWA*), a special area of storage used by the routine. Then, DL/I transfers the modified version of the segment to your program's I/O area.

When your program issues a call to add or replace a segment, the edit/compression routine accesses the program's I/O area, manipulates the data there into the form in which it will be stored on DASD, then moves it to the segment work area. From there, DL/I returns the segment to the buffer pool, and from there to disk.

Although using an edit/compression routine to compress and expand segment occurrences imposes additional processing overhead, it can result in a significant saving in DASD space. And if it can compress segments in such a way so all the segment occurrences in a data base record fit in a single physical record, the number of I/O operations to the data base data set will be reduced and performance will be improved. However, these are detailed data base design considerations that don't affect you as an application programmer.

Field level sensitivity

You already know that a program's view of a data base doesn't have to include all the segment types in the data base. That's called *segment level sensitivity*, and it's controlled by the SENSEG macros the data base administrator codes subordinate to the PCB macro for the data base in the program's PSBGEN. At a lower level, when *field level sensitivity* is used, a program isn't sensitive to all the fields within a segment. The DBA controls field level sensitivity by coding the SENFLD macro subordinate to the SENSEG macro in the PCB definition.

By using field level sensitivity, the DBA can adjust a program's view of a data base to just what the program needs. The fields in a segment as it's presented to an application program are a subset of all the fields in the segment. In addition, they can be *mapped* in the program's I/O area in a different sequence, with different spacing, or with a different format than they have in the actual segment.

Besides mapping the fields within a segment, the DBA can exercise a fine level of control over the program's ability to change the contents of those fields. On SENFLD macros, the DBA specifies the fields that can be changed and those that can't. Then, the program can make changes only to authorized fields in authorized segments. Although in most cases using field level sensitivity for a segment and then selectively allowing changes only for some sensitive fields is taking security to an extreme, it is appropriate for some applications. If you develop an update program that processes a data base that's defined like this, you need to know that if you issue a replace call for a segment and you try to change a field that isn't authorized for a replace, the call will fail with a DA status code.

When you insert segments defined with field level sensitivity, DL/I automatically fills in fields to which your program isn't sensitive. If your program isn't sensitive to a character field on an insert, DL/I fills it with blanks; if it isn't sensitive to a numeric field, the field's value is set to zero.

When field level sensitivity is used, some other advanced DL/I features are supported. One of these features is automatic data conversion. For example, a field stored as binary data in the data base can be converted automatically to packed decimal data in your program's view. It's also possible to specify a *user field exit routine* that's invoked whenever a field is accessed, much like an edit/ compression routine. And the data base administrator can specify a field in a program's view of a segment that doesn't actually exist in the physical segment. This *virtual field* can be assigned any initial value by the DBA. Keep in mind that these are advanced features of an advanced feature, and they're not regularly used in most shops. And in any event, they're all transparent to your application programs.

Discussion

Again, I want to stress that although the features this chapter presents are sophisticated, none of them except variable length segments has a significant effect on how you code your programs. For segment edit/compression routines and most of the features of field level sensitivity, you just have to realize that the data your program views as a segment may not be what's actually stored on disk. For variable length segments, however, you have to be aware of your application's conventions for handling variable length fields within the segments. Although the DL/I elements for fixed length and variable length segments are the same, the COBOL implications of processing variable length segments can be complex.

Terminology

variable length segment
length field
segment edit/compression routine
encryption
decryption
buffer pool
segment work area
SWA
segment level sensitivity
field level sensitivity
map
user field exit routine
virtual field

Objectives

1. Given complete specifications, code a program that processes a data base with variable length segments.

2. Describe the functions a segment edit/compression routine can perform and describe how such a routine works.

3. Describe field level sensitivity and these related features:

   a. DL/I data conversion facility
   b. user field exit routines
   c. virtual fields

Section 4

DL/I data base processing in interactive programs

This section introduces DL/I programming for the interactive environment. Chapter 11 describes the interactive system environment. Then, chapters 12 and 13 introduce the two IBM software products that are widely used to implement interactive applications: IMS/VS Data Communications and CICS/VS.

Chapters 12 and 13 are themselves introductions. To develop production programs for either environment, you need to know more. If you're going to be developing programs for IMS DC, you need the second part of this series, *IMS for the COBOL Programmer, Part 2: Data Communications and Message Format Service*. On the other hand, if you're going to be developing CICS programs, I recommend Doug Lowe's *CICS for the COBOL Programmer, Part 1: An Introductory Course* and *Part 2: An Advanced Course*.

Chapter 11

An introduction to interactive systems

So far, all of the program examples in this book have been batch programs. In batch processing, transactions are collected in groups, or batches, before they're processed. For example, inventory receipts for a full day, or even several days, might be accumulated before being posted to the inventory data base.

Batch processing for years was the rule in the data processing industry. Over the years, technological improvements have increased the capabilities of batch systems, but they haven't changed their fundamental nature. However, with the development of data communications facilities and display stations, interactive processing has become more and more common. In fact, most new systems today are interactive.

In an *interactive* (or *on-line*) *system*, a user working at a display station interacts with the computer. On a transaction by transaction basis, the user enters data and receives output back from the system. There's no longer a need to batch transactions, then process them all at once.

This chapter is divided into two main sections. The first describes four types of interactive programs you're likely to encounter, as well as four considerations common to all types of interactive systems. The second section describes the hardware components that support an interactive system: data communication networks and the 3270 Information Display System.

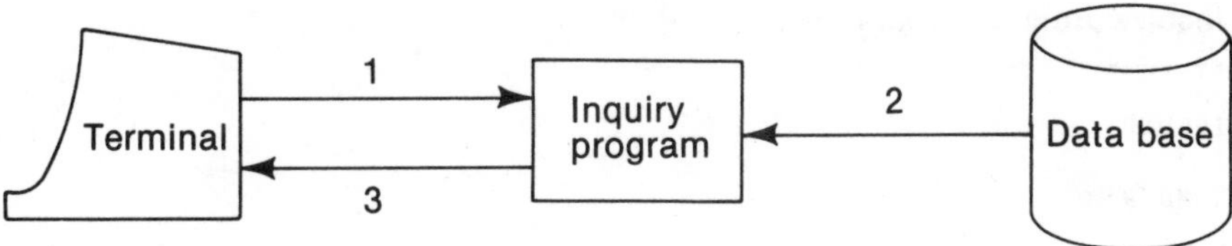

Explanation

1. The operator requests the data to be displayed.
2. The program retrieves the appropriate data from the data base.
3. The program displays the data at the terminal.

Figure 11-1 An inquiry program

INTERACTIVE PROGRAMS

This section is a brief introduction to the kinds of programs you're likely to find in an interactive system. First, I'll describe four main types of programs, grouped by general function. Then, I'll point out some design and programming considerations that are especially important in the interactive environment. If you're already familiar with interactive program types and considerations, you can skip this section.

Types of interactive programs

The kinds of programs you can find on interactive systems fall into four main categories: (1) inquiry programs, (2) data entry programs, (3) maintenance programs, and (4) menu programs. Although some interactive programs may combine functions and, as a result, fall into two or more of these groups, these are the basic categories. Now, I'll describe each.

Inquiry programs An *inquiry program* is designed to respond to a user's inquiry. Figure 11-1 illustrates a typical inquiry program. As you can see, the inquiry program here requires three steps: (1) the operator enters some value to identify the data to be retrieved, such as a segment key; (2) the program retrieves the appropriate segments from the data base; and (3) the program displays the data at the terminal.

The customer inquiry program awaits operator input

```
CUSTOMER INQUIRY                                                    10/31/85

CUSTOMER NUMBER: _

NAME:                                         CURRENT BALANCE DUE:
ADDRESS:
                                              YEAR-TO-DATE SALES:
                                              MONTH-TO-DATE SALES:

     INVOICE    DATE    DUE DATE    AMOUNT    BALANCE









PRESS CLEAR TO END SESSION
```

Figure 11-2 Operation of an inquiry program (part 1 of 3)

Figure 11-2 shows three screens from a typical inquiry program. This program displays information for a selected customer. In the first screen (part 1), the terminal is waiting for the operator to enter a customer number. The second screen (part 2) shows the customer number the operator entered. When the operator presses the enter key, the program retrieves and displays the data for the specified customer (part 3).

The inquiry program in figure 11-2 is relatively simple; it accesses just one data base and, for each transaction, just one data base record. Even the most complicated part of the program's logic (determining month-to-date and year-to-date sales for the customer) is straightforward. However, it's possible to develop complex inquiry programs that provide a variety of display options and that combine data extracted from several DL/I data bases. Even so, the basic operation of an inquiry program is what figure 11-1 shows.

Data entry programs Although inquiry programs are widely used, they don't let users key in data that's added to a system's data bases. For that, *data entry programs* are used. Figure 11-3 illustrates a simple data

The operator enters a customer number

```
CUSTOMER INQUIRY                                                  10/31/85

CUSTOMER NUMBER: 1050_

NAME:                                       CURRENT BALANCE DUE:
ADDRESS:
                                            YEAR-TO-DATE SALES:
                                            MONTH-TO-DATE SALES:

    INVOICE     DATE     DUE DATE     AMOUNT     BALANCE








PRESS CLEAR TO END SESSION
```

Figure 11-2 Operation of an inquiry program (part 2 of 3)

The program retrieves the customer's record and displays it

```
CUSTOMER INQUIRY                                                  10/31/85

CUSTOMER NUMBER: 01050

NAME:       BARRY'S HARDWARE STORE          CURRENT BALANCE DUE:   2,049.50
ADDRESS:    2105 N. FIRST STREET
            FRESNO      CA 93726            YEAR-TO-DATE SALES:   10,118.68
                                            MONTH-TO-DATE SALES:   3,328.55

    INVOICE     DATE     DUE DATE     AMOUNT     BALANCE
     078666   08/27/85   09/27/85     149.50      149.50
     079026   09/16/85   10/16/85   1,200.00    1,200.00
     080028   10/01/85   11/01/85     250.00      250.00
     081374   10/27/85   11/27/85   3,078.55      450.00




PRESS CLEAR TO END SESSION
```

Figure 11-2 Operation of an inquiry program (part 3 of 3)

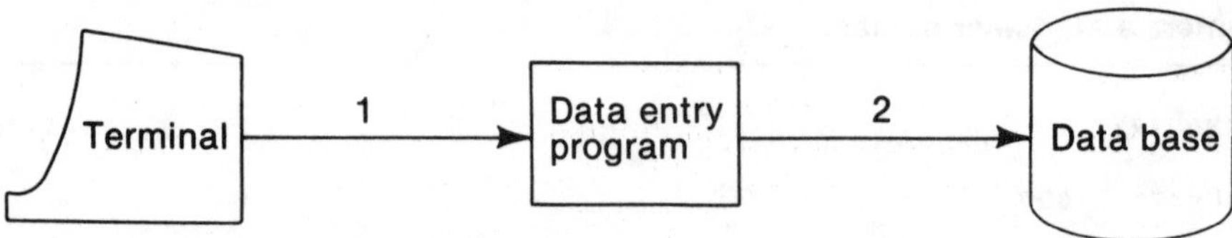

Explanation

1. The operator enters the data for one transaction at the terminal.
2. The program updates any related data bases.

Figure 11-3 A data entry program

entry program that requires only two steps. First, the operator enters data for one transaction at the terminal, and then the program updates any related data bases.

Frankly, this is as simple as a data entry program can get. More sophisticated programs involve interaction with the operator, requiring him to verify the data he entered by comparing it with information the program extracted from data bases. Other data entry programs integrate inquiry and data entry functions.

Maintenance programs A *maintenance program* can update a data base by adding, replacing, or deleting segments. Figure 11-4 shows a typical maintenance program. In this case, the program allows only changes to existing segment occurrences. In step 1, the operator enters a key value to identify the data to be changed. Then, the program extracts the necessary information from the data base (step 2) and displays it for the operator to review (step 3). The operator enters the changes that need to be made to the data (step 4), and the program issues the necessary calls to record the changes in the data base (step 5).

You can think of a maintenance program as a combination of an inquiry program and a data entry program. Like an inquiry program, a maintenance program accepts a key value and retrieves data for display. And like a data entry program, a maintenance program accepts data the operator keys in and uses it to update affected data bases.

Menu programs A *menu program* lets an operator select the functions he wants to perform. Figure 11-5 shows a typical menu program. Three steps are required: (1) the program sends a list of

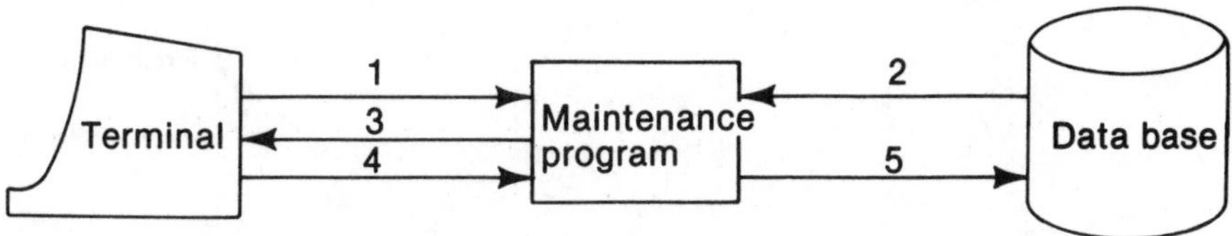

Explanation

1. The operator requests the data to be updated.
2. The program retrieves the appropriate data from the data base.
3. The program displays the data at the terminal.
4. The operator enters the required changes to the data.
5. The program rewrites the changes to the data base.

Figure 11-4 A maintenance program

processing selections to the terminal; (2) the operator chooses one of the selections; and (3) the menu program passes control to the program the operator selected. An application that's built around a set of menu programs is called a *menu-driven system*.

Figure 11-6 shows a typical menu screen. In many interactive systems, several layers of menus are required. For example, if the operator selects number 1 in figure 11-6, another menu showing selections related to order entry might be displayed.

Some interactive systems don't use menus. Instead, the operator invokes programs using explicit commands. For example, the operator might enter

```
ORD1
```

to begin an order entry program. In some cases, the command can include data the program will use as it executes. Systems that use programs that work like this are called *command-driven systems*.

Interactive program considerations

Now that you're familiar with the kinds of programs that can make up an interactive system, you need to be aware of some of the special

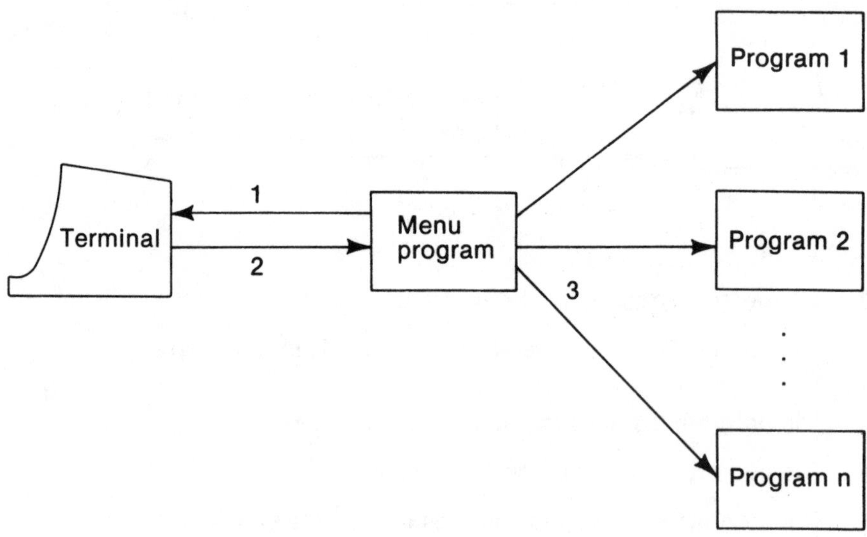

Explanation

1. The menu program sends a list of selections to the terminal.
2. The operator chooses one of the selections.
3. Control is transferred to the appropriate program.

Figure 11-5 A menu program

problems interactive programs must be able to handle. In this section, I'll cover four basic problems common to all interactive systems: shared data, response time, security, and recovery.

Shared data A batch program has exclusive control over the data bases it processes, so there's no chance that another program can interfere with its processing. In an interactive system, however, many terminal operators use the system at the same time, and they all must have access to the data bases they need. As a result, an interactive system must provide for *shared data* by coordinating updates so two programs don't update the same data at the same time.

Response time *Response time* is another special consideration for interactive systems that isn't a concern with batch systems. Quite simply, response time is how long an operator has to wait for a

```
                    MASTER MENU

                    1. ORDER ENTRY

                    2. CUSTOMER MAINTENANCE

                    3. CUSTOMER INQUIRY

                    4. INVOICING

                    YOUR SELECTION: _



PRESS CLEAR TO END SESSION
```

Figure 11-6 A typical menu screen

transaction to be processed. A response time of several seconds is probably good, while several minutes probably isn't.

Many factors affect response time: the number of users on the system, the storage available, the speed of the disk units in use, how system parameters are set, how fast telecommunications lines are, and how application programs are written. There are some important program design considerations you need to know for IMS and particularly for CICS that affect response time. In both cases, as in the batch environment, keeping your DL/I calls few and simple will improve your programs' response times.

Security In a batch system, *security* is easy to maintain because there's only one access to the computer system: the computer room. However, in an interactive system, terminals are located in many places, and security is a problem. Both CICS and IMS DC (and the telecommunications access method VTAM) provide security (1) with basic logon controls that keep unauthorized users off the system and (2) with access control features that restrict users to just the data they need.

Recovery Recovery from system and program failures is complex enough in the batch environment, but the additional requirements of interactive processing make it even more complicated. Both CICS and IMS DC include sophisticated recovery features that make recovery as fast and efficient as possible. For the most part, recovery is transparent to the application programmer, so I mention it here just for perspective.

DATA COMMUNICATIONS NETWORKS

A *data communications network* (often called a *telecommunications network*) lets users at *local terminals* (terminals that are located at the computer site) or *remote terminals* (terminals that aren't located at the computer site) access a *host computer* (or *host system*). In this section, I'll briefly describe the components of a data communications network, with emphasis on the most common type of terminal on IBM systems: the 3270 Information Display System.

Elements of a data communications network

Figure 11-7 is a schematic representation of a typical telecommunications network. Basically, five elements make up a network: (1) a host system, (2) a communication controller, (3) modems, (4) telecommunication lines, and (5) terminal systems. A single *terminal system* consists of one or more CRT display stations connected to the network through a terminal controller.

At the center of the network in figure 11-7 is the host system. For both IMS DC and CICS, the host system is a System/370 family processor, such as a 3080 or 4300 model. The *telecommunications monitor* (IMS DC, CICS, or, on some large OS systems, both) runs in the host system processor to control interactive application programs and to manage data base and file processing.

To control physical communication functions, the host system uses a *telecommunications* (or *TC*) *access method.* The TC access method serves as an interface between the physical operation of the terminal network and programs, much as the other access methods are interfaces between I/O units like DASDs and programs. The most common TC access methods are *BTAM* (*Basic Telecommunications Access Method*) and *VTAM* (*Virtual Telecommunications Access Method*).

Figure 11-7 shows two remote terminal systems attached to the host through a 3705 *communication controller.* The 3705 is at the host site and is connected to the two remote sites by *telecommunication lines* that have modems on each end. A *modem* is a device that translates

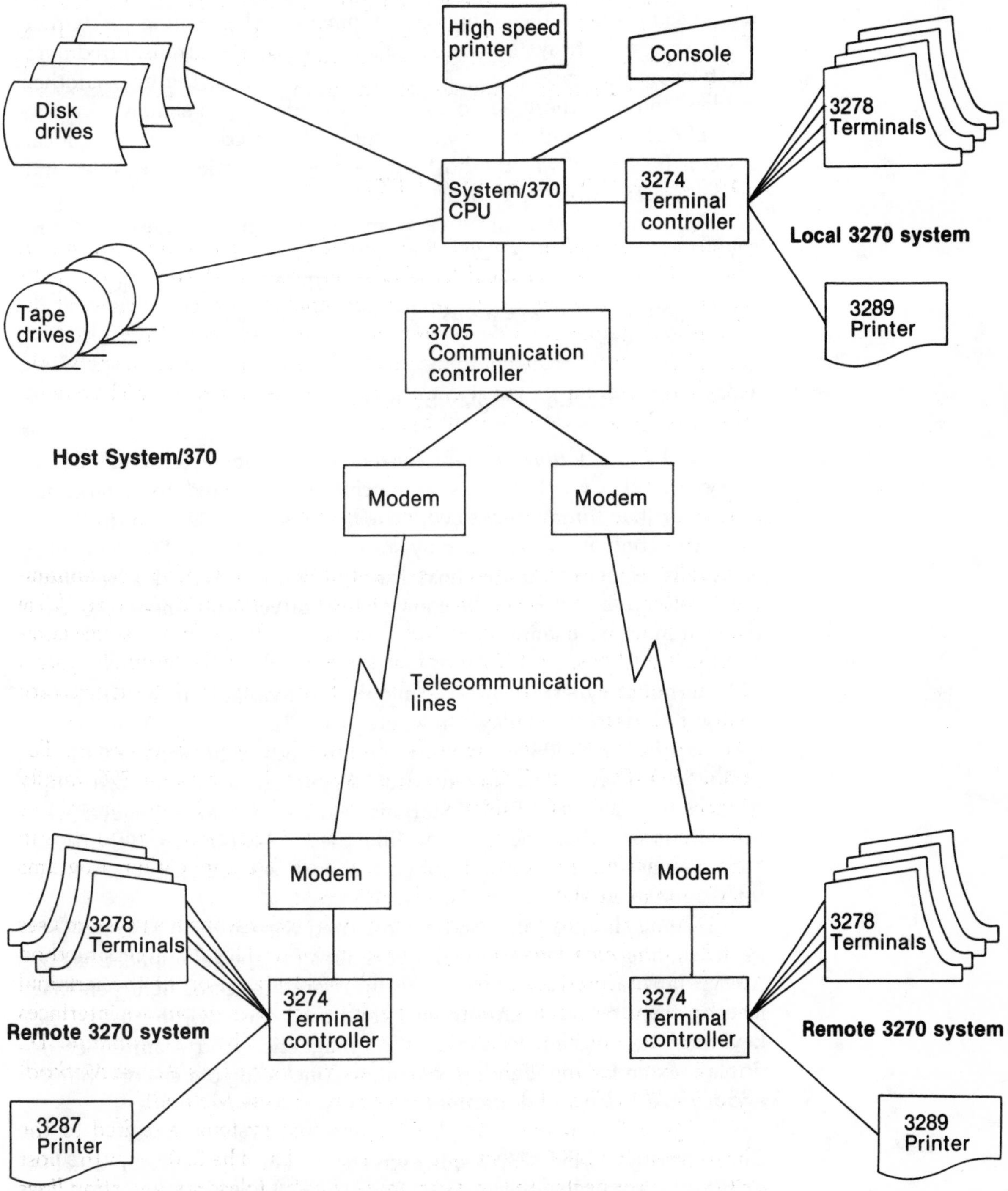

Figure 11-7 A typical System/370 and 3270 configuration

digital signals from the computer equipment at the sending end (either the host or remote system) into audio signals that are transmitted over the telecommunication line. At the receiving end of the line, another modem converts those audio signals back into digital signals.

The third terminal system in figure 11-7 is configured as a local system. Because it's at the host site, a communication controller and modems aren't necessary for it.

As you can see, all three terminal systems in figure 11-7 are 3270-type systems. The 3270 Information Display System is the most common type of terminal system used with IMS DC and CICS. As a result, you need to have a basic understanding of it.

The 3270 Information Display System

The *3270 Information Display System* isn't a single terminal, but a subsystem of CRT terminals and printers connected to a *terminal controller* that communicates with the host. A single 3270 controller, a 3274, can control up to 32 display stations and printers. The controller is usually attached to the host through a modem and a telecommunication line, but it can be equipped for direct attachment to one of the host system's channels.

3270 terminal types 3270 terminals are available in a variety of configurations that display anywhere from 12 lines of 40 characters each to 43 lines of 80 characters, with one model that displays 27 lines of 132 characters. One advanced 3270-type terminal, the 3290, can serve as four separate display stations at the same time. However, the most common 3270-type terminals (like the 3278 Model 2 and the 3178) have screens with 24 usable display lines, each with 80 characters, for a total screen size of 1920 characters.

3270 display stations can be configured with a variety of options, including alternate keyboard configurations for special applications or foreign languages. Less common features are a selector light pen that lets the operator communicate with the host system without using the keyboard, a magnetic slot reader or magnetic hand scanner, color display, extended highlighting capabilities (including underscore, blink, and reverse video), and graphics.

Characteristics of the 3270 display screen The 3270 screen is a *field-oriented display*. In other words, the screen consists of a number of user-defined fields. As in a record or segment description, a field on a

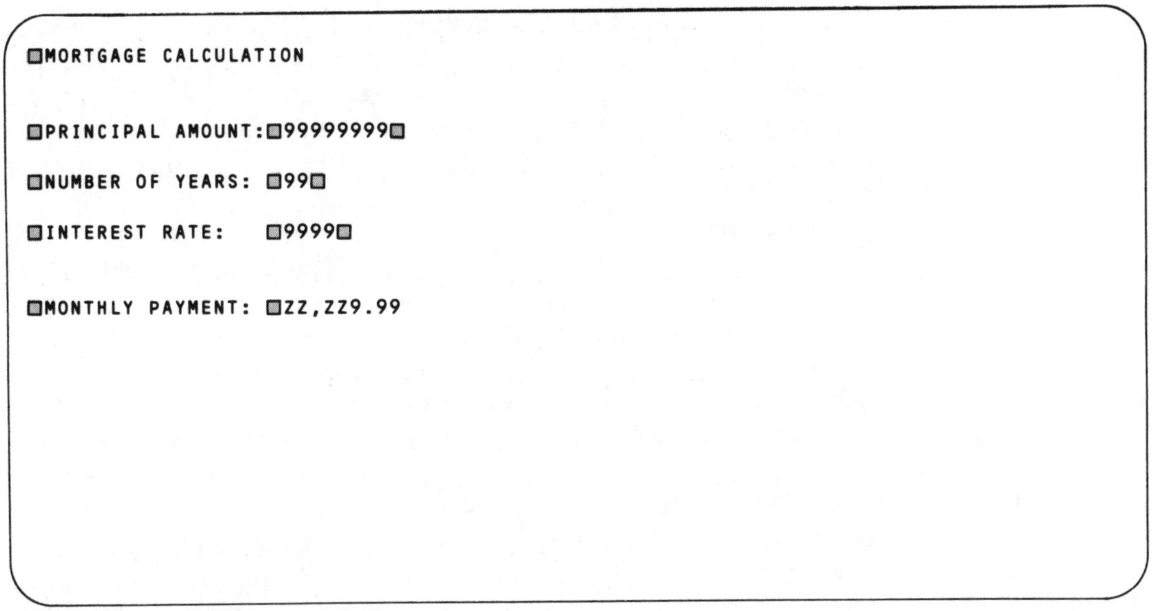

```
▣MORTGAGE CALCULATION

▣PRINCIPAL AMOUNT:▣99999999▣

▣NUMBER OF YEARS: ▣99▣

▣INTEREST RATE:   ▣9999▣

▣MONTHLY PAYMENT: ▣ZZ,ZZ9.99
```

Figure 11-8 Attribute bytes in a 3270 display

screen is a specified area that contains a particular category of information. Some screen fields let the operator key data into them, while others are protected from data entry.

A special character called an *attribute byte* (or *attribute character*) marks the beginning of a field. The attribute byte takes up one position on the screen—the position immediately to the left of the field it defines—but it's displayed on the screen as a space. The end of a field is defined by another attribute byte. So the length of a screen field depends on the position of the next attribute byte. If there is no subsequent attribute byte, the field continues to the end of the screen.

Figure 11-8 shows the placement of attribute bytes in a sample 3270 display. Here, the small shaded boxes represent attribute bytes. These small boxes don't actually appear on the screen. Instead, spaces appear in the attribute byte positions.

The screen in figure 11-8 has three data entry fields: principal amount (99999999), number of years (99), and interest rate (9999). (Don't confuse these data entry fields with the captions that identify the data the operator should key into them.) These data entry fields each require *two* attribute bytes: one to mark the start of the field, the other to mark the end.

On the other hand, display-only fields—like captions and data displayed by the program—require only one attribute byte. For example, the monthly payment field in figure 11-8 (ZZ,ZZ9.99) doesn't require an attribute byte to mark where it ends because it's a display-only field. However, if it were a data entry field, it would require a terminating attribute byte.

As its name implies, the attribute byte does more than just mark the beginning or end of a field. It also determines a field's characteristics, called its *attributes*. A field's attributes are determined by the values of the bits in its attribute byte.

For example, the attribute byte can make a field display with regular or bright intensity, or not display at all. The attribute byte determines whether a field is protected (display only) or unprotected (data entry). And, for an unprotected field, the attribute byte determines the shift of the field (shift controls the kind of data that can be keyed into the field: alphanumeric or numeric only). A field can have almost any combination of these attributes. In addition, on terminals that support basic color operations, the attribute byte determines the display color of a field.

As an application programmer, you can set the values of attribute bytes to control the appearance and function of the screen. Both IMS DC and CICS include facilities to do this; but they're advanced features I won't cover in depth in the chapters that follow. I present the concept of attribute bytes here because it's basic information that's referred to commonly, and you should be familiar with it.

Discussion

This chapter is just an introduction to interactive systems. Although the next two chapters expand what you've learned here with more specific information on IMS DC and CICS, they too are just introductions. Before you can develop interactive application programs for either telecommunications monitor, you'll need more background and information.

Terminology

interactive system
on-line system
inquiry program
data entry program
maintenance program
menu program
menu-driven system
command-driven system
shared data
response time
security
data communications network
telecommunications network
local terminal
remote terminal
host computer
host system
terminal system
telecommunications monitor
telecommunications access method
TC access method
BTAM
Basic Telecommunications Access Method
VTAM
Virtual Telecommunications Access Method
communication controller
telecommunication line
modem
3270 Information Display System
terminal controller
field-oriented display
attribute byte
attribute character
attribute

Objectives

1. Describe the four basic types of interactive programs.
2. Describe the four considerations that take on special importance in interactive systems.
3. Describe the main components of a data communications network.
4. Describe the characteristics of a 3270 display station's screen.

Chapter 12

Interactive programs in the IMS/VS DC environment

Although all of the programs you've seen so far in this book use IMS/VS facilities, they use only a subset of them. In a full-function IMS system, data base (DB) processing is combined with data communications (DC) processing. This chapter introduces you to the IMS DC environment and the DL/I calls you can use for interactive functions, and it presents a simple IMS DC inquiry program.

Keep in mind that this chapter isn't a thorough treatment of IMS DC. Its purpose is to help you understand the features and facilities of a complete IMS system. To be able to code production application programs for the DC environment, you need to know much more, which you can learn from *Part 2* of this series.

How IMS DC works

To understand how an application program works in an IMS DC system, you need to be familiar with three concepts: IMS regions, messages and message queueing, and program scheduling.

IMS regions In the batch environment, a DL/I program executes in its own region, just like any other batch job. In contrast, an application program in the DC environment executes in a *dependent region*. It's dependent upon the *IMS control region* (or just *CTL region*), where the

IMS control program resides. The IMS control program manages the execution of other IMS components (called *modules*) that also run in the control region. These modules provide a variety of services to support the IMS terminal network and the processing done in dependent regions.

To illustrate, figure 12-1 shows how the IMS control region provides services for its dependent regions. Here, IMS modules that reside in the control region handle all application program requests for data base and terminal I/O operations. All data base data sets and terminals used by DC programs are allocated to the control region, as are a single set of log data sets that are used for the entire IMS DC system rather than for individual application programs. As a result, IMS DC has centralized control over its data bases, terminals, and logs.

The number of dependent regions used in an IMS DC system varies from installation to installation. In figure 12-1, there's one *batch message processing (BMP) region* and two *message processing program (MPP) regions*. I'll describe the differences between the programs that can run in these kinds of regions in a moment. First, you need to know what "messages" are and how IMS handles them.

Messages and message queueing A *message* is a unit of data that's transmitted between a program and a terminal. The primary inputs to and outputs from DC programs are messages. To understand how this compares with batch programs, consider figure 12-2. For a batch program, shown in the top section of the figure, typical input is a transaction from a file containing a collection of transaction records. For each input record, a batch program does predictable processing against its data bases and writes a line on a report, its typical output.

The bottom section of figure 12-2 shows the corresponding elements for a DC program. Although the DC program may do the same data base processing as the batch program, its input is an *input message* entered by a user at a terminal. In IMS terms, this is a *transaction*: an input message destined for an application program. In fact, the data in the first eight characters of the input message is a *transaction code* that IMS associates with the particular application program that will process the message. The output of the DC program in figure 12-2 is an *output message* sent back to the terminal, perhaps verification that the requested processing was successfully completed by a maintenance program, much like a report line on a batch program's output.

Actually, figure 12-2 is a simplification. Figure 12-3 shows more accurately how transactions are supplied to a DC program, although

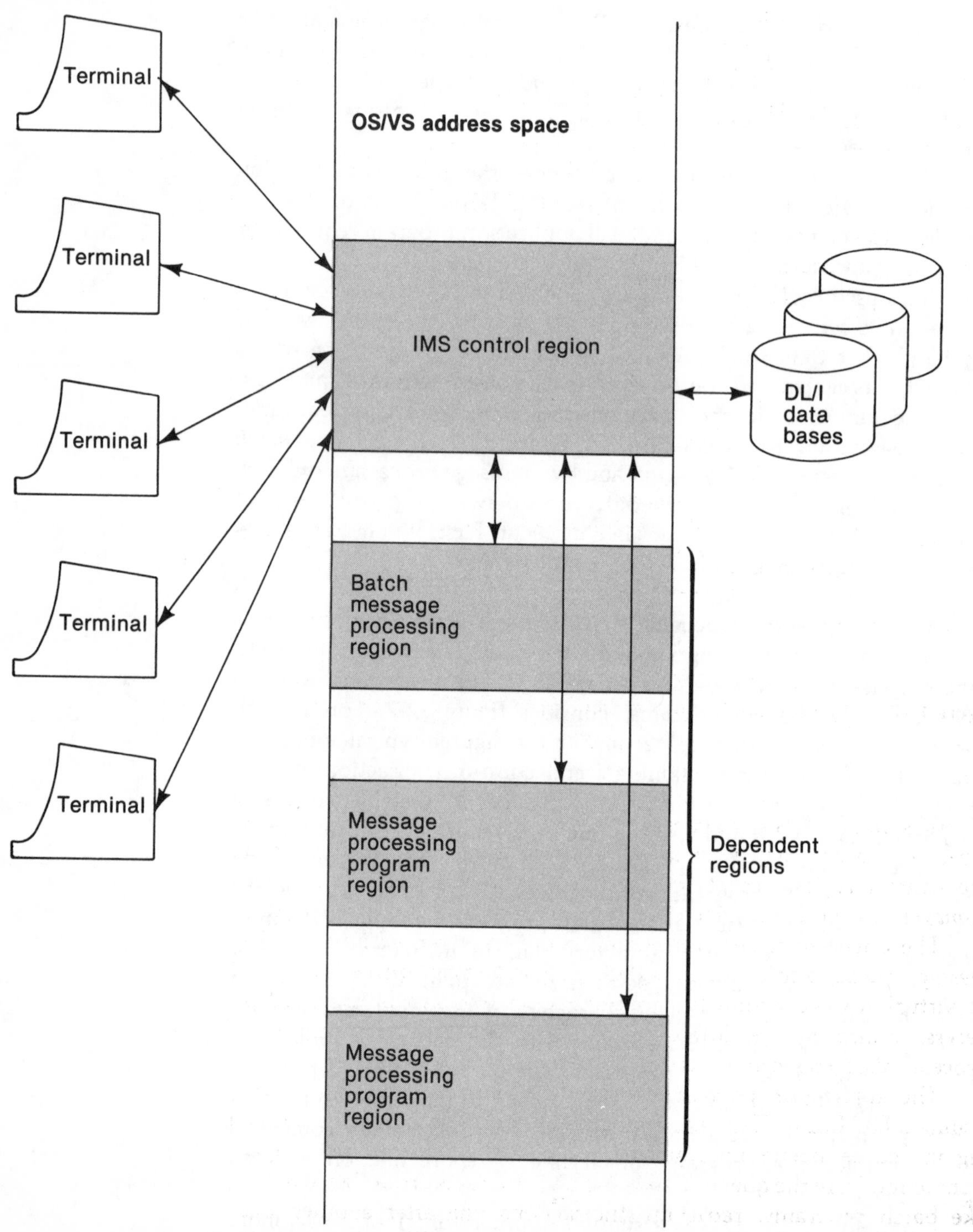

Figure 12-1 How the IMS control region provides services for dependent regions

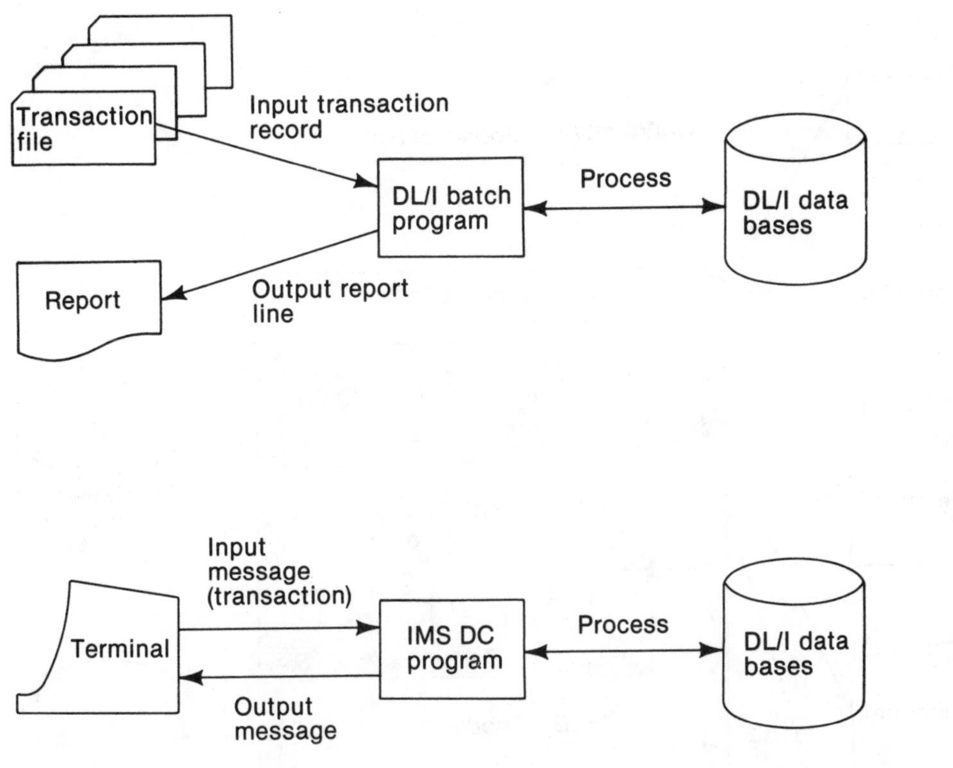

Figure 12-2 Typical input, process, and output for DL/I batch and IMS DC programs

it's still simplified. As you can see, a message doesn't go directly from a terminal to a program. First, *data communications modules* running in the control region accept the terminal input and pass it to *queue management modules,* which are also executing in the control region.

The queue management modules store the terminal input in the *message queue,* also called the *QPOOL.* The message queue is an area of virtual storage within the control region that can be extended if necessary into an overflow data set on DASD. Storing messages, a process called *message queueing,* is a major IMS DC function.

The application program requests a transaction (a message) by issuing a DL/I call. Then, DL/I modules, which also reside in the CTL region, cause queue management modules to retrieve the proper transaction from the queue. Typically, DC programs are designed much like batch programs, retrieving transactions one after another and doing the same basic processing for each. Such a DC program ends when there are no more input messages for it on the queue.

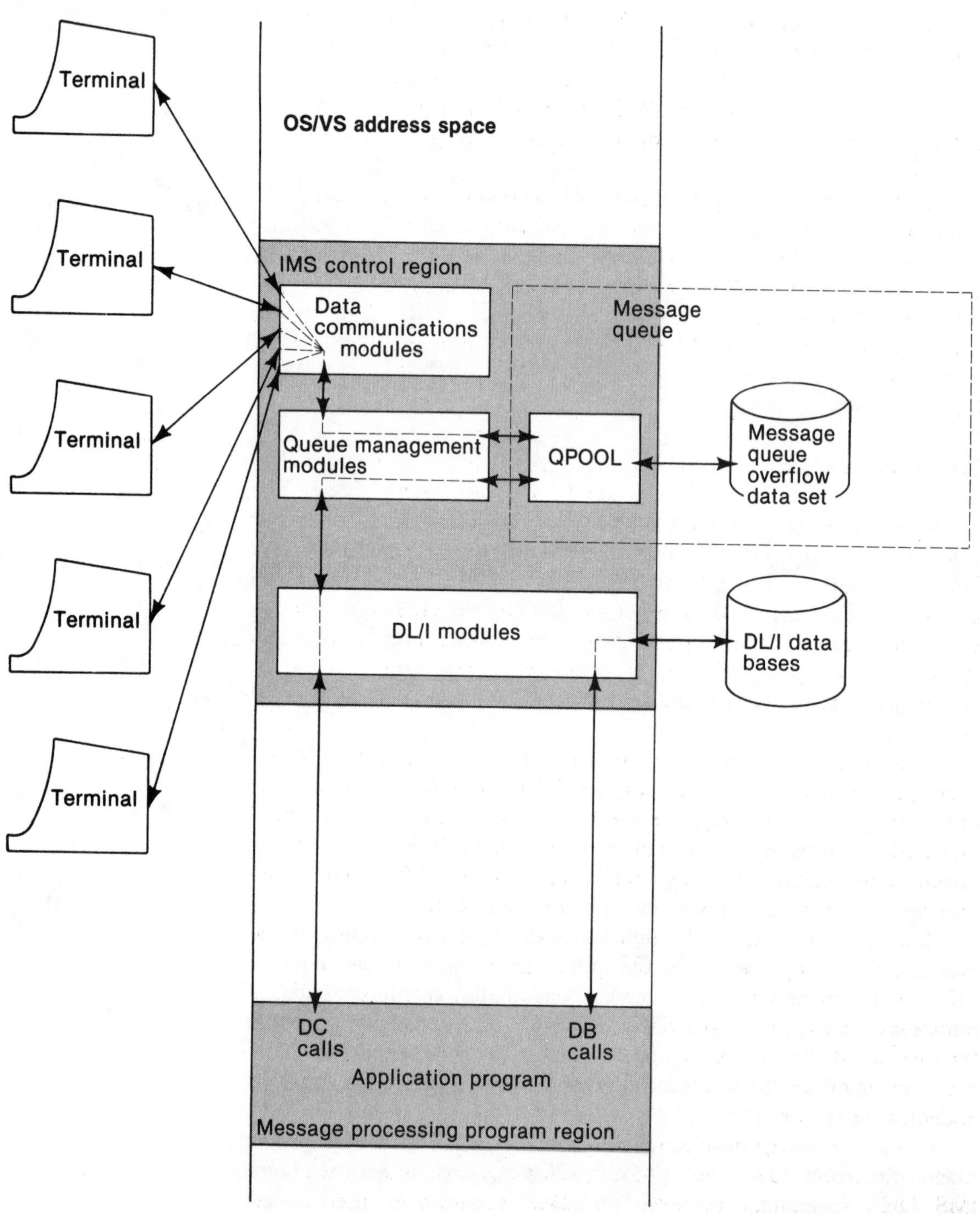

Figure 12-3 Message queueing

To send an output message back to a terminal, the application program issues another DL/I call. The DL/I modules in the CTL region pass the message to queue management, which stores the output message in the message queue. IMS DC then takes care of routing the message back to the proper terminal through its data communications modules.

To control the format of messages transmitted to a terminal or to interpret the format of messages received from a terminal, *Message Format Service* (*MFS*) modules, also residing in the CTL region, may be used. In other words, MFS provides a manageable way of utilizing the formatted display capabilities of 3270 devices. By coding special programs that create MFS blocks, you can define complex formatted screens and improve processing efficiency. *Part 2* of this series covers MFS in detail.

Program scheduling To enter a transaction that will be processed by an application program, the user has to send an input message that contains the proper transaction code in the first eight positions, followed by transaction data. In the simplest case, the operator actually keys the eight-character transaction code in the first eight screen positions and follows it with the other data elements that make up the complete message. (If MFS is used, it can insert the transaction code in the message automatically so the operator doesn't have to enter it, provided the screen is formatted properly. Don't worry about that for now, though.)

Once the input message, beginning with the transaction code, has been queued, IMS DC's *scheduling modules* determine when to cause the corresponding message processing program to be loaded and executed. If an input message is queued for an MPP that isn't already running and a suitable MPP dependent region is free, IMS *schedules* the program into that region without operator intervention.

Usually, when an MPP is scheduled, it quickly processes the message or messages for it on the queue, then ends. However, some MPPs may process complex transactions that are entered in large numbers by many terminal users working at the same time. When that's the case, an MPP can execute for an extended period of time. While the program processes its oldest input messages, new ones are constantly added to the queue.

A batch message processing program also uses input transactions from the message queue, but is scheduled by JCL, not automatically by IMS DC's scheduling modules. A BMP program is used when transactions entered on-line can be held without being posted to the data base immediately. Many input messages for a BMP program are accumulated on the queue over a period of time (perhaps a day), then posted in a single run. Although this is like a batch program running in an independent DL/I region, a BMP program can access the IMS message queue. And since all BMP program data base processing is done through the IMS control region, the data bases it uses can be accessed by other programs while the BMP program is running.

DL/I calls for message processing

As I've already mentioned, your IMS DC programs issue DL/I calls, much like data base calls, to perform message processing functions. This section presents the considerations you need to keep in mind when you code DL/I calls for message processing.

As you know, DL/I data base calls operate at the segment level. The same is true for data communications calls: both input and output messages are made up of segments. However, the segments that make up a message aren't organized hierarchically, as in a data base record. Instead, they just represent parts of a message. Often, a message consists of just one segment.

Figure 12-4 compares a DL/I data base call and a DL/I data communications call. Both specify a DL/I function, a PCB mask, and an I/O area. In this section, I'll describe how you use each of these three elements in a DC call. (The fourth element of a DB call, the SSA, isn't used on a DC call.)

DL/I function Just as in a data base call, the first argument you code on a DC call is the name of a four-character working-storage field that contains the proper function code value for the operation you want DL/I to perform. The basic DC call functions are get unique (GU), get next (GN), and insert (ISRT). You issue a GU call to retrieve the first (or only) segment of an input message. If an input message contains multiple segments, you retrieve subsequent ones with GN calls. And to send an output message, you issue one ISRT call for each segment in the message.

PCB mask As with a DB call, a DC call must specify a Linkage Section PCB mask. DL/I knows a particular call is a DC call because the PCB mask you specify is one it associates with message processing. When the DBA creates a PSBGEN job for an MPP, she codes an option on the PSBGEN macro to cause a special PCB called the *I/O PCB* to be generated.

A data base call

```
CALL 'CBLTDLI' USING DLI-GU
                     CR-PCB-MASK
                     RECEIVABLE-SEGMENT
                     INVOICE-NO-SSA.
```

A data communication call

```
CALL 'CBLTDLI' USING DLI-GU
                     IO-PCB-MASK
                     INPUT-MESSAGE-SEGMENT.
```

Figure 12-4 A data base call and a data communication call

Just like a data base PCB, the I/O PCB resides outside your program. To provide addressability to the I/O PCB mask, then, you must list it along with your program's data base PCBs on the ENTRY statement. For the I/O PCB to be addressed properly, it must be the first PCB listed on the ENTRY statement.

The data elements that make up an I/O PCB differ from those in a data base PCB. Figure 12-5 shows you how to code a complete I/O PCB mask in COBOL. For basic DC applications, the only I/O PCB field you need to worry about is the status code field. As in a data base PCB, it's two bytes long and is located in positions 11 and 12. When I describe how to use message processing calls later in this chapter, I'll present status code values you can expect.

The other fields in the I/O PCB mask are for advanced functions you probably won't often use. They contain such information as the name of the terminal that initiated the transaction, the date and time the message was sent, a message sequence number assigned to the message by IMS, the name of a special control block called a MOD that's used by Message Format Service, and the user-id of the user who initiated the transaction. As I said, you probably won't use these fields often.

Segment I/O area A DC call specifies a segment I/O area, just like a DB call. When you issue a GU or GN call to retrieve an input message segment, DL/I places the segment data in the I/O area the call names. Similarly, when you issue an ISRT call to send an output message segment, DL/I gets the data from the I/O area. Of course, as with a data base ISRT call, you must first build the output data in the I/O area.

```
*
 01  IO-PCB-MASK.
*
     05  IO-PCB-LOGICAL-TERMINAL PIC X(8).
     05  FILLER                  PIC XX.
     05  IO-PCB-STATUS-CODE      PIC XX.
     05  IO-PCB-DATE             PIC S9(7)       COMP-3.
     05  IO-PCB-TIME             PIC S9(6)V9     COMP-3.
     05  IO-PCB-MSG-SEQ-NUMBER   PIC S9(5)       COMP.
     05  IO-PCB-MOD-NAME         PIC X(8).
     05  IO-PCB-USER-ID          PIC X(8).
*
```

Figure 12-5 COBOL code for an I/O PCB mask

A problem you might have when you develop a DC program is deciding how to code its I/O area fields. Because message segments can vary in size, the I/O areas you use must be large enough to contain the largest segment that will be processed through them. Also, you have to provide additional control fields in both input and output messages. As I show you how to retrieve and send messages, I'll describe the I/O area format requirements in more detail. At any rate, when you receive specifications for a DC program, they should indicate the formats of its I/O areas.

How to retrieve an input message

To retrieve an input message, an application program issues either a single GU call or a GU call followed by one or more GN calls. The technique you use depends on how many segments the input message contains. That's a decision the system designer makes, and it should be indicated in your program specifications.

How to retrieve single-segment input messages If an input message consists of just one segment occurrence, all you need to do is issue one GU call to retrieve it. When this is the case, your MPP is much like a batch transaction processing program. The batch program executes a READ statement to retrieve a transaction record from an input file, then does predictable data base processing and reporting based upon the data in the transaction. The program repeats this cycle for each record in the transaction file. When the batch program encounters the AT END condition when it attempts a READ for the transaction file, it ends.

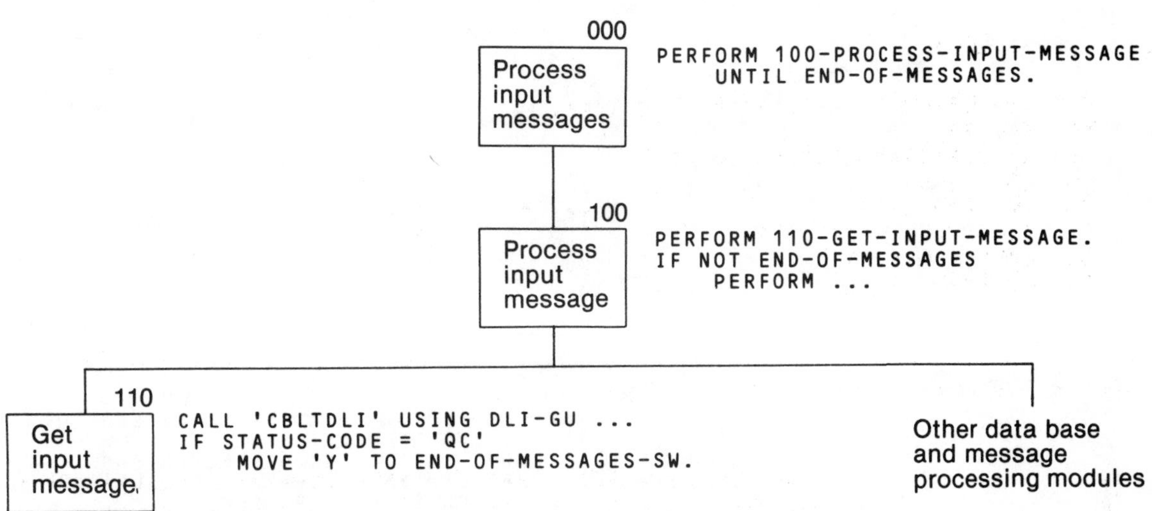

Figure 12-6 A partial program structure chart and sample COBOL code for a program that processes single-segment input messages

An MPP works similarly, but instead of being driven by transaction records in a transaction file, it's driven by messages in the message queue. Figure 12-6 presents a partial structure chart and sample COBOL source code to illustrate this. The MPP issues a DC GU call to retrieve the input message from the IMS message queue, then it does predictable data base processing based on the input message. Usually, it sends a reply message back to the originating terminal. When the program gets a QC status code (instead of blanks) as a result of its DC GU call, it knows there are no more messages on the queue, and it ends.

How to retrieve multiple-segment input messages The situation is only slightly more complicated when your program processes multiple-segment input messages. Figure 12-7 illustrates that the MPP is still driven by the presence of messages on the message queue and that it ends when no more messages are present. However, the programming technique required to retrieve a complete message has more steps. To retrieve the first segment of a multiple-segment message, your program issues a GU call. Then, to retrieve subsequent segments for that message, it issues GN calls repeatedly until it encounters a QD status code.

The structure of an input message segment The input message segment IMS passes to your program begins with two two-byte fields:

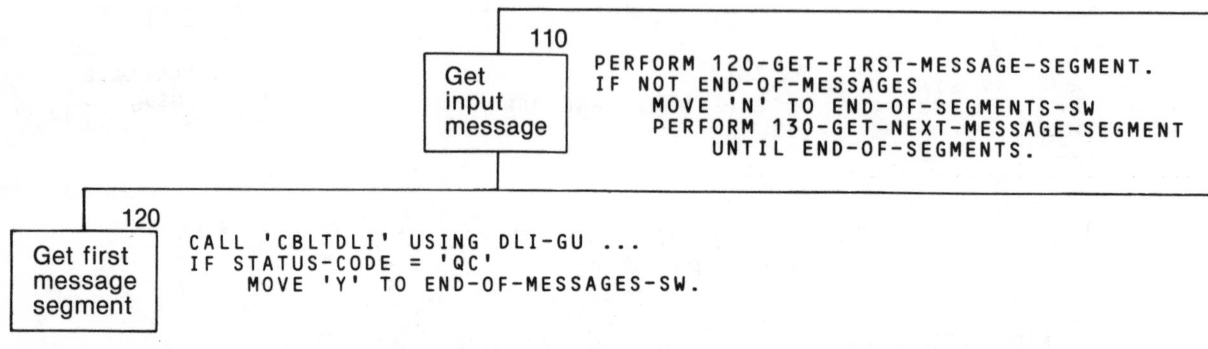

Figure 12-7 A partial program structure chart and sample COBOL code for a program that processes multiple-segment input messages

the *LL field* followed by the *ZZ field*. After the ZZ field comes the actual data in the message segment, which can be variable length.

The LL field contains, in binary format, the length of the entire input message segment, including the LL and ZZ fields. Typically, you define the LL field with PIC S9(3) and COMP usage. The ZZ field is reserved for use by IMS, so although you define it in the I/O area, you don't do anything with it. You should define the ZZ field with PIC XX or PIC S9(3) and COMP usage. The structure of the data component of the input message varies depending on the application.

How the data that's passed to your program relates to what the terminal operator entered depends on how IMS edits the message. In other words, the format of the message your program receives can be just like what the operator entered at the terminal, or it can vary significantly. As I've already mentioned, MFS can be used to alter the format of data transferred between programs and terminals. Then, what the operator keys in at the terminal and the transaction the application program receives can look quite different. In *Part 2*, I'll

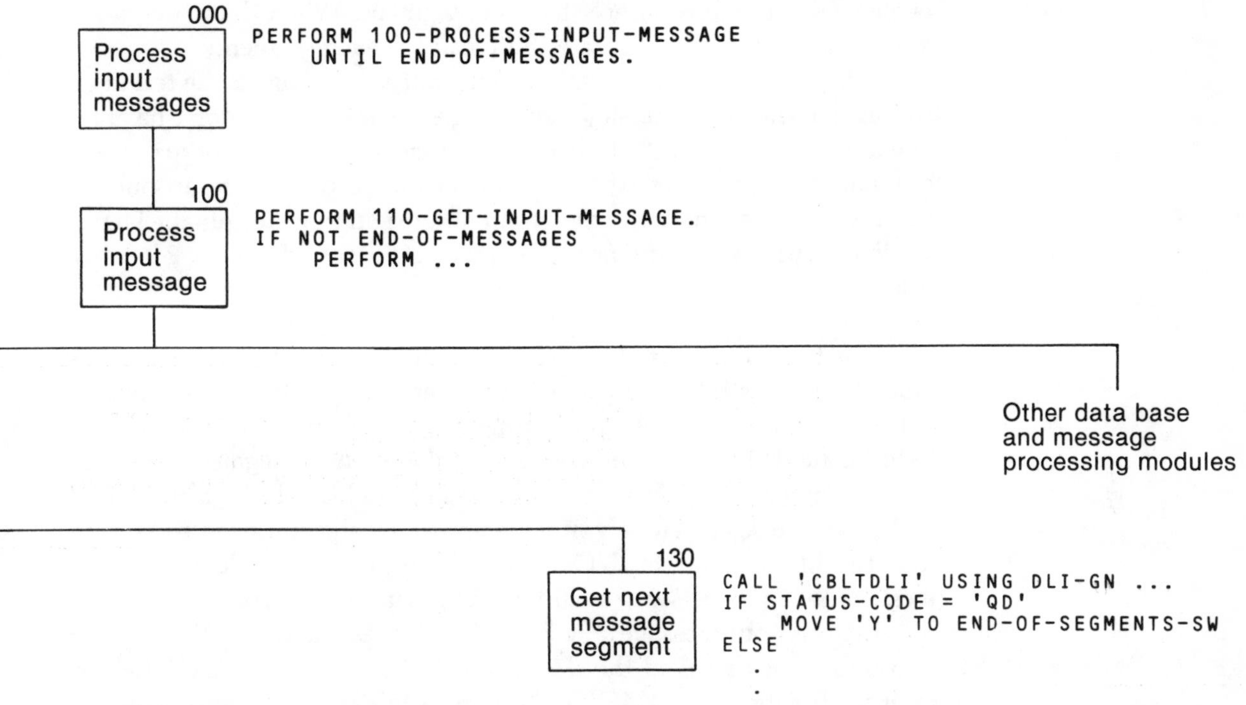

show you how to use MFS to do this kind of formatting. (Although the input message for the program example in this chapter is processed by MFS, its format isn't changed from what the operator enters.)

When you get specifications for a DC program, be sure they provide all the information you need about the input messages it will process. Particularly, you need to know how many segments a message can contain. That's necessary to determine how to code the calls to retrieve them. Also, you must know the segments' formats so you can code their layouts in the Working-Storage Section.

How to send an output message

As I've already mentioned, you send output message segments by issuing ISRT calls that specify the I/O PCB. Before you issue an ISRT call, you build the output message segment in the I/O area you name on the call. Although many output messages consist of just a single segment, some require more than one segment. When that's the case, your program issues a separate ISRT call for each segment.

In most cases, the destination of the output message is the terminal from which the input message came. When that's so, you don't have to take any special action to insure that the message is sent to the correct terminal. In some cases, though, you might need to route an output message to a destination other than the originating terminal. That's possible—but it's an advanced DC feature I'll cover in *Part 2* of this series.

The structure of an output message segment An output message has much the same structure as an input message: its first four bytes contain data required by IMS. An output message segment begins with a two-byte LL field that contains the length of the entire segment. Like an input segment, you define an output segment's LL field with PIC S9(3) and COMP usage. Before you issue an ISRT call, you need to be sure that the LL field in the I/O area contains the actual length of the message that's to be sent, including the initial four bytes.

In an output message, the ZZ field in bytes 3 and 4 is divided into two binary fields called the *Z1 field* and the *Z2 field*. The Z1 field is reserved for the use of IMS, and you must initialize it to zero. You can use the Z2 field to control some advanced terminal operations, but for most applications, it too should be set to zero. As a result, you can code the two fields together with PIC S9(3) and COMP usage and initialize the field with VALUE ZERO. Or, you can code it as PIC XX and specify VALUE LOW-VALUE.

After the first four bytes comes the actual output message data. As with an input message, this data can vary in length, and its format depends on the application. Also, if you use MFS, the format of the data in the message can differ from what's displayed at the user's terminal. On the other hand, if you don't use MFS, the output message contains all the data that's displayed, plus any format control characters required by the terminal device.

Before you code a DC program, be sure that its specifications indicate the format of its output messages. This includes the number of segments that make up an output message and the formats and lengths of those segments.

A sample IMS DC inquiry program

Now that you're familiar with the basics of IMS DC programming, I want to show you a simple inquiry program. This program lets the operator display the financial status of a receivable (an invoice) from a customer data base. (The customer data base is described in detail in chapter 7; if you haven't read chapter 7, I suggest you look at figures 7-1 and 7-2 to get an idea of the structure of the data base.)

The two screen layouts for the program are in figure 12-8. In part 1 of the figure, you can see how the user sends an input message. He keys in the transaction code (which in this case is DLIIINQ), then follows it with the number of the invoice to be displayed. The operator has to key in two spaces between the transaction code and the invoice number to make sure the input message is properly formatted when it's presented to the program. (If more sophisticated MFS editing were being used here, this wouldn't necessarily be the case.)

Part 2 of figure 12-8 shows the format of the output the program will send back to the terminal. After retrieving the requested receivable segment from the customer data base, the program formats data from it, calculates the original billing total and total payments and adjustments, and sends the results to the terminal. The MFS editing in effect for the program requires that each screen line be a separate output message segment. They're displayed beginning on line 3 of the screen.

Figure 12-9 gives more specific information about the formats of the message segments the program will handle. As you can see, the input message, which consists of just one segment occurrence, has to be defined with 79 bytes for text in addition to the LL and ZZ fields. The first seven characters of the text contain the transaction code DLIIINQ, and two spaces follow in positions 8 and 9. Then, in positions 10 through 15 is the invoice number. The program will use it to construct an SSA for use in a GU call to retrieve the requested receivable segment from the customer data base.

The output message consists of nine segments. As I just mentioned, each segment is displayed on a successive screen line, beginning with line 3. The program will have to format both the constant and variable data on each display line. (Again, if more sophisticated MFS editing were being used, this wouldn't necessarily be so.) In this case, none of the segments may be longer than 79 bytes, the length of a display line on the 3270 screen minus one for an attribute byte in position 1. However, the program can send shorter segments if trailing positions don't contain data.

Figure 12-10 presents the structure chart for the program. As you can see, it's similar to the partial structure chart in figure 12-6. The program is driven by the presence of input messages on the message queue. For each input message it retrieves (in module 110), it tries to retrieve the proper receivable segment occurrence from the customer

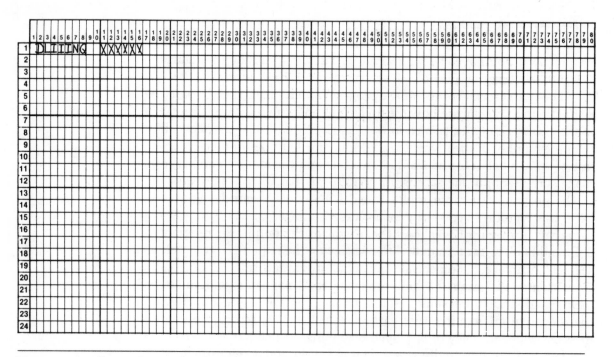

```
DLIIINQ  XXXXXX
```

Figure 12-8 Screen layout for the IMS DC inquiry program (part 1 of 2)

```
 INVOICE:  999999   DATE:  99/99/99     SUBTOTAL:        ZZZZZ.99-
                                        DISCOUNT:        ZZZZZ.99-
                                        SALES TAX:       ZZZZZ.99-
                                        FREIGHT:         ZZZZZ.99-
                                                         ---------
                                        BILLING:         ZZZZZ.99-
                                        PMTS/ADJS:       ZZZZZ.99-
                                                         ---------
                                        DUE:             ZZZZZ.99-
```

Figure 12-8 Screen layout for the IMS DC inquiry program (part 2 of 2)

Input message specifications

Will consist of one segment.
Will contain the transaction code DLIIINQ in positions 1 through 7.
Will contain blanks in positions 8 and 9.
Will contain the number of the invoice (receivable) to be displayed in positions 10 through 15.
Will contain no more than 79 bytes of text.

Output message specifications

Will consist of nine segments, mapped to the screen beginning at line 3.
May contain no more than 79 characters of text.
May contain fewer than 79 characters of text.

Figure 12-9 Message specifications for the IMS DC inquiry program

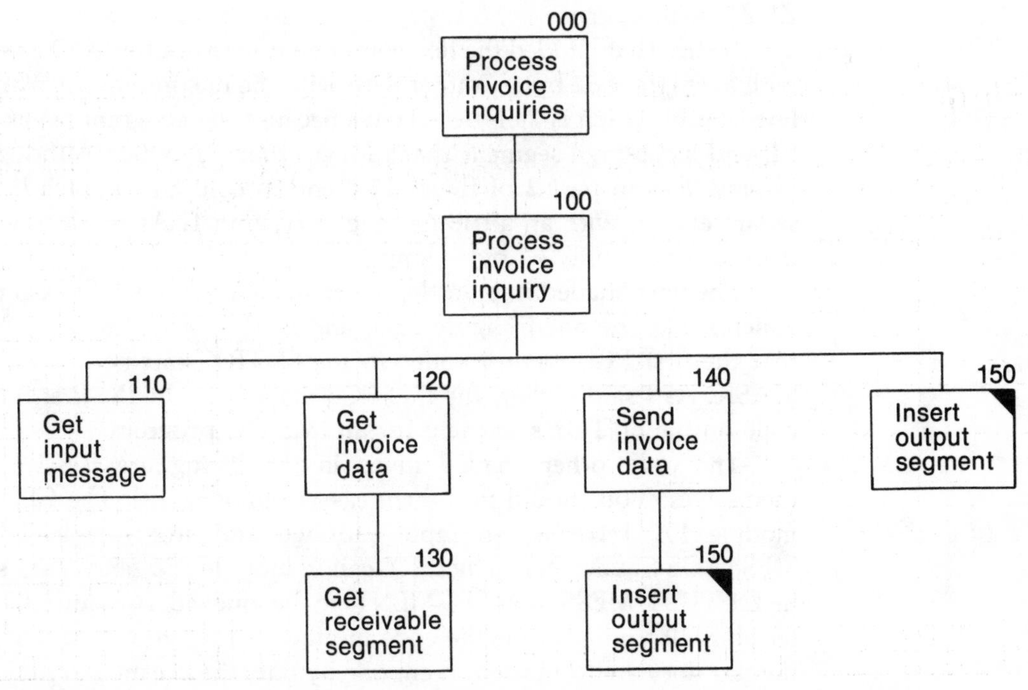

Figure 12-10 Structure chart for the IMS DC inquiry program

data base (module 120). If the data base GU call is successful, the program formats the data from the receivable segment (module 140) and repeatedly inserts output message segments (module 150 invoked from module 140) to build the complete message. On the other hand, if the requested receivable segment isn't found, the program issues a single insert call to send an error message (module 150 invoked from module 100).

Now, consider figure 12-11, the complete source listing for the IMS DC inquiry program. I've shaded the parts of the program I particularly want you to notice.

The field INPUT-MESSAGE-SEGMENT is used by the DC GU call. It's 83 bytes long, beginning with the 2-byte LL field and the 2-byte ZZ field, followed by the 79-byte user text area. Notice that I didn't assign initial values to the LL and ZZ fields; that's because IMS stores data in them after each call.

Next is the field OUTPUT-MESSAGE-SEGMENT, which is the I/O area used by the DC ISRT call. It also begins with two 2-byte fields: LL and the combination of Z1 and Z2. Because IMS depends on the values stored in those fields to process an output message segment properly, I coded initial values for them. The initial value of the LL field is the length of the entire I/O area (66 bytes), and the initial value of the Z1-Z2 field is zero.

Notice that I coded the text component in the output I/O area field with a length of 62 bytes, rather than with the maximum display screen line length, which is 79 bytes. That's because the program never needs to send a message segment that's longer than 62 bytes. Although the display lines in part 2 of figure 12-8 end in column 63, each line is a separate field, with an attribute byte in column 1. As result, the fields themselves are only 62 bytes long.

The next shaded item in the program listing is the I/O PCB mask, which is like the one in figure 12-5, and the ENTRY statement. Notice that the first PCB name I coded in the ENTRY statement is IO-PCB-MASK. As I said earlier, the I/O PCB mask must be the first one you code on the ENTRY statement for an IMS DC program.

The only other shaded items in the listing are the DC calls themselves. You should find them easy to understand. The GU call in module 110 retrieves an input message and stores it in INPUT-MESSAGE-SEGMENT. The ISRT call in module 150 sends data stored in OUTPUT-MESSAGE-SEGMENT to be queued for output to the terminal. If you examine the code in module 140, you'll see that all of the text lines are formatted; then, one by one, they're moved to the I/O area and inserted.

```
 IDENTIFICATION DIVISION.
*
 PROGRAM-ID.  DLIIINQ.
*
 ENVIRONMENT DIVISION.
*
 DATA DIVISION.
*
 WORKING-STORAGE SECTION.
*
 01  SWITCHES.
*
     05  INVOICE-FOUND-SW              PIC X        VALUE 'Y'.
         88  INVOICE-FOUND                          VALUE 'Y'.
     05  END-OF-MESSAGES-SW            PIC X        VALUE 'N'.
         88  END-OF-MESSAGES                        VALUE 'Y'.
*
 01  INPUT-MESSAGE-SEGMENT.
*
     05  INPUT-MSG-LL                  PIC S9(3)    COMP.
     05  INPUT-MSG-ZZ                  PIC S9(3)    COMP.
     05  INPUT-MSG-TRANS-CODE          PIC X(9).
     05  INPUT-MSG-INVOICE-NO          PIC X(6).
     05  FILLER                        PIC X(64).
*
 01  OUTPUT-MESSAGE-SEGMENT.
*
     05  OUTPUT-MSG-LL                 PIC S9(3)    COMP  VALUE +66.
     05  OUTPUT-MSG-Z1-Z2              PIC S9(3)    COMP  VALUE ZERO.
     05  OUTPUT-MSG-TEXT               PIC X(62).
*
 01  INVOICE-DATA-LINE-1.
*
     05  FILLER            PIC X(10)    VALUE 'INVOICE: '.
     05  IDL1-INV-NUMBER   PIC X(6).
     05  FILLER            PIC X(10)    VALUE '    DATE: '.
     05  IDL1-INV-DATE     PIC 99/99/99.
     05  FILLER            PIC X(5)     VALUE SPACE.
     05  FILLER            PIC X(14)    VALUE 'SUBTOTAL:     '.
     05  IDL1-PROD-TOTAL   PIC Z(5).99-.
*
 01  INVOICE-DATA-LINE-2.
*
     05  FILLER            PIC X(39)    VALUE SPACE.
     05  FILLER            PIC X(14)    VALUE 'DISCOUNT:     '.
     05  IDL2-CASH-DISC    PIC Z(5).99-.
*
 01  INVOICE-DATA-LINE-3.
*
     05  FILLER            PIC X(39)    VALUE SPACE.
     05  FILLER            PIC X(14)    VALUE 'SALES TAX:    '.
     05  IDL3-SALES-TAX    PIC Z(5).99-.
*
```

Figure 12-11 Source listing for the IMS DC inquiry program (part 1 of 5)

```
 01  INVOICE-DATA-LINE-4.
*
     05  FILLER              PIC X(39)    VALUE SPACE.
     05  FILLER              PIC X(14)    VALUE 'FREIGHT:      '.
     05  IDL4-FREIGHT        PIC Z(5).99-.
*
 01  INVOICE-DATA-LINE-5.
*
     05  FILLER              PIC X(53)    VALUE SPACE.
     05  FILLER              PIC X(9)     VALUE '-------- '.
*
 01  INVOICE-DATA-LINE-6.
*
     05  FILLER              PIC X(39)    VALUE SPACE.
     05  FILLER              PIC X(14)    VALUE 'BILLING:      '.
     05  IDL6-BILLING        PIC Z(5).99-.
*
 01  INVOICE-DATA-LINE-7.
*
     05  FILLER              PIC X(39)    VALUE SPACE.
     05  FILLER              PIC X(14)    VALUE 'PMTS/ADJS:    '.
     05  IDL7-PMTS-ADJS      PIC Z(5).99-.
*
 01  INVOICE-DATA-LINE-8.
*
     05  FILLER              PIC X(53)    VALUE SPACE.
     05  FILLER              PIC X(9)     VALUE '-------- '.
*
 01  INVOICE-DATA-LINE-9.
*
     05  FILLER              PIC X(39)    VALUE SPACE.
     05  FILLER              PIC X(14)    VALUE 'DUE:          '.
     05  IDL9-BALANCE        PIC Z(5).99-.
*
 01  ERROR-LINE.
*
     05  FILLER              PIC X(8)     VALUE 'INVOICE '.
     05  EL-INVOICE-NO       PIC X(6).
     05  FILLER              PIC X(10)    VALUE ' NOT FOUND'.
     05  FILLER              PIC X(38)    VALUE SPACE.
*
 01  DLI-FUNCTIONS.
*
     05  DLI-GU                        PIC X(4)     VALUE 'GU  '.
     05  DLI-GHU                       PIC X(4)     VALUE 'GHU '.
     05  DLI-GN                        PIC X(4)     VALUE 'GN  '.
     05  DLI-GHN                       PIC X(4)     VALUE 'GHN '.
     05  DLI-GNP                       PIC X(4)     VALUE 'GNP '.
     05  DLI-GHNP                      PIC X(4)     VALUE 'GHNP'.
     05  DLI-ISRT                      PIC X(4)     VALUE 'ISRT'.
     05  DLI-DLET                      PIC X(4)     VALUE 'DLET'.
     05  DLI-REPL                      PIC X(4)     VALUE 'REPL'.
     05  DLI-CHKP                      PIC X(4)     VALUE 'CHKP'.
     05  DLI-XRST                      PIC X(4)     VALUE 'XRST'.
     05  DLI-PCB                       PIC X(4)     VALUE 'PCB '.
```

Figure 12-11 Source listing for the IMS DC inquiry program (part 2 of 5)

```
*
 01   RECEIVABLE-SEGMENT.
*
      05   RS-INVOICE-NUMBER         PIC X(6).
      05   RS-INVOICE-DATE           PIC X(6).
      05   RS-PO-NUMBER              PIC X(25).
      05   RS-PRODUCT-TOTAL          PIC S9(5)V99      COMP-3.
      05   RS-CASH-DISCOUNT          PIC S9(5)V99      COMP-3.
      05   RS-SALES-TAX              PIC S9(5)V99      COMP-3.
      05   RS-FREIGHT                PIC S9(5)V99      COMP-3.
      05   RS-BALANCE-DUE            PIC S9(5)V99      COMP-3.
*
 01   INVOICE-NO-SSA.
*
      05   FILLER                    PIC X(9)     VALUE 'CRRECSEG('.
      05   FILLER                    PIC X(10)    VALUE 'CRRECXNO ='.
      05   INVOICE-NO-SSA-VALUE      PIC X(6).
      05   FILLER                    PIC X        VALUE ')'.
*
 LINKAGE SECTION.
*
 01   IO-PCB-MASK.
*
      05   IO-PCB-LOGICAL-TERMINAL PIC X(8).
      05   FILLER                    PIC XX.
      05   IO-PCB-STATUS-CODE        PIC XX.
      05   IO-PCB-DATE               PIC S9(7)         COMP-3.
      05   IO-PCB-TIME               PIC S9(6)V9       COMP-3.
      05   IO-PCB-MSG-SEQ-NUMBER     PIC S9(5)         COMP.
      05   IO-PCB-MOD-NAME           PIC X(8).
      05   IO-PCB-USER-ID            PIC X(8).
*
 01   CR-PCB-MASK.
*
      05   CR-PCB-DBD-NAME           PIC X(8).
      05   CR-PCB-SEGMENT-LEVEL      PIC XX.
      05   CR-PCB-STATUS-CODE        PIC XX.
      05   CR-PCB-PROC-OPTIONS       PIC X(4).
      05   FILLER                    PIC S9(5)         COMP.
      05   CR-PCB-SEGMENT-NAME       PIC X(8).
      05   CR-PCB-KEY-LENGTH         PIC S9(5)         COMP.
      05   CR-PCB-NUMB-SENS-SEGS     PIC S9(5)         COMP.
      05   CR-PCB-KEY                PIC X(22).
*
 PROCEDURE DIVISION.
*
      ENTRY 'DLITCBL' USING IO-PCB-MASK
                            CR-PCB-MASK.
*
 000-PROCESS-INVOICE-INQUIRIES.
*
      PERFORM 100-PROCESS-INVOICE-INQUIRY
          UNTIL END-OF-MESSAGES.
      GOBACK.
*
```

Figure 12-11 Source listing for the IMS DC inquiry program (part 3 of 5)

```
 100-PROCESS-INVOICE-INQUIRY.
*
     PERFORM 110-GET-INPUT-MESSAGE.
     IF NOT END-OF-MESSAGES
         PERFORM 120-GET-INVOICE-DATA
         IF INVOICE-FOUND
             PERFORM 140-SEND-INVOICE-DATA
         ELSE
             MOVE INPUT-MSG-INVOICE-NO TO EL-INVOICE-NO
             MOVE ERROR-LINE           TO OUTPUT-MSG-TEXT
             PERFORM 150-INSERT-OUTPUT-SEGMENT.
*
 110-GET-INPUT-MESSAGE.
*
     CALL 'CBLTDLI' USING DLI-GU
                          IO-PCB-MASK
                          INPUT-MESSAGE-SEGMENT.
     IF IO-PCB-STATUS-CODE = 'QC'
         MOVE 'Y' TO END-OF-MESSAGES-SW.
*
 120-GET-INVOICE-DATA.
*
     MOVE 'Y'                    TO INVOICE-FOUND-SW.
     MOVE INPUT-MSG-INVOICE-NO TO INVOICE-NO-SSA-VALUE.
     PERFORM 130-GET-RECEIVABLE-SEGMENT.
*
 130-GET-RECEIVABLE-SEGMENT.
*
     CALL 'CBLTDLI' USING DLI-GU
                          CR-PCB-MASK
                          RECEIVABLE-SEGMENT
                          INVOICE-NO-SSA.
     IF CR-PCB-STATUS-CODE NOT = SPACE
         MOVE 'N' TO INVOICE-FOUND-SW.
*
 140-SEND-INVOICE-DATA.
*
     MOVE RS-INVOICE-NUMBER   TO IDL1-INV-NUMBER.
     MOVE RS-INVOICE-DATE     TO IDL1-INV-DATE.
     MOVE RS-PRODUCT-TOTAL    TO IDL1-PROD-TOTAL.
     MOVE RS-CASH-DISCOUNT    TO IDL2-CASH-DISC.
     MOVE RS-SALES-TAX        TO IDL3-SALES-TAX.
     MOVE RS-FREIGHT          TO IDL4-FREIGHT.
     COMPUTE IDL6-BILLING =    RS-PRODUCT-TOTAL -
                               RS-CASH-DISCOUNT +
                               RS-SALES-TAX +
                               RS-FREIGHT.
     COMPUTE IDL7-PMTS-ADJS =  RS-BALANCE-DUE -
                              (RS-PRODUCT-TOTAL -
                               RS-CASH-DISCOUNT +
                               RS-SALES-TAX +
                               RS-FREIGHT).
```

Figure 12-11 Source listing for the IMS DC inquiry program (part 4 of 5)

```
      MOVE RS-BALANCE-DUE       TO IDL9-BALANCE.
      MOVE INVOICE-DATA-LINE-1 TO OUTPUT-MSG-TEXT.
      PERFORM 150-INSERT-OUTPUT-SEGMENT.
      MOVE INVOICE-DATA-LINE-2 TO OUTPUT-MSG-TEXT.
      PERFORM 150-INSERT-OUTPUT-SEGMENT.
      MOVE INVOICE-DATA-LINE-3 TO OUTPUT-MSG-TEXT.
      PERFORM 150-INSERT-OUTPUT-SEGMENT.
      MOVE INVOICE-DATA-LINE-4 TO OUTPUT-MSG-TEXT.
      PERFORM 150-INSERT-OUTPUT-SEGMENT.
      MOVE INVOICE-DATA-LINE-5 TO OUTPUT-MSG-TEXT.
      PERFORM 150-INSERT-OUTPUT-SEGMENT.
      MOVE INVOICE-DATA-LINE-6 TO OUTPUT-MSG-TEXT.
      PERFORM 150-INSERT-OUTPUT-SEGMENT.
      MOVE INVOICE-DATA-LINE-7 TO OUTPUT-MSG-TEXT.
      PERFORM 150-INSERT-OUTPUT-SEGMENT.
      MOVE INVOICE-DATA-LINE-8 TO OUTPUT-MSG-TEXT.
      PERFORM 150-INSERT-OUTPUT-SEGMENT.
      MOVE INVOICE-DATA-LINE-9 TO OUTPUT-MSG-TEXT.
      PERFORM 150-INSERT-OUTPUT-SEGMENT.
*
 150-INSERT-OUTPUT-SEGMENT.
*
      CALL 'CBLTDLI' USING DLI-ISRT
                           IO-PCB-MASK
                           OUTPUT-MESSAGE-SEGMENT.
*
```

Figure 12-11 Source listing for the IMS DC inquiry program (part 5 of 5)

Discussion

Writing application programs for the IMS DC environment is complicated. Although the program example in this chapter is a functional DC program, it's a simple one. As a result, I don't encourage you to try to develop a production DC program using it alone as an example. Instead, you should read *Part 2* of this series.

Terminology

dependent region
IMS control region
CTL region
IMS control program
modules
batch message processing region

BMP region
message processing program region
MPP region
message
input message
transaction
transaction code
output message
data communications modules
queue management modules
message queue
QPOOL
message queueing
Message Format Service
MFS
scheduling modules
scheduling
I/O PCB
LL field
ZZ field
Z1 field
Z2 field

Objectives

1. Compare and contrast the following types of DL/I programs:

   a. DL/I batch program
   b. batch message processing program
   c. message processing program

2. Describe the steps a typical IMS DC message processing program goes through as it processes one transaction.

3. Compare the COBOL requirements for issuing DL/I data base calls and those for issuing DL/I message processing calls.

4. Given complete specifications, design and code an IMS DC program of complexity comparable to that of the program example in this chapter.

Chapter 13

Interactive programs in the CICS/VS environment

If you're already familiar with CICS, this chapter will show you what you need to know to develop CICS programs that process DL/I data bases. If you aren't familiar with CICS, this chapter won't show you all you need to know about it, although it will introduce you to the CICS environment. In the first section of the chapter, I'll describe CICS and introduce the basic concepts and terms you need to know to understand the sample program in the second section of the chapter, which focuses on the DL/I considerations for CICS programming. If you already have CICS experience, you can skip the first section.

CICS CONCEPTS AND TERMINOLOGY

This section briefly describes how CICS works. Then, it presents some basic considerations all CICS programmers must keep in mind.

How CICS/VS works

CICS is designed to support multiple users running a variety of interactive programs at the same time. Simply put, CICS is an interface between the application programs in an interactive system and the host operating system, as figure 13-1 shows. Application programs commu-

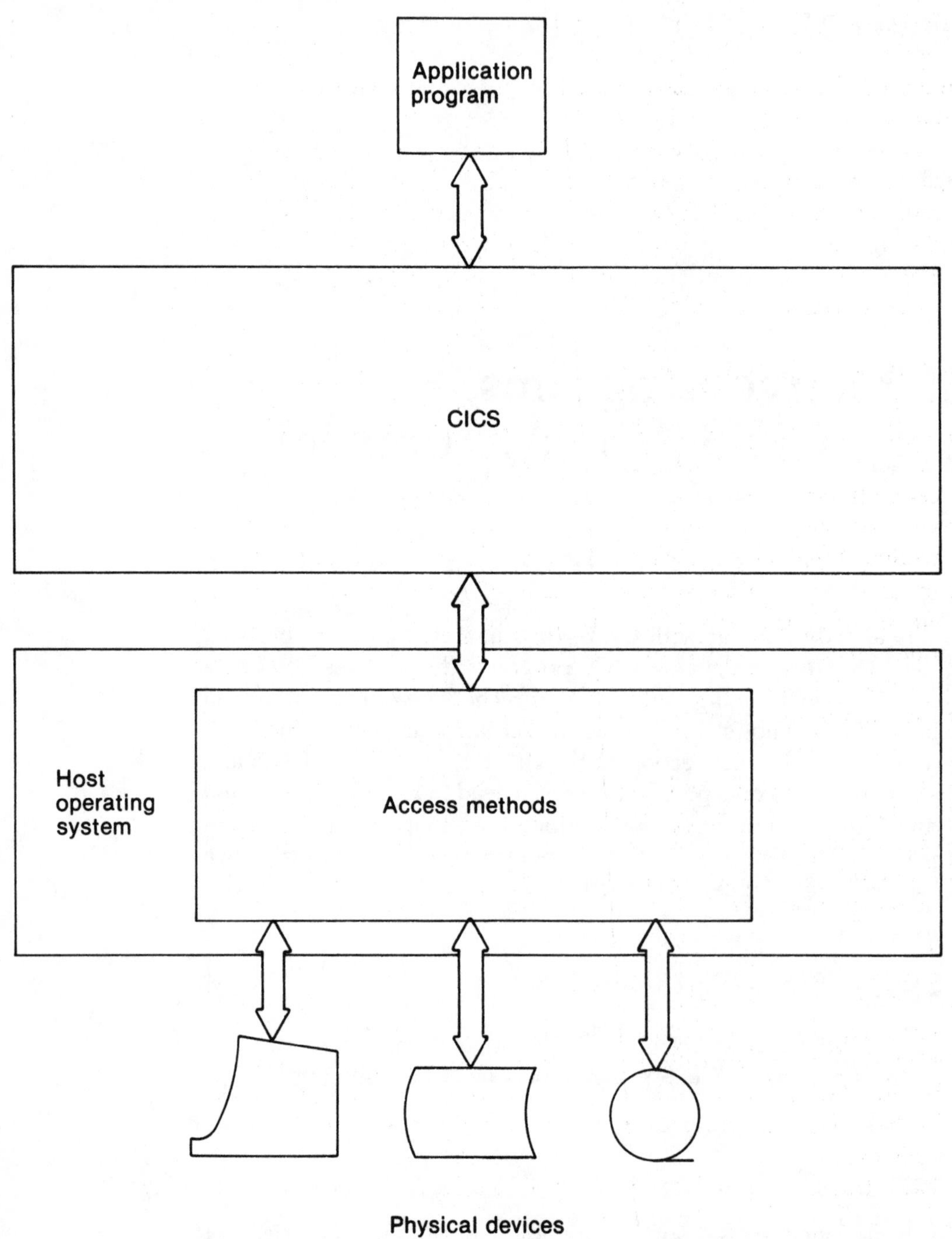

Figure 13-1 How CICS acts as an interface between the operating system and application programs

nicate with CICS, which in turn communicates with access methods through the host operating system. As far as the operating system is concerned, CICS is itself an application program. That means CICS runs in one of the system's partitions or regions.

For example, in figure 13-2, CICS is running on a DOS/VSE system in the foreground-2 partition. Usually, CICS requires a large partition or region (five megabytes of virtual storage isn't unusual) because it's a complex software product with many modules and because it allows many user application programs (or tasks) to execute at the same time.

Multitasking In CICS, a *task* is the execution of an application program (or perhaps several application programs) for a specific user. One of the basic features of CICS is multitasking. *Multitasking* simply means that CICS allows more than one task to execute at the same time. For example, in figure 13-2, six tasks are running in the CICS production partition.

Multitasking is similar to multiprogramming. Basically, multiprogramming means that an operating system allows several programs to execute at the same time. In contrast, multitasking means that a program running in a single partition or region lets several tasks execute at the same time. For all practical purposes, multitasking is the same thing as multiprogramming one level down.

Notice in figure 13-2 that three of the CICS terminal users (1, 3, and 6) are running the same application program: order entry. If the same program were loaded into storage at three different locations, valuable virtual storage would be wasted. CICS uses a concept called *multithreading* so only one copy of a program is loaded into storage, regardless of how many users are running it. Fortunately, this is transparent to you as an application programmer.

Transactions and task initiation A *transaction* is a predefined unit of work a terminal user can invoke. When a transaction is invoked, a specified application program is loaded into storage (if it isn't already there) and a task is started. The difference between a transaction and a task is that while many users can invoke the same transaction, each is given his own task.

Each transaction is identified by a unique four-character code called a *transaction identifier* (or just *trans-id*). An operator initiates a transaction by entering its trans-id into the terminal. For example, to run an order entry program, the operator might enter a trans-id like ORD1.

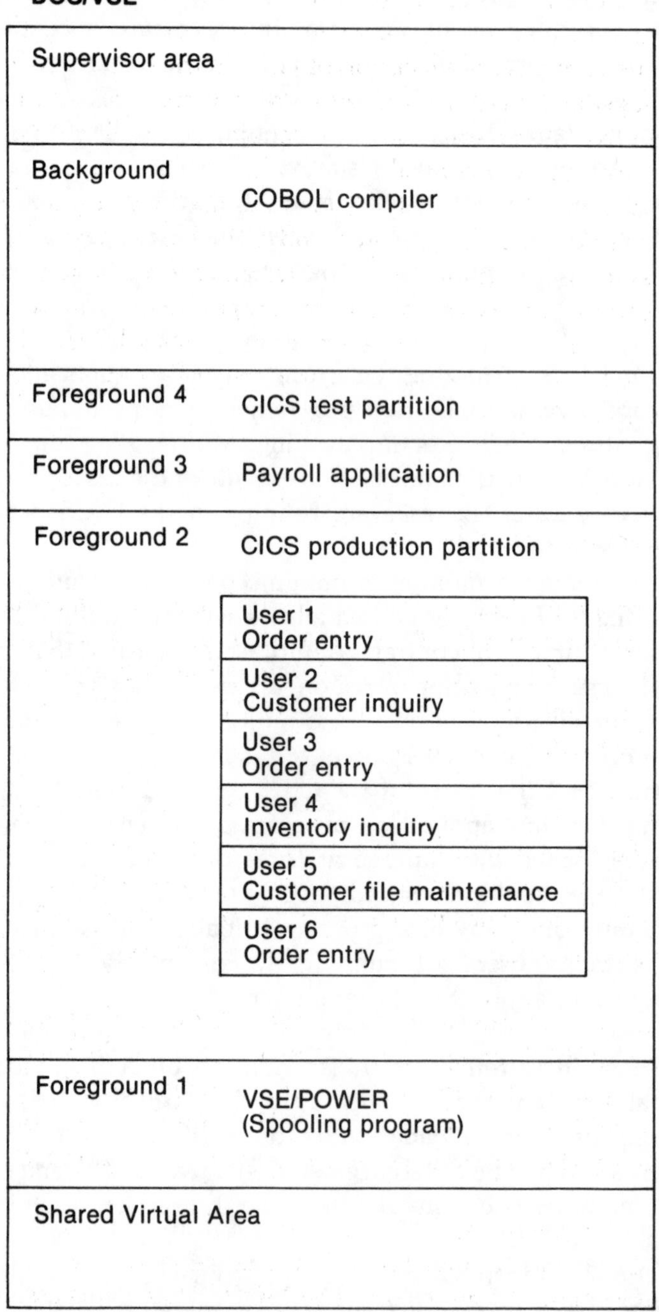

Figure 13-2 Multiprogramming and multitasking in a CICS partition

CICS modules CICS is a complicated software product that consists of many components called *management modules*. For example, the task control module controls the execution of tasks in the CICS system. Other CICS management modules are terminal control, file control, transient data control, temporary storage control, journal control, program control, and interval control.

When DL/I is used with CICS, DL/I modules are loaded into the CICS partition or region and are executed under the control of CICS. There are some systems programming considerations for making the DL/I-CICS connection, but as an application programmer, you don't have to worry about them. Your program simply issues DL/I calls, which are processed by the DL/I modules within the CICS partition just as if you'd issued the calls in a batch program.

Basic CICS programming considerations

An application program that executes under CICS is somewhat different from a batch program. Although you can use most standard COBOL features in a CICS program, including the DL/I call, to perform many functions (like terminal or VSAM file I/O), your program has to issue *CICS commands*.

CICS commands The top section of figure 13-3 shows a typical CICS command. This command (RECEIVE) causes data from the user's terminal to be moved to a working-storage area in the program. As you can see, a CICS command begins with EXEC CICS and ends with END-EXEC. There are dozens of CICS commands, and, as you'd expect, their formats vary.

Because CICS commands aren't standard COBOL, they don't make sense to the COBOL compiler. As a result, to compile a CICS COBOL program, you first must process your source code with the *CICS command-level translator* to convert CICS commands to a form that's meaningful to the COBOL compiler. Figure 13-4 shows this process.

The translator converts each CICS command into a series of COBOL MOVE statements followed by a CALL statement, as you can see in the bottom section of figure 13-3. The MOVE statements assign values to the fields that are the arguments of the CALL statement. The CALL statement activates the CICS command-level interface to invoke the required CICS services. As you can see, the source code for the

Original source code

```
 EXEC CICS
      RECEIVE MAP('MORMAP1')
              MAPSET('MORSET1')
              INTO(MORTGAGE-CALCULATION-MAP)
 END-EXEC.
```

Translated source code

```
*EXEC CICS
*     RECEIVE MAP('MORMAP1')
*             MAPSET('MORSET1')
*             INTO(MORTGAGE-CALCULATION-MAP)
*END-EXEC.
      MOVE '              00079    ' TO DFHEIVO
      MOVE 'MORMAP1' TO DFHC0070
      MOVE 'MORSET1' TO DFHC0071
     CALL 'DFHEI1' USING DFHEIVO  DFHC0070
      MORTGAGE-CALCULATION-MAP DFHDUMMY DFHC0071.
```

Figure 13-3 Sample source and translated code

original command is included as comments in the translated version of the program; it's there only to help you read the translated program.

In addition to converting all CICS commands to MOVE and CALL statements, the translator inserts other code in your program's Working-Storage and Linkage Sections. Most of it isn't relevant to you.

Basic Mapping Support A part of CICS that you'll probably use is *Basic Mapping Support*, or *BMS*. BMS is an interface within CICS between the application program and the terminal control module. To receive data from or send data to a terminal, the application program issues a CICS command that invokes BMS.

To format terminal data, BMS uses map definitions you code in a special kind of assembler language program called a *mapset*. When you use BMS, you can exercise a high degree of control over the format of data displayed on and retrieved from a terminal. Although I'm not going to show you how to code and use BMS mapsets, you should realize that most CICS programs do formatted terminal I/O through BMS and that you'll probably have to use it in your CICS programs.

Pseudo-conversational program design Most CICS application programs have to be written so they don't tie up valuable virtual storage resources. Although a single CICS system can support hundreds

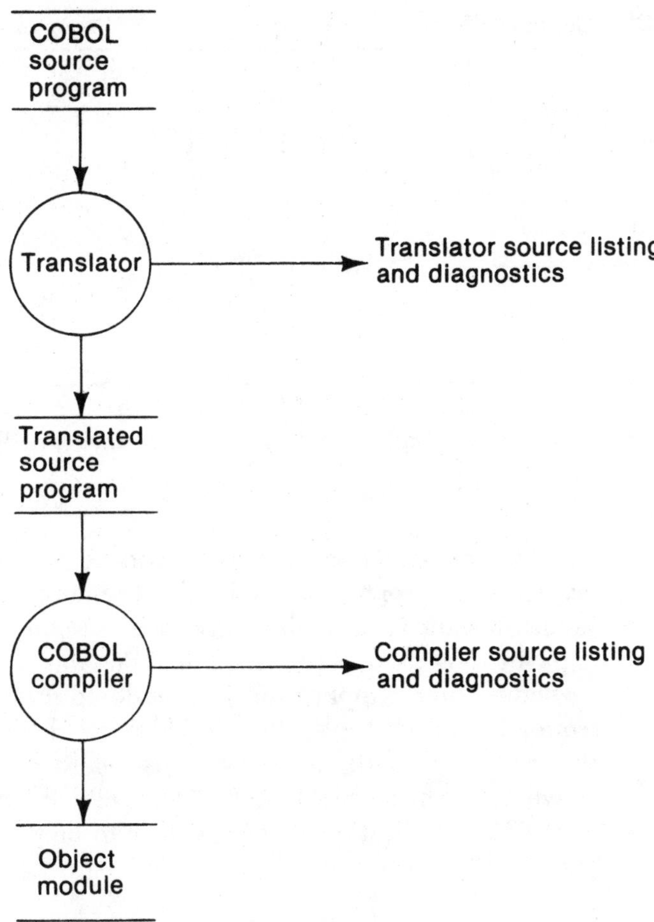

Figure 13-4 The translation and compilation process

of terminals, it can't operate efficiently if programs remain in storage while they wait for data from terminals. As a result, most CICS programs are written using the *pseudo-conversational programming* technique.

With pseudo-conversational programming, a program ends after it sends data to a terminal. Then, it's restarted when the operator completes an entry. This is called "pseudo-conversational" because although the program appears to be carrying on a conversation with the terminal user, it's actually not present in storage. The terminal user doesn't realize that the program ends each time it sends output to the terminal.

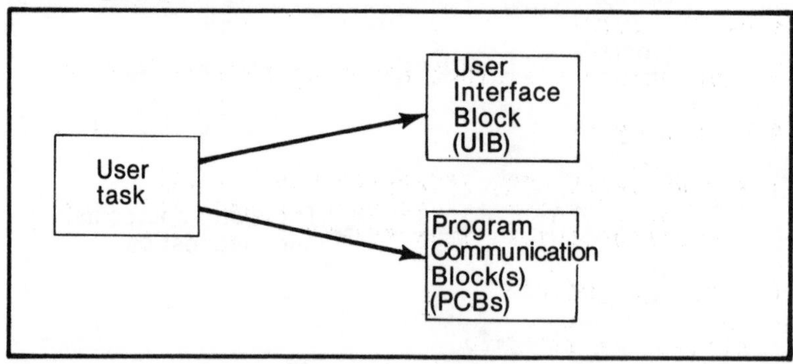

Figure 13-5 A DL/I task must establish addressability to the User Interface Block and one or more PCBs

This programming technique can be confusing and complicated because your program has to be able to figure out where it is when it is restarted. Much of the difficulty in developing a CICS program is in implementing pseudo-conversational design.

For some applications, pseudo-conversational design isn't required. For example, the program in this chapter isn't pseudo-conversational and, as a result, is relatively easy to understand. However, keep in mind that this program is unusual in that respect; most CICS application programs have to be pseudo-conversational.

DL/I CONSIDERATIONS FOR CICS PROGRAMMING

If you've developed CICS programs, you'll have little trouble learning how to code a DL/I program for execution under CICS. In fact, as I've already mentioned, DL/I calls in a CICS program are just like those in a batch program. However, there are two differences you need to know before you write a CICS DL/I program. First, your program must issue a special DL/I call—the *scheduling call*—before it can issue any other DL/I call. And second, DL/I error checking under CICS is more complicated than it is in batch programs.

How to schedule a PSB

Figure 13-5 shows that before your program can issue a DL/I call to process a data base, it must have access to two types of virtual storage

```
*************************************************************************
*                                                                       *
*       MODULE-NAME = DLIUIB                                            *
*                                                                       *
*       DESCRIPTIVE NAME = STRUCTURE FOR USER INTERFACE BLOCK           *
*                                                                       *
*       STATUS = VERSION 1.5                                    @D15D38D*
*                                                                       *
*       FUNCTION = DESCRIBE USER INTERFACE BLOCK FIELDS.                *
*                  THE UIB CONTAINS SCHEDULING AND SYSTEM CALL          *
*                  STATUS INFORMATION RETURNED TO THE USER.             *
*                                                                       *
*       MODULE-TYPE = STRUCTURE                                         *
*                                                                       *
*       CHANGE ACTIVITY = @BCAC80A                                      *
*                                                                       *
*************************************************************************
 01    DLIUIB.
*      DLIUIB    EXTENDED CALL USER INTERFACE BLOCK
       02 UIBPCBAL PICTURE S9(8) USAGE IS COMPUTATIONAL.
*         UIBPCBAL      PCB ADDRESS LIST
       02 UIBRCODE.
*         UIBRCODE      DL/I RETURN CODES
            03 UIBFCTR PICTURE X.
*              UIBFCTR     RETURN CODES
               88  FCNORESP     VALUE ' '.
               88  FCNOTOPEN    VALUE ' '.
               88  FCINVREQ     VALUE ' '.
            03 UIBDLTR PICTURE X.
*              UIBDLTR     ADDITIONAL INFORMATION
               88  DLPSBNF      VALUE ' '.
               88  DLTASKNA     VALUE ' '.
               88  DLPSBSCH     VALUE ' '.
               88  DLLANGCON    VALUE ' '.
               88  DLPSBFAIL    VALUE ' '.
               88  DLPSBNA      VALUE ' '.
               88  DLTERMNS     VALUE ' '.
               88  DLFUNCNS     VALUE ' '.
               88  DLINA        VALUE '\'.
```

Figure 13-6 The DLIUIB copy book

areas: one or more Program Communication Blocks, which you already know about, and the *User Interface Block*, or *UIB*. The UIB is an interface area between your program and the CICS routines that communicate with DL/I. Each DL/I program requires a single UIB under CICS.

Figure 13-6 shows an IBM-supplied copy book named DLIUIB you can include in your program to define the UIB. If you'll study it for a moment, you'll see that the User Interface Block consists of just two fields. They're the 02-level items shaded in figure 13-6: UIBPCBAL and

UIBRCODE. You'll see how both of these fields are used later in this chapter. I use this copy book as it is, but you can code your own simplified version if you like.

Linkage Section fields in CICS programs As figure 13-5 indicates, the UIB and PCB are data areas that exist outside of your program's storage. In other words, the UIB and PCB are in storage that's owned by CICS, not by your application program. As a result, you must define them in your program's Linkage Section rather than in its Working-Storage Section. When you define a field in your program's Linkage Section, you are *not* allocating storage for it. Instead, you're defining how the field's contents are organized. The storage the field uses is allocated by CICS, outside of your program. This shouldn't be new to you: the PCB mask you define in the Linkage Section of a batch DL/I program defines an area of storage outside your program.

When CICS loads and executes a program, it expects to find two fields defined in the Linkage Section: the Execute Interface Block (DFHEIB) and the Communication Area (DFHCOMMAREA). The COBOL that defines the Execute Interface Block is automatically inserted by the command-level translator, so you don't have to code it yourself. And DFHCOMMAREA is optional; if you omit it, the translator inserts a one-byte communication area.

Because these fields are required in all CICS programs (whether they use DL/I or not), CICS automatically provides *addressability* to them. However, if you define other fields in the Linkage Section (like the UIB and PCB), you must establish addressability to them yourself. If you don't, your program won't be able to access the information stored in them. In a batch program, this addressability is established when you code the ENTRY statement at the beginning of your program; but you don't code the ENTRY statement in a CICS DL/I program.

How to use BLL cells to access CICS areas To establish addressability to a field outside your program under CICS, you use a convention called *Base Locator for Linkage* (or *BLL*). Figure 13-7 illustrates this convention. Quite simply, you must define an 01-level item in the Linkage Section following DFHCOMMAREA. In figure 13-7, I call this item BLL-CELLS, but the name doesn't matter. Each field in BLL-CELLS is a pointer that stores the address of a subsequent Linkage Section field. These pointers must be defined as binary fullwords (PIC S9(8) COMP).

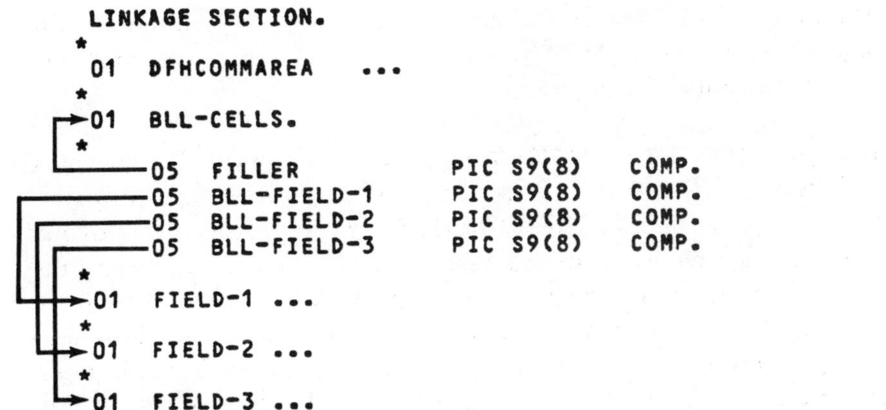
```
LINKAGE SECTION.
*
 01  DFHCOMMAREA    ...
*
 01  BLL-CELLS.
*
     05  FILLER          PIC S9(8)   COMP.
     05  BLL-FIELD-1     PIC S9(8)   COMP.
     05  BLL-FIELD-2     PIC S9(8)   COMP.
     05  BLL-FIELD-3     PIC S9(8)   COMP.
*
 01  FIELD-1 ...
*
 01  FIELD-2 ...
*
 01  FIELD-3 ...
```

Figure 13-7 BLL cells are used to address data areas described in the Linkage Section

The first pointer (FILLER) contains the address of the BLL-CELLS item itself. Then, each subsequent pointer contains the address of an 01-level item that follows in the Linkage Section. In figure 13-7, the pointer named BLL-FIELD-1 is used to establish addressability to FIELD-1. Similarly, BLL-FIELD-2 is used for FIELD-2 and BLL-FIELD-3 is used for FIELD-3. The names of the BLL cells don't matter; what does matter is the order in which you code them.

How to obtain the address of the UIB and PCBs Before you can use Linkage Section fields (other than the Execute Interface Block or the Communication Area), you must load the BLL-cell fields with their addresses. The question is, how do you obtain the addresses of the UIB and PCBs? Figure 13-8 gives part of the answer. Here, you can see that one of the UIB fields (UIBPCBAL) points indirectly to the PCBs. UIBPCBAL contains the address of another data area that contains a list of PCB addresses. In other words, the UIB points to a PCB address list which, in turn, points to all of the PCBs.

Why does PCB addressing work that way? Simply, to provide for a variable number of PCBs within a PSB. Although the User Interface Block is a fixed length area, it needs to point to a variable number of PCBs. That's why the variable length PCB address list is used. It contains one pointer for each PCB in the program's PSB. In figure 13-8, two PCBs are defined, so the PCB address list contains two pointers.

An implication of the addressing scheme in figure 13-8 is that you must define an additional Linkage Section field for the PCB address list.

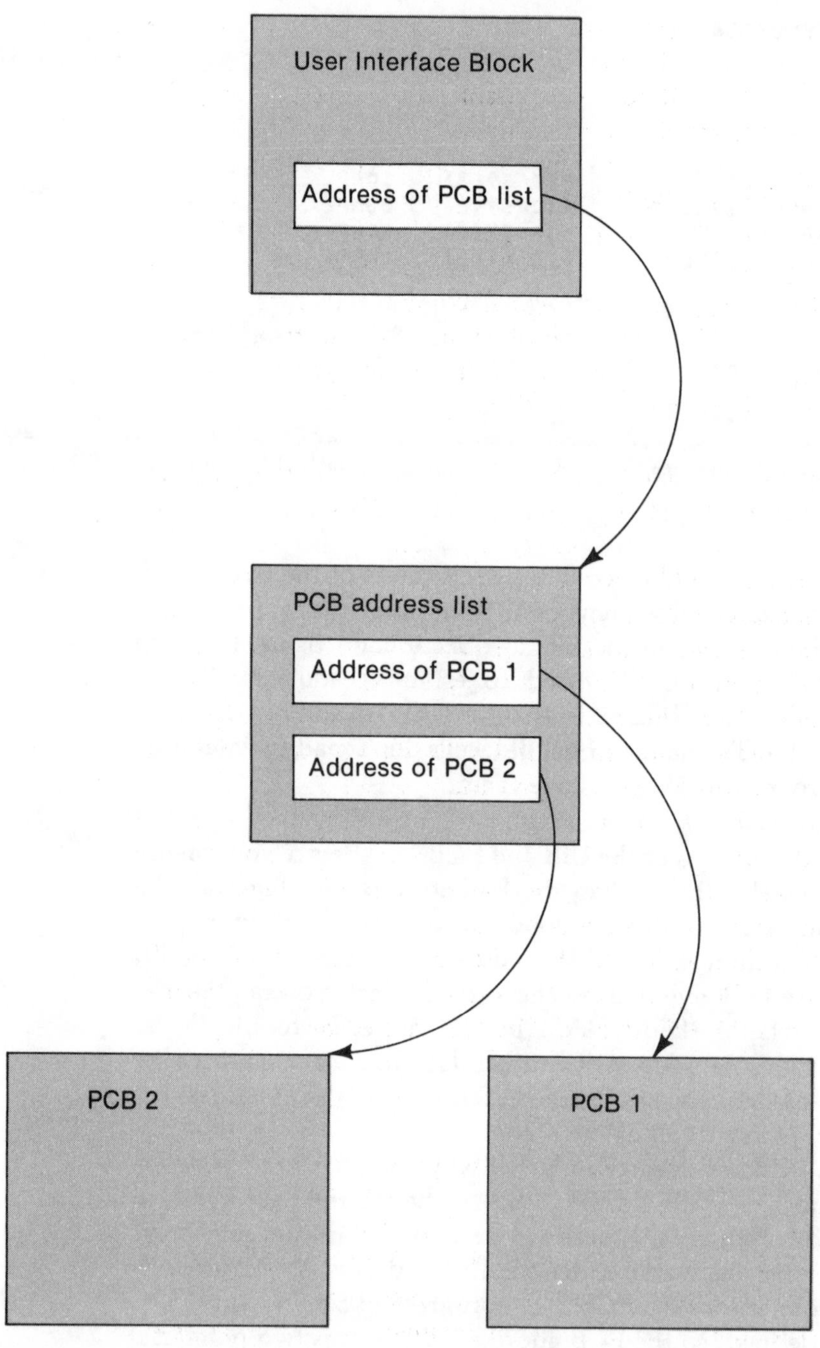

Figure 13-8 A field in the UIB points to a list of PCB addresses

In fact, for the example shown in figure 13-8, you'd define four Linkage Section fields: one for the UIB, one for the PCB address list, and one for each of the two PCBs. In addition, you'd define four corresponding BLL cells to establish addressability to those fields.

Figure 13-8 shows that if you know the address of the UIB, you can establish addressability to the PCBs by using the pointer addresses in the PCB address list. The part of the addressing question left unanswered by figure 13-8 is how you get the address of the UIB to begin with. That's where the scheduling call comes in: its function is to acquire storage for the User Interface Block and return its address to your program. So once you've issued a scheduling call, you can address the UIB, then the PCB address list, and finally the PCBs themselves.

Because I want to be sure you understand how PCB scheduling works, look at figure 13-9. The four parts of this figure show how your program establishes addressability to the required DL/I areas. The top section of each part shows the COBOL statement issued by the program. The bottom section shows the relationship of Linkage Section entries to actual storage areas. The areas that are addressable after each COBOL statement executes are shaded. (For the sake of the illustration, assume the PSB contains two PCBs, called PCB-1 and PCB-2.)

Part 1 of figure 13-9 shows the scheduling call. DLI-PCB is the name of a four-character field defined in the Working-Storage Section that contains the function code required for a scheduling call: PCB. PSB-NAME is an eight-character working-storage field that contains the name of the PSB this program uses. The scheduling call returns the address of the UIB in BLL-UIB. As the shading indicates, the Linkage Section field DLIUIB masks the actual UIB.

To establish addressability to the PCB address list, all you do is move the pointer (UIBPCBAL) to the BLL cell for the address list. That's what part 2 of figure 13-9 illustrates. The MOVE statement

```
MOVE UIBPCBAL TO BLL-PCB-AL
```

loads the address of the PCB address list into BLL-PCB-AL. As a result, PCB-ADDRESS-LIST now masks the actual address list.

Part 3 shows how to establish addressability to the first PCB: a MOVE statement loads the first pointer in the PCB address list into the BLL cell for PCB-1. After the MOVE statement executes, PCB-1 correctly masks the first PCB. In a similar manner, part 4 shows how addressability is established for the second PCB.

To summarize, the scheduling call places the UIB address in its BLL cell. Then, it's just a matter of moving pointers into appropriate BLL cells so that all of the required fields are addressable. In fact, as you've

The program issues the scheduling call:

```
CALL 'CBLTDLI' USING DLI-PCB
                     PSB-NAME
                     BLL-UIB.
MOVE UIBPCBAL    TO BLL-PCB-AL.
MOVE PCB-1-ADDR TO BLL-PCB-1.
MOVE PCB-2-ADDR TO BLL-PCB-2.
```

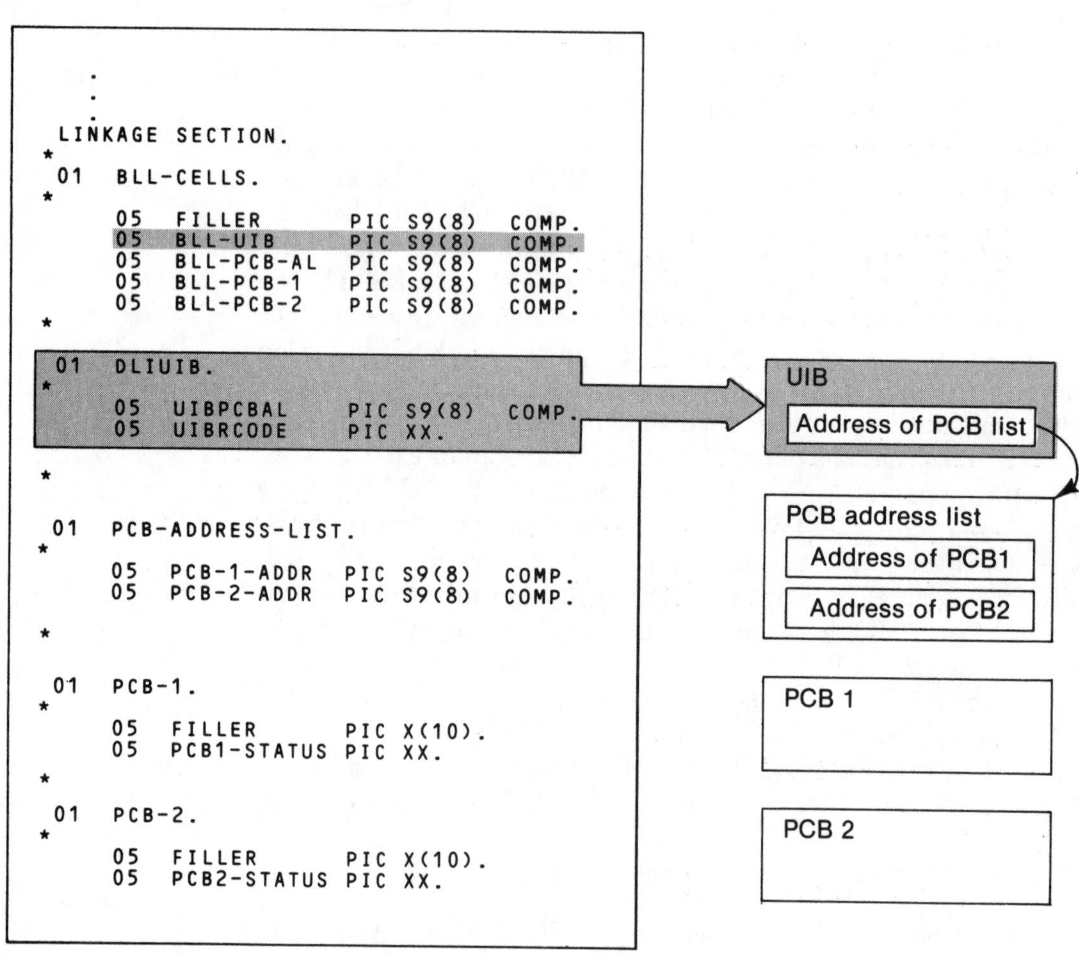

Figure 13-9 Addressing DL/I control blocks (part 1 of 4)

seen in figure 13-9, the COBOL coding required to establish addressability to all of the DL/I areas is simple; it's just a CALL statement followed by a series of MOVE statements. With the background in this

The program loads the BLL cell for the PCB address list:

```
CALL 'CBLTDLI' USING DLI-PCB
                     PSB-NAME
                     BLL-UIB.
MOVE UIBPCBAL    TO BLL-PCB-AL.
MOVE PCB-1-ADDR TO BLL-PCB-1.
MOVE PCB-2-ADDR TO BLL-PCB-2.
```

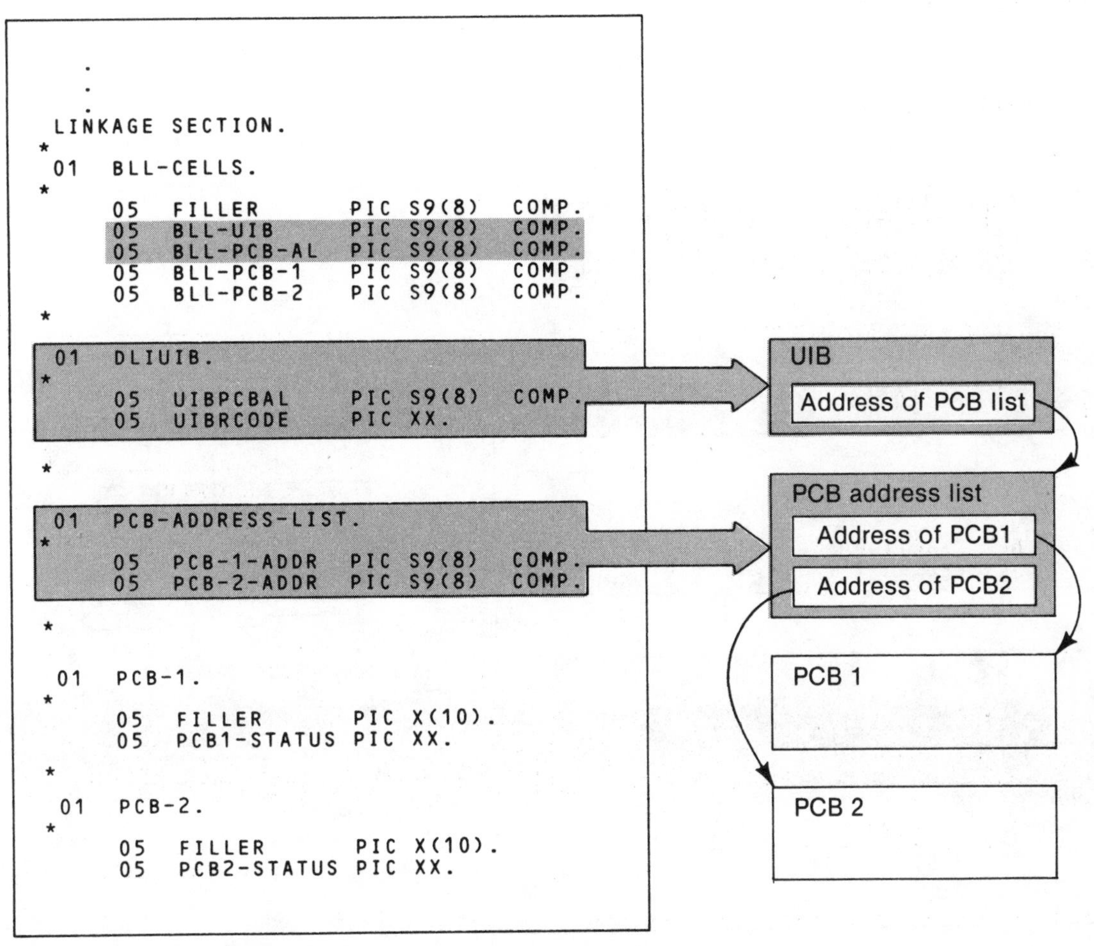

Figure 13-9 Addressing DL/I control blocks (part 2 of 4)

section, though, you'll better understand what this simple code really accomplishes when you see it used in the program example later in this chapter.

The program loads the BLL cell for PCB-1:

```
CALL 'CBLTDLI' USING DLI-PCB
                     PSB-NAME
                     BLL-UIB.
MOVE UIBPCBAL    TO BLL-PCB-AL.
MOVE PCB-1-ADDR TO BLL-PCB-1.
MOVE PCB-2-ADDR TO BLL-PCB-2.
```

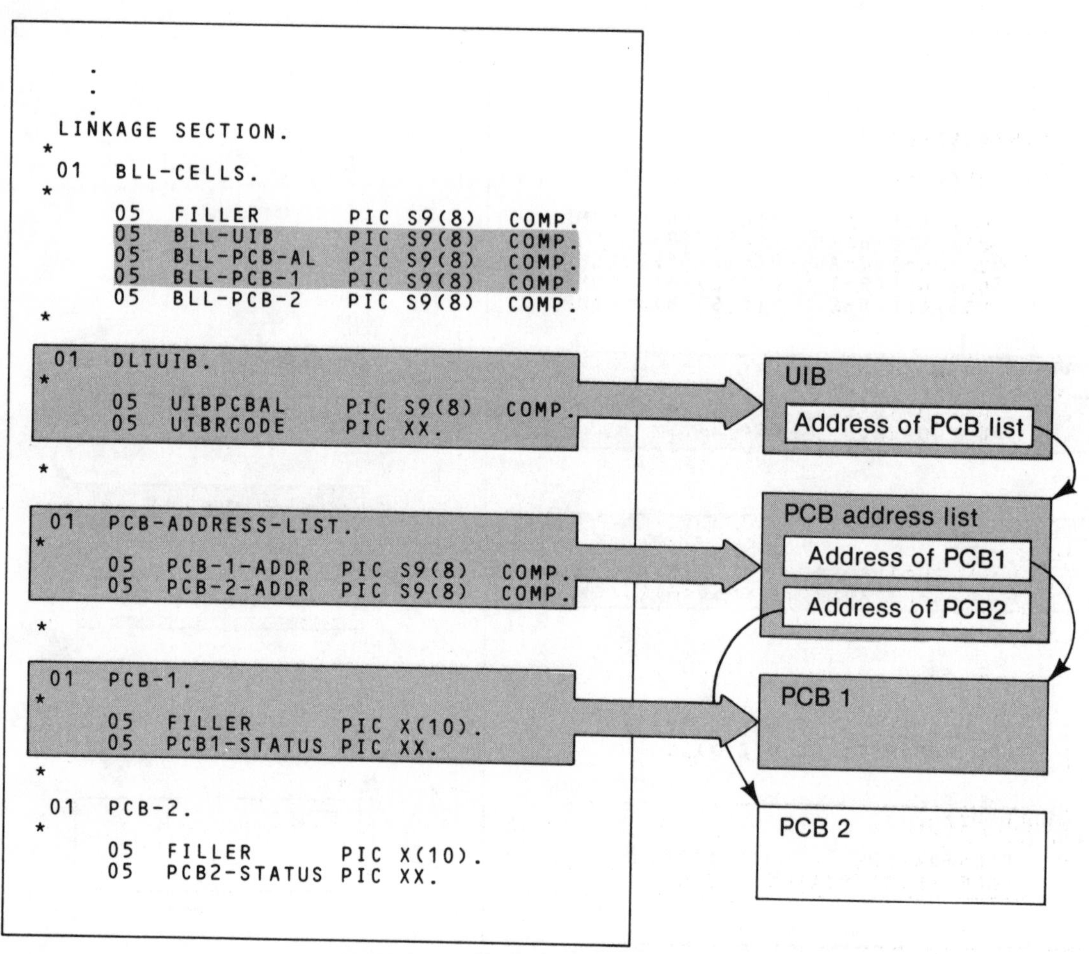

Figure 13-9 Addressing DL/I control blocks (part 3 of 4)

Considerations for the VS COBOL II compiler If your installation uses the new VS COBOL II compiler (that's the new IBM compiler based on the 198X COBOL standards), you'll have to code your scheduling statements a little differently than I've shown. That's

The program loads the BLL cell for PCB-2:

```
CALL 'CBLTDLI' USING DLI-PCB
                     PSB-NAME
                     BLL-UIB.
MOVE UIBPCBAL    TO BLL-PCB-AL.
MOVE PCB-1-ADDR  TO BLL-PCB-1.
MOVE PCB-2-ADDR  TO BLL-PCB-2.
```

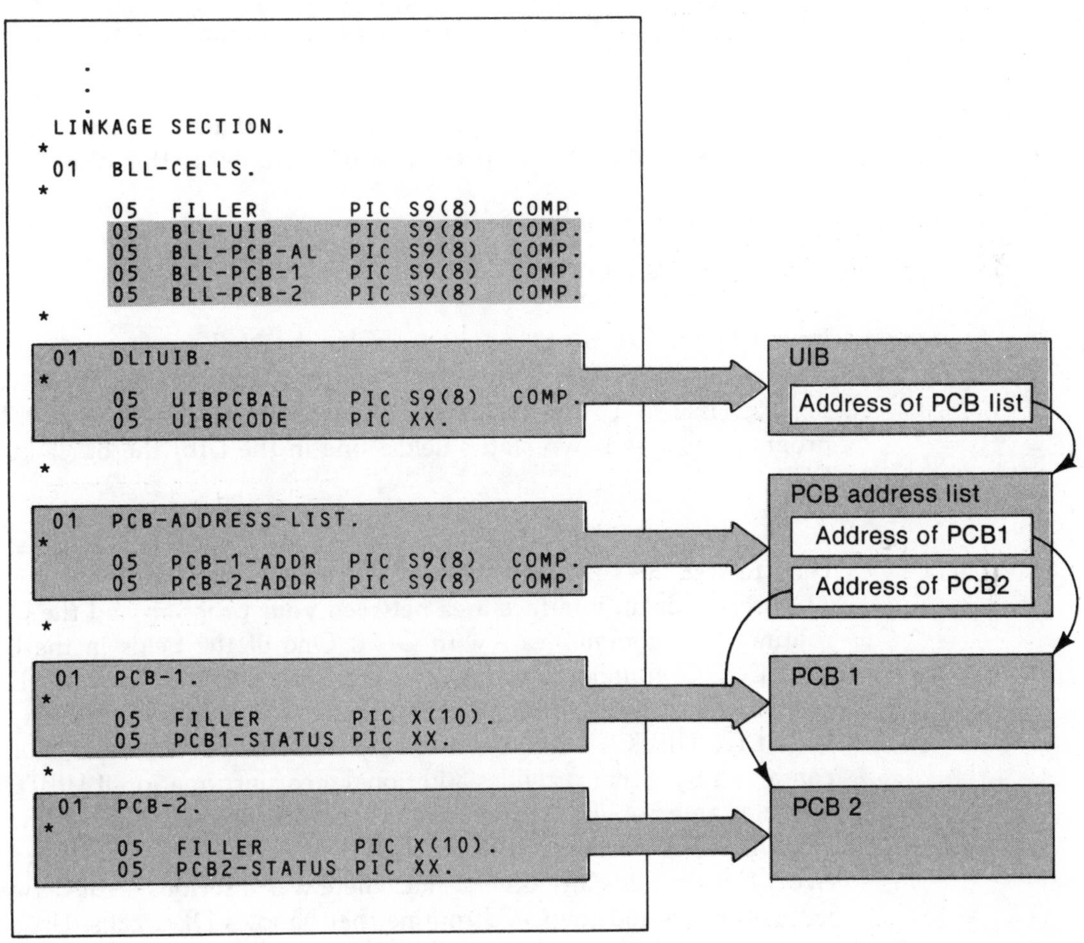

Figure 13-9 Addressing DL/I control blocks (part 4 of 4)

because VS COBOL II doesn't support the BLL-cell linkage convention for addressing Linkage Section fields. Instead, it uses a new language feature: the ADDRESS special register.

When you use the ADDRESS special register, you don't code BLL-cell entries in the Linkage Section. And you code your scheduling statements like this:

```
CALL 'CBLTDLI' USING DLI-PCB
                     PSB-NAME
                     ADDRESS OF DLIUIB.
MOVE UIBPCBAL   TO ADDRESS OF PCB-ADDRESS-LIST.
MOVE PCB-1-ADDR TO ADDRESS OF PCB-1.
MOVE PCB-2-ADDR TO ADDRESS OF PCB-2.
```

As you can see if you compare this code to that in figure 13-9, the function of the ADDRESS special register is similar to that of BLL cells.

How to handle DL/I errors

In a CICS DL/I program, as in a batch DL/I program, you are responsible for checking for error conditions after each DL/I call your program issues. To determine if a DL/I call is successful, your CICS program must test two status fields: one in the UIB, the other in the PCB.

How to test the UIB status code The User Interface Block (figure 13-6) serves as an interface area between your program and the CICS routines that communicate with DL/I. One of the fields in the UIB, UIBRCODE, contains a status code that indicates whether your DL/I call was successful. UIBRCODE contains two subfields: UIBFCTR and UIBDLTR. UIBFCTR contains a one-byte response code, and UIBDLTR contains a byte that provides additional error information if UIBFCTR indicates an error. Usually, you're only concerned with UIBFCTR.

UIBFCTR normally contains LOW-VALUE. If it does, there's no error. If it contains any other value, there was a serious error between your program and the CICS routine that handles DL/I calls. Usually, the cause of this type of error is that the scheduling call failed. An error indicated by UIBFCTR is always serious, so you should issue a CICS ABEND command to terminate the task.

The ABEND command causes your program to abend just as if CICS had detected some type of processing error: a message is written to the terminal, an optional transaction dump is created, and the task is terminated. Normally, CICS abends a task automatically when a serious error occurs, but that's not the case with DL/I.

How to test the PCB status code Following the test of UIBFCTR, your program should check the PCB status code just as a batch program would do. At the very least, if you don't expect an operation to cause any return codes to be generated, you should test the status code field to make sure it contains blanks.

A sample CICS/VS-DL/I inquiry program

Now that you know how to schedule a PSB for a CICS DL/I program and how to handle DL/I errors under CICS, take a look at figures 13-10 through 13-12. Here, I present a simple CICS program that lets an operator display the current status of a receivable (an invoice) from a customer data base. (The customer data base is described in detail in chapter 7; if you haven't read chapter 7, I suggest you look at figures 7-1 and 7-2 to get an idea of the data base structure.)

Figure 13-10 presents the screen layouts for this program. As you can see in part 1, the operator enters little information: the trans-id DLII, followed by a space and the six-digit invoice number. This is a simple screen layout. A more typical application would use a BMS mapset and would have the operator enter data on a screen formatted with fields and captions. However, the approach this program uses is simpler to let you focus more on DL/I considerations than on CICS elements.

Part 2 of figure 13-10 shows the output the program sends to the user. After retrieving the requested receivable segment from the customer data base, the program formats data from it, calculates the original billing total and total payments and adjustments, and sends the results to the terminal. Again, this is a simple display; a production program would more likely use BMS to format the screen.

Figure 13-11 gives the structure chart for the inquiry program. The basic functions of the program are to schedule its single PSB (module 1000), get the operator's entry (module 2000), retrieve the proper receivable segment from the customer data base (module 3000), and send the output display back to the terminal (module 4000). If the program detects an error, it performs module 5000 to send an error message back to the user.

Figure 13-12 is the complete source listing for this program. Module 1000 schedules the PSB. If you look at the Linkage Section, you'll see that the entries I coded there are similar to those in figure 13-9. But instead of using a generalized name like PCB-1 or PCB-2, I

```
 DLII XXXXXX
```

Figure 13-10 Screen layout for the CICS inquiry program (part 1 of 2)

```
 INVOICE:  999999    DATE:  99/99/99      SUBTOTAL:      ZZZZZ.99-
                                          DISCOUNT:      ZZZZZ.99-
                                          SALES TAX:     ZZZZZ.99-
                                          FREIGHT:       ZZZZZ.99-
                                                         ---------
                                          BILLING:       ZZZZZ.99-
                                          PMTS/ADJS:     ZZZZZ.99-
                                                         ---------
                                          DUE:           ZZZZZ.99-
```

Figure 13-10 Screen layout for the CICS inquiry program (part 2 of 2)

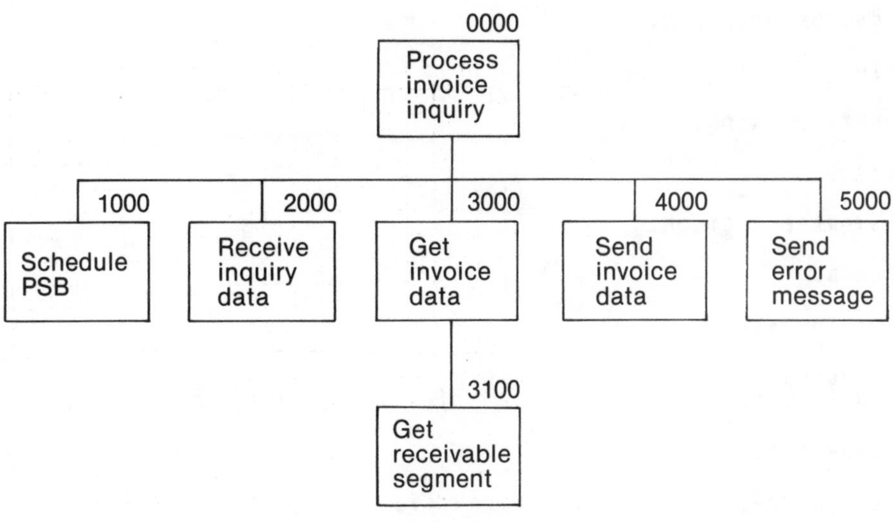

Figure 13-11 Structure chart for the CICS inquiry program

refer to the PCB with a specific name: CR-PCB-MASK. Module 1000 first issues a scheduling call to get the address of the UIB. Then, it tests UIBFCTR to make sure the scheduling call worked. If it didn't, an ABEND command terminates the program. Otherwise, two MOVE statements load addresses into the appropriate BLL cells so the PCB-POINTERS and CR-PCB-MASK fields in the Linkage Section are addressable.

Module 2000 issues the CICS commands required to retrieve the data the operator entered and to check for some error conditions. Here, I just want you to notice that the RECEIVE command causes the data the operator entered to be placed in the working-storage field COMMAND-LINE.

Module 3000 uses the invoice number value in the field CL-INVOICE-NUMBER to format an SSA to retrieve the receivable segment, then invokes module 3100, where a GU call that specifies INVOICE-NO-SSA retrieves a specific receivable segment from the customer data base. The retrieval is based on the secondary index I described in chapter 7. If the field CR-PCB-STATUS-CODE has any value other than space after the call, it means the call was unsuccessful, so an appropriate switch is set. The most likely cause of a non-blank status code here is an invalid invoice number; that's treated as an operator error, not a data base error.

```
 IDENTIFICATION DIVISION.
*
 PROGRAM-ID.  DLIIINQ.
*
 ENVIRONMENT DIVISION.
*
 DATA DIVISION.
*
 WORKING-STORAGE SECTION.
*
 01  SWITCHES.
*
     05  VALID-DATA-SW             PIC X       VALUE 'Y'.
         88  VALID-DATA                        VALUE 'Y'.
     05  INVOICE-FOUND-SW          PIC X       VALUE 'Y'.
         88  INVOICE-FOUND                     VALUE 'Y'.
*
 01  COMMAND-LINE.
*
     05  CL-TRANS-ID               PIC X(4).
     05  FILLER                    PIC X.
     05  CL-INVOICE-NUMBER         PIC X(6)  VALUE SPACE.
*
 01  COMMAND-LENGTH                PIC S9(4) VALUE +11  COMP.
*
 01  INVOICE-DATA-LINES.
*
     05  IDL-LINE-1.
         10  FILLER                PIC X(10) VALUE 'INVOICE: '.
         10  IDL1-INV-NUMBER       PIC X(6).
         10  FILLER                PIC X(10) VALUE '   DATE: '.
         10  IDL1-INV-DATE         PIC 99/99/99.
         10  FILLER                PIC X(5)  VALUE SPACE.
         10  FILLER                PIC X(14) VALUE 'SUBTOTAL:     '.
         10  IDL1-PRODUCT-TOTAL    PIC Z(5).99-.
         10  FILLER                PIC X(18) VALUE SPACE.
*
     05  IDL-LINE-2.
         10  FILLER                PIC X(39) VALUE SPACE.
         10  FILLER                PIC X(14) VALUE 'DISCOUNT:     '.
         10  IDL2-CASH-DISCOUNT    PIC Z(5).99-.
         10  FILLER                PIC X(18) VALUE SPACE.
*
     05  IDL-LINE-3.
         10  FILLER                PIC X(39) VALUE SPACE.
         10  FILLER                PIC X(14) VALUE 'SALES TAX:    '.
         10  IDL3-SALES-TAX        PIC Z(5).99-.
         10  FILLER                PIC X(18) VALUE SPACE.
*
```

Figure 13-12 Source listing for the CICS inquiry program (part 1 of 5)

```
       05  IDL-LINE-4.
           10  FILLER                     PIC X(39) VALUE SPACE.
           10  FILLER                     PIC X(14) VALUE 'FREIGHT:      '.
           10  IDL4-FREIGHT               PIC Z(5).99-.
           10  FILLER                     PIC X(18) VALUE SPACE.
      *
       05  IDL-LINE-5.
           10  FILLER                     PIC X(53) VALUE SPACE.
           10  FILLER                     PIC X(9)  VALUE '-------- '.
           10  FILLER                     PIC X(18) VALUE SPACE.
      *
       05  IDL-LINE-6.
           10  FILLER                     PIC X(39) VALUE SPACE.
           10  FILLER                     PIC X(14) VALUE 'BILLING:      '.
           10  IDL6-BILLING               PIC Z(5).99-.
           10  FILLER                     PIC X(18) VALUE SPACE.
      *
       05  IDL-LINE-7.
           10  FILLER                     PIC X(39) VALUE SPACE.
           10  FILLER                     PIC X(14) VALUE 'PMTS/ADJS:    '.
           10  IDL7-PMTS-ADJS             PIC Z(5).99-.
           10  FILLER                     PIC X(18) VALUE SPACE.
      *
       05  IDL-LINE-8.
           10  FILLER                     PIC X(53) VALUE SPACE.
           10  FILLER                     PIC X(9)  VALUE '-------- '.
           10  FILLER                     PIC X(18) VALUE SPACE.
      *
       05  IDL-LINE-9.
           10  FILLER                     PIC X(39) VALUE SPACE.
           10  FILLER                     PIC X(14) VALUE 'DUE:          '.
           10  IDL9-BALANCE-DUE           PIC Z(5).99-.
           10  FILLER                     PIC X(18) VALUE SPACE.
      *
       01  ERROR-MESSAGE                  PIC X(34).
      *
       01  DLI-FUNCTIONS.
      *
           05  DLI-GU                     PIC X(4)  VALUE 'GU  '.
           05  DLI-GHU                    PIC X(4)  VALUE 'GHU '.
           05  DLI-GN                     PIC X(4)  VALUE 'GN  '.
           05  DLI-GHN                    PIC X(4)  VALUE 'GHN '.
           05  DLI-GNP                    PIC X(4)  VALUE 'GNP '.
           05  DLI-GHNP                   PIC X(4)  VALUE 'GHNP'.
           05  DLI-ISRT                   PIC X(4)  VALUE 'ISRT'.
           05  DLI-DLET                   PIC X(4)  VALUE 'DLET'.
           05  DLI-REPL                   PIC X(4)  VALUE 'REPL'.
           05  DLI-CHKP                   PIC X(4)  VALUE 'CHKP'.
           05  DLI-XRST                   PIC X(4)  VALUE 'XRST'.
           05  DLI-PCB                    PIC X(4)  VALUE 'PCB '.
      *
```

Figure 13-12 Source listing for the CICS inquiry program (part 2 of 5)

```
 01  PSB-NAME                   PIC X(8)  VALUE 'CRSI    '.
*
 01  RECEIVABLE-SEGMENT.
*
     05  RS-INVOICE-NUMBER      PIC X(6).
     05  RS-INVOICE-DATE        PIC X(6).
     05  RS-PO-NUMBER           PIC X(25).
     05  RS-PRODUCT-TOTAL       PIC S9(5)V99  COMP-3.
     05  RS-CASH-DISCOUNT       PIC S9(5)V99  COMP-3.
     05  RS-SALES-TAX           PIC S9(5)V99  COMP-3.
     05  RS-FREIGHT             PIC S9(5)V99  COMP-3.
     05  RS-BALANCE-DUE         PIC S9(5)V99  COMP-3.
*
 01  INVOICE-NO-SSA.
*
     05  FILLER                 PIC X(9)  VALUE 'CRRECSEG('.
     05  FILLER                 PIC X(10) VALUE 'CRRECXNO ='.
     05  INVOICE-NO-SSA-VALUE   PIC X(6).
     05  FILLER                 PIC X     VALUE ')'.
*
 LINKAGE SECTION.
*
 01  BLL-CELLS.
*
     05  FILLER                 PIC S9(8)     COMP.
     05  BLL-UIB                PIC S9(8)     COMP.
     05  BLL-PCB-POINTERS       PIC S9(8)     COMP.
     05  BLL-CUSTOMER-PCB       PIC S9(8)     COMP.
*
 COPY DLIUIB.
*
 01  PCB-POINTERS.
*
     05  CUSTOMER-PCB-POINTER   PIC S9(8)     COMP.
*
 01  CR-PCB-MASK.
*
     05  CR-PCB-DBD-NAME        PIC X(8).
     05  CR-PCB-SEGMENT-LEVEL   PIC XX.
     05  CR-PCB-STATUS-CODE     PIC XX.
     05  CR-PCB-PROC-OPTIONS    PIC X(4).
     05  FILLER                 PIC S9(5)     COMP.
     05  CR-PCB-SEGMENT-NAME    PIC X(8).
     05  CR-PCB-KEY-LENGTH      PIC S9(5)     COMP.
     05  CR-PCB-NUMB-SENS-SEGS  PIC S9(5)     COMP.
     05  CR-PCB-KEY             PIC X(22).
*
 PROCEDURE DIVISION.
*
```

Figure 13-12 Source listing for the CICS inquiry program (part 3 of 5)

```
0000-PROCESS-INVOICE-INQUIRY SECTION.
*
     PERFORM 1000-SCHEDULE-PSB.
     PERFORM 2000-RECEIVE-INQUIRY-DATA.
     IF VALID-DATA
         PERFORM 3000-GET-INVOICE-DATA
         IF INVOICE-FOUND
             PERFORM 4000-SEND-INVOICE-DATA.
     IF NOT VALID-DATA
         PERFORM 5000-SEND-ERROR-MESSAGE.
     EXEC CICS
         RETURN
     END-EXEC.
*
 1000-SCHEDULE-PSB SECTION.
*
     CALL 'CBLTDLI' USING DLI-PCB
                          PSB-NAME
                          BLL-UIB.
     IF UIBFCTR NOT = LOW-VALUE
         EXEC CICS
             ABEND ABCODE('DLI1')
         END-EXEC.
     MOVE UIBPCBAL             TO BLL-PCB-POINTERS.
     MOVE CUSTOMER-PCB-POINTER TO BLL-CUSTOMER-PCB.
*
 2000-RECEIVE-INQUIRY-DATA SECTION.
*
     EXEC CICS
         HANDLE CONDITION LENGERR(2000-LENGERR)
     END-EXEC.
     EXEC CICS
         RECEIVE INTO(COMMAND-LINE)
                 LENGTH(COMMAND-LENGTH)
     END-EXEC.
     IF     CL-INVOICE-NUMBER = SPACE
         OR CL-INVOICE-NUMBER = LOW-VALUE
         MOVE 'N' TO VALID-DATA-SW
         MOVE ' YOU MUST SUPPLY AN INVOICE NUMBER'
             TO ERROR-MESSAGE.
     GO TO 2000-EXIT.
*
 2000-LENGERR.
*
     MOVE 'N' TO VALID-DATA-SW.
     MOVE ' TOO MUCH DATA ENTERED' TO ERROR-MESSAGE.
*
 2000-EXIT.
*
     EXIT.
*
```

Figure 13-12 Source listing for the CICS inquiry program (part 4 of 5)

```
 3000-GET-INVOICE-DATA SECTION.
*
     MOVE CL-INVOICE-NUMBER TO INVOICE-NO-SSA-VALUE.
     PERFORM 3100-GET-RECEIVABLE-SEGMENT.
*
  3100-GET-RECEIVABLE-SEGMENT SECTION.
*
     CALL 'CBLTDLI' USING DLI-GU
                          CR-PCB-MASK
                          RECEIVABLE-SEGMENT
                          INVOICE-NO-SSA.
     IF CR-PCB-STATUS-CODE NOT = SPACE
         MOVE ' INVOICE NOT FOUND' TO ERROR-MESSAGE
         MOVE 'N'                  TO INVOICE-FOUND-SW
                                      VALID-DATA-SW.
*
 4000-SEND-INVOICE-DATA SECTION.
*
     MOVE RS-INVOICE-NUMBER TO IDL1-INV-NUMBER.
     MOVE RS-INVOICE-DATE   TO IDL1-INV-DATE.
     MOVE RS-PRODUCT-TOTAL  TO IDL1-PRODUCT-TOTAL.
     MOVE RS-CASH-DISCOUNT  TO IDL2-CASH-DISCOUNT.
     MOVE RS-SALES-TAX      TO IDL3-SALES-TAX.
     MOVE RS-FREIGHT        TO IDL4-FREIGHT.
     COMPUTE IDL6-BILLING = RS-PRODUCT-TOTAL -
                            RS-CASH-DISCOUNT +
                            RS-SALES-TAX +
                            RS-FREIGHT.
     COMPUTE IDL7-PMTS-ADJS =  RS-BALANCE-DUE -
                              (RS-PRODUCT-TOTAL -
                               RS-CASH-DISCOUNT +
                               RS-SALES-TAX +
                               RS-FREIGHT).
     MOVE RS-BALANCE-DUE    TO IDL9-BALANCE-DUE.
     EXEC CICS
         SEND FROM(INVOICE-DATA-LINES)
              LENGTH(720)
              ERASE
     END-EXEC.
*
 5000-SEND-ERROR-MESSAGE SECTION.
*
     EXEC CICS
         SEND FROM(ERROR-MESSAGE)
              LENGTH(34)
     END-EXEC.
```

Figure 13-12 Source listing for the CICS inquiry program (part 5 of 5)

Module 4000 formats the invoice data for the display and issues a SEND command to send the entire display area INVOICE-DATA-LINES to the terminal. Although this isn't the most efficient way to send data to a terminal, it's the easiest to understand for a CICS novice.

DISCUSSION

Although the DL/I processing this program does is trivial, it should be clear to you that there's little difference between DL/I processing in a CICS program and in a batch program. As long as you establish addressability to your PCBs properly, issuing other calls shouldn't present problems for you.

However, DL/I considerations aside, CICS programming is a complicated subject. Frankly, if this is your first exposure to CICS, you're not ready to start writing CICS programs, although this chapter should put you in a good position to start learning CICS. On the other hand, if you are an experienced CICS programmer, this chapter will help you apply your DL/I batch programming skills in the CICS environment.

Terminology

task
multitasking
multithreading
transaction
transaction identifier
trans-id
management module
CICS command
CICS command-level translator
Basic Mapping Support
BMS
mapset
pseudo-conversational programming
scheduling call
User Interface Block
UIB
addressability
Base Locator for Linkage
BLL

Objectives

1. Explain the function of the DL/I User Interface Block in a CICS DL/I program.

2. Explain how the scheduling call establishes addressability to the PCBs used by a CICS DL/I program.

3. If you're an experienced CICS programmer, develop a CICS program that processes DL/I data bases according to program and data base specifications supplied to you.

Section 5

DL/I data base organizations and access methods

This section presents information about the various DL/I data base organizations. You've been able to learn how to develop sophisticated data base processing programs without a thorough knowledge of data base structure because DL/I insulates you from it. Frankly, it's the data base administrator, not the application programmer, who has to be completely familiar with data base structure.

However, I believe that you'll be able to do a better job of application programming with a basic background in DL/I data base organizations. For example, if you know how much work the system has to do when you issue certain kinds of calls, you might think twice before you use them. In addition, knowing the fundamentals of how DL/I data bases are organized will help you contribute in conversations with your data base administrator. And, if you're faced with having to do DBA work yourself, you'll be better able to find the more detailed information you need from the IBM manuals.

This section has three chapters. Chapter 14 gives you an overview of DL/I access methods. Then, chapters 15 and 16 describe the sequential and direct data base access methods.

Chapter 14

An introduction to the DL/I data base organizations

This chapter gives you a brief overview of the DL/I data base organizations and access methods. In it, you'll learn just what the DL/I access methods are and how they fit into the overall system software picture. You'll also learn the basic terms and concepts you need to know to understand the more technical information in chapters 15 and 16.

The DL/I organizations and access methods

In standard file processing, there's a difference between a file's organization and the access method that's used to process it. (Frankly, the difference is more academic than practical, but it's a difference nonetheless.) For instance, a file might have sequential organization and be accessed by the operating system's sequential access method, such as QSAM on an OS system or SAM on a DOS system. When VSAM is the access method, a file can have one of three organizations: sequential (in an entry-sequenced data set), indexed (in a key-sequenced data set), or random (in a relative-record data set). The point is that an organization is a generalized description of how a file is processed, while an access method is the software used to implement that processing.

The same is true for DL/I data bases. DL/I provides two basic data base organizations: hierarchic sequential and hierarchic direct. For each organization, different access methods are available.

Hierarchic sequential organizations In a data base with *hierarchic sequential organization,* or *HS organization,* the segments that make up a data base record are related to one another by their physical locations. In other words, hierarchic sequential data bases are stored in hierarchical sequence.

HS data bases can be implemented using one of the HS access methods. Normally, one of two is used: the *Hierarchical Sequential Access Method* (*HSAM*) or the *Hierarchical Indexed Sequential Access Method* (*HISAM*). Usually, a hierarchic sequential data base implemented with HSAM is called an HSAM data base. And an HS data base implemented with HISAM is called a HISAM data base.

An HSAM data base is much like a sequential file. To process an HSAM data base, a program works through it sequentially from beginning to end. Because of the sequential nature of an HSAM data base, application programs cannot replace or delete segments without copying the entire data base. As a result, HSAM isn't as commonly used as HISAM.

In a HISAM data base, data is stored with hierarchic sequential organization, so sequential processing is efficient. In addition, an index is maintained to allow random access to any data base record. So you can think of a HISAM data base as being much like an ISAM file or a VSAM KSDS.

Two other access methods are available to implement a data base with hierarchic sequential organization: *SHSAM* (*Simple Hierarchical Sequential Access Method*) and *SHISAM* (*Simple Hierarchical Indexed Sequential Access Method*). As their names imply, these access methods are variations of HSAM and HISAM. However, while HSAM and HISAM can support complex hierarchical structures, SHSAM and SHISAM can support data bases that consist only of root segments. SHSAM and SHISAM are of limited value; they're used primarily when converting standard files to DL/I data bases.

The next chapter shows you how HSAM and HISAM data bases are structured. For now, I want you to realize that these access methods aren't used for most data bases. HSAM is particularly limited because it doesn't allow random access at all. HISAM is more powerful, but it's restricted because some of the most useful advanced DL/I features (like full function logical relationships and secondary indexing) are available only for data bases with direct organization.

Hierarchic direct organizations If a data base is going to do much random processing, the data base administrator will probably implement it with *hierarchic direct organization,* or *HD organization.* When HD organization is used, segment occurrences include prefixes that contain direct address pointers to related segments. Depending on how complex the data base structure is, these pointers can be extensive.

There are two access methods that can be used to implement a data base with HD organization. The first, *HDAM*, or the *Hierarchical Direct Access Method,* stores root segment occurrences based on a randomizing routine. In this respect, it's similar to direct processing using DAM. Occurrences of dependent segments are related to the root and one another by the system of pointers the HD organization is based upon. Because root segments are *not* typically stored sequentially in an HDAM data base, HDAM data bases aren't generally appropriate for sequential processing.

If some mix of sequential and random processing is required, *HIDAM*, or the *Hierarchical Indexed Direct Access Method* is appropriate. Segment data in a HIDAM data base is stored just as in an HDAM data base, but the root segment is located through an index. As a result, a randomizing routine isn't used in a HIDAM data base. And, because of the index, root segments can be retrieved in sequence.

How DL/I and operating system access methods are related

It's easy to make a comparison like "a DL/I data base with sequential organization can be implemented with HISAM just like a standard sequential file can be implemented with VSAM." This kind of comparison can help you learn about the DL/I access methods by relating them to something familiar. However, don't let the parallel terminology mislead you. The relationship between data bases and their related DL/I access methods is above and in addition to the relationship between standard files and their operating system access methods; it does *not* replace it.

This shouldn't cause you problems as long as you keep two points in mind. First, DL/I access methods are internal to DL/I itself. They aren't available for use outside the DL/I environment. And second, DL/I data bases—whatever their organization—are stored in data sets that DL/I accesses by invoking the services of the standard operating system access methods like SAM, QSAM, ISAM, or, more commonly, VSAM.

Sample data bases

In the next two chapters, I'll show you how HSAM, HISAM, HDAM, and HIDAM data bases are structured. To help you understand this

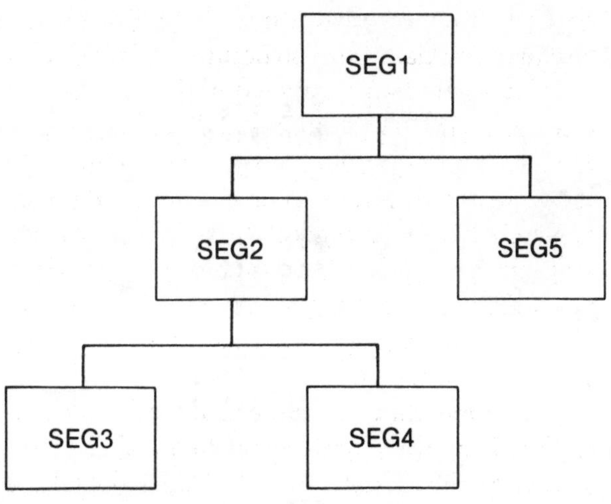

Figure 14-1 Hierarchical structure for the sample data bases

material, I've created a simple five-segment hierarchical structure, shown in figure 14-1, that I'll use as the basis for generating sample data bases with each of the four main access methods. Each of the sample data bases will contain the same segment occurrences. As a result, when I show you listings of the data sets that contain the data bases, you'll be able to compare their structures more easily.

Figure 14-2 gives the segment descriptions for each of the five segment types. Each of the segment types begins with a six-byte sequence field. To help you identify where segments begin and end in the sample data bases, the first four characters of each sequence field will contain a value that identifies the segment type (SEG1, SEG2, SEG3, SEG4, or SEG5). Key position 5 indicates the data base record (1, 2, or 3). And key position 6 is used to distinguish between twin segment occurrences. This kind of segment identification isn't used in a production data base, but it will help you in the examples that follow.

Figure 14-3 contains the data I'll use to load each of the sample data bases. One line of data here corresponds to one segment occurrence in a sample data base, and they're in hierarchical sequence in the figure. The three shaded lines contain the data that will be used to load the three root segment occurrences. Of course, in a production data base, you'd expect hundreds or thousands of data base records. Even so, these three data base records illustrate what I want you to learn and will make the sample data bases easier for you to study.

```
*
 01  SAMPLE-SEGMENT-1.
*
     05  SS1-KEY                     PIC X(6).
     05  SS1-DATA                    PIC X(42).
*
 01  SAMPLE-SEGMENT-2.
*
     05  SS2-KEY                     PIC X(6).
     05  SS2-DATA                    PIC X(26).
*
 01  SAMPLE-SEGMENT-3.
*
     05  SS3-KEY                     PIC X(6).
     05  SS3-DATA                    PIC X(10).
*
 01  SAMPLE-SEGMENT-4.
*
     05  SS4-KEY                     PIC X(6).
     05  SS4-DATA                    PIC X(26).
*
 01  SAMPLE-SEGMENT-5.
*
     05  SS5-KEY                     PIC X(6).
     05  SS5-DATA                    PIC X(42).
*
```

Figure 14-2 Segment layouts for the sample data bases

Additional IMS access methods

The access methods I've already described (HSAM, SHSAM, HISAM, SHISAM, HDAM, and HIDAM) are available under both DL/I DOS/VS and IMS/VS. However, IMS supports three other data base types: GSAM data bases and two kinds of "Fast Path" data bases.

GSAM data bases *GSAM,* the *Generalized Sequential Access Method,* lets application programs treat OS sequential files (using BSAM or VSAM) as data bases. A GSAM data base is not considered to be hierarchical; data is processed on a record by record basis, but through DL/I calls. Processing of the data base is sequential; ISRT calls add data only at the end of the data base, and REPL and DLET calls aren't supported.

As with SHSAM and SHISAM data bases, GSAM data bases are typically used during conversion from a system that uses standard files to one that uses data bases. However, if a program needs to access both standard DL/I data bases and OS/VS files, the files can be defined as

```
SEG111|111111111111111111111111111111111111111111
SEG211|22222222222222222222222222
SEG311|3333333333
SEG312|3333333333
SEG411|44444444444444444444444444
SEG212|22222222222222222222222222
SEG311|3333333333
SEG312|3333333333
SEG411|44444444444444444444444444
SEG412|44444444444444444444444444
SEG511|555555555555555555555555555555555555555555
SEG121|111111111111111111111111111111111111111111
SEG221|22222222222222222222222222
SEG321|3333333333
SEG322|3333333333
SEG421|44444444444444444444444444
SEG222|22222222222222222222222222
SEG321|3333333333
SEG322|3333333333
SEG421|44444444444444444444444444
SEG422|44444444444444444444444444
SEG521|555555555555555555555555555555555555555555
SEG131|111111111111111111111111111111111111111111
SEG231|22222222222222222222222222
SEG331|3333333333
SEG332|3333333333
SEG431|44444444444444444444444444
SEG232|22222222222222222222222222
SEG331|3333333333
SEG332|3333333333
SEG431|44444444444444444444444444
SEG432|44444444444444444444444444
SEG531|555555555555555555555555555555555555555555
```

Figure 14-3 Test data for the sample data bases

GSAM data bases. Then, because the files are considered by IMS to be data bases, IMS recovery facilities can be used for them.

Fast Path data bases For some IMS data communications applications, especially fast response time is necessary for terminal users. When that's the case, the data base administrator can use *Fast Path data bases*. The *Fast Path feature*, which is available only with IMS DC (not IMS batch or DL/I with CICS), provides fast processing for simple data structures. There are two kinds of Fast Path data bases: MSDBs and DEDBs.

A data base administrator can use an *MSDB* (*main storage data base*) to store an application's most intensively used data. As you can tell from the name, an MSDB resides in virtual storage. As a result, it's possible to access data in it very quickly. However, because an MSDB uses the system's most valuable resource, it probably contains a small amount of data.

A typical use for an MSDB would be for accumulating general-ledger control values in a large network. Whenever an application program processes a transaction, the same general-ledger segments are retrieved and updated. Because this kind of data base activity can be intense in a large system, implementing a data base like this as an MSDB might be desirable for performance reasons.

MSDBs are root-segment-only data bases. As a result, the GNP and GHNP calls aren't supported for them, although the other basic data base calls are. In addition, a special call (FLD) is unique to MSDBs. It lets a program operate on a single field rather than an entire segment.

When it's necessary to store a large quantity of data, the data base administrator can use a *DEDB* (*data entry data base*). Unlike an MSDB, a DEDB is stored on disk and has a hierarchical structure, with up to 127 segment types. Most of these are organized in the typical DL/I fashion, as *direct dependent segment types*. However, within a data base, one *sequential dependent segment type* can be defined.

When occurrences of the sequential dependent segment type are inserted, they're added in a separate area of the data base and in chronological rather than hierarchical sequence. Sequential dependent segments can be inserted more rapidly than if they were direct dependents, but it's inefficient to retrieve them. Usually, they're used to collect a large volume of data that doesn't need to be immediately accessible. Then, off-line jobs are used later to process that data and, if necessary, reformat it.

DEDBs also use a complicated storage scheme that involves separating the data base into as many as 240 *areas*, each in its own data set with its own space management characteristics. This not only makes for more efficient processing, but allows for very large data bases.

It's possible to duplicate areas in a DEDB using the *area data set replication feature*. For retrieval operations, that can improve response time. However, when a change is made to one area, IMS has to make the same change to all duplicate areas to insure data base integrity. As a result, it's practical to use area data set replication only when the duplicated data isn't highly volatile.

Discussion

Again, I want to stress that it's the data base administrator, not the application programmer, who has to worry about the technical details of data base organizations. By the time you receive specifications for an application program, the data base design and organization questions have already been answered. However, you should have a general understanding of how the basic, full function DL/I data bases are organized. So that's what the next two chapters will give you.

Terminology

hierarchic sequential organization
HS organization
Hierarchical Sequential Access Method
HSAM
Hierarchical Indexed Sequential Access Method
HISAM
SHSAM
Simple Hierarchical Sequential Access Method
SHISAM
Simple Hierarchical Indexed Sequential Access Method
hierarchic direct organization
HD organization
HDAM
Hierarchical Direct Access Method
HIDAM
Hierarchical Indexed Direct Access Method
GSAM
Generalized Sequential Access Method
Fast Path data base
Fast Path feature
MSDB
main storage data base
DEDB
data entry data base
direct dependent segment type
sequential dependent segment type
area
area data set replication feature

Objectives

1. Distinguish between sequential data base organization and direct data base organization.

2. Describe the relationships among DL/I access methods, DL/I data bases, operating system access methods, and data sets that contain data bases.

3. Describe when it's appropriate for a data base administrator to implement a data base:

   a. using SHSAM
   b. using SHISAM
   c. using GSAM
   d. as an MSDB
   e. as a DEDB

Chapter 15

The sequential data base access methods

This chapter describes the two main DL/I access methods for data bases with sequential organization: HSAM and HISAM. It shows you the structures of data bases implemented with those access methods. In addition, it explains why HS data bases are well suited for some kinds of processing, but not for others.

HSAM

The simplest of the main DL/I organizations, and also the most limited in the processing it supports, is HSAM, the Hierarchical Sequential Access Method. In this section, I'll show you how to define an HSAM data base, how data is stored in it, and how HSAM data bases are used. But first, let me tell you about the processing restrictions you have to be aware of when you develop application programs that process HSAM data bases.

The thing about HSAM data bases you need to keep in mind is that DL/I always processes them sequentially. Although you can issue a GU call for an HSAM data base, DL/I scans the entire data base to find the segment you requested. You can use the ISRT call to add segments to an HSAM data base, but only when loading a new copy of the data base;

you can't insert segments in the middle of an existing HSAM data base. Also, the REPL and DLET calls aren't supported at all for HSAM data bases. After you've seen a sample HSAM data base, you'll better understand these restrictions.

How to define an HSAM data base Figure 15-1 shows the output of the HSAM DBDGEN job for the sample data base I described in the last chapter. This output is from an MVS system, but it would be almost identical under DOS/VSE. As you can see, the DBD macro specifies the data base should be HSAM (ACCESS=HSAM).

The second macro, DATASET, describes the characteristics of the files that will be used for the data base. When the DBA defines an HSAM data base, she must specify two data sets: one for input processing (DD1) and one for output processing (DD2). When an application program accesses data in an existing HSAM data base, it retrieves records from the data set associated in the invoking JCL with the DD1 name. On the other hand, when an application program creates a new data base, it writes data to the data set associated in the JCL with the DD2 name.

When an application program updates an HSAM data base, both data sets are active. That's because HSAM doesn't allow segments to be deleted or updated in place. So whenever segments in an HSAM data base are updated or deleted, the entire data base must be copied from the input data set to the output data set. When the update program finishes, the output data set becomes the current version of the data base.

The data sets that store an HSAM data base use the host operating system's native sequential access method. For IMS/VS, that's either BSAM or QSAM; for DL/I DOS/VS, it's SAM. For the DEVICE parameter of the DATASET macro, the DBA codes the unit type that will contain the BSAM/QSAM or SAM files. In figure 15-1, that value is 3380. Rather than specify the model number of a supported DASD, the DBA can code DEVICE=TAPE to cause the data base to be stored on magnetic tape. Only HSAM (and SHSAM) data bases can be stored on tape; DL/I data bases that use any of the other access methods must be stored on DASD.

The last parameter on the DATASET macro specifies the size of the QSAM/BSAM or SAM record that will contain HSAM data. One of the values is for records in the input data set, the other for records in the output data set. In general, it's most efficient to specify a record size that's equal to the track size of the DASD that contains the data base.

```
STMT   SOURCE STATEMENT

   1            PRINT NOGEN
   2  DBD             NAME=EXHSAM,ACCESS=HSAM
   3  DATASET         DD1=EXHSAMI,DD2=EXHSAMO,DEVICE=3380,RECORD=(512,512)
  4+*,                  3380 DISK STORAGE
   5 *
   6  SEGM            NAME=SEG1,BYTES=48
   7  FIELD           NAME=(SEG1KEY,SEQ),BYTES=6,START=1,TYPE=C
   8 *
   9  SEGM            NAME=SEG2,PARENT=SEG1,BYTES=32
  10  FIELD           NAME=(SEG2KEY,SEQ),BYTES=6,START=1,TYPE=C
  11 *
  12  SEGM            NAME=SEG3,PARENT=SEG2,BYTES=16
  13  FIELD           NAME=(SEG3KEY,SEQ),BYTES=6,START=1,TYPE=C
  14 *
  15  SEGM            NAME=SEG4,PARENT=SEG2,BYTES=32
  16  FIELD           NAME=(SEG4KEY,SEQ),BYTES=6,START=1,TYPE=C
  17 *
  18  SEGM            NAME=SEG5,PARENT=SEG1,BYTES=48
  19  FIELD           NAME=(SEG5KEY,SEQ),BYTES=6,START=1,TYPE=C
  20 *
  21  DBDGEN
 171+*,****** SEQUENCE FIELD ******
 178+*,****** SEQUENCE FIELD ******
 185+*,****** SEQUENCE FIELD ******
 192+*,****** SEQUENCE FIELD ******
 199+*,****** SEQUENCE FIELD ******
 256  FINISH
 257  END
```

Figure 15-1 DBDGEN output for the HSAM data base

However, in this example, I specified an unusually small record size to make it easier to illustrate how data is stored in an HSAM data base.

How an HSAM data base is structured HSAM data bases have the simplest structure of all the DL/I data base types: segments are stored in strict hierarchical sequence. To understand, consider figure 15-2. This is a listing of the data set that contains the data base I described in the last chapter.

Notice that the data set has three 512-byte records. The record size agrees with the value I specified in the DBDGEN job. It's just a coincidence that the data set has three records and the data base has three data base records. In HSAM, there's no fixed relationship between the number of data base records and the number of records in the data set that contains the data base.

```
LISTING OF DATA SET -MMA2.EXHSAMO

RECORD SEQUENCE NUMBER - 1
000000  0100E2C5 C7F1F1F1 F1F1F1F1 F1F1F1F1  F1F1F1F1 F1F1F1F1 F1F1F1F1 F1F1F1F1  *..SEG111111111111111111111111111*
000020  F1F1F1F1 F1F1F1F1 F1F1F1F1 F1F1F1F1  F1F10200 E2C5C7F2 F1F1F2F2 F2F2F2F2  *111111111111111111..SEG211222222*
000040  F2F2F2F2 F2F2F2F2 F2F2F2F2 F2F2F2F2  F2F2F2F2 0300E2C5 C7F3F1F1 F3F3F3F3  *22222222222222222222..SEG3113333*
000060  F3F3F3F3 F3F30300 E2C5C7F3 F1F2F3F3  F3F3F3F3 F3F3F3F3 0400E2C5 C7F4F1F1  *333333..SEG3123333333333..SEG411*
000080  F4F4F4F4 F4F4F4F4 F4F4F4F4 F4F4F4F4  F4F4F4F4 F4F4F4F4 F4F40200 E2C5C7F2  *44444444444444444444444444..SEG2*
0000A0  F1F2F2F2 F2F2F2F2 F2F2F2F2 F2F2F2F2  F2F2F2F2 F2F2F2F2 F2F2F2F2 0300E2C5  *1222222222222222222222222222..SE*
0000C0  C7F3F1F1 F3F3F3F3 F3F3F3F3 F3F30300  E2C5C7F3 F1F2F3F3 F3F3F3F3 F3F3F3F3  *G3113333333333..SEG3123333333333*
0000E0  0400E2C5 C7F4F1F1 F4F4F4F4 F4F4F4F4  F4F4F4F4 F4F4F4F4 F4F4F4F4 F4F4F4F4  *..SEG411444444444444444444444444*
000100  F4F40400 E2C5C7F4 F1F2F4F4 F4F4F4F4  F4F4F4F4 F4F4F4F4 F4F4F4F4 F4F4F4F4  *44..SEG4124444444444444444444444*
000120  F4F4F4F4 0500E2C5 C7F5F1F1 F5F5F5F5  F5F5F5F5 F5F5F5F5 F5F5F5F5 F5F5F5F5  *4444..SEG51155555555555555555555*
000140  F5F5F5F5 F5F5F5F5 F5F5F5F5 F5F5F5F5  F5F5F5F5 F5F50100 E2C5C7F1 F2F1F1F1  *5555555555555555555555..SEG12111*
000160  F1F1F1F1 F1F1F1F1 F1F1F1F1 F1F1F1F1  F1F1F1F1 F1F1F1F1 F1F1F1F1 F1F1F1F1  *11111111111111111111111111111111*
000180  F1F1F1F1 F1F1F1F1 0200E2C5 C7F2F2F1  F2F2F2F2 F2F2F2F2 F2F2F2F2 F2F2F2F2  *11111111..SEG2212222222222222222*
0001A0  F2F2F2F2 F2F2F2F2 F2F20300 E2C5C7F3  F2F1F3F3 F3F3F3F3 F3F3F3F3 0300E2C5  *2222222222..SEG3213333333333..SE*
0001C0  C7F3F2F2 F3F3F3F3 F3F3F3F3 F3F30400  E2C5C7F4 F2F1F4F4 F4F4F4F4 F4F4F4F4  *G3223333333333..SEG4214444444444*
0001E0  F4F4F4F4 F4F4F4F4 F4F4F4F4 F4F4F4F4  00000000 00000000 00000000 00000000  *4444444444444444................*

RECORD SEQUENCE NUMBER - 2
000000  0200E2C5 C7F2F2F2 F2F2F2F2 F2F2F2F2  F2F2F2F2 F2F2F2F2 F2F2F2F2 F2F2F2F2  *..SEG222222222222222222222222222*
000020  F2F20300 E2C5C7F3 F2F1F3F3 F3F3F3F3  F3F3F3F3 0300E2C5 C7F3F2F2 F3F3F3F3  *22..SEG3213333333333..SEG3223333*
000040  F3F3F3F3 F3F30400 E2C5C7F4 F2F1F4F4  F4F4F4F4 F4F4F4F4 F4F4F4F4 F4F4F4F4  *333333..SEG421444444444444444444*
000060  F4F4F4F4 F4F4F4F4 0400E2C5 C7F4F2F2  F4F4F4F4 F4F4F4F4 F4F4F4F4 F4F4F4F4  *44444444..SEG4224444444444444444*
000080  F4F4F4F4 F4F4F4F4 F4F40500 E2C5C7F5  F2F1F5F5 F5F5F5F5 F5F5F5F5 F5F5F5F5  *4444444444..SEG52155555555555555*
0000A0  F5F5F5F5 F5F5F5F5 F5F5F5F5 F5F5F5F5  F5F5F5F5 F5F5F5F5 F5F5F5F5 0100E2C5  *5555555555555555555555555555..SE*
0000C0  C7F1F3F1 F1F1F1F1 F1F1F1F1 F1F1F1F1  F1F1F1F1 F1F1F1F1 F1F1F1F1 F1F1F1F1  *G1311111111111111111111111111111*
0000E0  F1F1F1F1 F1F1F1F1 F1F1F1F1 F1F10200  E2C5C7F2 F3F1F2F2 F2F2F2F2 F2F2F2F2  *11111111111111..SEG2312222222222*
000100  F2F2F2F2 F2F2F2F2 F2F2F2F2 F2F2F2F2  0300E2C5 C7F3F3F1 F3F3F3F3 F3F3F3F3  *2222222222222222..SEG33133333333*
000120  F3F30300 E2C5C7F3 F3F2F3F3 F3F3F3F3  F3F3F3F3 0400E2C5 C7F4F3F1 F4F4F4F4  *33..SEG3323333333333..SEG4314444*
000140  F4F4F4F4 F4F4F4F4 F4F4F4F4 F4F4F4F4  F4F4F4F4 F4F40200 E2C5C7F2 F3F2F2F2  *4444444444444444444444..SEG23222*
000160  F2F2F2F2 F2F2F2F2 F2F2F2F2 F2F2F2F2  F2F2F2F2 F2F2F2F2 0300E2C5 C7F3F3F1  *222222222222222222222222..SEG331*
000180  F3F3F3F3 F3F3F3F3 F3F30300 E2C5C7F3  F3F2F3F3 F3F3F3F3 F3F3F3F3 0400E2C5  *3333333333..SEG3323333333333..SE*
0001A0  C7F4F3F1 F4F4F4F4 F4F4F4F4 F4F4F4F4  F4F4F4F4 F4F4F4F4 F4F4F4F4 F4F40400  *G43144444444444444444444444444..*
0001C0  E2C5C7F4 F3F2F4F4 F4F4F4F4 F4F4F4F4  F4F4F4F4 F4F4F4F4 F4F4F4F4 F4F4F4F4  *SEG43244444444444444444444444444*
0001E0  00000000 00000000 00000000 00000000  00000000 00000000 00000000 00000000  *................................*

RECORD SEQUENCE NUMBER - 3
000000  0500E2C5 C7F5F3F1 F5F5F5F5 F5F5F5F5  F5F5F5F5 F5F5F5F5 F5F5F5F5 F5F5F5F5  *..SEG531555555555555555555555555*
000020  F5F5F5F5 F5F5F5F5 F5F5F5F5 F5F5F5F5  F5F50000 00000000 00000000 00000000  *555555555555555555..............*
000040  00000000 00000000 00000000 00000000  00000000 00000000 00000000 00000000  *................................*
000060  00000000 00000000 00000000 00000000  00000000 00000000 00000000 00000000  *................................*
000080  00000000 00000000 00000000 00000000  00000000 00000000 00000000 00000000  *................................*
0000A0  00000000 00000000 00000000 00000000  00000000 00000000 00000000 00000000  *................................*
0000C0  00000000 00000000 00000000 00000000  00000000 00000000 00000000 00000000  *................................*
0000E0  00000000 00000000 00000000 00000000  00000000 00000000 00000000 00000000  *................................*
000100  00000000 00000000 00000000 00000000  00000000 00000000 00000000 00000000  *................................*
000120  00000000 00000000 00000000 00000000  00000000 00000000 00000000 00000000  *................................*
000140  00000000 00000000 00000000 00000000  00000000 00000000 00000000 00000000  *................................*
```

Data base record 1

Data base record 2

Data base record 3

Figure 15-2 Contents of the HSAM data base's data set (part 1 of 2)

```
IDCAMS   SYSTEM SERVICES                                               TIME: 19:08:58          09/04/85      PAGE    5

LISTING OF DATA SET -MMA2.EXHSAMO
000160  00000000 00000000 00000000 00000000   00000000 00000000 00000000 00000000   *................................*
000180  00000000 00000000 00000000 00000000   00000000 00000000 00000000 00000000   *................................*
0001A0  00000000 00000000 00000000 00000000   00000000 00000000 00000000 00000000   *................................*
0001C0  00000000 00000000 00000000 00000000   00000000 00000000 00000000 00000000   *................................*
0001E0  00000000 00000000 00000000 00000000   00000000 00000000 00000000 00000000   *................................*

IDC0005I NUMBER OF RECORDS PROCESSED WAS 3

IDC0001I FUNCTION COMPLETED, HIGHEST CONDITION CODE WAS 0
```

Figure 15-2 Contents of the HSAM data base's data set (part 2 of 2)

That's because DL/I packs segment occurrences as densely as it can into each data set record. To understand, take a closer look at figure 15-2. Here, I've boxed the segment occurrences that make up the second of the three data base records in the sample data base. As you can see, this data base record is split between the first and second data set records.

What happened is that after the segment occurrences for the first record were added to the first data set record, space was left over in it. DL/I used the remaining space for the segment occurrences from the second data base record that would fit (keys SEG121, SEG221, SEG321, SEG322, and SEG421). Even then, 16 free bytes were still left in the first data set record, but that wasn't enough space for the next segment occurrence (SEG222), which required 34 bytes. As a result, DL/I separated the segments in the second data base record, so the rest of its segment occurrences (keys SEG222, SEG321, SEG322, SEG421, SEG422, and SEG521) are stored in the second data set record.

How does DL/I know where segments begin and end? DL/I adds a two-byte *segment prefix* to each segment occurrence, according to the format in figure 15-3. In figure 15-2, I've highlighted the hex values of the segment prefixes in the second data base record.

The first byte of a prefix is the *segment identifier,* and the second is the *delete byte.* The segment identifier indicates the hierarchical position of a segment type. For the root segment, the segment identifier is hex 01; for the second segment type in hierarchical sequence, it's hex 02; and so on. (DL/I uses the segment type specified on an ISRT call to determine the correct value for the segment identifier.) The maximum value of the segment identifier is hex FF, which corresponds to 255: the maximum number of segment types DL/I supports in one data base. The segment identifier values in the segments in figure 15-2 range from hex 01 to hex 05, for each of the five segment types in the sample data base.

The segment identifier tells DL/I what kind of segment it's working with. Then, DL/I determines the segment length from DBD data. The byte after the last byte of a segment occurrence will be the first byte of the next segment occurrence: its segment identifier. If that byte contains low value (hex 00), DL/I knows there are no more segment occurrences in the data set record. (In figure 15-2, that's the case with byte 497 in the first data set record, byte 481 in the second, and byte 51 in the third.)

The delete byte in the segment prefix isn't used in HSAM because HSAM doesn't support delete processing. As a result, the delete bytes in each of the segment occurrences in figure 15-2 have hex 00 as their value.

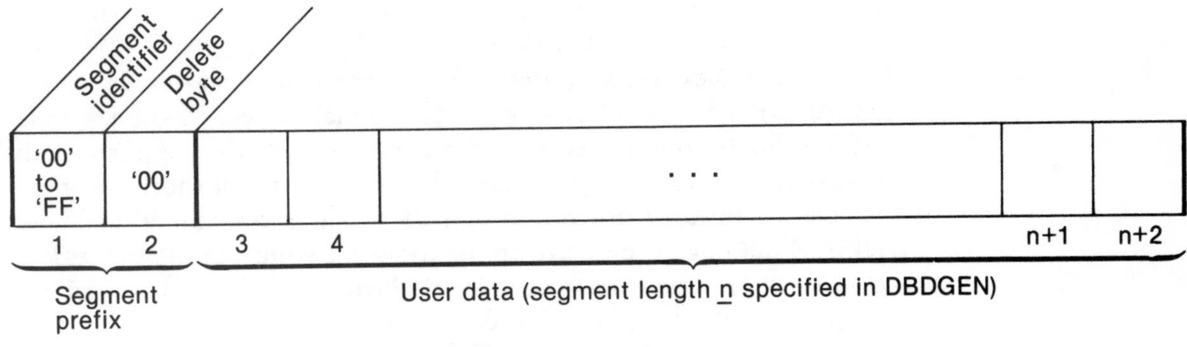

Figure 15-3 Format of a segment in a data base with HS organization

How a SHSAM data base is structured SHSAM, the Simple Hierarchical Sequential Access Method, is a functional subset of HSAM, so if you understand HSAM, you'll understand SHSAM. Basically, a SHSAM data base consists only of root segments. As a result, no segment prefix is necessary to identify segment types. Otherwise, data is stored in a SHSAM data base just like it is in an HSAM data base.

How HSAM and SHSAM data bases can be used Because access to data stored in an HSAM data base is sequential only, you can imagine that the data base's usefulness is limited. As a result, HSAM isn't an appropriate access method for data bases that will have any random processing activity. Although it's possible to issue random retrieval calls against an HSAM data base, performance is usually unacceptable because all preceding segment occurrences have to be read.

HSAM can be appropriate for applications in which (1) large amounts of data that aren't accessed regularly need to be archived for permanent storage and (2) access to that data, when it occurs, is strictly sequential. This is a case when it's also useful to store a data base on tape, a capability that's available only with HSAM.

Because SHSAM supports root-segment-only structures, it's even more limited in application than HSAM. However, the DBA can use SHSAM to treat a standard sequential file as a data base. Then, DL/I recovery facilities can apply to the file.

HISAM

A more complex and powerful data base access method than HSAM is HISAM, the Hierarchical Indexed Sequential Access Method. While HSAM limits you to sequential processing, HISAM supports both sequential and random processing. In this section, I'll show you how the DBA defines a HISAM data base, how data is stored in it, and how HISAM data bases are used. In addition, I'll point out the processing considerations you need to keep in mind when you develop application programs that process HISAM data bases.

How to define a HISAM data base Figure 15-4 is the output of an MVS DBDGEN job for the sample data base implemented with HISAM. Again, the DOS/VSE job would be almost the same. The DBD macro specifies that the access method for the data base is HISAM and that VSAM data sets will be used for it.

A HISAM data base requires two separate data sets: a *primary data set* and an *overflow data set*. They're specified in the DATASET macro in figure 15-4 with these parameters:

```
DD1=HISAMPR
```

for the primary data set and

```
OVFLW=HISAMOV
```

for the overflow data set. In a moment, you'll see how DL/I uses the two data sets to store a single data base.

The DEVICE parameter of the DATASET macro for a HISAM data base must specify a DASD unit. Here again, it's 3380, but it could as well be any of the supported DASD types. Finally, the RECORD parameter specifies the record sizes for the primary and overflow data sets. To make the illustration easy to understand, I've used unrealistically small record sizes here. The other macros in this DBDGEN job are the same as in figure 15-1.

How a HISAM data base is structured The primary data set of a HISAM data base is a keyed file (either a VSAM KSDS or an ISAM file) that contains one record for each data base record. The key of the KSDS or ISAM file is the sequence field of the root segment. As a result, DL/I can directly access the primary data set record that contains a specific root segment occurrence.

```
STMT   SOURCE STATEMENT

  1          PRINT NOGEN
  2  DBD           NAME=EXHISAM,ACCESS=(HISAM,VSAM)
  3  DATASET       DD1=HISAMPR,OVFLW=HISAMOV,DEVICE=3380,RECORD=(128,128)
 4+*,                3380 DISK STORAGE
  5 *
  6  SEGM          NAME=SEG1,BYTES=48
  7  FIELD         NAME=(SEG1KEY,SEQ),BYTES=6,START=1,TYPE=C
  8 *
  9  SEGM          NAME=SEG2,PARENT=SEG1,BYTES=32
 10  FIELD         NAME=(SEG2KEY,SEQ),BYTES=6,START=1,TYPE=C
 11 *
 12  SEGM          NAME=SEG3,PARENT=SEG2,BYTES=16
 13  FIELD         NAME=(SEG3KEY,SEQ),BYTES=6,START=1,TYPE=C
 14 *
 15  SEGM          NAME=SEG4,PARENT=SEG2,BYTES=32
 16  FIELD         NAME=(SEG4KEY,SEQ),BYTES=6,START=1,TYPE=C
 17 *
 18  SEGM          NAME=SEG5,PARENT=SEG1,BYTES=48
 19  FIELD         NAME=(SEG5KEY,SEQ),BYTES=6,START=1,TYPE=C
 20 *
 21  DBDGEN
63+*,* * * * * * * * * * * * * * * * * * * * * * * * * *
64+*,*
65+*,   RECOMMENDED VSAM DEFINE CLUSTER PARAMETERS
66+*,*
67+*,* * * * * * * * * * * * * * * * * * * * * * * * * *
69+*,* * * * * * * * * * * * * * * * * * * * * * * * * *
70+*,*
71+*,*                          *NOTE1
72+*,*   DEFINE CLUSTER (NAME(HISAMPR) -
73+*,*          INDEXED KEYS (6,6) -
74+*,*          RECORDSIZE (128,128)) -
75+*,*          DATA (CONTROLINTERVALSIZE (4096))
76+*,*
77+*,* *NOTE1 - SHOULD SPECIFY DSNAME FOR DD HISAMPR
78+*,*
79+*,* * * * * * * * * * * * * * * * * * * * * * * * * *
81+*,* * * * * * * * * * * * * * * * * * * * * * * * * *
82+*,*
83+*,*                          *NOTE2
84+*,*   DEFINE CLUSTER (NAME(HISAMOV) NONINDEXED -
85+*,*          RECORDSIZE (128,128) -
86+*,*          CONTROLINTERVALSIZE (512))
87+*,*
88+*,* *NOTE2 - SHOULD SPECIFY DSNAME FOR DD HISAMOV
89+*,*
90+*,* * * * * * * * * * * * * * * * * * * * * * * * * *
201+*,****** SEQUENCE FIELD ******
208+*,****** SEQUENCE FIELD ******
215+*,****** SEQUENCE FIELD ******
222+*,****** SEQUENCE FIELD ******
229+*,****** SEQUENCE FIELD ******
286  FINISH
287  END
```

Figure 15-4 DBDGEN output for the HISAM data base

In figure 15-4, you can see that part of the output of the DBDGEN job is a brief listing that describes the characteristics of the data sets that will contain the data base. Look at the information for the KSDS (the primary data set). Its name is HISAMPR, its VSAM control interval size is 4096, and its record length is 128 (specified in the RECORD parameter of the DATASET macro). Its key length is 6 (that's the length of the sequence field of the root segment), and the relative key position is 6 (the first byte in the KSDS record is position 0). The first four bytes of each record contain a pointer to a related record in the overflow data set (more about this in a moment), and the fifth and sixth bytes contain the segment prefix for the root segment.

Now, take a look at part 1 of figure 15-5 to see the contents of the primary data set. The three records in it correspond to the three data base records loaded into the data base. (In a HISAM data base, there's a one-to-one correspondence between data base records and records in the primary data set, unlike HSAM.) The sequence field values of the root segments of these three data base records are SEG111, SEG121, and SEG131. If you look at the key field in positions 6 through 11 of each record, you'll see that those are the values they contain.

Look more closely at the contents of the second primary data set record, the one that corresponds to the second data base record. In this record, there's space for four segment occurrences: the root itself plus three of its dependents. As in an HSAM data base, dependent segments under HISAM are stored in hierarchical sequence. However, when the primary data set record doesn't have enough space to contain all of its root segment's dependents, the dependents that won't fit are stored in the overflow data set.

To relate records in the primary and overflow data sets, HISAM uses the four-byte direct address pointer at the beginning of each record in the primary data set. In the KSDS record for the second data base record in part 1 of figure 15-5, the value of that pointer is hex 300, which converts to decimal 768. That's the relative byte address (RBA) of an overflow record in the overflow data set, which is usually a VSAM ESDS. (The RBA is the displacement of the record from the beginning of the file.)

Now, look to parts 2 and 3 of figure 15-5. This is the overflow data set. As you can see, the record with RBA 768 (decimal) contains the segment occurrences that follow in hierarchical sequence after those in the record in the primary data set.

```
IDCAMS   SYSTEM SERVICES                                                TIME: 15:30:52         09/05/85      PAGE    2

LISTING OF DATA SET -MMA2.HISAMPR

KEY OF RECORD - E2C5C7F1F1F1
000000   00000200 0100E2C5 C7F1F1F1 F1F1F1F1   F1F1F1F1 F1F1F1F1 F1F1F1F1 F1F1F1F1   *......SEG11111111111111111111111*
000020   F1F1F1F1 F1F1F1F1 F1F1F1F1 F1F1F1F1   F1F1F1F1 F1F10200 E2C5C7F2 F1F1F2F2   *1111111111111111111111..SEG21122*
000040   F2F2F2F2 F2F2F2F2 F2F2F2F2 F2F2F2F2   F2F2F2F2 F2F2F2F2 0300E2C5 C7F3F1F1   *222222222222222222222222..SEG311*
000060   F3F3F3F3 F3F3F3F3 F3F30300 E2C5C7F3   F1F2F3F3 F3F3F3F3 F3F3F3F3 00000000   *3333333333..SEG3123333333333....*

KEY OF RECORD - E2C5C7F1F2F1
000000   00000300 0100E2C5 C7F1F2F1 F1F1F1F1   F1F1F1F1 F1F1F1F1 F1F1F1F1 F1F1F1F1   *......SEG12111111111111111111111*
000020   F1F1F1F1 F1F1F1F1 F1F1F1F1 F1F1F1F1   F1F1F1F1 F1F10200 E2C5C7F2 F2F1F2F2   *1111111111111111111111..SEG22122*
000040   F2F2F2F2 F2F2F2F2 F2F2F2F2 F2F2F2F2   F2F2F2F2 F2F2F2F2 0300E2C5 C7F3F2F1   *222222222222222222222222..SEG321*
000060   F3F3F3F3 F3F3F3F3 F3F30300 E2C5C7F3   F2F2F3F3 F3F3F3F3 F3F3F3F3 00000000   *3333333333..SEG3223333333333....*

KEY OF RECORD - E2C5C7F1F3F1
000000   00000480 0100E2C5 C7F1F3F1 F1F1F1F1   F1F1F1F1 F1F1F1F1 F1F1F1F1 F1F1F1F1   *......SEG13111111111111111111111*
000020   F1F1F1F1 F1F1F1F1 F1F1F1F1 F1F1F1F1   F1F1F1F1 F1F10200 E2C5C7F2 F3F1F2F2   *1111111111111111111111..SEG23122*
000040   F2F2F2F2 F2F2F2F2 F2F2F2F2 F2F2F2F2   F2F2F2F2 F2F2F2F2 0300E2C5 C7F3F3F1   *222222222222222222222222..SEG331*
000060   F3F3F3F3 F3F3F3F3 F3F30300 E2C5C7F3   F3F2F3F3 F3F3F3F3 F3F3F3F3 00000000   *3333333333..SEG3323333333333....*

IDC0005I NUMBER OF RECORDS PROCESSED WAS 3

IDC0001I FUNCTION COMPLETED, HIGHEST CONDITION CODE WAS 0
```

Figure 15-5 Contents of the HISAM data base's data sets (part 1 of 3)

```
IDCAMS  SYSTEM SERVICES                                              TIME: 15:30:52        09/05/85     PAGE   4

LISTING OF DATA SET -MMA2.HISAMOV

RBA OF RECORD - 0
000000  85248F15 3046020F 00000000 00000000   00000000 00000000 00000500 C4C6E2F1   *............................DFS1*
000020  4BF24BF0 00000080 00000000 E2000000   00000000 00000000 00000000 00000000   *.2.0........S...................*
000040  00000000 00000000 00000000 00000000   00000000 00000000 00000000 00000000   *................................*
000060  00000000 00000000 00000000 00000000   00000000 00000000 00000000 00000000   *................................*

RBA OF RECORD - 128
000000  00000000 00000000 00000000 00000000   00000000 00000000 00000000 00000000   *................................*
000020  00000000 00000000 00000000 00000000   00000000 00000000 00000000 00000000   *................................*
000040  00000000 00000000 00000000 00000000   00000000 00000000 00000000 00000000   *................................*
000060  00000000 00000000 00000000 00000000   00000000 00000000 00000000 00000000   *................................*

RBA OF RECORD - 256
000000  00000000 00000000 00000000 00000000   00000000 00000000 00000000 00000000   *................................*
000020  00000000 00000000 00000000 00000000   00000000 00000000 00000000 00000000   *................................*
000040  00000000 00000000 00000000 00000000   00000000 00000000 00000000 00000000   *................................*
000060  00000000 00000000 00000000 00000000   00000000 00000000 00000000 00000000   *................................*

RBA OF RECORD - 512
000000  00000280 0400E2C5 C7F4F1F1 F4F4F4F4   F4F4F4F4 F4F4F4F4 F4F4F4F4 F4F4F4F4   *......SEG41144444444444444444444*
000020  F4F4F4F4 F4F40200 E2C5C7F2 F1F2F2F2   F2F2F2F2 F2F2F2F2 F2F2F2F2 F2F2F2F2   *444444..SEG212222222222222222222*
000040  F2F2F2F2 F2F2F2F2 0300E2C5 C7F3F1F1   F3F3F3F3 F3F3F3F3 F3F30300 E2C5C7F3   *22222222..SEG3113333333333..SEG3*
000060  F1F2F3F3 F3F3F3F3 F3F3F3F3 00000000   00000000 00000000 00000000 00000000   *123333333333....................*

RBA OF RECORD - 640
000000  00000000 0400E2C5 C7F4F1F1 F4F4F4F4   F4F4F4F4 F4F4F4F4 F4F4F4F4 F4F4F4F4   *......SEG41144444444444444444444*
000020  F4F4F4F4 F4F40400 E2C5C7F4 F1F2F4F4   F4F4F4F4 F4F4F4F4 F4F4F4F4 F4F4F4F4   *444444..SEG412444444444444444444*
000040  F4F4F4F4 F4F4F4F4 0500E2C5 C7F5F1F1   F5F5F5F5 F5F5F5F5 F5F5F5F5 F5F5F5F5   *44444444..SEG5115555555555555555*
000060  F5F5F5F5 F5F5F5F5 F5F5F5F5 F5F5F5F5   F5F5F5F5 F5F5F5F5 F5F50000 00000000   *55555555555555555555555555......*

RBA OF RECORD - 768
000000  00000400 0400E2C5 C7F4F2F1 F4F4F4F4   F4F4F4F4 F4F4F4F4 F4F4F4F4 F4F4F4F4   *......SEG42144444444444444444444*
000020  F4F4F4F4 F4F40200 E2C5C7F2 F2F2F2F2   F2F2F2F2 F2F2F2F2 F2F2F2F2 F2F2F2F2   *444444..SEG222222222222222222222*
000040  F2F2F2F2 F2F2F2F2 0300E2C5 C7F3F2F1   F3F3F3F3 F3F3F3F3 F3F30300 E2C5C7F3   *22222222..SEG3213333333333..SEG3*
000060  F2F2F3F3 F3F3F3F3 F3F3F3F3 00000000   00000000 00000000 00000000 00000000   *223333333333....................*

RBA OF RECORD - 1024
000000  00000000 0400E2C5 C7F4F2F1 F4F4F4F4   F4F4F4F4 F4F4F4F4 F4F4F4F4 F4F4F4F4   *......SEG42144444444444444444444*
000020  F4F4F4F4 F4F40400 E2C5C7F4 F2F2F4F4   F4F4F4F4 F4F4F4F4 F4F4F4F4 F4F4F4F4   *444444..SEG422444444444444444444*
000040  F4F4F4F4 F4F4F4F4 0500E2C5 C7F5F2F1   F5F5F5F5 F5F5F5F5 F5F5F5F5 F5F5F5F5   *44444444..SEG5215555555555555555*
000060  F5F5F5F5 F5F5F5F5 F5F5F5F5 F5F5F5F5   F5F5F5F5 F5F5F5F5 F5F50000 00000000   *55555555555555555555555555......*

RBA OF RECORD - 1152
000000  00000500 0400E2C5 C7F4F3F1 F4F4F4F4   F4F4F4F4 F4F4F4F4 F4F4F4F4 F4F4F4F4   *......SEG43144444444444444444444*
000020  F4F4F4F4 F4F40200 E2C5C7F2 F3F2F2F2   F2F2F2F2 F2F2F2F2 F2F2F2F2 F2F2F2F2   *444444..SEG232222222222222222222*
000040  F2F2F2F2 F2F2F2F2 0300E2C5 C7F3F3F1   F3F3F3F3 F3F3F3F3 F3F30300 E2C5C7F3   *22222222..SEG3313333333333..SEG3*
000060  F3F2F3F3 F3F3F3F3 F3F3F3F3 00000000   00000000 00000000 00000000 00000000   *323333333333....................*
```

Figure 15-5 Contents of the HISAM data base's data sets (part 2 of 3)

```
IDCAMS   SYSTEM SERVICES                                        TIME: 15:30:52        09/05/85      PAGE    5

LISTING OF DATA SET -MMA2.HISAMOV

RBA OF RECORD - 1280
000000   00000000 0400E2C5 C7F4F3F1 F4F4F4F4   F4F4F4F4 F4F4F4F4 F4F4F4F4 F4F4F4F4   *......SEG43144444444444444444444*
000020   F4F4F4F4 F4F40400 E2C5C7F4 F3F2F4F4   F4F4F4F4 F4F4F4F4 F4F4F4F4 F4F4F4F4   *444444..SEG432444444444444444444*
000040   F4F4F4F4 F4F4F4F4 0500E2C5 C7F5F3F1   F5F5F5F5 F5F5F5F5 F5F5F5F5 F5F5F5F5   *44444444..SEG5315555555555555555*
000060   F5F5F5F5 F5F5F5F5 F5F5F5F5 F5F5F5F5   F5F5F5F5 F5F5F5F5 F5F50000 00000000   *55555555555555555555555555......*

IDC0005I NUMBER OF RECORDS PROCESSED WAS 9

IDC0001I FUNCTION COMPLETED, HIGHEST CONDITION CODE WAS 0
```

Figure 15-5 Contents of the HISAM data base's data sets (part 3 of 3)

Each record in the overflow data set also begins with a four-byte RBA field. Its value points to the next ESDS record that contains more dependent segments for the same data base record. As a result, as many data set records as are necessary can be chained together in the overflow data set to accommodate all the segment occurrences in a single data base record. In part 2 of figure 15-5, the pointer field in the first overflow record for the second data base record points to the record with RBA hex 400, or decimal 1024. It just happens here that it's the next ESDS record in sequence, but it doesn't have to be.

The overflow record with RBA 1024 contains the last of the segment occurrences that make up the second data base record. The hex zeros in its pointer field indicate the end of the chain; there are no more overflow records for this data base record.

In this example, both of the data sets are VSAM files. VSAM is the only option under DL/I DOS/VS. However, under IMS/VS, you can use ISAM for the primary data set and OSAM (the Overflow Sequential Access Method) for the overflow data set. OSAM is a special sequential access method that uses RBA addressing, much like a VSAM ESDS. Although the ISAM/OSAM option is available under IMS, most HISAM data bases are implemented with VSAM data sets.

How a SHISAM data base is structured A SHISAM data base contains only root segments. Since root segments are always stored in the primary data set, there's no overflow data set for a SHISAM data base, nor are overflow pointers required. As a result, a data base administrator can use SHISAM to process a standard VSAM KSDS or an ISAM file using DL/I calls and DL/I recovery facilities.

How HISAM and SHISAM data bases can be used HISAM data bases are appropriate when it's necessary to store data that will be accessed both randomly and sequentially. However, there are some detailed design considerations that can affect the performance of applications that the DBA needs to keep in mind. For example, HISAM is best suited for applications with uniform data base records. If a HISAM data base record contains many segment occurrences, it will use many records in the overflow data set, and retrieval will be time consuming. Similarly, volatile data bases aren't well suited for implementation with HISAM. That's because when data is added to a HISAM data base, segment occurrences may have to be shuffled around, records split, and pointers readjusted; that's inefficient.

Delete processing, although supported under HISAM, doesn't physically remove a segment from the data base. Instead, it sets the segment's delete byte to mark the segment as deleted. Dependents of the deleted segment aren't marked as deleted, but since access to them would be through the deleted parent, they're inaccessible. However, because the deleted segments and their dependents remain in the data sets, they use valuable space. In addition, they reduce performance because DL/I still processes them when it performs certain calls, even though that's transparent to the application program. As a result, HISAM data bases that have update activity must be reorganized periodically.

Discussion

Historically, HSAM and HISAM are the oldest DL/I access methods. With the first releases of IMS, HISAM was the most sophisticated and powerful DL/I access method. However, with IMS/VS, HD access methods were introduced. As you'll see in the next chapter, they provide more flexible and efficient data base structures and support more advanced DL/I features than do HSAM and HISAM.

Terminology

segment prefix
segment identifier
delete byte
primary data set
overflow data set

Objective

Describe the physical structure of and appropriate uses for:

a. a SHSAM data base
b. a HSAM data base
c. a SHISAM data base
d. a HISAM data base

Chapter 16

The direct data base access methods

This chapter describes the structure of the two main DL/I access methods for data bases with direct organization: HDAM and HIDAM. These two access methods differ primarily in how they provide access to root segments. Once a root segment occurrence has been accessed, the mechanisms used to store and retrieve dependent segment occurrences in data bases with direct organizations are basically the same under both HDAM and HIDAM. As a result, this chapter first describes the structure of an HD data base. Then, it describes the differences between HDAM and HIDAM. Finally, it describes how logical relationships are maintained in an HD data base.

STRUCTURE OF A DATA BASE WITH DIRECT ORGANIZATION

As you learned in the last chapter, segments in HSAM and HISAM data bases are related by their physical positions. As a result, segments in a data base with HS organization often have to be moved to keep the hierarchical structure intact when new segments are added to the data base.

In a data base with HD organization, the relationships among segments don't rely on their physical positions in the data set. Instead, segments are related to one another by pointer values stored with them.

The pointer values are four-byte relative byte addresses (RBAs), much like the addresses used in HISAM data bases. However, the direct address pointer values in HISAM point to records in the data base's overflow data set. In contrast, each HD pointer, which is stored in a segment's prefix, points directly to another segment occurrence, whether that segment is at the beginning of a record or not.

After a segment has been inserted into an HD data base, its position is fixed; it isn't moved when other segments are added, as in an HSAM or a HISAM data base. That's because pointers in other segments chain to it, and moving it would cause those pointers to become inaccurate. Also, when a segment is deleted from a data base with HD organization, the space it used is immediately available to store another segment. That's not the case with HISAM.

The system of pointers that the data base administrator can use in a data base with HD organization is complicated. In this chapter, you'll learn the options that are available, and you'll see what DL/I is doing for you as you issue certain calls against an HD data base.

Pointers

IMS/VS provides two main groups of pointers: *hierarchical pointers* and *child/twin pointers*; under DL/I DOS/VS, hierarchical pointers aren't supported. Hierarchical pointers chain individual segment occurrences together and are appropriate when segments are usually retrieved sequentially. So in a sense, the processing characteristics of a data base implemented with hierarchical pointers are much like those of an HSAM or HISAM data base. Child/twin pointers, on the other hand, are a better choice when most processing is random, and they work well when processing is sequential. It is possible to mix pointers of the two types in one IMS data base, but for a given segment type, pointers from only one of the two groups are allowed. In any event, the data base administrator indicates what types of pointers are to be used by coding special parameters in the DBDGEN job. Now, I want to describe pointers of both types in more detail.

Hierarchical pointers To implement a basic hierarchical structure, the IMS DBA can specify *hierarchical forward (HF) pointers*. These are direct address pointers that set up the same hierarchical sequence of segment occurrences that's implemented via physical sequencing in an HSAM or a HISAM data base. For additional flexibility in handling delete processing, the DBA can, along with HF pointers, specify *hierarchical backward (HB) pointers*. These are direct address pointers that chain to the previous segment occurrence in hierarchical sequence.

As I've already mentioned, hierarchical pointers aren't as appropriate for random processing as child/twin pointers. As a result, it's more common for HD data bases to be implemented with the more powerful child/twin pointer types. And VSE users don't have an option because DL/I DOS/VS doesn't support hierarchical pointers.

Child and twin pointers There are four kinds of child/twin pointers. The *physical child first* (*PCF*) *pointer* is the only one of the four that's required whenever child/twin pointers are used. It's part of the prefix of a parent segment, and its value is the RBA of the first occurrence of the related child segment subordinate to the parent segment. If a parent segment has more than one directly dependent segment type, there's one PCF pointer for each.

The *physical child last* (*PCL*) *pointer* is optional. It points to the last occurrence of the specified segment type subordinate to a given parent segment occurrence and can improve performance when calls qualified with the L command code are issued or when processing rules for the segment specify "last."

The two other pointers in this group are twin pointers. They chain to occurrences of the same segment type subordinate to the same parent segment occurrence. If only a single occurrence of a segment type subordinate to a given parent is allowed in a particular data base, a twin pointer isn't required. However, that's unusual. It's more likely that multiple twin segment occurrences may be present. Then, their prefixes must include the *physical twin forward* (*PTF*) *pointer*. Its function is like that of the hierarchical forward pointer: it chains to the next twin segment occurrence in hierarchical sequence. The *physical twin backward* (*PTB*) *pointer* is optional. The DBA might specify it for reasons similar to those for specifying the HB pointer.

Figure 16-1 shows how all of the child/twin pointers that can be present in a segment prefix are organized. As with the other DL/I access methods, the prefix begins with the segment identifier and the delete byte that, together, use two bytes. Then, between the delete byte and the user data, all of the specified pointers are stored. Remember, each HD pointer is an RBA value and, as a result, is four bytes long.

The first pointer in the prefix in figure 16-1 is the physical twin forward pointer. It's almost always present. The next pointer could be the physical twin backward pointer. It probably won't be present, but if it is, it immediately follows the PTF pointer. If a segment type is not a

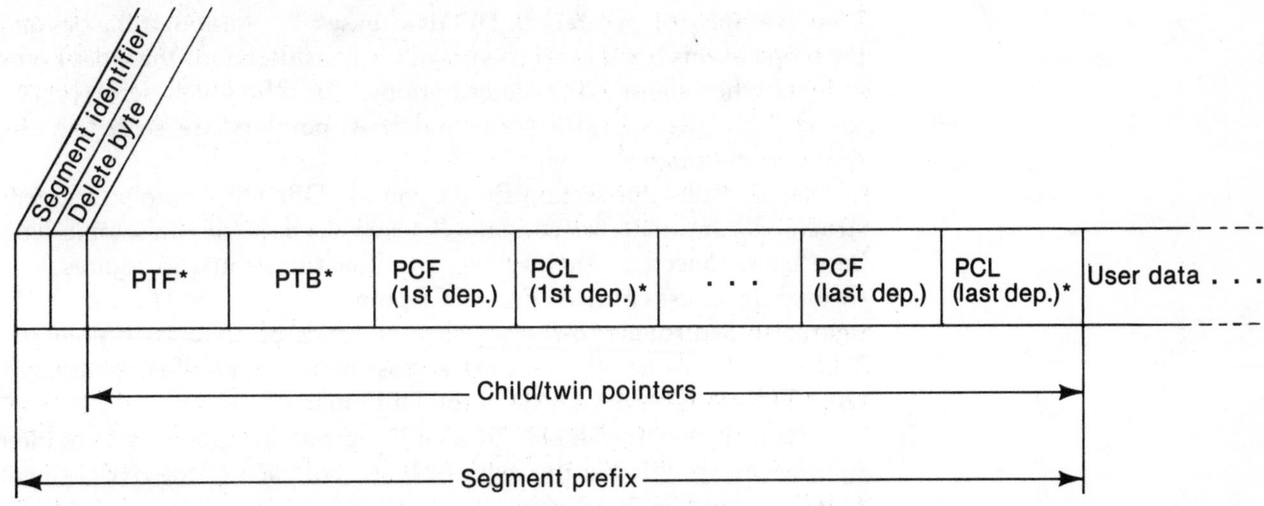

Figure 16-1 Format of a parent segment in a data base with HD organization

parent, user data follows the PTB pointer or, if the PTB pointer is absent, the PTF pointer.

On the other hand, if a segment type is a parent, the specified child pointers are stored between the twin pointer(s) and the user data. At the least, there's one physical child first (PCF) pointer for each segment type that can be subordinate to the parent. They're stored in the parent's segment prefix in hierarchical sequence. In addition, one or more physical child last pointers can be present, depending on the DBA's specifications. If a PCL pointer is present for a child segment type, it immediately follows its corresponding PCF pointer.

As you can imagine, a parent segment with several child segment types can have a long segment prefix. For example, the prefix of a parent segment with the maximum number of pointers and six child segment types is 58 bytes long. And that's overhead that's present in *each* occurrence of the parent segment, not just once in the data base or once in each data base record. Of course, the more pointers that are used, the more work DL/I has to do when the data base is updated to insure that they're all accurate.

It's a challenge for the DBA to select the best pointers for a given data base. Obviously, the pointers the DBA selects have to meet the requirements of the application. However, they also should use as little DASD space and as few DL/I resources as possible.

Two examples of pointers in HD data bases Although it's beyond the scope of this book to teach you all the considerations the DBA keeps in mind when she selects pointer options, I still think it's useful for you to see how she specifies them and how pointers are stored in the resulting data bases.

As a result, this section shows you the DBDGEN output, segment structures, and data set contents for two versions of the sample data base I introduced in chapter 14. The first (illustrated in figures 16-2 through 16-4) uses only PTF and PCF pointers; the second (illustrated in figures 16-5 through 16-7) uses all four kinds of child/twin pointers. Both data bases use the HDAM access method and VSAM data sets (ACCESS=(HDAM,VSAM) in the DBD macro).

As you can see in the DBDGEN output in figure 16-2, pointer options are specified at the segment level. For each of the five segment types in figure 16-2, I coded

```
POINTER=TWIN
```

This means that PTF pointers will be included in the prefixes of occurrences of all five segment types. If I had coded

```
POINTER=TWINBWD
```

PTB as well as PTF pointers would have been included. If one or more of these segment types would never have twin occurrences, I could have coded

```
POINTER=NOTWIN
```

to suppress twin pointers altogether. However, that's uncommon.

To specify whether just PCF or both PCF and PCL pointers should be stored in parent segments, the DBA codes specifications in the PARENT parameter of the SEGM macros for the child segments. Besides the name of the parent segment, the PARENT parameter also indicates whether only a PCF pointer should be part of the parent's prefix (the default) or whether the prefix should include both a PCF and a PCL pointer for the child segment type. If the PARENT parameter specifies SNGL (or doesn't specify a pointer option at all), only the PCF pointer is used for the child segment. On the other hand, if the PARENT parameter specifies DBLE, both PCF and PCL pointers are used. In figure 16-2, the SEGM macros for segment types 2 through 5 specify SNGL, so no PCL pointers will be used in this version of the data base.

```
STMT   SOURCE STATEMENT

   1            PRINT NOGEN
   2  DBD             NAME=EXHDAM,ACCESS=(HDAM,VSAM),RMNAME=(DFSHDC10,,10)
   3  DATASET         DD1=EXHDAM,DEVICE=3380
  4+*,                  3380 DISK STORAGE
   5 *
   6  SEGM            NAME=SEG1,BYTES=48,POINTER=TWIN
   7  FIELD           NAME=(SEG1KEY,SEQ),BYTES=6,START=1,TYPE=C
   8 *
   9  SEGM            NAME=SEG2,PARENT=((SEG1,SNGL)),BYTES=32,POINTER=TWIN
  10  FIELD           NAME=(SEG2KEY,SEQ),BYTES=6,START=1,TYPE=C
  11 *
  12  SEGM            NAME=SEG3,PARENT=((SEG2,SNGL)),BYTES=16,POINTER=TWIN
  13  FIELD           NAME=(SEG3KEY,SEQ),BYTES=6,START=1,TYPE=C
  14 *
  15  SEGM            NAME=SEG4,PARENT=((SEG2,SNGL)),BYTES=32,POINTER=TWIN
  16  FIELD           NAME=(SEG4KEY,SEQ),BYTES=6,START=1,TYPE=C
  17 *
  18  SEGM            NAME=SEG5,PARENT=((SEG1,SNGL)),BYTES=48,POINTER=TWIN
  19  FIELD           NAME=(SEG5KEY,SEQ),BYTES=6,START=1,TYPE=C
  20 *
  21  DBDGEN
 63+*,* * * * * * * * * * * * * * * * * * * * * * * * * *
 64+*,*
 65+*,    RECOMMENDED VSAM DEFINE CLUSTER PARAMETERS
 66+*,*
 67+*,* * * * * * * * * * * * * * * * * * * * * * * * * *
 69+*,* * * * * * * * * * * * * * * * * * * * * * * * * *
 70+*,*
 71+*,*                       *NOTE2
 72+*,*    DEFINE CLUSTER (NAME(EXHDAM) NONINDEXED -
 73+*,*           RECORDSIZE (2041,2041) -
 74+*,*           CONTROLINTERVALSIZE (2048))
 75+*,*
 76+*,* *NOTE2 - SHOULD SPECIFY DSNAME FOR DD EXHDAM
 77+*,*
 78+*,* * * * * * * * * * * * * * * * * * * * * * * * * *
189+*,****** SEQUENCE FIELD ******
196+*,****** SEQUENCE FIELD ******
203+*,****** SEQUENCE FIELD ******
210+*,****** SEQUENCE FIELD ******
217+*,****** SEQUENCE FIELD ******
283   FINISH
284   END
```

Figure 16-2 DBDGEN ouput for the HDAM data base (version 1)

Notice in the bottom of figure 16-2 that the data set that will contain this data base is a VSAM entry-sequenced data set. Also, notice that the record length for it is 2041 bytes.

Before I show you the listing of the data set that contains this data base, I want you to think for a moment about what the formats of its segments are. Figure 16-3 shows that all of the segments have a PTF pointer, and it's the first pointer in each segment. Because segments 3, 4, and 5 aren't parent segments, they don't have any other pointers; user data immediately follows the PTF pointer in them. However, segments 1 and 2 do have additional pointers: one PCF pointer for each segment type that's subordinate to them. For segment 1, there's a PCF pointer for segment 2 and another for segment 5. And for segment 2, there's a PCF pointer for segment 3 and one for segment 4.

Now that you know what to expect in the data set, take a look at figure 16-4. This is part of the listing of the ESDS that contains the HDAM data base. I've selected just the record that includes the segment occurrences themselves.

Before I discuss the individual pointer values, I want you to recall that an RBA is a displacement from the beginning of a data set. In this example, the segments are in the third record in the data set, which begins at RBA 4096. The displacements shown down the left side of the listing, given in hexadecimal, are from the beginning of the third record, not from the beginning of the data set. As a result, to calculate the displacement from the beginning of the data set, you add the hex value for 4096 (1000) to the displacements in the listing. Then, the values in the pointers will make sense.

In both the hex and character sections of figure 16-4, I've drawn a box around the segment occurrences that make up the second data base record in the sample data base. Then, in the hex portion, I've shaded the segment prefix of each segment in that record and marked its parts. Remember that each segment prefix begins with the segment identifier, the delete byte, and the PTF pointer (a total of 6 bytes). In addition, the prefixes for segment types 1 and 2 have two PCF pointers, so they're 14 bytes long.

Now, look at the first shaded prefix. It's for the data base record's root segment, as the hex value 01 in the segment identifier field tells you. The first pointer chains to the next twin of this segment, which is the third data base record's root segment. As the arrow shows, it begins immediately after the boxed data, at RBA hex 133C. (Remember, for this data set record, you add hex 1000 to the displacement values on the left side of the listing to get the displacement from the beginning of the data set, which is what the pointer values specify.) The other two pointer values in the shaded root segment prefix, hex 11E0 and 1306, are PCF pointers. They're the RBAs of the first occurrences within this data base record of segment types 2 and 5.

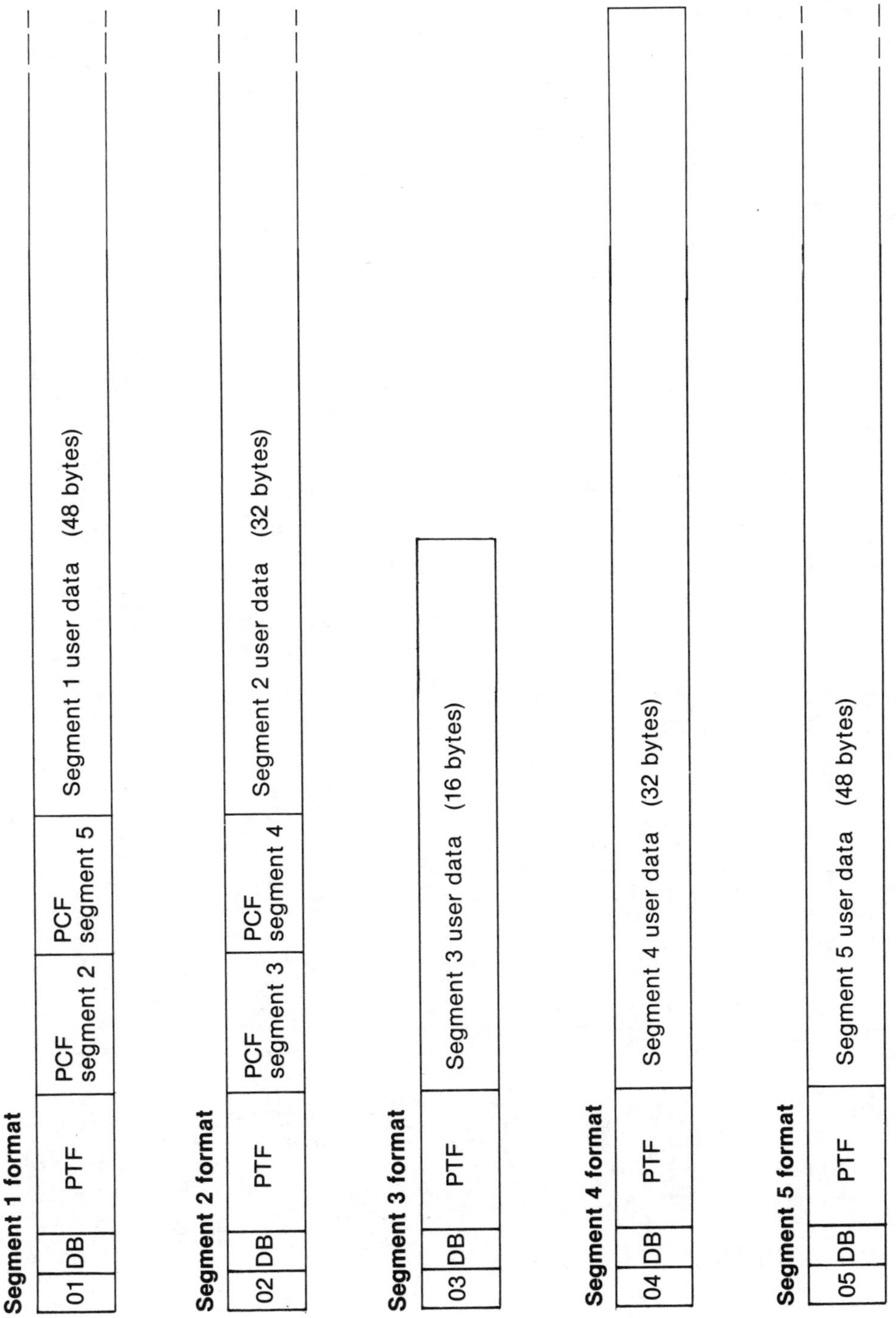

Segment 1 format

01	DB	PTF	PCF segment 2	PCF segment 5	Segment 1 user data (48 bytes)

Segment 2 format

02	DB	PTF	PCF segment 3	PCF segment 4	Segment 2 user data (32 bytes)

Segment 3 format

03	DB	PTF	Segment 3 user data (16 bytes)

Segment 4 format

04	DB	PTF	Segment 4 user data (32 bytes)

Segment 5 format

05	DB	PTF	Segment 5 user data (48 bytes)

Figure 16-3 Segment formats for the HDAM data base (version 1)

```
IDCAMS  SYSTEM SERVICES                                          TIME: 13:13:04        09/07/85     PAGE   2

LISTING OF DATA SET -MMA2.EXHDAM

RBA OF RECORD - 4096
000000  04D60000 00001008 01000000 11A20000   10460000 116CE2C5 C7F1F1F1 F1F1F1F1   *.O...................%SEG1111111*
000020  F1F1F1F1 F1F1F1F1 F1F1F1F1 F1F1F1F1   F1F1F1F1 F1F1F1F1 F1F1F1F1 F1F1F1F1   *11111111111111111111111111111111*
000040  F1F1F1F1 F1F10200 000010C6 00001074   000010A0 E2C5C7F2 F1F1F2F2 F2F2F2F2   *111111.....F........SEG211222222*
000060  F2F2F2F2 F2F2F2F2 F2F2F2F2 F2F2F2F2   F2F2F2F2 03000000 108AE2C5 C7F3F1F1   *22222222222222222222......SEG311*
000080  F3F3F3F3 F3F3F3F3 F3F30300 00000000   E2C5C7F3 F1F2F3F3 F3F3F3F3 F3F3F3F3   *3333333333......SEG3123333333333*
0000A0  04000000 0000E2C5 C7F4F1F1 F4F4F4F4   F4F4F4F4 F4F4F4F4 F4F4F4F4 F4F4F4F4   *......SEG41144444444444444444444*
0000C0  F4F4F4F4 F4F40200 00000000 000010F4   00001120 E2C5C7F2 F1F2F2F2 F2F2F2F2   *444444.........4....SEG212222222*
0000E0  F2F2F2F2 F2F2F2F2 F2F2F2F2 F2F2F2F2   F2F2F2F2 03000000 110AE2C5 C7F3F1F1   *22222222222222222222......SEG311*
000100  F3F3F3F3 F3F3F3F3 F3F30300 00000000   E2C5C7F3 F1F2F3F3 F3F3F3F3 F3F3F3F3   *3333333333......SEG3123333333333*
000120  04000000 1146E2C5 C7F4F1F1 F4F4F4F4   F4F4F4F4 F4F4F4F4 F4F4F4F4 F4F4F4F4   *......SEG41144444444444444444444*
000140  F4F4F4F4 F4F40400 00000000 E2C5C7F4   F1F2F4F4 F4F4F4F4 F4F4F4F4 F4F4F4F4   *444444......SEG41244444444444444*
000160  F4F4F4F4 F4F4F4F4 F4F4F4F4 05000000   0000E2C5 C7F5F1F1 F5F5F5F5 F5F5F5F5   *444444444444......SEG51155555555*
000180  F5F5F5F5 F5F5F5F5 F5F5F5F5 F5F5F5F5   F5F5F5F5 F5F5F5F5 F5F5F5F5 F5F5F5F5   *55555555555555555555555555555555*
0001A0  F5F50100 0000133C 000011E0 00001306   E2C5C7F1 F2F1F1F1 F1F1F1F1 F1F1F1F1   *55..............SEG1211111111111*
0001C0  F1F1F1F1 F1F1F1F1 F1F1F1F1 F1F1F1F1   F1F1F1F1 F1F1F1F1 F1F1F1F1 F1F1F1F1   *11111111111111111111111111111111*
0001E0  02000000 12600000 120E0000 123AE2C5   C7F2F2F1 F2F2F2F2 F2F2F2F2 F2F2F2F2   *.....-........SEG221222222222222*
000200  F2F2F2F2 F2F2F2F2 F2F2F2F2 F2F20300   00001224 E2C5C7F3 F2F1F3F3 F3F3F3F3   *22222222222222......SEG321333333*
000220  F3F3F3F3 03000000 0000E2C5 C7F3F2F2   F3F3F3F3 F3F3F3F3 F3F30400 00000000   *3333......SEG3223333333333......*
000240  E2C5C7F4 F2F1F4F4 F4F4F4F4 F4F4F4F4   F4F4F4F4 F4F4F4F4 F4F4F4F4 F4F4F4F4   *SEG42144444444444444444444444444*
000260  02000000 00000000 128E0000 12BAE2C5   C7F2F2F2 F2F2F2F2 F2F2F2F2 F2F2F2F2   *..............SEG222222222222222*
000280  F2F2F2F2 F2F2F2F2 F2F2F2F2 F2F20300   000012A4 E2C5C7F3 F2F1F3F3 F3F3F3F3   *22222222222222......SEG321333333*
0002A0  F3F3F3F3 03000000 0000E2C5 C7F3F2F2   F3F3F3F3 F3F3F3F3 F3F30400 000012E0   *3333......SEG3223333333333......*
0002C0  E2C5C7F4 F2F1F4F4 F4F4F4F4 F4F4F4F4   F4F4F4F4 F4F4F4F4 F4F4F4F4 F4F4F4F4   *SEG42144444444444444444444444444*
0002E0  04000000 0000E2C5 C7F4F2F2 F4F4F4F4   F4F4F4F4 F4F4F4F4 F4F4F4F4 F4F4F4F4   *......SEG42244444444444444444444*
000300  F4F4F4F4 F4F40500 00000000 E2C5C7F5   F2F1F5F5 F5F5F5F5 F5F5F5F5 F5F5F5F5   *444444......SEG52155555555555555*
000320  F5F5F5F5 F5F5F5F5 F5F5F5F5 F5F5F5F5   F5F5F5F5 F5F5F5F5 F5F5F5F5 01000000   *5555555555555555555555555555....*
000340  00000000 137A0000 14A0E2C5 C7F1F3F1   F1F1F1F1 F1F1F1F1 F1F1F1F1 F1F1F1F1   *.....:....SEG1311111111111111111*
000360  F1F1F1F1 F1F1F1F1 F1F1F1F1 F1F1F1F1   F1F1F1F1 F1F1F1F1 F1F10200 000013FA   *11111111111111111111111111......*
000380  000013A8 000013D4 E2C5C7F2 F3F1F2F2   F2F2F2F2 F2F2F2F2 F2F2F2F2 F2F2F2F2   *.......MSEG231222222222222222222*
0003A0  F2F2F2F2 F2F2F2F2 03000000 13BEE2C5   C7F3F3F1 F3F3F3F3 F3F3F3F3 F3F30300   *22222222......SEG3313333333333..*
0003C0  00000000 E2C5C7F3 F3F2F3F3 F3F3F3F3   F3F3F3F3 04000000 0000E2C5 C7F4F3F1   *....SEG3323333333333......SEG431*
0003E0  F4F4F4F4 F4F4F4F4 F4F4F4F4 F4F4F4F4   F4F4F4F4 F4F4F4F4 F4F40200 00000000   *44444444444444444444444444......*
000400  00001428 00001454 E2C5C7F2 F3F2F2F2   F2F2F2F2 F2F2F2F2 F2F2F2F2 F2F2F2F2   *........SEG232222222222222222222*
000420  F2F2F2F2 F2F2F2F2 03000000 143EE2C5   C7F3F3F1 F3F3F3F3 F3F3F3F3 F3F30300   *22222222......SEG3313333333333..*
000440  00000000 E2C5C7F3 F3F2F3F3 F3F3F3F3   F3F3F3F3 04000000 147AE2C5 C7F4F3F1   *....SEG3323333333333.....:SEG431*
000460  F4F4F4F4 F4F4F4F4 F4F4F4F4 F4F4F4F4   F4F4F4F4 F4F4F4F4 F4F40400 0000000C   *44444444444444444444444444......*
000480  E2C5C7F4 F3F2F4F4 F4F4F4F4 F4F4F4F4   F4F4F4F4 F4F4F4F4 F4F4F4F4 F4F4F4F4   *SEG43244444444444444444444444444*
0004A0  05000000 0000E2C5 C7F5F3F1 F5F5F5F5   F5F5F5F5 F5F5F5F5 F5F5F5F5 F5F5F5F5   *......SEG53155555555555555555555*
0004C0  F5F5F5F5 F5F5F5F5 F5F5F5F5 F5F5F5F5   F5F5F5F5 F5F50000 03220000 00000000   *5555555555555555555555..........*
0004E0  00000000 00000000 00000000 00000000   00000000 00000000 00000000 00000000   *................................*
000500  00000000 00000000 00000000 00000000   00000000 00000000 00000000 00000000   *................................*
000520  00000000 00000000 00000000 00000000   00000000 00000000 00000000 00000000   *................................*
000540  00000000 00000000 00000000 00000000   00000000 00000000 00000000 00000000   *................................*
000560  00000000 00000000 00000000 00000000   00000000 00000000 00000000 00000000   *................................*
000580  00000000 00000000 00000000 00000000   00000000 00000000 00000000 00000000   *................................*
0005A0  00000000 00000000 00000000 00000000   00000000 00000000 00000000 00000000   *................................*
0005C0  00000000 00000000 00000000 00000000   00000000 00000000 00000000 00000000   *................................*
```

Figure 16-4 Contents of the HDAM data base's data set (version 1) (part 1 of 2)

```
IDCAMS   SYSTEM SERVICES                                                  TIME: 13:13:04        09/07/85     PAGE    3

LISTING OF DATA SET -MMA2.EXHDAM

0005E0  00000000 00000000 00000000 00000000   00000000 00000000 00000000 00000000   *................................*
000600  00000000 00000000 00000000 00000000   00000000 00000000 00000000 00000000   *................................*
000620  00000000 00000000 00000000 00000000   00000000 00000000 00000000 00000000   *................................*
000640  00000000 00000000 00000000 00000000   00000000 00000000 00000000 00000000   *................................*
000660  00000000 00000000 00000000 00000000   00000000 00000000 00000000 00000000   *................................*
000680  00000000 00000000 00000000 00000000   00000000 00000000 00000000 00000000   *................................*
0006A0  00000000 00000000 00000000 00000000   00000000 00000000 00000000 00000000   *................................*
0006C0  00000000 00000000 00000000 00000000   00000000 00000000 00000000 00000000   *................................*
0006E0  00000000 00000000 00000000 00000000   00000000 00000000 00000000 00000000   *................................*
000700  00000000 00000000 00000000 00000000   00000000 00000000 00000000 00000000   *................................*
000720  00000000 00000000 00000000 00000000   00000000 00000000 00000000 00000000   *................................*
000740  00000000 00000000 00000000 00000000   00000000 00000000 00000000 00000000   *................................*
000760  00000000 00000000 00000000 00000000   00000000 00000000 00000000 00000000   *................................*
000780  00000000 00000000 00000000 00000000   00000000 00000000 00000000 00000000   *................................*
0007A0  00000000 00000000 00000000 00000000   00000000 00000000 00000000 00000000   *................................*
0007C0  00000000 00000000 00000000 00000000   00000000 00000000 00000000 00000000   *................................*
0007E0  00000000 00000000 00000000 00000000   00000000 00000000 00                  *.........................       *

IDC0005I NUMBER OF RECORDS PROCESSED WAS 1

IDC0001I FUNCTION COMPLETED, HIGHEST CONDITION CODE WAS 0
```

Figure 16-4 Contents of the HDAM data base's data set (version 1) (part 2 of 2)

The next shaded prefix is for the first occurrence of segment 2 in this data base record. It begins at RBA 11E0, as the PCF pointer in the segment 1 prefix indicates. The PTF pointer in this segment 2 prefix points ahead to the next occurrence of segment 2 in the data base record (RBA 1260). Its other two pointer values, 120E and 123A, are the RBAs of the first subordinate occurrences of segment types 3 and 4.

The first occurrence of segment 3, the third shaded segment prefix, contains only a PTF pointer, which chains ahead to the next occurrence of segment 3, at RBA 1224. That occurrence, whose segment prefix is the fourth one in figure 16-4, is the last segment 3 occurrence subordinate to the current parent, so its PTF pointer contains hex zeros.

The fifth segment prefix in the figure is for the only segment 4 occurrence subordinate to the current parent. As a result, its PTF pointer contains hex zeros. The sixth segment prefix is for another occurrence of segment 2. The PTF value in the previous segment 2 occurrence (RBA 1260) chains to it. And the system of pointers continues on throughout the segment occurrences. If you take a moment and study the addresses in each of the shaded cells in figure 16-4, I think the scheme for direct addressing will be clearer to you.

To help you understand implementations that use more complicated pointer structures, consider figures 16-5 through 16-7. This is the same data base as in figures 16-2 through 16-4, but with physical twin backward and physical child last pointers as well as PTF and PCF pointers.

Figure 16-5 is the DBDGEN output for the data base version with these pointers. As you can see, I specified

```
POINTER=TWINBWD
```

for each of the five segment types to insure that both PTF and PTB pointers would be used. In addition, for each child segment, I coded DBLE on the PARENT parameter of the SEGM macro to insure that both physical child first and physical child last pointers would be used.

The resulting segment structures are in figure 16-6. Notice in each case that the PTB pointer immediately follows the PTF pointer. And PCL pointers immediately follow their related PCF pointers.

Figure 16-7 shows the part of the data base ESDS that contains the second data base record. I'm not going to describe all the pointer relationships in this example; you can review them yourself. However, notice that in this example, even more than in figure 16-4, a relatively large percentage of each data base record is occupied not by user data, but by pointers.

```
STMT   SOURCE STATEMENT

   1           PRINT NOGEN
   2  DBD            NAME=EXHDAM,ACCESS=(HDAM,VSAM),RMNAME=(DFSHDC10,,10)
   3  DATASET        DD1=EXHDAM,DEVICE=3380
   4+*,                3380 DISK STORAGE
   5 *
   6  SEGM           NAME=SEG1,BYTES=48,POINTER=TWINBWD
   7  FIELD          NAME=(SEG1KEY,SEQ),BYTES=6,START=1,TYPE=C
   8 *
   9  SEGM           NAME=SEG2,PARENT=((SEG1,DBLE)),BYTES=32,POINTER=TWINBWD
  10  FIELD          NAME=(SEG2KEY,SEQ),BYTES=6,START=1,TYPE=C
  11 *
  12  SEGM           NAME=SEG3,PARENT=((SEG2,DBLE)),BYTES=16,POINTER=TWINBWD
  13  FIELD          NAME=(SEG3KEY,SEQ),BYTES=6,START=1,TYPE=C
  14 *
  15  SEGM           NAME=SEG4,PARENT=((SEG2,DBLE)),BYTES=32,POINTER=TWINBWD
  16  FIELD          NAME=(SEG4KEY,SEQ),BYTES=6,START=1,TYPE=C
  17 *
  18  SEGM           NAME=SEG5,PARENT=((SEG1,DBLE)),BYTES=48,POINTER=TWINBWD
  19  FIELD          NAME=(SEG5KEY,SEQ),BYTES=6,START=1,TYPE=C
  20 *
  21  DBDGEN
  63+*,* * * * * * * * * * * * * * * * * * * * * * * * * *
  64+*,*
  65+*,   RECOMMENDED VSAM DEFINE CLUSTER PARAMETERS
  66+*,*
  67+*,* * * * * * * * * * * * * * * * * * * * * * * * * *
  69+*,* * * * * * * * * * * * * * * * * * * * * * * * * *
  70+*,*
  71+*,*                    *NOTE2
  72+*,*   DEFINE CLUSTER (NAME(EXHDAM) NONINDEXED -
  73+*,*          RECORDSIZE (2041,2041) -
  74+*,*          CONTROLINTERVALSIZE (2048))
  75+*,*
  76+*,* *NOTE2 - SHOULD SPECIFY DSNAME FOR DD EXHDAM
  77+*,*
  78+*,* * * * * * * * * * * * * * * * * * * * * * * * * *
 189+*,****** SEQUENCE FIELD ******
 196+*,****** SEQUENCE FIELD ******
 203+*,****** SEQUENCE FIELD ******
 210+*,****** SEQUENCE FIELD ******
 217+*,****** SEQUENCE FIELD ******
 283  FINISH
 284  END
```

Figure 16-5 DBDGEN output for the HDAM data base (version 2)

Space management in HD data bases

In addition to providing direct access to segments based on pointers, the HD access methods also manage space more efficiently than HSAM and HISAM. This section describes how DL/I manages free space in an HD

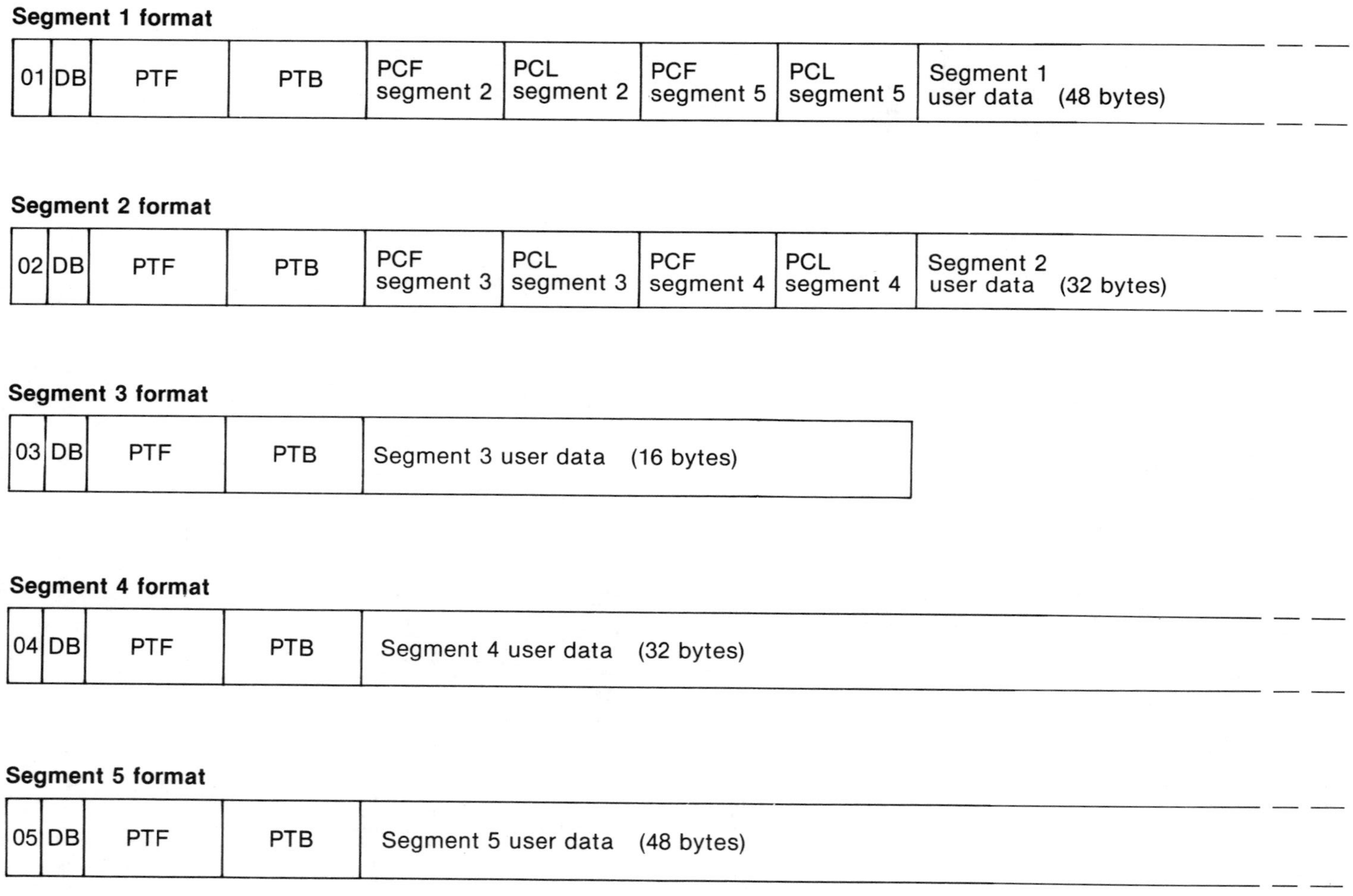

Segment 1 format

01	DB	PTF	PTB	PCF segment 2	PCL segment 2	PCF segment 5	PCL segment 5	Segment 1 user data (48 bytes)

Segment 2 format

02	DB	PTF	PTB	PCF segment 3	PCL segment 3	PCF segment 4	PCL segment 4	Segment 2 user data (32 bytes)

Segment 3 format

03	DB	PTF	PTB	Segment 3 user data (16 bytes)

Segment 4 format

04	DB	PTF	PTB	Segment 4 user data (32 bytes)

Segment 5 format

05	DB	PTF	PTB	Segment 5 user data (48 bytes)

Figure 16-6 Segment formats for the HDAM data base (version 2)

data base both within a single physical record and within the entire data base data set.

Space management at the physical record level In each physical record in an HD data base's data set, DL/I maintains fields to keep track of where free space is located. To help you understand how this works, I'm going to use the same data set record illustrated in figure 16-7.

In figure 16-8, I've shaded the fields DL/I uses for HD free space management. Each physical record in an HD data base that contains user data begins with a two-byte *free space element anchor point* (*FSEAP*). The value in the FSEAP is a pointer to the first available free space within the physical record. In figure 16-8, the FSEAP's value is 5A2. If you look to displacement 5A2 within this record, you'll find that it's the byte that follows the last segment stored in the record.

The first eight bytes in a section of free space in a physical record is a *free space element* (*FSE*). In figure 16-8, the FSE pointed to by the FSEAP is shaded. Let me describe the format of the FSE working backwards. The four-byte field on the right is the *task-id field*; it's used in interactive applications to let programs reuse space they free without having to compete with other programs for it. In this example, the task-id field contains hex zeros.

The FSE's middle field, which uses two bytes, contains the total size of the section of free space. It's called the *available space field*. In figure 16-8, its value is hex 256, or decimal 598. If you count the number of free bytes remaining in the record after the last segment occurrence (including the FSE), you'll see that the total is 599. However, only 598 are available because HD operations are in increments of even numbers (all segments are stored on halfword boundaries).

The first two-byte field in an FSE is the *chain pointer field*. It points to the next section of free space in the record. In the FSE in figure 16-8, the pointer contains hex zeros. That means there are no more free spaces in the record. However, if a segment is deleted from this data set record, the situation changes.

For example, figure 16-9 shows the same data set record after the second data base record has been deleted (a DLET call was issued for the root segment). The FSEAP in figure 16-9 points not to the original free space in the physical record, but to what was the beginning position of the first segment in the second data base record: displacement hex 1E6. DL/I wrote a new FSE in that location that indicates the amount of free space that follows is 478 bytes (hex 1DE). In addition, the chain pointer value in the new FSE points to the original FSE (displacement hex 5A2).

```
IDCAMS  SYSTEM SERVICES                                    TIME: 13:23:07        09/07/85     PAGE   2

LISTING OF DATA SET -MMA2.EXHDAM

RBA OF RECORD - 4096
000000  05A20000 00001008 01000000 11E60000  00000000 10520000 10EA0000 11AC0000  *.............W..................*
000020  11ACE2C5 C7F1F1F1 F1F1F1F1 F1F1F1F1  F1F1F1F1 F1F1F1F1 F1F1F1F1 F1F1F1F1  *..SEG111111111111111111111111111*
000040  F1F1F1F1 F1F1F1F1 F1F1F1F1 F1F1F1F1  F1F10200 000010EA 00000000 0000108C  *111111111111111111..............*
000060  000010A6 000010C0 000010C0 E2C5C7F2  F1F1F2F2 F2F2F2F2 F2F2F2F2 F2F2F2F2  *............SEG21122222222222222*
000080  F2F2F2F2 F2F2F2F2 F2F2F2F2 03000000  10A60000 0000E2C5 C7F3F1F1 F3F3F3F3  *222222222222..........SEG3113333*
0000A0  F3F3F3F3 F3F30300 00000000 0000108C  E2C5C7F3 F1F2F3F3 F3F3F3F3 F3F3F3F3  *333333..........SEG3123333333333*
0000C0  04000000 00000000 0000E2C5 C7F4F1F1  F4F4F4F4 F4F4F4F4 F4F4F4F4 F4F4F4F4  *..........SEG4114444444444444444*
0000E0  F4F4F4F4 F4F4F4F4 F4F40200 00000000  00001052 00001124 0000113E 00001158  *4444444444......................*
000100  00001182 E2C5C7F2 F1F2F2F2 F2F2F2F2  F2F2F2F2 F2F2F2F2 F2F2F2F2 F2F2F2F2  *....SEG21222222222222222222222222*
000120  F2F2F2F2 03000000 113E0000 0000E2C5  C7F3F1F1 F3F3F3F3 F3F3F3F3 F3F30300  *2222..........SEG3113333333333..*
000140  00000000 00001124 E2C5C7F3 F1F2F3F3  F3F3F3F3 F3F3F3F3 04000000 11820000  *........SEG3123333333333........*
000160  0000E2C5 C7F4F1F1 F4F4F4F4 F4F4F4F4  F4F4F4F4 F4F4F4F4 F4F4F4F4 F4F4F4F4  *..SEG411444444444444444444444444*
000180  F4F40400 00000000 00001158 E2C5C7F4  F1F2F4F4 F4F4F4F4 F4F4F4F4 F4F4F4F4  *44..........SEG41244444444444444*
0001A0  F4F4F4F4 F4F4F4F4 F4F4F4F4 05000000  00000000 0000E2C5 C7F5F1F1 F5F5F5F5  *444444444444..........SEG5115555*
0001C0  F5F5F5F5 F5F5F5F5 F5F5F5F5 F5F5F5F5  F5F5F5F5 F5F5F5F5 F5F5F5F5 F5F5F5F5  *55555555555555555555555555555555*
0001E0  F5F5F5F5 F5F50100 000013C4 00001008  00001230 000012C8 0000138A 0000138A  *555555.....D...........H........*
000200  E2C5C7F1 F2F1F1F1 F1F1F1F1 F1F1F1F1  F1F1F1F1 F1F1F1F1 F1F1F1F1 F1F1F1F1  *SEG12111111111111111111111111111*
000220  F1F1F1F1 F1F1F1F1 F1F1F1F1 F1F1F1F1  02000000 12C80000 00000000 126A0000  *1111111111111111.....H..........*
000240  12840000 129E0000 129EE2C5 C7F2F2F1  F2F2F2F2 F2F2F2F2 F2F2F2F2 F2F2F2F2  *..........SEG2212222222222222222*
000260  F2F2F2F2 F2F2F2F2 F2F20300 00001284  00000000 E2C5C7F3 F2F1F3F3 F3F3F3F3  *2222222222..........SEG321333333*
000280  F3F3F3F3 03000000 00000000 126AE2C5  C7F3F2F2 F3F3F3F3 F3F3F3F3 F3F30400  *3333..........SEG3223333333333..*
0002A0  00000000 00000000 E2C5C7F4 F2F1F4F4  F4F4F4F4 F4F4F4F4 F4F4F4F4 F4F4F4F4  *........SEG421444444444444444444*
0002C0  F4F4F4F4 F4F4F4F4 02000000 00000000  12300000 13020000 131C0000 13360000  *44444444........................*
0002E0  1360E2C5 C7F2F2F2 F2F2F2F2 F2F2F2F2  F2F2F2F2 F2F2F2F2 F2F2F2F2 F2F2F2F2  *.-SEG222222222222222222222222222*
000300  F2F20300 0000131C 00000000 E2C5C7F3  F2F1F3F3 F3F3F3F3 F3F3F3F3 03000000  *22..........SEG3213333333333....*
000320  00000000 1302E2C5 C7F3F2F2 F3F3F3F3  F3F3F3F3 F3F30400 00001360 00000000  *......SEG3223333333333.....-....*
000340  E2C5C7F4 F2F1F4F4 F4F4F4F4 F4F4F4F4  F4F4F4F4 F4F4F4F4 F4F4F4F4 F4F4F4F4  *SEG42144444444444444444444444444*
000360  04000000 00000000 1336E2C5 C7F4F2F2  F4F4F4F4 F4F4F4F4 F4F4F4F4 F4F4F4F4  *..........SEG4224444444444444444*
000380  F4F4F4F4 F4F4F4F4 F4F40500 00000000  00000000 E2C5C7F5 F2F1F5F5 F5F5F5F5  *4444444444..........SEG521555555*
0003A0  F5F5F5F5 F5F5F5F5 F5F5F5F5 F5F5F5F5  F5F5F5F5 F5F5F5F5 F5F5F5F5 F5F5F5F5  *55555555555555555555555555555555*
0003C0  F5F5F5F5 01000000 00000000 11E60000  140E0000 14A60000 15680000 1568E2C5  *5555.........W................SE*
0003E0  C7F1F3F1 F1F1F1F1 F1F1F1F1 F1F1F1F1  F1F1F1F1 F1F1F1F1 F1F1F1F1 F1F1F1F1  *G1311111111111111111111111111111*
000400  F1F1F1F1 F1F1F1F1 F1F1F1F1 F1F10200  000014A6 00000000 00001448 00001462  *11111111111111..................*
000420  0000147C 0000147C E2C5C7F2 F3F1F2F2  F2F2F2F2 F2F2F2F2 F2F2F2F2 F2F2F2F2  *...@...@SEG231222222222222222222*
000440  F2F2F2F2 F2F2F2F2 03000000 14620000  0000E2C5 C7F3F3F1 F3F3F3F3 F3F3F3F3  *22222222..........SEG33133333333*
000460  F3F30300 00000000 00001448 E2C5C7F3  F3F2F3F3 F3F3F3F3 F3F3F3F3 04000000  *33..........SEG3323333333333....*
000480  00000000 0000E2C5 C7F4F3F1 F4F4F4F4  F4F4F4F4 F4F4F4F4 F4F4F4F4 F4F4F4F4  *......SEG43144444444444444444444*
0004A0  F4F4F4F4 F4F40200 00000000 0000140E  000014E0 000014FA 00001514 0000153E  *444444..........................*
0004C0  E2C5C7F2 F3F2F2F2 F2F2F2F2 F2F2F2F2  F2F2F2F2 F2F2F2F2 F2F2F2F2 F2F2F2F2  *SEG23222222222222222222222222222*
0004E0  03000000 14FA0000 0000E2C5 C7F3F3F1  F3F3F3F3 F3F3F3F3 F3F30300 00000000  *..........SEG3313333333333......*
000500  000014E0 E2C5C7F3 F3F2F3F3 F3F3F3F3  F3F3F3F3 04000000 153E0000 0000E2C5  *....SEG3323333333333..........SE*
000520  C7F4F3F1 F4F4F4F4 F4F4F4F4 F4F4F4F4  F4F4F4F4 F4F4F4F4 F4F4F4F4 F4F40400  *G43144444444444444444444444444..*
000540  00000000 00001514 E2C5C7F4 F3F2F4F4  F4F4F4F4 F4F4F4F4 F4F4F4F4 F4F4F4F4  *........SEG432444444444444444444*
000560  F4F4F4F4 F4F4F4F4 05000000 00000000  0000E2C5 C7F5F3F1 F5F5F5F5 F5F5F5F5  *44444444..........SEG53155555555*
000580  F5F5F5F5 F5F5F5F5 F5F5F5F5 F5F5F5F5  F5F5F5F5 F5F5F5F5 F5F5F5F5 F5F5F5F5  *55555555555555555555555555555555*
0005A0  F5F50000 02560000 00000000 00000000  00000000 00000000 00000000 00000000  *55..............................*
0005C0  00000000 00000000 00000000 00000000  00000000 00000000 00000000 00000000  *................................*
```

Figure 16-7 Contents of the HDAM data base's data set (version 2) (part 1 of 2)

```
IDCAMS  SYSTEM SERVICES                                              TIME: 13:23:07         09/07/85      PAGE    3

LISTING OF DATA SET -MMA2.EXHDAM

0005E0  00000000 00000000 00000000 00000000   00000000 00000000 00000000 00000000   *................................*
000600  00000000 00000000 00000000 00000000   00000000 00000000 00000000 00000000   *................................*
000620  00000000 00000000 00000000 00000000   00000000 00000000 00000000 00000000   *................................*
000640  00000000 00000000 00000000 00000000   00000000 00000000 00000000 00000000   *................................*
000660  00000000 00000000 00000000 00000000   00000000 00000000 00000000 00000000   *................................*
000680  00000000 00000000 00000000 00000000   00000000 00000000 00000000 00000000   *................................*
0006A0  00000000 00000000 00000000 00000000   00000000 00000000 00000000 00000000   *................................*
0006C0  00000000 00000000 00000000 00000000   00000000 00000000 00000000 00000000   *................................*
0006E0  00000000 00000000 00000000 00000000   00000000 00000000 00000000 00000000   *................................*
000700  00000000 00000000 00000000 00000000   00000000 00000000 00000000 00000000   *................................*
000720  00000000 00000000 00000000 00000000   00000000 00000000 00000000 00000000   *................................*
000740  00000000 00000000 00000000 00000000   00000000 00000000 00000000 00000000   *................................*
000760  00000000 00000000 00000000 00000000   00000000 00000000 00000000 00000000   *................................*
000780  00000000 00000000 00000000 00000000   00000000 00000000 00000000 00000000   *................................*
0007A0  00000000 00000000 00000000 00000000   00000000 00000000 00000000 00000000   *................................*
0007C0  00000000 00000000 00000000 00000000   00000000 00000000 00000000 00000000   *................................*
0007E0  00000000 00000000 00000000 00000000   00000000 00000000 00                  *.........................       *

IDC0005I NUMBER OF RECORDS PROCESSED WAS 1

IDC0001I FUNCTION COMPLETED, HIGHEST CONDITION CODE WAS 0
```

Figure 16-7 Contents of the HDAM data base's data set (version 2) (part 2 of 2)

```
IDCAMS   SYSTEM SERVICES                                          TIME: 13:23:07        09/07/85      PAGE    2
LISTING OF DATA SET -MMA2.EXHDAM

RBA OF RECORD - 4096
000000  05A20000 00001008 01000000 11E60000   00000000 10520000 10EA0000 11AC0000   *............W....................*
000020  11ACE2C5 C7F1F1F1 F1F1F1F1 F1F1F1F1   F1F1F1F1 F1F1F1F1 F1F1F1F1 F1F1F1F1   *..SEG11111111111111111111111111111*
000040  F1F1F1F1 F1F1F1F1 F1F1F1F1 F1F1F1F1   F1F10200 000010EA 00000000 0000108C   *111111111111111111...............*
000060  000010A6 000010C0 000010C0 E2C5C7F2   F1F1F2F2 F2F2F2F2 F2F2F2F2 F2F2F2F2   *............SEG211222222222222222*
000080  F2F2F2F2 F2F2F2F2 F2F2F2F2 03000000   10A60000 0000E2C5 C7F3F1F1 F3F3F3F3   *222222222222..........SEG3113333*
0000A0  F3F3F3F3 F3F30300 00000000 0000108C   E2C5C7F3 F1F2F3F3 F3F3F3F3 F3F3F3F3   *333333...........SEG312333333333333*
0000C0  04000000 00000000 0000E2C5 C7F4F1F1   F4F4F4F4 F4F4F4F4 F4F4F4F4 F4F4F4F4   *..........SEG41144444444444444444*
0000E0  F4F4F4F4 F4F4F4F4 F4F40200 00000000   00001052 00001124 0000113E 00001158   *4444444444......................*
000100  00001182 E2C5C7F2 F1F2F2F2 F2F2F2F2   F2F2F2F2 F2F2F2F2 F2F2F2F2 F2F2F2F2   *....SEG212222222222222222222222222*
000120  F2F2F2F2 03000000 113E0000 0000E2C5   C7F3F1F1 F3F3F3F3 F3F3F3F3 F3F30300   *2222..........SEG3113333333333..*
000140  00000000 00001124 E2C5C7F3 F1F2F3F3   F3F3F3F3 F3F3F3F3 04000000 11820000   *........SEG3123333333333.........*
000160  0000E2C5 C7F4F1F1 F4F4F4F4 F4F4F4F4   F4F4F4F4 F4F4F4F4 F4F4F4F4 F4F4F4F4   *..SEG4114444444444444444444444444*
000180  F4F40400 00000000 00001158 E2C5C7F4   F1F2F4F4 F4F4F4F4 F4F4F4F4 F4F4F4F4   *44..........SEG41244444444444444*
0001A0  F4F4F4F4 F4F4F4F4 F4F4F4F4 05000000   00000000 0000E2C5 C7F5F1F1 F5F5F5F5   *444444444444..........SEG5115555*
0001C0  F5F5F5F5 F5F5F5F5 F5F5F5F5 F5F5F5F5   F5F5F5F5 F5F5F5F5 F5F5F5F5 F5F5F5F5   *55555555555555555555555555555555*
0001E0  F5F5F5F5 F5F50100 000013C4 00001008   00001230 000012C8 0000138A 0000138A   *555555.....D............H........*
000200  E2C5C7F1 F2F1F1F1 F1F1F1F1 F1F1F1F1   F1F1F1F1 F1F1F1F1 F1F1F1F1 F1F1F1F1   *SEG1211111111111111111111111111111*
000220  F1F1F1F1 F1F1F1F1 F1F1F1F1 F1F1F1F1   02000000 12C80000 00000000 126A0000   *1111111111111111.....H..........*
000240  12840000 129E0000 129EE2C5 C7F2F2F1   F2F2F2F2 F2F2F2F2 F2F2F2F2 F2F2F2F2   *..........SEG2212222222222222222*
000260  F2F2F2F2 F2F2F2F2 F2F20300 00001284   00000000 E2C5C7F3 F2F1F3F3 F3F3F3F3   *2222222222..........SEG321333333*
000280  F3F3F3F3 03000000 00000000 126AE2C5   C7F3F2F2 F3F3F3F3 F3F3F3F3 F3F30400   *3333...........SEG3223333333333..*
0002A0  00000000 00000000 E2C5C7F4 F2F1F4F4   F4F4F4F4 F4F4F4F4 F4F4F4F4 F4F4F4F4   *........SEG42144444444444444444*
0002C0  F4F4F4F4 F4F4F4F4 02000000 00000000   12300000 13020000 131C0000 13360000   *44444444........................*
0002E0  1360E2C5 C7F2F2F2 F2F2F2F2 F2F2F2F2   F2F2F2F2 F2F2F2F2 F2F2F2F2 F2F2F2F2   *.-SEG2222222222222222222222222222*
000300  F2F20300 0000131C 00000000 E2C5C7F3   F2F1F3F3 F3F3F3F3 F3F3F3F3 03000000   *22..........SEG3213333333333....*
000320  00000000 1302E2C5 C7F3F2F2 F3F3F3F3   F3F3F3F3 F3F30400 00001360 00000000   *......SEG3223333333333.....-....*
000340  E2C5C7F4 F2F1F4F4 F4F4F4F4 F4F4F4F4   F4F4F4F4 F4F4F4F4 F4F4F4F4 F4F4F4F4   *SEG4214444444444444444444444444*
000360  04000000 00000000 1336E2C5 C7F4F2F2   F4F4F4F4 F4F4F4F4 F4F4F4F4 F4F4F4F4   *..........SEG42244444444444444444*
000380  F4F4F4F4 F4F4F4F4 F4F40500 00000000   00000000 E2C5C7F5 F2F1F5F5 F5F5F5F5   *4444444444..........SEG521555555*
0003A0  F5F5F5F5 F5F5F5F5 F5F5F5F5 F5F5F5F5   F5F5F5F5 F5F5F5F5 F5F5F5F5 F5F5F5F5   *55555555555555555555555555555555*
0003C0  F5F5F5F5 01000000 00000000 11E60000   140E0000 14A60000 15680000 1568E2C5   *5555............W...............SE*
0003E0  C7F1F3F1 F1F1F1F1 F1F1F1F1 F1F1F1F1   F1F1F1F1 F1F1F1F1 F1F1F1F1 F1F1F1F1   *G13111111111111111111111111111111*
000400  F1F1F1F1 F1F1F1F1 F1F1F1F1 F1F10200   000014A6 00000000 00001448 00001462   *11111111111111..................*
000420  0000147C 0000147C E2C5C7F2 F3F1F2F2   F2F2F2F2 F2F2F2F2 F2F2F2F2 F2F2F2F2   *...@...@SEG23122222222222222222*
000440  F2F2F2F2 F2F2F2F2 03000000 14620000   0000E2C5 C7F3F3F1 F3F3F3F3 F3F3F3F3   *22222222..........SEG33133333333*
000460  F3F30300 00000000 00001448 E2C5C7F3   F3F2F3F3 F3F3F3F3 F3F3F3F3 04000000   *33..........SEG3323333333333....*
000480  00000000 0000E2C5 C7F4F3F1 F4F4F4F4   F4F4F4F4 F4F4F4F4 F4F4F4F4 F4F4F4F4   *......SEG43144444444444444444444*
0004A0  F4F4F4F4 F4F40200 00000000 0000140E   000014E0 000014FA 00001514 0000153E   *444444..........................*
0004C0  E2C5C7F2 F3F2F2F2 F2F2F2F2 F2F2F2F2   F2F2F2F2 F2F2F2F2 F2F2F2F2 F2F2F2F2   *SEG2322222222222222222222222222222*
0004E0  03000000 14FA0000 0000E2C5 C7F3F3F1   F3F3F3F3 F3F3F3F3 F3F30300 00000000   *..........SEG3313333333333......*
000500  000014E0 E2C5C7F3 F3F2F3F3 F3F3F3F3   F3F3F3F3 04000000 153E0000 0000E2C5   *....SEG3323333333333..........SE*
000520  C7F4F3F1 F4F4F4F4 F4F4F4F4 F4F4F4F4   F4F4F4F4 F4F4F4F4 F4F4F4F4 F4F40400   *G4314444444444444444444444444..*
000540  00000000 00001514 E2C5C7F4 F3F2F4F4   F4F4F4F4 F4F4F4F4 F4F4F4F4 F4F4F4F4   *........SEG43244444444444444444*
000560  F4F4F4F4 F4F4F4F4 05000000 00000000   0000E2C5 C7F5F3F1 F5F5F5F5 F5F5F5F5   *44444444..........SEG53155555555*
000580  F5F5F5F5 F5F5F5F5 F5F5F5F5 F5F5F5F5   F5F5F5F5 F5F5F5F5 F5F5F5F5 F5F5F5F5   *55555555555555555555555555555555*
0005A0  F5F50000 02560000 00000000 00000000   00000000 00000000 00000000 00000000   *55..............................*
0005C0  00000000 00000000 00000000 00000000   00000000 00000000 00000000 00000000   *................................*
```

Free space element anchor point (FSEAP)

Chain pointer field — Available space field — Task id field

Free space element (FSE)

Figure 16-8 HD free space management: Contents of the HDAM data base's data set (version 2) before a deletion (part 1 of 2)

```
IDCAMS  SYSTEM SERVICES                                                  TIME: 13:23:07        09/07/85     PAGE   3

LISTING OF DATA SET -MMA2.EXHDAM

0005E0  00000000 00000000 00000000 00000000   00000000 00000000 00000000 00000000   *................................*
000600  00000000 00000000 00000000 00000000   00000000 00000000 00000000 00000000   *................................*
000620  00000000 00000000 00000000 00000000   00000000 00000000 00000000 00000000   *................................*
000640  00000000 00000000 00000000 00000000   00000000 00000000 00000000 00000000   *................................*
000660  00000000 00000000 00000000 00000000   00000000 00000000 00000000 00000000   *................................*
000680  00000000 00000000 00000000 00000000   00000000 00000000 00000000 00000000   *................................*
0006A0  00000000 00000000 00000000 00000000   00000000 00000000 00000000 00000000   *................................*
0006C0  00000000 00000000 00000000 00000000   00000000 00000000 00000000 00000000   *................................*
0006E0  00000000 00000000 00000000 00000000   00000000 00000000 00000000 00000000   *................................*
000700  00000000 00000000 00000000 00000000   00000000 00000000 00000000 00000000   *................................*
000720  00000000 00000000 00000000 00000000   00000000 00000000 00000000 00000000   *................................*
000740  00000000 00000000 00000000 00000000   00000000 00000000 00000000 00000000   *................................*
000760  00000000 00000000 00000000 00000000   00000000 00000000 00000000 00000000   *................................*
000780  00000000 00000000 00000000 00000000   00000000 00000000 00000000 00000000   *................................*
0007A0  00000000 00000000 00000000 00000000   00000000 00000000 00000000 00000000   *................................*
0007C0  00000000 00000000 00000000 00000000   00000000 00000000 00000000 00000000   *................................*
0007E0  00000000 00000000 00000000 00000000   00000000 00000000 00                  *.........................       *

IDC0005I NUMBER OF RECORDS PROCESSED WAS 1

IDC0001I FUNCTION COMPLETED, HIGHEST CONDITION CODE WAS 0
```

Figure 16-8 HD free space management: Contents of the HDAM data base's data set (version 2) before a deletion (part 2 of 2)

```
IDCAMS  SYSTEM SERVICES                              TIME: 17:49:55       09/07/85      PAGE   2

LISTING OF DATA SET -MMA2.EXHDAM

RBA OF RECORD - 4096
000000  01E60000 00001008 01000000 13C40000   00000000 10520000 10EA0000 11AC0000  *.W...........D..................*
000020  11ACE2C5 C7F1F1F1 F1F1F1F1 F1F1F1F1   F1F1F1F1 F1F1F1F1 F1F1F1F1 F1F1F1F1  *..SEG111111111111111111111111111*
000040  F1F1F1F1 F1F1F1F1 F1F1F1F1 F1F1F1F1   F1F10200 000010EA 00000000 0000108C  *111111111111111111..............*
000060  000010A6 000010C0 000010C0 E2C5C7F2   F1F1F2F2 F2F2F2F2 F2F2F2F2 F2F2F2F2  *............SEG21122222222222222*
000080  F2F2F2F2 F2F2F2F2 F2F2F2F2 03000000   10A60000 0000E2C5 C7F3F1F1 F3F3F3F3  *222222222222..........SEG3113333*
0000A0  F3F3F3F3 F3F30300 00000000 0000108C   E2C5C7F3 F1F2F3F3 F3F3F3F3 F3F3F3F3  *333333..........SEG3123333333333*
0000C0  04000000 00000000 0000E2C5 C7F4F1F1   F4F4F4F4 F4F4F4F4 F4F4F4F4 F4F4F4F4  *..........SEG4114444444444444444*
0000E0  F4F4F4F4 F4F4F4F4 F4F40200 00000000   00001052 00001124 0000113E 00001158  *4444444444......................*
000100  00001182 E2C5C7F2 F1F2F2F2 F2F2F2F2   F2F2F2F2 F2F2F2F2 F2F2F2F2 F2F2F2F2  *....SEG2122222222222222222222222*
000120  F2F2F2F2 03000000 113E0000 0000E2C5   C7F3F1F1 F3F3F3F3 F3F3F3F3 F3F30300  *2222..........SEG3113333333333..*
000140  00000000 00001124 E2C5C7F3 F1F2F3F3   F3F3F3F3 F3F3F3F3 04000000 11820000  *........SEG3123333333333........*
000160  0000E2C5 C7F4F1F1 F4F4F4F4 F4F4F4F4   F4F4F4F4 F4F4F4F4 F4F4F4F4 F4F4F4F4  *..SEG411444444444444444444444444*
000180  F4F40400 00000000 00001158 E2C5C7F4   F1F2F4F4 F4F4F4F4 F4F4F4F4 F4F4F4F4  *44..........SEG41244444444444444*
0001A0  F4F4F4F4 F4F4F4F4 F4F4F4F4 05000000   00000000 0000E2C5 C7F5F1F1 F5F5F5F5  *444444444444..........SEG5115555*
0001C0  F5F5F5F5 F5F5F5F5 F5F5F5F5 F5F5F5F5   F5F5F5F5 F5F5F5F5 F5F5F5F5 F5F5F5F5  *55555555555555555555555555555555*
0001E0  F5F5F5F5 F5F505A2 01DE0000 00001008   00000000 00000000 00000000 00000000  *555555..........................*
000200  E2C5C7F1 F2F1F1F1 F1F1F1F1 F1F1F1F1   F1F1F1F1 F1F1F1F1 F1F1F1F1 F1F1F1F1  *SEG12111111111111111111111111111*
000220  F1F1F1F1 F1F1F1F1 F1F1F1F1 F1F1F1F1   05A20194 00000000 00000000 00000000  *1111111111111111................*
000240  00000000 00000000 0000E2C5 C7F2F2F1   F2F2F2F2 F2F2F2F2 F2F2F2F2 F2F2F2F2  *..........SEG2212222222222222222*
000260  F2F2F2F2 F2F2F2F2 F2F205A2 005E0000   00000000 E2C5C7F3 F2F1F3F3 F3F3F3F3  *2222222222...;......SEG321333333*
000280  F3F3F3F3 03000000 00000000 0000E2C5   C7F3F2F2 F3F3F3F3 F3F3F3F3 F3F30400  *3333..........SEG3223333333333..*
0002A0  00000000 00000000 E2C5C7F4 F2F1F4F4   F4F4F4F4 F4F4F4F4 F4F4F4F4 F4F4F4F4  *........SEG421444444444444444444*
0002C0  F4F4F4F4 F4F4F4F4 02000000 00000000   00000000 00000000 00000000 00000000  *44444444........................*
0002E0  0000E2C5 C7F2F2F2 F2F2F2F2 F2F2F2F2   F2F2F2F2 F2F2F2F2 F2F2F2F2 F2F2F2F2  *..SEG222222222222222222222222222*
000300  F2F205A2 00800000 00000000 E2C5C7F3   F2F1F3F3 F3F3F3F3 F3F3F3F3 03000000  *22..........SEG3213333333333....*
000320  00000000 0000E2C5 C7F3F2F2 F3F3F3F3   F3F3F3F3 F3F30400 00001360 00000000  *......SEG3223333333333.....-....*
000340  E2C5C7F4 F2F1F4F4 F4F4F4F4 F4F4F4F4   F4F4F4F4 F4F4F4F4 F4F4F4F4 F4F4F4F4  *SEG42144444444444444444444444444*
000360  04000000 00000000 0000E2C5 C7F4F2F2   F4F4F4F4 F4F4F4F4 F4F4F4F4 F4F4F4F4  *..........SEG4224444444444444444*
000380  F4F4F4F4 F4F4F4F4 F4F40500 00000000   00000000 E2C5C7F5 F2F1F5F5 F5F5F5F5  *4444444444..........SEG521555555*
0003A0  F5F5F5F5 F5F5F5F5 F5F5F5F5 F5F5F5F5   F5F5F5F5 F5F5F5F5 F5F5F5F5 F5F5F5F5  *55555555555555555555555555555555*
0003C0  F5F5F5F5 01000000 00000000 10080000   140E0000 14A60000 15680000 1568E2C5  *5555..........................SE*
0003E0  C7F1F3F1 F1F1F1F1 F1F1F1F1 F1F1F1F1   F1F1F1F1 F1F1F1F1 F1F1F1F1 F1F1F1F1  *G1311111111111111111111111111111*
000400  F1F1F1F1 F1F1F1F1 F1F1F1F1 F1F10200   000014A6 00000000 00001448 00001462  *11111111111111..................*
000420  0000147C 0000147C E2C5C7F2 F3F1F2F2   F2F2F2F2 F2F2F2F2 F2F2F2F2 F2F2F2F2  *...@...@SEG231222222222222222222*
000440  F2F2F2F2 F2F2F2F2 03000000 14620000   0000E2C5 C7F3F3F1 F3F3F3F3 F3F3F3F3  *22222222..........SEG33133333333*
000460  F3F30300 00000000 00001448 E2C5C7F3   F3F2F3F3 F3F3F3F3 F3F3F3F3 04000000  *33..........SEG3323333333333....*
000480  00000000 0000E2C5 C7F4F3F1 F4F4F4F4   F4F4F4F4 F4F4F4F4 F4F4F4F4 F4F4F4F4  *......SEG43144444444444444444444*
0004A0  F4F4F4F4 F4F40200 00000000 0000140E   000014E0 000014FA 00001514 0000153E  *444444..........................*
0004C0  E2C5C7F2 F3F2F2F2 F2F2F2F2 F2F2F2F2   F2F2F2F2 F2F2F2F2 F2F2F2F2 F2F2F2F2  *SEG23222222222222222222222222222*
0004E0  03000000 14FA0000 0000E2C5 C7F3F3F1   F3F3F3F3 F3F3F3F3 F3F30300 00000000  *..........SEG3313333333333......*
000500  000014E0 E2C5C7F3 F3F2F3F3 F3F3F3F3   F3F3F3F3 04000000 153E0000 0000E2C5  *....SEG3323333333333..........SE*
000520  C7F4F3F1 F4F4F4F4 F4F4F4F4 F4F4F4F4   F4F4F4F4 F4F4F4F4 F4F4F4F4 F4F40400  *G43144444444444444444444444444..*
000540  00000000 00001514 E2C5C7F4 F3F2F4F4   F4F4F4F4 F4F4F4F4 F4F4F4F4 F4F4F4F4  *........SEG432444444444444444444*
000560  F4F4F4F4 F4F4F4F4 05000000 00000000   0000E2C5 C7F5F3F1 F5F5F5F5 F5F5F5F5  *44444444..........SEG53155555555*
000580  F5F5F5F5 F5F5F5F5 F5F5F5F5 F5F5F5F5   F5F5F5F5 F5F5F5F5 F5F5F5F5 F5F5F5F5  *55555555555555555555555555555555*
0005A0  F5F50000 02560000 00000000 00000000   00000000 00000000 00000000 00000000  *55..............................*
0005C0  00000000 00000000 00000000 00000000   00000000 00000000 00000000 00000000  *................................*
```

Figure 16-9 HD free space management: Contents of the HDAM data base's data set (version 2) after a deletion (part 1 of 2)

```
IDCAMS   SYSTEM SERVICES                                  TIME: 17:49:55        09/07/85     PAGE   3

LISTING OF DATA SET -MMA2.EXHDAM

0005E0  00000000 00000000 00000000 00000000   00000000 00000000 00000000 00000000   *................................*
000600  00000000 00000000 00000000 00000000   00000000 00000000 00000000 00000000   *................................*
000620  00000000 00000000 00000000 00000000   00000000 00000000 00000000 00000000   *................................*
000640  00000000 00000000 00000000 00000000   00000000 00000000 00000000 00000000   *................................*
000660  00000000 00000000 00000000 00000000   00000000 00000000 00000000 00000000   *................................*
000680  00000000 00000000 00000000 00000000   00000000 00000000 00000000 00000000   *................................*
0006A0  00000000 00000000 00000000 00000000   00000000 00000000 00000000 00000000   *................................*
0006C0  00000000 00000000 00000000 00000000   00000000 00000000 00000000 00000000   *................................*
0006E0  00000000 00000000 00000000 00000000   00000000 00000000 00000000 00000000   *................................*
000700  00000000 00000000 00000000 00000000   00000000 00000000 00000000 00000000   *................................*
000720  00000000 00000000 00000000 00000000   00000000 00000000 00000000 00000000   *................................*
000740  00000000 00000000 00000000 00000000   00000000 00000000 00000000 00000000   *................................*
000760  00000000 00000000 00000000 00000000   00000000 00000000 00000000 00000000   *................................*
000780  00000000 00000000 00000000 00000000   00000000 00000000 00000000 00000000   *................................*
0007A0  00000000 00000000 00000000 00000000   00000000 00000000 00000000 00000000   *................................*
0007C0  00000000 00000000 00000000 00000000   00000000 00000000 00000000 00000000   *................................*
0007E0  00000000 00000000 00000000 00000000   00000000 00000000 00                  *.........................       *

IDC0005I NUMBER OF RECORDS PROCESSED WAS 1

IDC0001I FUNCTION COMPLETED, HIGHEST CONDITION CODE WAS 0
```

Figure 16-9 HD free space management: Contents of the HDAM data base's data set (version 2) after a deletion (part 2 of 2)

Notice that DL/I did not overwrite the data from the second data base record. It's still present in the record. However, because it's in a location that's marked as free space, DL/I ignores it and can store new segment occurrences in the now logically unused space.

That's how DL/I manages free space within a single physical record in an HD data base's data set. Although it's not critical that you have a detailed understanding of the mechanics of space management, you should realize that if you list the data set that contains an HD data base, what you see on first glance may not really be what's there as far as DL/I is concerned.

Space management at the data set level DL/I also keeps track of what parts of the data set contain free space. If the data set is a VSAM ESDS, the "parts" are control intervals (CIs); if it's an OSAM file, they're blocks. Since most HD data bases are implemented with VSAM, as is the example in this chapter, I'll use the VSAM term "control interval." In the sample data base, the control interval size is 2048, and the record size is 2041, so there's a one-to-one relationship between records and control intervals.

The first control interval in an HD data base's data set contains a *bit map* that DL/I uses to determine which subsequent control intervals contain free space. A control interval is considered to have usable free space if it contains at least one unused space large enough to hold an occurrence of the largest segment type in the data base.

Figure 16-10 shows the values you'd find in the first 16 bytes of the bit map control interval in the sample data base. The first two bytes, the FSEAP, contain hex zeros because there's no free space in the CI for user data. The second two bytes contain hex 1 in the low-order position. This indicates that the CI is a bit map. In other CIs, these two bytes contain hex zeros.

The bit map itself begins in byte 9 in figure 16-10. Each bit position in the bit map corresponds to one control interval in the data set. The first bit position corresponds to the bit map control interval itself, the second bit position corresponds to the next control interval, and so on. If the value of a bit is 0, the corresponding control interval doesn't contain a usable free space. Since the first bit corresponds to the bit map control interval, its value is 0: No user data can be stored in the bit map CI. The bit map in figure 16-10 shows that all the subsequent CIs do contain free space adequate for at least one occurrence of the largest segment in the data base; that's what the binary 1's indicate.

The bit map in the sample data base uses the rest of its control interval, so its total size is 2033 bytes. Since each byte indicates the free

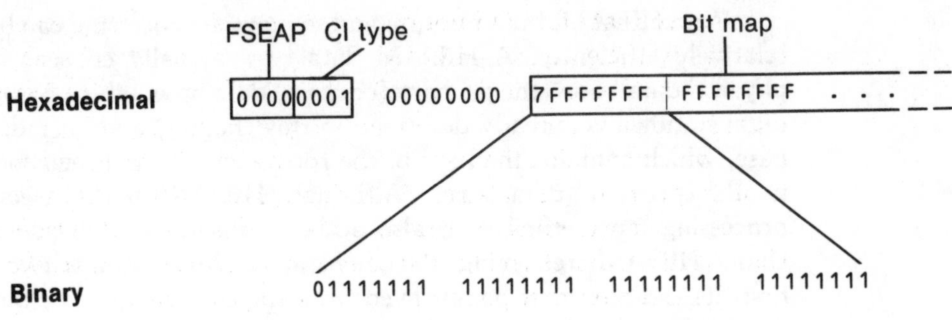

Figure 16-10 Values in the first 16 bytes of the bit map control interval in the HDAM data base's data set

space status of eight control intervals, this bit map can be used for space management of 16,264 CIs, each with 2041 bytes, or a total of more than 33 megabytes. If the data base requires more space, another bit map control interval will follow the last control interval managed by the first bit map, and so on.

Both of the DL/I direct access methods (HDAM and HIDAM) use the pointers and free space management features I've just described. However, they differ in how they provide access to the root segment. Now, I'll describe those two techniques.

HOW HDAM AND HIDAM DIFFER

In both HDAM and HIDAM data bases, once a root segment has been located, retrieval of dependent segments is usually fast. Often, many if not all dependents are stored in the same control interval as the root, so after that CI has been read, those dependents can be accessed at virtual storage speed. However, how the root is accessed to begin with varies between the two access methods.

Under HDAM, root segment occurrences are located based on calculations done by a randomizing module that's written by the user or, more likely, supplied by IBM as part of DL/I. Regardless, when root segment positions are determined by a randomizing module, they're most likely *not* stored in sequence in the data set, but rather are distributed throughout it. That's fine if access to the data base is almost always random. However, for sequential processing, random positioning of root segments can be a source of inefficiency. As a result, although HDAM data bases are efficient for random access, they're not as useful when sequential retrieval is required.

With HIDAM, both random and sequential processing can be done relatively efficiently. A HIDAM data base actually consists of two physical data bases: the primary (or main) data base, which has the HD organization I've already described in this chapter, and an index data base, which contains the keys of the root segments and their locations in the primary data base. Although HIDAM makes sequential processing more efficient, it also adds overhead to DL/I processing. Under HIDAM, retrieving a segment at random requires two steps: first, its location must be retrieved from the index data base; then, the record that contains it must be retrieved from the primary data base. Under HDAM, the index data base access isn't part of the process.

Now, I'll describe the differences in structure between HDAM and HIDAM data bases. Remember as you read this discussion that the relationships among segments within a data base record and the way DL/I manages free space within the data base are the same for both access methods.

How DL/I accesses an HDAM root segment

Most HDAM data bases are separated by the DBA into two sections: the *root addressable area* and the *overflow area*. Don't let these terms confuse you: they aren't separate data sets, like the primary and overflow data sets in a HISAM data base. Instead, they're separate areas of a single data set.

In each control interval in the root addressable area, DL/I creates one or more *root anchor points* (*RAPs*). A RAP is a four-byte field that contains an RBA, just like the pointers you're already familiar with. RAPs point to occurrences of root segments, and they're stored in the control interval immediately after the two-byte FSEAP and the two-byte CI type indicator fields. The maximum number of RAPs that can be defined in a CI is 255, but typically, five or fewer are used.

When a root segment is inserted in an HDAM data base, the HDAM randomizing routine that's being used calculates two values: (1) the CI that should contain the segment and (2) the RAP within the CI that should point to it. Then, if adequate space is available in the CI and the RAP isn't already in use for another root segment occurrence, DL/I adds the segment to the control interval and stores its beginning RBA in the RAP. If the RAP is in use, DL/I uses a physical twin forward pointer to chain to the new root segment from one of the roots that's already using the RAP. And if enough space isn't available in the CI for

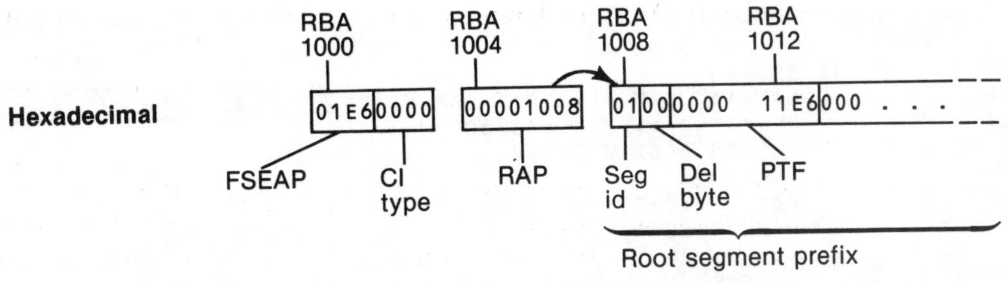

Figure 16-11 Hex values of the first 16 bytes of the first control interval in the sample data base that contains user data

the root segment, DL/I stores it in a nearby CI that does have enough free space.

Look for a moment at figure 16-11. This figure shows the hex contents of the first 16 bytes in the sample data base control interval that contains user data. (If you'd like, you can turn back to figure 16-4, 16-7, or 16-8 to see this small part of the control interval in context.) Because this data base was defined with only one RAP per CI, that's what you see in the figure. Its value points to the first associated root segment, which begins immediately after the RAP, at RBA 1008. If multiple root segment occurrences are associated with the same RAP, they're chained from the first occurrence by PTF pointers. In figure 16-11, the value at RBA 1012 (11E6), which is the PTF pointer, is itself an RBA that points to the next root segment occurrence.

To help you put this information into perspective, figures 16-12 and 16-13 illustrate still another variation of the sample HDAM data base. Figure 16-12, the DBDGEN output for the data base, is the same as the DBDGEN for the simpler version of the original data base (figure 16-2), except for the RMNAME parameter on the DBD macro:

```
RMNAME=(DFSHDC10,5,3,200)
```

DFSHDC10 is the name of the IBM-supplied randomizing module DL/I will use when it processes this data base.

The other three values specify what the structure of the HDAM data base will be. The 5 tells DL/I to use five RAPs per control interval in the data base's root addressable area. The 3 specifies that the root addressable area should use three control intervals. Obviously, this would be an unrealistically small number for a production data base; the limit is over 16 million. The last value in the RMNAME parameter,

```
STMT    SOURCE STATEMENT                                              ASM 0201 21.02

   1              PRINT NOGEN
   2   DBD              NAME=EXHDAM,ACCESS=(HDAM,VSAM),RMNAME=(DFSHDC10,5,3,200)
   3   DATASET          DD1=EXHDAM,DEVICE=3380
   4+*,                   3380 DISK STORAGE
   5 *
   6   SEGM             NAME=SEG1,BYTES=48,POINTER=TWIN
   7   FIELD            NAME=(SEG1KEY,SEQ),BYTES=6,START=1,TYPE=C
   8 *
   9   SEGM             NAME=SEG2,PARENT=((SEG1,SNGL)),BYTES=32,POINTER=TWIN
  10   FIELD            NAME=(SEG2KEY,SEQ),BYTES=6,START=1,TYPE=C
  11 *
  12   SEGM             NAME=SEG3,PARENT=((SEG2,SNGL)),BYTES=16,POINTER=TWIN
  13   FIELD            NAME=(SEG3KEY,SEQ),BYTES=6,START=1,TYPE=C
  14 *
  15   SEGM             NAME=SEG4,PARENT=((SEG2,SNGL)),BYTES=32,POINTER=TWIN
  16   FIELD            NAME=(SEG4KEY,SEQ),BYTES=6,START=1,TYPE=C
  17 *
  18   SEGM             NAME=SEG5,PARENT=((SEG1,SNGL)),BYTES=48,POINTER=TWIN
  19   FIELD            NAME=(SEG5KEY,SEQ),BYTES=6,START=1,TYPE=C
  20 *
  21   DBDGEN
  63+*,* * * * * * * * * * * * * * * * * * * * * * * * * *
  64+*,*
  65+*,    RECOMMENDED VSAM DEFINE CLUSTER PARAMETERS
  66+*,*
  67+*,* * * * * * * * * * * * * * * * * * * * * * * * * *
  69+*,* * * * * * * * * * * * * * * * * * * * * * * * * *
  70+*,*
  71+*,*                    *NOTE2
  72+*,*   DEFINE CLUSTER (NAME(EXHDAM) NONINDEXED -
  73+*,*          RECORDSIZE (2041,2041) -
  74+*,*          CONTROLINTERVALSIZE (2048))
  75+*,*
  76+*,* *NOTE2 - SHOULD SPECIFY DSNAME FOR DD EXHDAM
  77+*,*
  78+*,* * * * * * * * * * * * * * * * * * * * * * * * * *
 189+*,****** SEQUENCE FIELD ******
 196+*,****** SEQUENCE FIELD ******
 203+*,****** SEQUENCE FIELD ******
 210+*,****** SEQUENCE FIELD ******
 217+*,****** SEQUENCE FIELD ******
 283   FINISH
 284   END
```

Figure 16-12 DBDGEN output for the HDAM data base (version 3)

200, indicates that no more than 200 bytes of a single data base record may be added to the root addressable area by an unbroken series of insert calls. By specifying an appropriate value for this option, the DBA controls when dependent segments are written to the overflow area of the data set (as you'll see in a moment).

Now, take a look at figure 16-13. This is a partial listing of the data set that contains the HDAM data base defined in figure 16-12. As I said a moment ago, I've limited the root addressable area in this example to three control intervals (RBAs 2048, 4096, and 6144). The first of the three is the bit map, so it doesn't contain any user data. However, it does contain RAPs which may point to root segment occurrences stored in nearby control intervals. In all three of these records, I've shaded the RAPs DL/I created. (Remember, I specified that five RAPs should be created in each CI.)

As DL/I loaded the segments, the randomizing module generated a different control interval and RAP for each root segment occurrence. As a result, none of the root segment occurrences in figure 16-13 had to be chained together by PTF pointers. The first root segment is pointed to by RAP 2 in the CI with RBA 6144, the second by RAP 2 in the CI with RBA 4096, and the third by RAP 2 in the CI with RBA 2048.

I want you to notice two things about how these root segments are stored. First, their physical positions in the data base data set aren't what you'd expect based on their key field values. That's because the randomizing module did just what its name implies: it generated an apparently random location for each root segment. The practical result of this is that a program that issues calls to retrieve root segments from an HDAM data base sequentially will actually get them in what appears to be a random order.

Second, notice that the third root segment is addressed through a RAP in the bit map CI. Because there was no free space in the bit map CI, the third root segment couldn't be stored there. As a result, DL/I stored it in a nearby CI, the one with RBA 6144.

After each root segment, its dependent segments were inserted. However, because I specified a limit of 200 bytes of successive inserts in the root addressable area for this version of the data base, not all the dependent segments for these roots fit into it. In each case, 190 bytes of data could be stored in the root addressable area, but subsequent segments had to be written to the overflow area.

The overflow area in this data set begins with the control interval at RBA decimal 8192. If you look carefully at it, you'll see that it contains an FSEAP, but no RAPs. Immediately after the two-byte FSEAP is the first segment occurrence that wouldn't fit in the root addressable area: the second occurrence of segment type 2 for the first data base record.

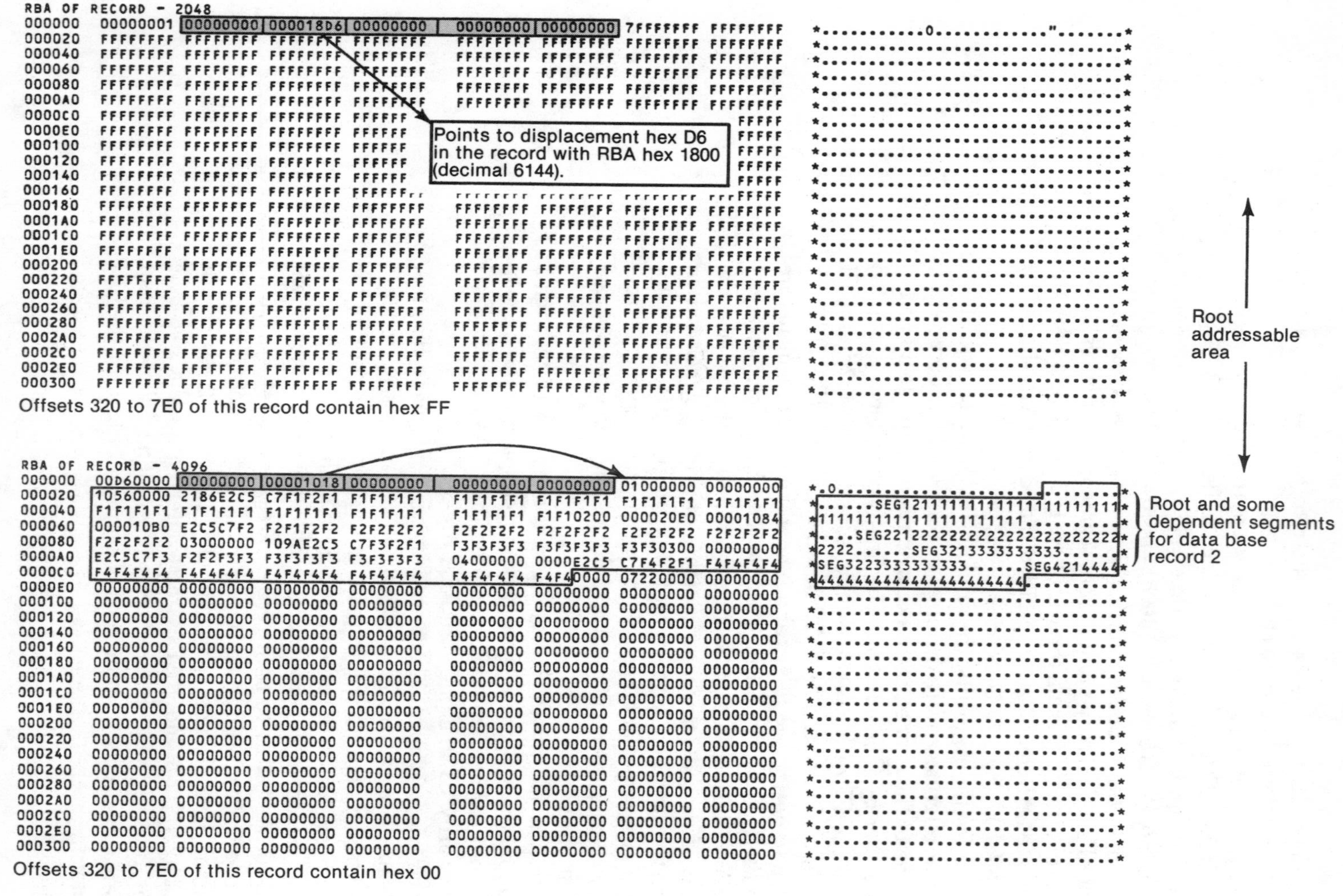

Figure 16-13 The root addressable area and the overflow area in the sample HDAM data base's data set (version 3) (part 1 of 2)

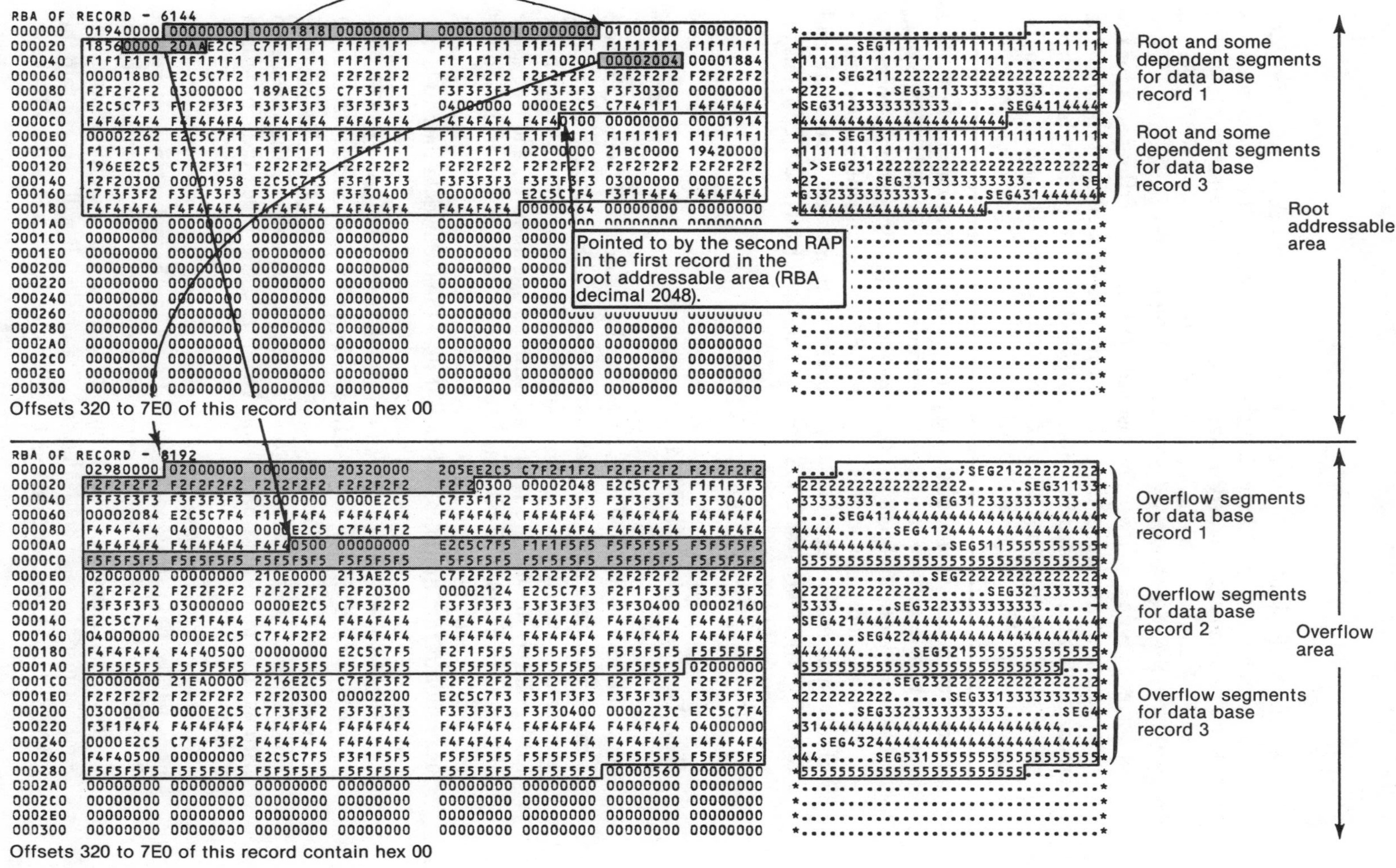

Figure 16-13 The root addressable area and the overflow area in the sample HDAM data base's data set (version 3) (part 2 of 2)

If you look at the segments from that record that are in the root addressable area, you'll see that the PTF pointer in the first occurrence of segment type 2 (shaded in figure 16-13) points to the overflow area (hex 2004 converts to displacement 4 in the record with RBA decimal 8192). In the overflow area, all the dependents of the second occurrence of segment type 2 follow. The last segment in the overflow area for the first data base record is the only occurrence of segment type 5 in the record (it's also shaded in figure 16-13). The PCF pointer in the root segment points to it (hex 20AA converts to displacement hex AA in the record with RBA decimal 8192).

Because HDAM uses this scheme of randomized access to root segments, access to a specific occurrence of the root can be fast. As a result, if a data base will be used primarily for random processing, HDAM is the best choice for it. However, when sequential processing in root segment sequence is required, HDAM's advantage becomes a disadvantage. For applications that have a mix of sequential and random processing, the DBA can use the last of the main DL/I access methods: HIDAM.

How DL/I accesses a HIDAM root segment

As you know, a HIDAM data base is really made up of two data bases: a main data base and an *index data base*. Within the main data base, user data is stored in much the same way as in an HDAM data base: RBA pointers are used to relate segments to one another, and free space elements, FSEAPs, and bit maps are used to manage free space. So the main difference between HIDAM and HDAM is that HIDAM doesn't use randomizing modules. Instead, it uses the index data base to locate root segment occurrences in the main data base.

Because two data bases make up a HIDAM data base, the DBA has to use two DBDGEN jobs to define it. Figures 16-14 and 16-15 present the output of the DBDGEN jobs for the sample main HIDAM data base and its index data base. As you can see at the ends of the these two listings, the main data base is an ESDS and the index data base is a KSDS.

The index data base has a single segment type that contains one user-defined field. As you can see in figure 16-15, that segment is named POINTER. For each root segment occurrence in the main data base, there's one occurrence of the segment POINTER in the index data base. And because the segment is defined as an index, it will also contain the RBA of the related root segment occurrence in the main data base.

```
STMT   SOURCE STATEMENT

   1            PRINT NOGEN
   2  DBD             NAME=EXHIDAM,ACCESS=(HIDAM,VSAM)
   3  DATASET         DD1=HIDAMD,DEVICE=3380
  4++,                   3380 DISK STORAGE
   5 *
   6  SEGM            NAME=SEG1,BYTES=48,POINTER=TWINBWD
   7  LCHILD          NAME=(POINTER,EXHIIND),POINTER=INDX
   8  FIELD           NAME=(SEG1KEY,SEQ),BYTES=6,START=1,TYPE=C
   9 *
  10  SEGM            NAME=SEG2,PARENT=((SEG1,DBLE)),BYTES=32,POINTER=TWINBWD
  11  FIELD           NAME=(SEG2KEY,SEQ),BYTES=6,START=1,TYPE=C
  12 *
  13  SEGM            NAME=SEG3,PARENT=((SEG2,DBLE)),BYTES=16,POINTER=TWINBWD
  14  FIELD           NAME=(SEG3KEY,SEQ),BYTES=6,START=1,TYPE=C
  15 *
  16  SEGM            NAME=SEG4,PARENT=((SEG2,DBLE)),BYTES=32,POINTER=TWINBWD
  17  FIELD           NAME=(SEG4KEY,SEQ),BYTES=6,START=1,TYPE=C
  18 *
  19  SEGM            NAME=SEG5,PARENT=((SEG1,DBLE)),BYTES=48,POINTER=TWINBWD
  20  FIELD           NAME=(SEG5KEY,SEQ),BYTES=6,START=1,TYPE=C
  21 *
  22  DBDGEN
 64++,* * * * * * * * * * * * * * * * * * * * * * * * *
 65++,*
 66++,   RECOMMENDED VSAM DEFINE CLUSTER PARAMETERS
 67++,*
 68++,* * * * * * * * * * * * * * * * * * * * * * * * *
 70++,* * * * * * * * * * * * * * * * * * * * * * * * *
 71++,*
 72++,*                    *NOTE2
 73++,*   DEFINE CLUSTER (NAME(HIDAMD) NONINDEXED -
 74++,*          RECORDSIZE (2041,2041) -
 75++,*          CONTROLINTERVALSIZE (2048))
 76++,*
 77++,* *NOTE2 - SHOULD SPECIFY DSNAME FOR DD HIDAMD
 78++,*
 79++,* * * * * * * * * * * * * * * * * * * * * * * * *
190++,****** SEQUENCE FIELD ******
197++,****** SEQUENCE FIELD ******
204++,****** SEQUENCE FIELD ******
211++,****** SEQUENCE FIELD ******
218++,****** SEQUENCE FIELD ******
283   FINISH
284   END
```

Figure 16-14 DBDGEN output for the HIDAM data base's main data base

All this will make better sense if you look at figures 16-16 and 16-17; they're listings of the data sets that contain the main and index data bases for this HIDAM data base.

```
STMT   SOURCE STATEMENT

   1           PRINT NOGEN
   2  DBD           NAME=EXHIIND,ACCESS=(INDEX,VSAM)
   3  DATASET       DD1=HIDAMI,DEVICE=3380
  4++,                3380 DISK STORAGE
   5 *
   6  SEGM          NAME=POINTER,BYTES=6
   7  LCHILD        NAME=(SEG1,EXHIDAM),INDEX=SEG1KEY
   8  FIELD         NAME=(INDEXFLD,SEQ),BYTES=6,START=1
   9 *
  10  DBDGEN
 53++,* * * * * * * * * * * * * * * * * * * * * * * * *
 54++,*
 55++,    RECOMMENDED VSAM DEFINE CLUSTER PARAMETERS
 56++,*
 57++,* * * * * * * * * * * * * * * * * * * * * * * * *
 59++,* * * * * * * * * * * * * * * * * * * * * * * * *
 60++,*
 61++,*                 *NOTE1
 62++,*   DEFINE CLUSTER (NAME(HIDAMI) -
 63++,*          INDEXED KEYS (6,5) -
 64++,*          RECORDSIZE (12,12)) -
 65++,*          DATA (CONTROLINTERVALSIZE (1024))
 66++,*
 67++,* *NOTE1 - SHOULD SPECIFY DSNAME FOR DD HIDAMI
 68++,*
 69++,* * * * * * * * * * * * * * * * * * * * * * * * *
108++,****** SEQUENCE FIELD ******
 173  FINISH
 174  END
```

Figure 16-15 DBDGEN output for the HIDAM data base's index data base

Figure 16-16 is the control interval in the main data base that contains the three data base records in the sample data base. The CI begins with a two-byte FSEAP and a two-byte control interval identifier, as you'd expect in an HDAM data base. However, in an HDAM data base, you'd expect to find one or more four-byte RAPs next. But in this HIDAM data base, the first occurrence of a data base segment immediately follows the control interval identifier: RAPs typically aren't used in HIDAM data bases. In the figure, I've drawn boxes around the segment occurrences that make up the three data base records to help you see where the root segments for the three records are located.

Now, look at figure 16-17. This is the listing of the KSDS that contains the index data base. In the right side of this figure, I've shaded and labelled the key field of the KSDS. As you can see, each record contains the sequence field value from the root segment in one of the data base records (SEG111, SEG121, and SEG131).

Immediately before the key field value in each of these KSDS records is the four-byte RBA of the corresponding root segment occurrence in the main data base ESDS. For example, the second root segment is located at RBA hex 11E2 in the ESDS. If you look back to figure 16-16, you'll find the second root segment at that location.

From an application programmer's point of view, the organization of a HIDAM data base is the most flexible of all those available under DL/I. However, it can be inefficient when processing is mostly random. That's because two data sets have to be accessed and updated instead of one as data base activity occurs. However, when a mixture of sequential and random processing is required, HIDAM is usually the best choice.

POINTERS IN LOGICAL DATA RELATIONSHIPS

The mechanism DL/I uses to implement logical relationships depends on still another set of pointers, in addition to the hierarchical and child/twin pointer types this chapter has already described. This section introduces the pointers DL/I uses when the DBA specifies logical relationships. This isn't a complete discussion of implementing logical relationships; for more information, you should turn to the reference manuals I list in the discussion at the end of this chapter.

DL/I supports two kinds of logical pointers: *direct logical pointers* and *symbolic logical pointers*. Direct logical pointers contain specific RBAs and are used with HDAM and HIDAM data bases. It is possible to use HISAM data bases in some logical relationships, but when you do, pointers relating to it must be symbolic. A symbolic logical pointer contains the concatenated key of the related segment. In this section, I'm going to describe only direct logical pointers because they're more common.

You should recall from the chapter on logical data base processing that the link between two physical structures is through the logical child. In any logical relationship, it's possible to access the logical parent through the logical child. DL/I uses a *logical parent* (*LP*) *pointer* in the logical child segment to implement this path.

The LP pointer is required in any logical relationship. If the relationship is bidirectional, the logical parent segment contains a *logical child first* (*LCF*) *pointer*. By using it, the logical child can be accessed from its logical parent. In addition, the data base administrator can also specify that the logical parent include a *logical child last* (*LCL*) *pointer* for the logical child type. LCF and LCL pointers work like PCF and PCL pointers for physical children.

```
LISTING OF DATA SET -MMA2.HIDAMD

RBA OF RECORD - 4096
000000  05E80000 01000000 11E20000 00000000  104E0000 10E60000 11A80000 11A8E2C5  *.Y.......S.......+...W........SE*
000020  C7F1F1F1 F1F1F1F1 F1F1F1F1 F1F1F1F1  F1F1F1F1 F1F1F1F1 F1F1F1F1 F1F1F1F1  *G1111111111111111111111111111111*
000040  F1F1F1F1 F1F1F1F1 F1F1F1F1 F1F10200  000010E6 00000000 00001088 000010A2  *11111111111111.....W............*
000060  000010BC 000010BC E2C5C7F2 F1F1F2F2  F2F2F2F2 F2F2F2F2 F2F2F2F2 F2F2F2F2  *........SEG211222222222222222222*
000080  F2F2F2F2 F2F2F2F2 03000000 10A20000  0000E2C5 C7F3F1F1 F3F3F3F3 F3F3F3F3  *22222222..........SEG31133333333*
0000A0  F3F30300 00000000 00001088 E2C5C7F3  F1F2F3F3 F3F3F3F3 F3F3F3F3 04000000  *33..........SEG3123333333333....*
0000C0  00000000 0000E2C5 C7F4F1F1 F4F4F4F4  F4F4F4F4 F4F4F4F4 F4F4F4F4 F4F4F4F4  *......SEG41144444444444444444444*
0000E0  F4F4F4F4 F4F40200 00000000 0000104E  00001120 0000113A 00001154 0000117E  *444444.........+...............=*
000100  E2C5C7F2 F1F2F2F2 F2F2F2F2 F2F2F2F2  F2F2F2F2 F2F2F2F2 F2F2F2F2 F2F2F2F2  *SEG21222222222222222222222222222*
000120  03000000 113A0000 0000E2C5 C7F3F1F1  F3F3F3F3 F3F3F3F3 F3F30300 00000000  *..........SEG3113333333333......*
000140  00001120 E2C5C7F3 F1F2F3F3 F3F3F3F3  F3F3F3F3 04000000 117E0000 0000E2C5  *....SEG3123333333333.....=....SE*
000160  C7F4F1F1 F4F4F4F4 F4F4F4F4 F4F4F4F4  F4F4F4F4 F4F4F4F4 F4F4F4F4 F4F40400  *G41144444444444444444444444444..*
000180  00000000 00001154 E2C5C7F4 F1F2F4F4  F4F4F4F4 F4F4F4F4 F4F4F4F4 F4F4F4F4  *........SEG412444444444444444444*
0001A0  F4F4F4F4 F4F4F4F4 05000000 00000000  0000E2C5 C7F5F1F1 F5F5F5F5 F5F5F5F5  *44444444..........SEG51155555555*
0001C0  F5F5F5F5 F5F5F5F5 F5F5F5F5 F5F5F5F5  F5F5F5F5 F5F5F5F5 F5F5F5F5 F5F5F5F5  *55555555555555555555555555555555*
0001E0  F5F50100 000013C0 00001004 0000122C  000012C4 00001386 00001386 E2C5C7F1  *55.................D........SEG1*
000200  F2F1F1F1 F1F1F1F1 F1F1F1F1 F1F1F1F1  F1F1F1F1 F1F1F1F1 F1F1F1F1 F1F1F1F1  *21111111111111111111111111111111*
000220  F1F1F1F1 F1F1F1F1 F1F1F1F1 02000000  12C40000 00000000 12660000 12800000  *111111111111.....D..............*
000240  129A0000 129AE2C5 C7F2F2F1 F2F2F2F2  F2F2F2F2 F2F2F2F2 F2F2F2F2 F2F2F2F2  *......SEG22122222222222222222222*
000260  F2F2F2F2 F2F20300 00001280 00000000  E2C5C7F3 F2F1F3F3 F3F3F3F3 F3F3F3F3  *222222..........SEG3213333333333*
000280  03000000 00000000 1266E2C5 C7F3F2F2  F3F3F3F3 F3F3F3F3 F3F30400 00000000  *..........SEG3223333333333......*
0002A0  00000000 E2C5C7F4 F2F1F4F4 F4F4F4F4  F4F4F4F4 F4F4F4F4 F4F4F4F4 F4F4F4F4  *....SEG42144444444444444444444444*
0002C0  F4F4F4F4 02000000 00000000 122C0000  12FE0000 13180000 13320000 135CE2C5  *4444.........................*SE*
0002E0  C7F2F2F2 F2F2F2F2 F2F2F2F2 F2F2F2F2  F2F2F2F2 F2F2F2F2 F2F2F2F2 F2F20300  *G22222222222222222222222222222..*
000300  00001318 00000000 E2C5C7F3 F2F1F3F3  F3F3F3F3 F3F3F3F3 03000000 00000000  *........SEG3213333333333........*
000320  12FEE2C5 C7F3F2F2 F3F3F3F3 F3F3F3F3  F3F30400 0000135C 00000000 E2C5C7F4  *..SEG3223333333333.....*....SEG4*
000340  F2F1F4F4 F4F4F4F4 F4F4F4F4 F4F4F4F4  F4F4F4F4 F4F4F4F4 F4F4F4F4 04000000  *2144444444444444444444444444....*
000360  00000000 1332E2C5 C7F4F2F2 F4F4F4F4  F4F4F4F4 F4F4F4F4 F4F4F4F4 F4F4F4F4  *......SEG42244444444444444444444*
000380  F4F4F4F4 F4F40500 00000000 00000000  E2C5C7F5 F2F1F5F5 F5F5F5F5 F5F5F5F5  *444444..........SEG5215555555555*
0003A0  F5F5F5F5 F5F5F5F5 F5F5F5F5 F5F5F5F5  F5F5F5F5 F5F5F5F5 F5F5F5F5 F5F5F5F5  *55555555555555555555555555555555*
0003C0  01000000 159E0000 11E20000 140A0000  14A20000 15640000 1564E2C5 C7F1F3F1  *.........S................SEG131*
0003E0  F1F1F1F1 F1F1F1F1 F1F1F1F1 F1F1F1F1  F1F1F1F1 F1F1F1F1 F1F1F1F1 F1F1F1F1  *11111111111111111111111111111111*
000400  F1F1F1F1 F1F1F1F1 F1F10200 000014A2  00000000 00001444 0000145E 00001478  *1111111111.................;....*
000420  00001478 E2C5C7F2 F3F1F2F2 F2F2F2F2  F2F2F2F2 F2F2F2F2 F2F2F2F2 F2F2F2F2  *....SEG23122222222222222222222222*
000440  F2F2F2F2 03000000 145E0000 0000E2C5  C7F3F3F1 F3F3F3F3 F3F3F3F3 F3F30300  *2222.....;....SEG3313333333333..*
000460  00000000 00001444 E2C5C7F3 F3F2F3F3  F3F3F3F3 F3F3F3F3 04000000 00000000  *........SEG3323333333333........*
000480  0000E2C5 C7F4F3F1 F4F4F4F4 F4F4F4F4  F4F4F4F4 F4F4F4F4 F4F4F4F4 F4F4F4F4  *..SEG431444444444444444444444444*
0004A0  F4F40200 00000000 0000140A 000014DC  000014F6 00001510 0000153A E2C5C7F2  *44.................6........SEG2*
0004C0  F3F2F2F2 F2F2F2F2 F2F2F2F2 F2F2F2F2  F2F2F2F2 F2F2F2F2 F2F2F2F2 03000000  *3222222222222222222222222222....*
0004E0  14F60000 0000E2C5 C7F3F3F1 F3F3F3F3  F3F3F3F3 F3F30300 00000000 000014DC  *.6....SEG3313333333333..........*
000500  E2C5C7F3 F3F2F3F3 F3F3F3F3 F3F3F3F3  04000000 153A0000 0000E2C5 C7F4F3F1  *SEG3323333333333..........SEG431*
000520  F4F4F4F4 F4F4F4F4 F4F4F4F4 F4F4F4F4  F4F4F4F4 F4F4F4F4 F4F40400 00000000  *44444444444444444444444444......*
000540  00001510 E2C5C7F4 F3F2F4F4 F4F4F4F4  F4F4F4F4 F4F4F4F4 F4F4F4F4 F4F4F4F4  *....SEG43244444444444444444444444*
000560  F4F4F4F4 05000000 00000000 0000E2C5  C7F5F3F1 F5F5F5F5 F5F5F5F5 F5F5F5F5  *4444..........SEG531555555555555*
000580  F5F5F5F5 F5F5F5F5 F5F5F5F5 F5F5F5F5  F5F5F5F5 F5F5F5F5 F5F5F5F5 F5F50100  *555555555555555555555555555555..*
0005A0  00000000 000013C0 00000000 00000000  00000000 00000000 FFFFFFFF FFFF0000  *................................*
0005C0  00000000 00000000 00000000 00000000  00000000 00000000 00000000 00000000  *................................*
```

Data base record 1

Data base record 2

Data base record 3

Figure 16-16 Contents of the HIDAM main data base's data set (part 1 of 2)

```
IDCAMS  SYSTEM SERVICES                                            TIME: 21:15:16        10/18/85     PAGE   3

LISTING OF DATA SET -MMA2.HIDAMD

0005E0  00000000 00000000 00000210 00000000   00000000 00000000 00000000 00000000   *................................*
000600  00000000 00000000 00000000 00000000   00000000 00000000 00000000 00000000   *................................*
000620  00000000 00000000 00000000 00000000   00000000 00000000 00000000 00000000   *................................*
000640  00000000 00000000 00000000 00000000   00000000 00000000 00000000 00000000   *................................*
000660  00000000 00000000 00000000 00000000   00000000 00000000 00000000 00000000   *................................*
000680  00000000 00000000 00000000 00000000   00000000 00000000 00000000 00000000   *................................*
0006A0  00000000 00000000 00000000 00000000   00000000 00000000 00000000 00000000   *................................*
0006C0  00000000 00000000 00000000 00000000   00000000 00000000 00000000 00000000   *................................*
0006E0  00000000 00000000 00000000 00000000   00000000 00000000 00000000 00000000   *................................*
000700  00000000 00000000 00000000 00000000   00000000 00000000 00000000 00000000   *................................*
000720  00000000 00000000 00000000 00000000   00000000 00000000 00000000 00000000   *................................*
000740  00000000 00000000 00000000 00000000   00000000 00000000 00000000 00000000   *................................*
000760  00000000 00000000 00000000 00000000   00000000 00000000 00000000 00000000   *................................*
000780  00000000 00000000 00000000 00000000   00000000 00000000 00000000 00000000   *................................*
0007A0  00000000 00000000 00000000 00000000   00000000 00000000 00000000 00000000   *................................*
0007C0  00000000 00000000 00000000 00000000   00000000 00000000 00000000 00000000   *................................*
0007E0  00000000 00000000 00000000 00000000   00000000 00000000 00                  *.........................       *

IDC0005I NUMBER OF RECORDS PROCESSED WAS 1

IDC0001I FUNCTION COMPLETED, HIGHEST CONDITION CODE WAS 0
```

Figure 16-16 Contents of the HIDAM main data base's data set (part 2 of 2)

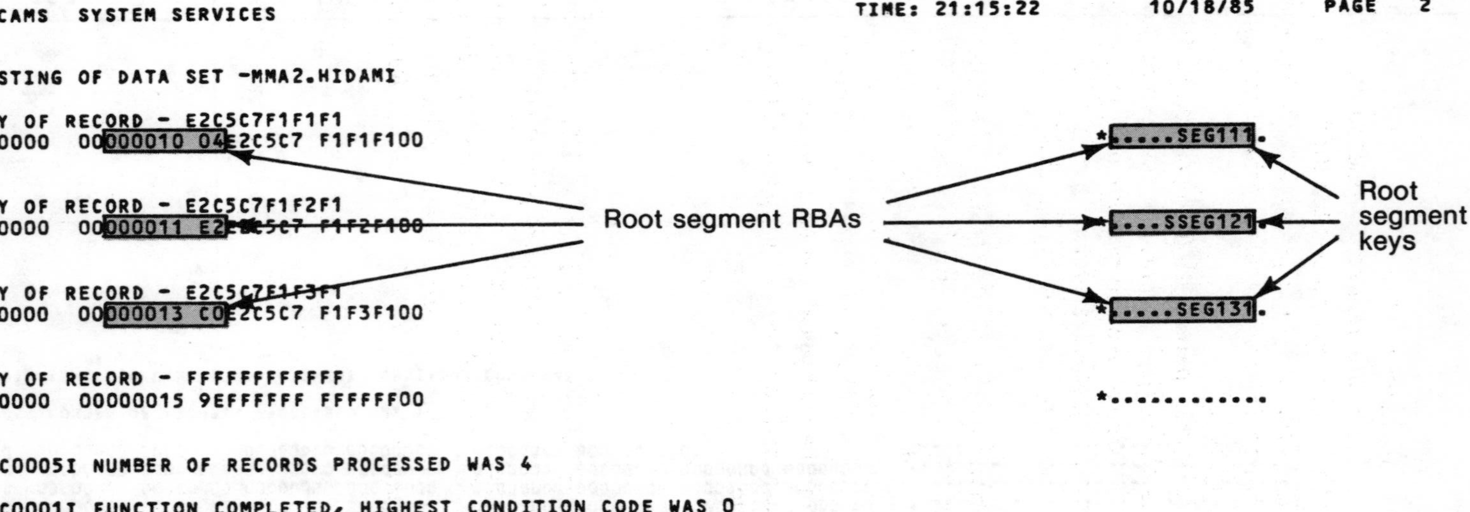

```
IDCAMS  SYSTEM SERVICES                                TIME: 21:15:22       10/18/85      PAGE    2

LISTING OF DATA SET -MMA2.HIDAMI

KEY OF RECORD - E2C5C7F1F1F1
000000  00000010 04E2C5C7 F1F1F100                              *.....SEG111.                  *

KEY OF RECORD - E2C5C7F1F2F1
000000  00000011 E2E2C5C7 F1F2F100                              *....SSEG121.                  *

KEY OF RECORD - E2C5C7F1F3F1
000000  00000013 C0E2C5C7 F1F3F100                              *.....SEG131.                  *

KEY OF RECORD - FFFFFFFFFFFF
000000  00000015 9EFFFFFF FFFFFF00                              *............                  *

IDC0005I NUMBER OF RECORDS PROCESSED WAS 4

IDC0001I FUNCTION COMPLETED, HIGHEST CONDITION CODE WAS 0
```


Figure 16-17 Contents of the HIDAM index data base's data set

When a logical parent can have multiple logical child segment occurrences, those logical children are related to one another with either *logical twin forward* (*LTF*) *pointers* or a combination of LTF and *logical twin backward* (*LTB*) *pointers*. These pointers serve the same function as PTF and PTB pointers in physical relationships: they chain twin segment occurrences together.

Finally, to allow the physical parent of a logical child to be retrieved when access is via the logical parent, the logical child can include a *physical parent* (*PP*) *pointer*. And to provide for the inverted hierarchical structure used by logical data bases, DL/I adds a PP pointer to each segment in the path from the logical child to the root segment.

Figure 16-18 is a schematic representation of how these pointers work. The darker set of arrows shows the path followed via the LCF and LTF pointers to retrieve all the logical children of a particular logical parent. Although this figure doesn't show it, logical pointers are always in addition to the physical pointers used to maintain the relationships of segments in their physical data bases. As you can imagine, when data bases are tied together with logical relationships, the pointers can be extensive.

DISCUSSION

If you want more information on how the pointers in HD data bases work, I encourage you to refer to the more detailed presentation in the manuals. If you're an MVS user, you should refer to *IMS/VS Version 1 Data Base Administration Guide* and *IMS/VS Version 1 Utilities Reference Manual*; if you're a VSE user, you should refer to *DL/I DOS/VS Data Base Administration* and *DL/I DOS/VS Resource Definition and Utilities*.

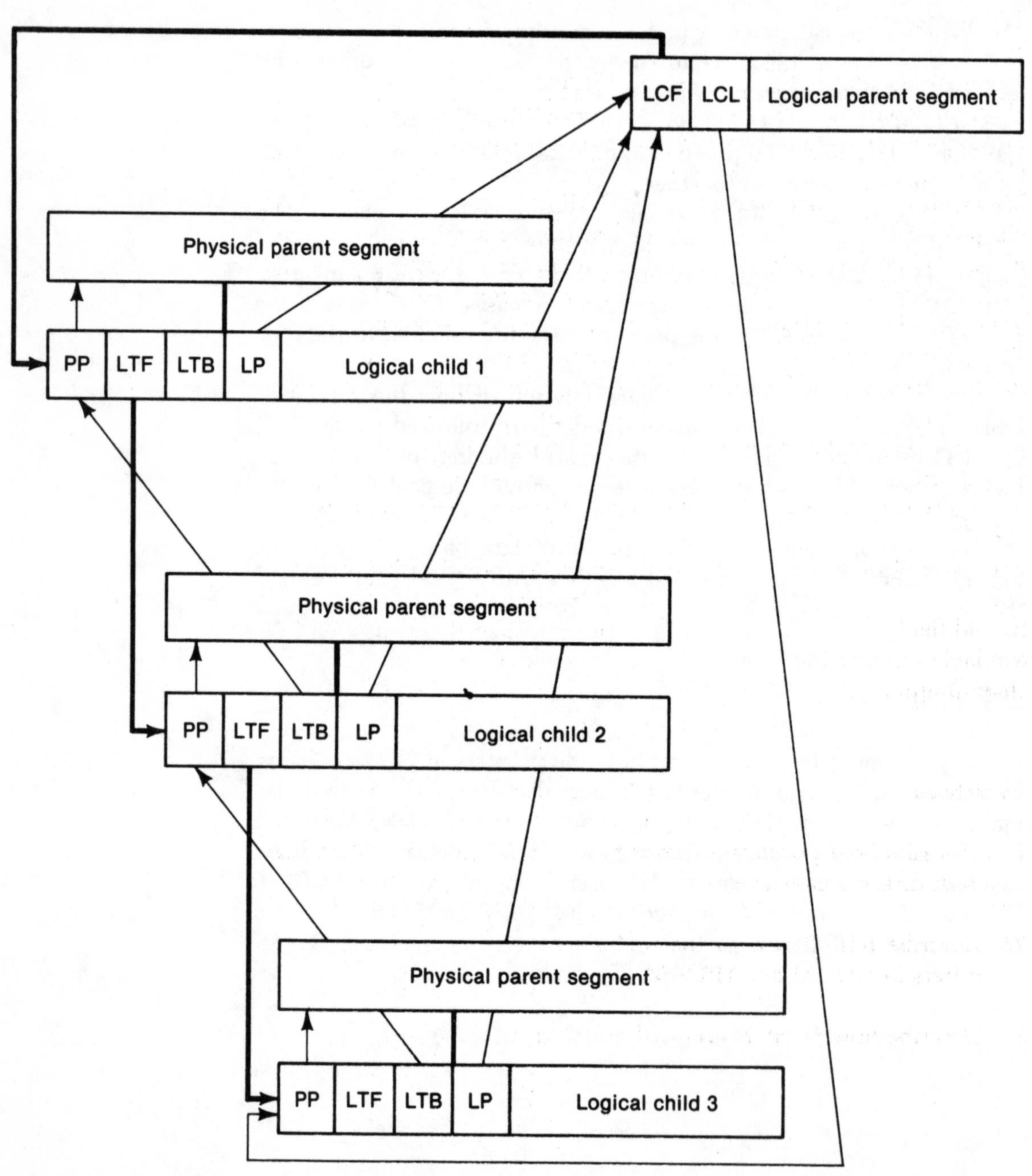

Figure 16-18 Pointers for logical relationships

Terminology

hierarchical pointer
child/twin pointer
hierarchical forward pointer
HF pointer
hierarchical backward pointer
HB pointer
physical child first pointer
PCF pointer
physical child last pointer
PCL pointer
physical twin forward pointer
PTF pointer
physical twin backward pointer
PTB pointer
free space element anchor point
FSEAP
free space element
FSE
task-id field
available space field
chain pointer field
bit map
root addressable area
overflow area
root anchor point
RAP
index data base
direct logical pointer
symbolic logical pointer
logical parent pointer
LP pointer
logical child first pointer
LCF pointer
logical child last pointer
LCL pointer
logical twin forward pointer
LTF pointer
logical twin backward pointer
LTB pointer
physical parent pointer
PP pointer

Objectives

1. Describe how pointers are used to relate segments in a data base with direct organization.

2. Describe how access to the root segment of a data base record differs in HDAM and HIDAM data bases.

3. Describe how pointers are used in logical relationships.

Appendix A

DL/I status codes

This appendix contains the DL/I status codes that can be returned as a result of calls issued against standard DL/I data bases. For each status code, there's a brief description followed by the call functions that can result in the code. (When one of the get functions is indicated for a status code, the get hold form of that call can also cause the condition to be raised; for example, if the GN call can cause a particular status code to be returned, the GHN call can too.) Although the descriptions that follow are brief, they're adequate for most problems. If you find that you need more information for a particular code, consult either the IMS/VS or DL/I DOS/VS application programming manual.

AB

The call did not specify a segment I/O area. This is a programming error.

Calls: All

AC

The call included an SSA with a hierarchical error. This is a programming error.

Calls: All get calls and ISRT

AD

The function code field specified for the call contains an incorrect value. This is a programming error.

Calls: All

AH

The call requires at least one SSA. This is a programming error.

Calls: ISRT

AI

An error occurred when trying to open the data base data set. The most common cause of the AI status code is an error in the JCL defining the data base data set. You might also get this status code if you try to load an existing data base or do other than load processing on an empty data set.

Calls: All

AJ

The call specifies an invalid SSA. This is a programming error. The PCB's segment level field contains the level number of the segment for which the SSA is invalid. The first thing you should check is the format of the SSA itself. If it seems to be correct, make sure the call doesn't specify an invalid SSA type. For an ISRT call, the lowest level SSA must be unqualified. For a REPL call, there may not be a qualified SSA. And for a DLET call, there may be only one SSA and it must be unqualified.

Calls: All

AK

The field you named on a qualified SSA isn't correct. This is a programming error.

Calls: All get calls and ISRT

AM

The call attempted an unauthorized operation, that is, one not allowed by the processing options or sensitive segments specified in the PCB. This is a programming error.

Calls: All

AO

The call caused an operation that resulted in a physical I/O error. This is a serious error that probably requires intervention by a system programmer.

Calls: All

AT

The I/O area the call specified is too large. This is usually a programming error, but the program's PSB may be incorrect.

Calls: DLET, REPL, and ISRT

AU

The SSAs specified on the call exceeded the maximum length allowed for them in the PSB. This usually is a programming error, but the PSB may be incorrect.

Calls: All

DA

The sequence field (or a non-replaceable field) has been changed in the program's I/O area. This is a programming error.

Calls: DLET and REPL

DJ

The call wasn't immediately preceded by a successful get hold call. This is a programming error.

Calls: DLET and REPL

DX

The call violated a delete rule for a segment. This is usually a programming error.

Calls: DLET

GA

A higher-level segment was retrieved during sequential retrieval. Usually a GA isn't an error but an expected condition.

Calls: Unqualified GN and GNP

GB

The end of the data base was reached during sequential retrieval.

Calls: GN

GD

Position was lost before the call could be completed, probably because a segment in the path to it was deleted through another PCB.

Calls: ISRT

GE

A segment occurrence meeting all the specified qualifications wasn't found (for a get call) or couldn't be added due to an error in the specified path (for an ISRT).

Calls: All get calls and ISRT

GK

A segment of a different type but at the same hierarchical level was retrieved during sequential retrieval. Usually a GK isn't an error but an expected condition.

Calls: Unqualified GN and GNP

GP

Proper parentage isn't in effect. This is usually a programming error.

Calls: GNP

II

The segment already exists in the data base.

Calls: ISRT

IX

The call violated an insert rule for a segment. This is usually a programming error.

Calls: ISRT

LB

The segment already exists in the data base.

Calls: ISRT

LC

The input data is not in hierarchical sequence.

Calls: ISRT

LD

One or more segments in the path to the segment being loaded are missing (an error in hierarchical sequence).

Calls: ISRT

LE

The sequence of segment types at the same level isn't the same as that specified in the DBD (an error in hierarchical sequence).

Calls: ISRT

NO

The call caused an operation that resulted in a physical I/O error on a secondary index. This is a serious error that probably requires intervention by a system programmer.

Calls: DLET, REPL, ISRT

RX

The call violated a replace rule for a segment. This is usually a programming error.

Calls: ISRT

V1

A variable length segment longer than the maximum segment size was specified. This is a programming error.

Calls: DLET, REPL, ISRT

bb (spaces)

The call was executed normally.

Calls: All

Appendix B

SSA command codes

Command code	Meaning
C	Use the complete concatenated key for the segment.
D	Path call.
F	Retrieve the first occurrence of the segment under its parent.
L	Retrieve the last occurrence of the segment under its parent.
N	Omit the segment from a path replace call.
P	Establish parentage at this level (above the lowest level segment returned by the call).
Q	Enqueue the segment.
U	Hold position for subsequent retrieval on this segment.
V	Hold position for subsequent retrieval on this segment and those above it.
-	The null command code; has the same effect as no command code at all.

Appendix C

JCL to compile and link batch COBOL programs that use DL/I data bases

This appendix presents sample job streams you can use as models for jobs you code to compile and link DL/I COBOL programs. The first job stream is for IMS/VS users; the second is for DL/I DOS/VS users. This appendix isn't a substitute for a working knowledge of JCL. As a result, if you aren't familiar with the JCL for your particular system, I encourage you to get a copy of either *OS JCL* by Wayne Clary or my book *DOS/VSE JCL*.

Compile and link job for IMS/VS users

Figure C-1 shows a job stream that uses the COBUCL procedure to compile and link a COBOL DL/I program. Here, the program name is INV2300. Although this job is much like the procedure to compile and link a non-DL/I program, a DD statment for LKED.SYSLMOD specifies the partitioned data set (PDS) that contains DL/I programs. In this case, it's MMA2.IMSVS.PGMLIB. Your program specifications should indicate the name of the library that will contain the load module.

You can specify the name of the load module in two places in the job. You can code it in parentheses after the PDS data set name on the DD statement for LKED.SYSLMOD, or you can supply a NAME linkage editor control statement after the LKED.SYSIN DD statement.

```
//MMA2COMP JOB  USER=...
//COBLK     EXEC  PROC=COBUCL,
//                PARM.COB='APOST',
//                PARM.LKED='MAP,LET,LIST'
//COB.SYSIN DD  *
       IDENTIFICATION DIVISION.
      *
       PROGRAM-ID.  INV2300.
      *
              .
              .
              .
/*
//LKED.SYSLMOD DD  DSN=MMA2.IMSVS.PGMLIB(INV2300),
//               DISP=SHR
//LKED.SYSIN   DD  *
   INCLUDE RESLIB(CBLTDLI)
   ENTRY   DLITCBL
   NAME    INV2300(R)
//LKED.RESLIB DD  DSN=IMS1.IMSVS.RESLIB,
//               DISP=SHR
//
```

Figure C-1 Job to compile and link an IMS/VS program

If you use the second technique and you want to replace an existing version of the member in the library, you have to follow the name with (R). If you like, you can use both techniques, as I did in figure C-1.

You need to include two other linkage editor control statements after the LKED.SYSIN DD statement:

```
INCLUDE RESLIB(CBLTDLI)
```

and

```
ENTRY DLITCBL
```

These are the same for all COBOL DL/I programs.

Finally, be sure to provide an overriding statement for LKED.RESLIB that specifies the correct data set name. Here, it's IMS1.IMSVS.RESLIB.

Your shop probably has a special procedure to compile and link DL/I programs. Or, IMSCOBOL, which is supplied with IMS, may be tailored to your installation's requirements. Check with a co-worker, your supervisor, or your DBA to find out if it or a similar procedure is available.

```
// JOB      COMPPGM
// OPTION   LIST,ERRS,CATAL,SXREF,NOSYM
   PHASE    INV2300,*
   INCLUDE DLZBPJRA
// EXEC     FCOBOL
       IDENTIFICATION DIVISION.
      *
       PROGRAM-ID.  INV2300.
      *
            .
            .
            .
/*
// LIBDEF   CL,TO=DLICIL
   ENTRY CBLCALLA
// EXEC     LNKEDT
/&
```

Figure C-2 Job to compile and link a DL/I DOS/VS program

Compile and link job for DL/I DOS/VS users

Figure C-2 is a job stream to compile and link a COBOL DL/I program on a VSE system. As with a non-DL/I compile and link job, you code a PHASE linkage editor control statement that specifies the name of the phase to be created before the EXEC statement for the compile step. After the PHASE statement but before the EXEC statement for the compiler, code an INCLUDE statement specifying DLZBPJRA (an interface module for use in DL/I COBOL programs). You can specify any options you want in effect on the JCL option statement (which is shown in figure C-2) or the COBOL CBL statement (which is not).

After the compile step, you code the statements for the link edit step. Be sure to code a LIBDEF statement to specify the TO core image library. (In figure C-2, it's DLICIL.) If the library isn't defined with a standard label, you need to supply a DLBL and an EXTENT statement for it. Also, any libraries required by the linkage editor must be specified in library search chains (usually, they're specified in a permanent search chain for the partition and, as a result, you don't need to code them explicitly in your jobs).

After the compile step but before the EXEC statement for the link edit step, you code an ENTRY linkage editor control statement that specifies CBLCALLA. Then, you can code the EXEC statement for the linkage editor.

Index

Comment Form

Your opinions count

If you have comments, criticisms, or suggestions, I'm eager to get them. Your opinions today will affect our products of tomorrow. If you have questions, you can expect an answer within one week of the time we receive them. And if you discover any errors in this book, typographical or otherwise, please point them out so we can make corrections when the book is reprinted.

Thanks for your help.

Mike Murach
Fresno, California

fold ---- fold

Book title: IMS for the COBOL Programmer, Part 1

Dear Mike: ______________________________

____

____

____

____

____

____

____

____

fold ---- fold

____

____

____

Name and Title ______________________________

Company (if any) ______________________________

Address ______________________________

City, State, & Zip ______________________________

Fold where indicated and seal.
No postage necessary if mailed in the United States.

fold

fold

NO POSTAGE
NECESSARY
IF MAILED
IN THE
UNITED STATES

BUSINESS REPLY MAIL

FIRST-CLASS MAIL PERMIT NO. 3063 FRESNO, CA

POSTAGE WILL BE PAID BY ADDRESSEE

Mike Murach & Associates, Inc.

4697 W JACQUELYN AVE
FRESNO CA 93722-9888

fold

fold

Order Form

Our Unlimited Guarantee

To our customers who order directly from us: You must be satisfied. Our books must work for you, or you can send them back for a full refund . . . no matter how many you buy, no matter how long you've had them.

Name & Title ______________________
Company (if company address) ______________________
Street Address ______________________
City, State, Zip ______________________
Phone number (including area code) ______________________

Qty	Product code and title		*Price
Data Base Processing			
______	IMS1	IMS for the COBOL Programmer Part 1: DL/I Data Base Processing	$34.50
______	IMS2	IMS for the COBOL Programmer Part 2: Data Communications and MFS	36.50
CICS			
______	CIC1	CICS for the COBOL Programmer: Part 1	$31.00
______	CIC2	CICS for the COBOL Programmer: Part 2	31.00
______	CREF	The CICS Programmer's Desk Reference	36.50
COBOL Language Elements			
______	SC1R	Structured ANS COBOL: Part 1	$31.00
______	SC2R	Structured ANS COBOL: Part 2	31.00
______	RW	Report Writer	17.50
______	VC2R	VS COBOL II (Second Edition)	27.50
VM Subjects			
______	VMCC	VM/CMS: Commands and Concepts	$25.00
______	VMXE	VM/CMS: XEDIT	25.00

- ☐ Bill me the appropriate price plus UPS shipping and handling (and sales tax in California) for each book ordered.
- ☐ Bill the appropriate book prices plus UPS shipping and handling (and sales tax in California) to my ________VISA ________MasterCard:
  Card number ______________________
  Valid thru (month/year) ______________________
  Cardowner's signature ______________________
  (not valid without signature)
- ☐ I want to **save** UPS shipping and handling charges. Here's my check or money order for $__________. California residents, please add 6¼% sales tax to your total. (Offer valid in the U.S. only.)

*** Prices are subject to change. Please call for current prices.**

Qty	Product code and title		*Price
OS/MVS Subjects			
______	MJCL	MVS JCL	$34.50
______	TSO	MVS TSO	27.50
______	OSUT	OS Utilities	17.50
DOS/VSE Subjects			
______	VJLR	DOS/VSE JCL (Second Edition)	$34.50
______	ICCF	DOS/VSE ICCF	31.00
VSAM			
______	VSMX	VSAM: Access Method Services and Application Programming	$27.50
______	VSMR	VSAM for the COBOL Programmer (Second Edition)	17.50
Assembler Language			
______	VBAL	DOS/VSE Assembler Language	$36.50
______	MBAL	MVS Assembler Language	36.50
System Development			
______	DDBS	How to Design and Develop Business Systems	$25.00

To order more quickly,

Call **toll-free** 1-800-221-5528
(Weekdays, 8:30 to 5 Pacific Std. Time)

Mike Murach & Associates, Inc.
4697 West Jacquelyn Avenue
Fresno, California 93722-6427
(209) 275-3335
Fax: (209) 275-9035

fold

fold

NO POSTAGE
NECESSARY
IF MAILED
IN THE
UNITED STATES

BUSINESS REPLY MAIL

FIRST-CLASS MAIL PERMIT NO. 3063 FRESNO, CA

POSTAGE WILL BE PAID BY ADDRESSEE

Mike Murach & Associates, Inc.

4697 W JACQUELYN AVE
FRESNO CA 93722-9888

fold

fold